Lecture Notes in Computer Science 14543

Founding Editors

Gerhard Goos
Juris Hartmanis

The series Lecture Notes in Computer Science (LNCS), including its subseries Lecture Notes in Artificial Intelligence (LNAI) and Lecture Notes in Bioinformatics (LNBI), has established itself as a medium for the publication of new developments in computer science and information technology research, teaching, and education.

LNCS enjoys close cooperation with the computer science R & D community, the series counts many renowned academics among its volume editors and paper authors, and collaborates with prestigious societies. Its mission is to serve this international community by providing an invaluable service, mainly focused on the publication of conference and workshop proceedings and postproceedings. LNCS commenced publication in 1973.

Yevgeni Koucheryavy · Ahmed Aziz
Editors

Internet of Things, Smart Spaces, and Next Generation Networks and Systems

23rd International Conference, NEW2AN 2023
and 16th Conference, ruSMART 2023
Dubai, United Arab Emirates, December 21–22, 2023
Proceedings, Part II

Editors
Yevgeni Koucheryavy 🆔
Tampere University
Tampere, Finland

Ahmed Aziz 🆔
Tashkent State University of Economics
Tashkent, Uzbekistan

ISSN 0302-9743   ISSN 1611-3349 (electronic)
Lecture Notes in Computer Science
ISBN 978-3-031-60996-1   ISBN 978-3-031-60997-8 (eBook)
https://doi.org/10.1007/978-3-031-60997-8

This Springer imprint is published by the registered company Springer Nature Switzerland AG
The registered company address is: Gewerbestrasse 11, 6330 Cham, Switzerland

Preface

We welcome you to the proceedings of the 23rd International Conference on Next Generation Wired/Wireless Networks and Systems (NEW2AN 2023) held at the American University in the Emirates, Dubai, UAE, December 21–22, 2023.

Originally, the NEW2AN conference was launched by the International Teletraffic Congress (ITC) in St. Petersburg in June 1993 as an ITC-Sponsored Regional International Teletraffic Seminar. The first edition was entitled "Traffic Management and Routing in SDH Networks" and held by the R&D Institute (LONIIS). In 2002, the event received its current name, NEW2AN. In 2008, NEW2AN acquired a new companion in Smart Spaces, ruSMART, hence boosting interaction between researchers, practitioners, and engineers across different areas of ICT. From 2012, the scope of ruSMART was extended to cover the Internet of the Things and related aspects.

Presently, NEW2AN is a well-established conference with a unique cross-disciplinary mixture of telecommunications-related research and science. NEW2AN is accompanied by outstanding keynotes from universities and companies across Europe, USA, and Asia.

The NEW2AN 2023 technical program addressed various aspects of next-generation data networks, while special attention is given to advanced wireless networking and applications. In particular, the authors demonstrated novel and innovative approaches to performance and efficiency analysis of 5G and beyond systems, advanced queuing theory, and machine learning. It is also worth mentioning the rich coverage of the Internet of Things, optics, signal processing, as well as Digital Economy and business aspects.

We would like to thank the Technical Program Committee members of the conference, as well as the invited reviewers, for their hard work and important contributions to the conference. This year, the conference program met the highest quality criteria with an acceptance ratio of around 26%. The number of submissions sent for peer review 258, while the number of full papers accepted was 67. A single-blind peer-review type was used for the review process and each submission received three reviews.

The current edition of the conference was organized in cooperation with Tampere University, Tashkent State University of Economics, and American University in the Emirates.

We believe that the NEW2AN 2023 conference delivered an informative, high-quality, and up-to-date scientific program. We also hope that participants enjoyed both the technical and social conference components, the UAE ways of hospitality, and the beautiful city of Dubai.

December 2023

Yevgeni Koucheryavy
Ahmed Aziz

Organization

International Advisory Committee

Sergei Balandin   FRUCT, Finland
Yevgeni Koucheryavy   Tampere University, Finland
Kongratbay Sharipov   Tashkent State University of Economics, Uzbekistan

Organizing Committee

Mansur Eshov   Tashkent State University of Economics, Uzbekistan
Gulnora Abdurakhmanova   Tashkent State University of Economics, Uzbekistan
Dilshodjon Rakhmonov   Tashkent State University of Economics, Uzbekistan
Maqsudjon Yuldashev   Tashkent State University of Economics, Uzbekistan
Ahmed Mohamed   Tashkent State University of Economics, Uzbekistan
Abbos Rakhmonaliev   Tashkent State University of Economics, Uzbekistan
Sanjar Mirzaliev   Tashkent State University of Economics, Uzbekistan
Mohammad Hammoudeh   King Fahd University of Petroleum & Minerals, Saudi Arabia

Technical Program Committee

Mari Carmen Aguayo-Torres   University of Malaga, Spain
Ozgur B. Akan   METU, Turkey
Khalid Al-Begain   University of Glamorgan, UK
Sergey Andreev (TPC Chair)   Tampere University of Technology, Finland
Tricha Anjali   Illinois Institute of Technology, USA
Konstantin Avrachenkov   Inria, France
Francisco Barcelo   UPC, Spain
Sergey Balandin   Nokia, Finland

Ivan Ganchev	University of Limerick, Ireland/University of Plovdiv Paisii Hilendarski, Bulgaria
Michele Pagano	University of Pisa, Italy
Veselin Rakocevic	City University London, UK
Dmitry Tkachenko	IEEE St. Petersburg BT/CE/COM Chapter, Russia
Edison Pignaton de Freitas	Federal University of Rio Grande do Sul, Brazil
Gianluca Reali	University of Perugia, Italy
Andrey Turlikov	State Univ. Aerospace Instrumentation, Russia
Takeshi Takahashi	National Institute of Information and Communications Technology, Japan
Anna Maria Vegni	Università Roma 3, Italy
Katarzyna Wac	University of Geneva, Switzerland

Contents – Part II

Contents – Part I

Models and Algorithms for Decision Making in Intelligent Control Systems

Murodjon Sultanov$^{(\boxtimes)}$ ⓘ and Gayrat Ishankhodjayev

Tashkent State University of Economics, Islam Karimov Street, 49, Tashkent, Uzbekistan
`murad.sultanov@tsue.uz`

Abstract. The article carries out a systematic analysis of decision making in intelligent control systems. Based on the methods of the systems approach, problems and shortcomings of decision-making processes in intelligent control systems have been identified. This paper outlines one of the main problems of intelligent control technologies, which is the reconstruction of intelligent reasoning and behavior using a computer, the creation of devices that simulate human management decisions under conditions of uncertainty and high risk, and a computational experiment was carried out to solve problems of a fuzzy decision-making model in intelligent control systems. The results of computational experiments for solving problems showed improvements in the quality, efficiency and reliability of decisions made in intelligent control systems.

Keywords: system analysis · model · task · method · decision-making · intelligent control systems · making semi-structured decisions

1 Introduction

Currently, in the world one can daily observe the intensive penetration of artificial intelligence methods and algorithms into all spheres of human activity to solve complex management problems and support decision-making. Firstly, interest in the class of intelligent control and decision-making systems is due to a number of reasons, which boil down to the fact that traditional information technologies cannot provide the required quality of control, since they do not take into account all the uncertainties affecting the object. Secondly, the potential of the theory of automatic control can be significantly expanded through the use of modern methods of information technology and data and knowledge processing technologies. Further development of intelligent control technologies both at the executive level and at the stage of organizing appropriate actions and behavior makes it possible to implement advanced technical systems with high performance characteristics and expanded functionality [1, 2].

One of the main problems of intelligent control technologies is the reconstruction of intelligent reasoning and behavior using a computer, the creation of devices that simulate human management decisions under conditions of uncertainty and high risk. The field of artificial intelligence, as a rule, includes those areas of activity that do not rely on accurate analytical models, methods and algorithms for solving problems characterized

© The Author(s), under exclusive license to Springer Nature Switzerland AG 2024
Y. Koucheryavy and A. Aziz (Eds.): NEW2AN/ruSMART 2023, LNCS 14543, pp. 1–11, 2024.
https://doi.org/10.1007/978-3-031-60997-8_1

by a high degree of uncertainty. The direction of intelligent control technologies is based on the following main scientific paradigms: fuzzy systems, artificial immune systems, artificial neural networks, evolutionary computing and swarm intelligence. Together with logic and deductive inference, machine learning, and expert systems, these methods and algorithms form the scientific direction of artificial intelligence. Intelligence is broadly defined as the ability to think, understand, and benefit from experience, including creativity, art, consciousness, emotion, and intuition [3, 4].

2   Formulation of the Problem

A large class of complex systems and processes, which include modern intelligent control systems, is characterized by integration, multi-level, distribution and a variety of performance indicators. The design of such systems, assessment of the quality of their structural and functional characteristics and control of the processes occurring in them in real conditions occurs under conditions of informational, procedural-functional, parametric and criterion uncertainties of various types. These, in particular, include fuzzy (vague) uncertainty, characterized by incompleteness, inaccuracy and linguistic vagueness (fuzziness) present in the initial information, criteria and assessments of customers and developers, as well as in the models and procedures used for describing and evaluating alternatives to the analyzed variants of objects and their states. The need to take into account several criteria in the process of selecting the best options, including the preferences of decision makers (DMs) in intelligent control systems, also characterizes one of the conditions of uncertainty.

This makes it advisable to develop and use models and methods for describing and evaluating options (alternatives) of the analyzed objects, as well as making decisions on choosing the best option under conditions of fuzzy uncertainty, which represent a special class of decision-making problems, called unstructured or weakly structured. Alternatives to decisions made in such problems are assessed on the basis of an analysis of soft estimates of the effectiveness indicators of the results of the implementation of decisions (outcomes) and the values of the risk of losses corresponding to certain decision outcomes.

The theoretical and methodological apparatus for solving such problems of intelligent control systems is the means of intelligent information technology "Soft Computing".

Below we will consider fuzzy-set approaches to constructing models for describing and evaluating alternatives, as well as problems of semi-structured decision making under conditions of fuzzy uncertainty [5, 6].

Let us introduce definitions of the basic concepts used in the problem of intelligent control systems under consideration.

An alternative is one of the options for many possible decisions made. Outcome is a possible result of the implementation of an alternative, that is, a consequence (the state of an object! that comes from the implementation of the decision made. Criterion and performance indicator are the type and characteristics of the measure in accordance with which the effectiveness of outcomes and their corresponding alternatives is assessed. Decision maker preferences are subjective criteria based on experience and personal assessment of the decision maker, both internal and external, of the current situation of the environment in which the analyzed objects (systems and processes of various natures) operate. A problem situation is a set of alternatives, their outcomes, that is, the states of the analyzed objects, as well as their corresponding types and values assessments of performance indicators. Environment is a set of types of uncertainties under which the analyzed problem situation is assessed and decisions are made. This problem considers a fuzzy environment.

The decision-making problem is conceptually formulated as follows. There are many possible solutions (alternatives), the implementation of which leads to the occurrence of certain outcomes: one - under conditions of certainty, and several possible ones - under conditions of uncertainty. The outcome can be characterized, for example, by the value of the state into which the object will go as a result of the implementation of this alternative. There are further indicators and performance criteria, as well as, importantly, subjective preferences of decision makers. Evaluation of outcomes according to selected performance criteria determines the degree of preference for alternatives corresponding to these outcomes. It is required to build a strategy for selecting the best alternative in accordance with the criteria for the effectiveness of outcomes and the preferences of decision makers [6, 7].

3   Methodology

Formal formulation of the DM problem under conditions of certainty:

Sets are given: $X = \{x_1, \ldots, x_i, \ldots, x_m\}$ - alternatives (decisions, actions), $Y = \{y_1, \ldots, y_i, \ldots, y_m\}$- outcomes of alternatives and $W = \{w_1, \ldots, w_i, \ldots, w_m\}$ - indicators of their effectiveness. Here we have the mappings $f: X \to Y, u: Y \to W$ and the resulting mapping $w: Y \to W = f, u$ which is a superposition of f and u.

In real conditions, alternatives and their outcomes are assessed by several performance indicators (criteria) $u_k: Y \to W, k = 1, \ldots, l$. Particular u_k criteria are usually contradictory and often incomparable.

It is required, under such initial conditions, to select from the set of acceptable options the best alternative x_{io} that provides the most acceptable, in a sense, value of the efficiency indicator w_i of the corresponding outcomes y_i, that is

$$x_{io} = \arg extr \, w_i, x_i \in X, y_i \in Y$$

where *extr* is interpreted as "best".

The choice of $x_i \in X$ under conditions of uncertainty in goals, criteria, situation models, and solution methods is a task of making unstructured or semi-structured decisions.

To describe and evaluate variants of problem situations of the analyzed objects, generated as a result of the implementation of corresponding alternatives in conditions of uncertainty (fuzzy environment), and to select them as the most acceptable according to the selected efficiency criteria, it is advisable to represent the problem of making semi-structured decisions of the given type with a multicriteria DM model [8, 9] as the following set

$$< T, D, W, \Theta(X), O, P, R > \tag{1}$$

where T is the type of DM problem, determined by the objective function and restrictions; $D = \{d_1, \ldots, d_i, \ldots, d_m\}$ - set of solution alternatives; $W = W(q(d), c(d), t(d)) = \{w_{ji}\}$ - vector of estimates of the effectiveness of the outcomes of alternatives D according to various indicators, for example, beneficial effect $q(d)$, energy costs $c(d)$ and time $t(d)$; $\Theta(X)$ - set of states (outcomes) described by parameters X of the object under study; O - probability distribution of outcomes; P - decision maker preference system; R - rules for forming alternatives.

In a fuzzy environment, each alternative may correspond to several outcomes that have fuzzy estimates. A problem situation with the same number of possible outcomes for all alternatives is considered. The generalized efficiency indicator $w_{ji} \in W$ of the outcomes of alternatives D is usually, as noted, a vector of several partial indicators. The specific values of assessments of the effectiveness of alternatives are determined both by the values of the alternatives themselves and by the current values of the problem situation. Therefore, the values of quantitative estimates $w_{ji} \in W$ of outcomes $\theta_j \in \Theta$ of alternatives $d_i \in D$ are represented by the matrix $W = \|w_{ji} = w(\theta_j, d_i)\|$ in the form

$$d_1 \ldots d_i \ldots d_m$$

$$\theta_1 w_{11} \ldots w_{1i} \ldots w_{1m}$$

$$\ldots \ldots \ldots \ldots \ldots \ldots \tag{2}$$

$$\theta_j w_{j1} \ldots w_{ji} \ldots w_{jm}$$

$$\ldots \ldots \ldots \ldots \ldots \ldots$$

$$\theta_n w_{n1} \ldots w_{ni} \ldots w_{nm}$$

This matrix characterizes in expanded form the situation of making semi-structured decisions.

In this case, the problematic situation in model (1) is represented by a set.

$$\{D, W, A_\Theta\}, \tag{3}$$

where $D = \{d_1, \ldots, d_i, \ldots, d_m\}$ set of solutions (alternatives); $\Theta = \{\theta_1, \ldots, \theta_n\}$ set of values of possible states (outcomes), into one of which the problem situation can go when implementing the alternative $d_i \in D$; $W = \{w_{ji}\}$ - matrix of the evaluation functional defined on $\Theta \times D$, the elements of which $w_{ji} = w(\theta_j, d_i)$ take values from R^i; A_Θ is a fuzzy set of estimates $A = \{w_{ji}\}$ on elements which is determined by specifying the mapping $\mu_{ji} = \mu_{A_\Theta}(w_{ji})$ values of elements w_{ji} in the interval [0,1], that is, A_Θ reflects a set of fuzzy estimates of performance indicators of states $\theta_j \in \Theta$; problematic situation resulting from the implementation of d_i.

Fuzzy estimates of performance indicators are usually given by fuzzy numbers, for example, such as: "about n", "approximately n", "a little more than n", "a little less than n", etc. In some cases, complex fuzzy estimates can be used, consisting of several simple ones connected by logical connectives AND, OR, NOT. Fuzzy numbers display qualitative ratings such as "low", "high", "average" and others. There may be intermediate estimates between those indicated. The number of such assessments is determined by the type of rating scale used: two-level, three-level, five-level and others, determined, in turn, by the number of selected alternatives, the specifics of the subject area, the types of criteria and performance indicators.

The set of values of such estimates - fuzzy numbers forms a term set $A = \{A_i\}$, $i = 1, 2, \ldots, m$ of a linguistic variable.

"Performance indicator assessments." Here m is the number of levels of the scale used, which is usually chosen equal to the number of alternatives. Each of these terms is represented by a fuzzy set

$$A_i = \mu_{A_i}(x_k)/x_k$$

where $x_k \in X$, $k = 1, 2, \ldots, K'$ are elements of the base set X, reflecting the possible numerical values of the fuzzy estimate (term $A_i \subset A$) of the efficiency indicator $w_{ji} \in W$; $\mu_{A_i}(x_k)$ - membership function of the element $x_k \in X$ fuzzy set - term $A_i \subset A$.

For a given situation $\{D, W, A_\Theta\}$ the problem of making multi-objective decisions in a fuzzy environment is reduced to the choice of decision makers of one decision, the best and most acceptable according to their chosen criterion.

Taking into account the above definitions of model elements (1) - (3), the formulation of the problem of making semi-structured decisions in general can be formulated as follows [9].

Given: sets $D = \{d_i\}$ -alternatives, $\Theta = \{\theta_j\}$ - states of the environment (outcomes) and $W(\Theta, D) = \{w_{ji} = w(\theta_j, d_i)\}$, $j = \overline{1, n}$, $i = \overline{1, m}$,- indicators of their effectiveness; fuzzy set A_Θ of estimates $w_{ji} = w(\theta_j, d_i)$; O - probability distribution of possible outcomes $\Theta = \{\theta_j\}$ for each alternative; P - decision maker preference system; R - rules for forming alternatives.

Required: choose the best option

$$d_{io} = \arg extr\left(w_{ji} = w(\theta_j, d_i)\right), d_i \in D, \theta_j \in \Theta \tag{4}$$

Here, the *extr* value is understood to be the best value that most satisfies both the selected criteria and the preferences of decision makers. In this case, the evaluation functional W will have a positive ingredient if decision makers choose the best alternative based on the condition $max\{w(\theta_j, d_i)\}$, $d_i \in D$, $\theta_j \in \Theta$. Otherwise it is a negative ingredient. The positive ingredient for the evaluation functional is used to express the categories of utility, gain, efficiency, probabilities of achieving target events, and so on. Negative ingredient - to express loss, loss, regret, damage, risk and so on.

Estimates of the vector of efficiency indicators of decisions made and environmental states can have both quantitative and qualitative (fuzzy) values. The specific type of elements of the objective function, as well as taking into account all or individual factors of finding the best value $w_{ji} = w(\theta_j, d_i) \in W(\Theta, D)$ determine the choice of appropriate solution methods, which leads to a wide variety of problems of making semi-structured decisions in a fuzzy environment, that is. in conditions of fuzzy uncertainty in goals, criteria, situation models and solution methods.

In this case, it is necessary to take into account the presence of the following assumptions in the initial conditions of the problem situation in the stated formulation of the problem of making semi-structured decisions in a fuzzy environment.

1. The set of alternatives (solutions) that can be implemented in order to transfer an object (process) from the current situation (state) $\theta_j \in \Theta, j = \overline{1, n}$, required, from a given set of situations, is given finite and fixed in the form $D = \{d_i\}\, i = \overline{1, m}$.
2. The set of possible states (situations), into one of which an object (process) can go as a result of the implementation of any alternative $d_i \in D, i = \overline{1, m}$ that is, the set of possible outcomes of alternatives, is also given as finite and fixed in the form $\Theta = \{\theta_j\}\, j = \overline{1, n}$.
3. The set of possible values of the axiological probabilities of the occurrence of outcomes $\theta_j \in \Theta, j = \overline{1, n}$ is formed in advance on the basis of expert opinions for the subject area under consideration and is specified by a matrix of the form $\overline{P} = \|\overline{p_{ji}}\|, j = \overline{1, n}, i = \overline{1, m}$.
4. The set of values for assessing the effectiveness indicator $w_{ji} = w(\theta_j, d_i)$ of the analyzed outcomes of the corresponding alternatives is also formed in advance on the basis of appropriate calculations (using models and expressions describing the dependencies between quantitative and/or qualitative parameters of states (situations) and those selected, determined by agreement based on of relevant goals and preferences) performance criteria. In the absence and/or impossibility, for some reason, of constructing such models and expressions, the required set of efficiency indicator estimates is formed on the basis of expert opinions in the form of linguistic variables with a corresponding term set reflecting the set of possible fuzzy estimates of the efficiency indicator.

The solution of the formulated problem (4) using models (1) - (3) is carried out in several stages. At the first stage, a statement of the problem is formed: goals, criteria, restrictions and preferences of decision makers. At the second stage, the rules are determined, on the basis of which the set of possible solutions for the situation under consideration and the corresponding outcomes are formed. At the third stage, the outcomes of alternatives are assessed for each of the selected criteria. At the fourth stage, a decision rule is constructed (or selected) - a strategy for identifying and selecting the best alternative in accordance with the criteria and preferences of decision makers. Based on this strategy, an ordered set of feasible alternatives is formed - the most preferable among those possible for the current situation. Analysis of feasible alternatives determines whether the required ordering of alternatives has been obtained. If not received, then they return to the previous stages to carry out appropriate refinements and adjustments to the parameters of the constructed models and the rules of the original problem. If the required ordering is obtained, then decision makers select the best solution from it, taking into account their personal preferences.

In many DM problems in a fuzzy environment, the result of choosing one or another alternative as a solution is estimated by a fuzzy number. For m alternatives, m basic fuzzy numbers-estimates are formed. If there are n possible outcomes for each alternative, *mcdotn* fuzzy number-estimates are formed. In this case, the number of their values will be equal to the number of base evaluation numbers (m). To solve such problems, modified fuzzy analogues of well-known criteria, for example, Bayesian and variance, are proposed.

If the vector $P = (p_1, \ldots, p_n)$ of the probability distribution on the set $\Theta = \{\theta_j\}$ is given, then to form the evaluation functional $W(\Theta, D) = \{w_{ji} = w(\theta_j, d_i)\}$ a select the best of them in conditions of a stochastic environment, the classical Bayes criterion is used, which has the form

$$B = \operatorname*{extr}_{d_i \in D} \left[\sum_{j=1}^{n} p_j w_{ji} \right] \tag{5}$$

Depending on the value of the ingredient of the used functional W (positive or negative), the maximum or minimum of criterion (5) is sought.

In a fuzzy environment, the vector $\overline{P} = (\overline{p_1}, \ldots, \overline{p_n})$ of axiological probability distributions and the vector $M = (\mu_1, \ldots, \mu_m)$ of membership functions of the values of the efficiency indicator estimates to fuzzy numbers-estimates (terms $A_i \subset A$) are specified on the set $\Theta \times D$. In this case, the evaluation functional is transformed to the form $w_{ji} = w(\theta_j, d_i)$. Then the static decision-making strategy is carried out in accordance with fuzzy analogues of the corresponding classical criteria: Bayes, variance, Wald, Hurwitz and others.

The proposed fuzzy analogue of the Bayes criterion is described, for the positive ingredient of the evaluation functional, by the expressions [9, 10]

$$B(\overline{p}, \mu, d_{i_0}) = \max_{d_i \in D}(\overline{p}, \mu, d_i) \tag{6}$$

where

$$B(\overline{p}, \mu, d_i) = \sum_{j=1}^{n} \overline{p_j} \sum_{s=1}^{k} \mu_{ji}^S w_{ji}^S / \sum_{j=1}^{n} \overline{p_j} \mu_j,$$

$$\mu_j = \sum_{s=1}^{k} \mu_{ji}^S.$$

Here: $w_{ji}^S = w^S(\theta_j, d_i)$ - discrete values of elements w_{ji} of the matrix $W(\Theta, D) = \{w_{ji} = w(\theta_j, d_i)\}$ of the evaluation functional, included in the set of corresponding fuzzy numbers-estimates and receiving values from R^1 with the corresponding membership function $\mu_{ji}^S = \mu_{A_i}\left(w_{ji}^S\right)$, $S = \overline{1, k}$ - domain of specifying discrete values that make up the base set of fuzzy numbers-estimates w_{ji}^S - corresponding fuzzy terms-sets of the linguistic variable "assessments of performance indicators". The latter can be characterized, for example, by qualitative assessments - fuzzy terms "high", "medium", "low", which, in turn, can be displayed by corresponding fuzzy numbers: "approximately 1", "approximately 3", "approximately 5".

A fuzzy analogue of a criterion such as the dispersion of the values of the evaluation functional W is represented in the form

$$\sigma^2(\overline{p}, \mu, d_{i_0}) = \min_{d_k \in D} \sigma^2(\overline{p}, \mu, d_i)$$

where

$$Bo^2(\overline{p}, \mu, d_{i_0}) = \sum_{j=1}^{n} [\sum_{s=1}^{k} \overline{p}_j \mu_{ji}^S w_{ji}^S / \sum_{j=1}^{n} \overline{p}_j \mu_j - B(\overline{p}, \mu, d_i)]^2 \overline{p}_j$$

Here μ_j and $B(\overline{p}, \mu, d_i)$ are determined in accordance with expressions (6).

In a more general form, a fuzzy environment is also characterized by a fuzzy (qualitative) assessment of states $\theta_j \in \Theta$. In this case, when calculating the corresponding criteria, one should take into account the expressions of fuzzy sets that display state estimates.

Currently, static models are mainly considered, the results of which are the initial stage of detailing assessments of problem situations and decision-making criteria. In various situational conditions, it is advisable to use dynamic (multi-step) models of decision-making processes [10, 11].

Let's consider the dynamic N-stage process of functioning of a controlled object. We will assume that at each stage $l(1 \leq l \leq N)$ the control body knows the following.

1. A set $A^l = \{a_1^l, \ldots, a_m^l\}$ of possible states of an object, into one of which the object can go from any state at the previous $(l - 1)$ th stage.
2. The set $D^l = \{d_1^l, \ldots, d_m^l\}$ of decisions that the control body can make, where d_m^l is understood as the decision of the control body at the l th stage to transfer the object to the d_m^l state and at l - At this stage, the control body can make only one decision from the set D^l.
3. The set $\theta^l = \{\theta_1^l, \ldots, \theta_m^l\}$ of characteristics of possible states of the environment at the l th stage.
4. A priori distribution $p^l = \{p_1^l, \ldots, p_m^l\}$ of states of the environment on the set Θ^l. That is $p_j^l = P\{\theta^l = \theta_j^l\}$.
5. Matrix $W(a_v^{i-1}) = \{f_{j,k}^i(a_v^{i-1})\}_{j,k=1}^{n,m}$
   Here:

$$f_{j,k}^i(a_v^{i-1}) = \sum_{S=1}^{k} \mu_{jk}^S w_{jk}^S(a_v^{i-1}) / \sum_{j=1}^{n} \mu_j, \mu_j \sum_{S=1}^{k} \mu_{jk}^S$$

values of the evaluation functional W for all possible states $a_v^{i-1} \in A^{i-1}$.
6. Conditional probability distribution $g_r^i(a_v^{i-1}, d_k^i) = P\{a_v^{i-1} \to a_r^i | d^i = d_k^i\}$ transition of an object to the state $a_v^{i-1} \in A^i$ from the state $a_v^{i-1} \in A^{i-1}$, if the decision $d_k^i \in D^i$. is made.

4 Results and Discussion

For the control body, the goal of the dynamic decision-making process is to transfer the controlled object from a given initial state a^0 to a given set of final states $\{a^0\}$ by selecting a sequence of optimal decisions by the control body in accordance with accepted criteria.

According to the Bayes-type criterion, the optimal strategy of a dynamic decision-making process $\{d_{k_l^o}^l(a_r^{l-1})\}_{r=1}^{m_{l-1}}$ can be sequentially found for $l = N, N-1, \ldots, 2, 1$ from the conditions

$$f_1\left(d_{k_l^o}^l\left(a_r^{l-1}\right), a_r^{l-1}\right) = \min_{d_k^i \in D^i} f_1\left(d_k^l\left(a_r^{l-1}\right), a_r^{l-1}\right)$$

in this case, the values satisfy the following $f_1\left(d_k^l(a_r^{l-1}), a_r^{l-1}\right)$ recurrence equations:

$$f_N\left(d_{k_N^o}^N\left(a_r^{N-1}\right), a_r^{l-1}\right) = \min_{d^{N_k} \in P^i} B^N\left(d_k^N, a_r^{N-1}\right),$$

$$f_1\left(d_{k_l^o}^l\left(a_r^{l-1}\right), a_r^{l-1}\right) = \min_{d^{lk} \in D^l} [B^l\left(d_k^l, a_r^{l-1}\right)+$$

$$\sum_{r_1=1}^{m_l} f_{l+1}(d_{k_{l+1}^o}^{l+1}\left(a_{r_1}^l\right), a_{r_1}^l) g_{r_1}^l(a_r^{l-1}, d_k^l)].$$

Here:

$$B^l\left(d_k^l, a_r^{l-1}\right) = \sum_{j=1}^{n_l} p_j^l f_{jk}^l(a_r^{l-1}),$$

$$f_{jk}^i\left(a_r^{i-1}\right) = \sum_{S=1}^{k} \mu_{jk}^S w_{jk}^S(a_r^{i-1}) / \sum_{j=1}^{n} \mu_j,$$

$$\mu_j = \sum_{S=1}^{k} \mu_{ji}^S.$$

For a Wald-type criterion, the recurrent equations for finding optimal strategies for a dynamic decision-making process have the form:

$$f_N^0\left(d_{k_N^o}^N\left(a_r^{N-1}\right), a_r^{l-1}\right) = \min_{d^{N_k} \in P^i} \max_{j=1,\ldots,n_N} f_{jk}^N\left(a_r^{N-1}\right),$$

$$f_l^0\left(d_{k_l^o}^l\left(a_r^{l-1}\right), a_r^{l-1}\right) = \min_{d^{lk} \in D^l} [\max_{j=1,\ldots,\eta_l} f_{jk}^l\left(a_r^{l-1}\right)+$$

$$+ \sum_{\eta=1}^{m_l} f_{l+1}^0(d_{k_{l+1}^o}^{l+1}\left(a_\eta^l\right), a_\eta^l) g_\eta^l(a_r^{l-1}, d_k^l)], l = N, N-1, \ldots, 2, 1.$$

Here:

$$f_{jk}^i\left(a_r^{i-1}\right) = \sum_{S=1}^{k} \mu_{jk}^S w_{jk}^S(a_r^{i-1}) / \sum_{j=1}^{n} \mu_j, \mu_j = \sum_{S=1}^{k} \mu_{ji}^S.$$

For a Hurwitz-type criterion, the optimal strategy for a dynamic decision-making process

$$D_0^l = \{d_{k_l^o}^l\left(a_r^{l-1}\right)\}_{r=1}^{m_{l-1}}, l = 1, \ldots, N$$

are found by solving recurrent equations of the form

$$f_{NN}^{\lambda}(d_{k_N^0}^N\left(a_r^{N-1}\right), a_r^{N-1}) = \min_{d_k^N \in D^N} [\lambda_N$$

$$\min_{j=1,\dots,\eta_N} f_{jk}^N\left(a_r^{N-1}\right) + (1+\lambda_N) \max_{j=1,\dots,\eta_N} f_{jk}^N(a_r^{N-1})],$$

$$f_{ll}^{\lambda}(d_{k_l^0}^l\left(a_r^{l-1}\right), a_r^{l-1}) = \min_{d_k^l \in D^l} [\lambda_l$$

$$\min_{j=1,\dots,\eta_l} f_{jk}^l\left(a_r^{l-1}\right) + (1+\lambda_l) \max_{j=1,\dots,\eta_l} f_{jk}^l\left(a_r^{l-1}\right) +$$

$$+ \sum_{r_l=1}^{m_l} f_{l+1}^{\lambda_l}(d_{k_{l+1}^0}^{l+1}\left(a_{r_l}^l\right), a_{r_l}^l)g_{r_l}^l(a_r^{l-1}, d_k^l)].$$

Here:

$$f_{jk}^i\left(a_r^{i-1}\right) = \sum_{S=1}^{k} \mu_{jk}^S w_{jk}^S(a_r^{i-1}) / \sum_{j=1}^{n} \mu_j, \; \mu_j = \sum_{S=1}^{k} \mu_{ji}^S.$$

5   Conclusion and Suggestions

A computational experiment was carried out to solve problems of a fuzzy decision-making model in intelligent control systems. The results of computational experiments for solving problems showed improvements in the quality, efficiency and reliability of decisions made in intelligent control systems.

A promising direction of research on the issues under consideration is the development of methods for solving problems of semi-structured decision making using a combination of "Soft Computing" technologies: fuzzy sets, neural networks, genetic algorithms, evolutionary modeling and programming.

References

1. Ishankhodjayev, G., Sultanov, M., Nurmamedov, B.: Issues of development of intelligent information electric power systems. Modern Innov. Syst. Technol. 2(2), 0251–0263. https://doi.org/10.47813/2782-2818-2022-2-2-0251-0263

2. Ishankhodjaev, G.K., Sultanov, M.B, Mirzaakhmedov, D.M. Azimov, D.T.: Optimization of information processes of multilevel intelligent systems. In: CMSCDE 2021: 1st International workshop on Communication management, Soft Computing and Digital Economy, December 15–16, 2021. Doi: https://doi.org/10.1145/3508072.3508212

3. Ishankhodjayev G.K., Sultanov M.B., Sultanov J. Development of an algorithm for optimizing energy-saving management processes in intelligent energy systems. In: International Conference on Information Science and Communications Technologies (ICISCT 2021): Applications, Trends and Opportunities, November 3–5, 2021. https://doi.org/10.1109/ICISCT52966.2021.9670247

4. Ishankhodjayev, G., Sultanov, M., Parpiyeva, R., Norboyeva, N.: Development of intelligent information decision support systems. In: the 6th International Conference on Future Networks & Distributed Systems has Processing Errors (2022). https://doi.org/10.1145/3584202.3584203

5. Ishankhodjayev, G., Sultanov, M., Parpiyeva, R., Norboyeva, N.: Creation of intelligent information decision support systems. In: IV International Scientific Conference "Construction Mechanics, Hydraulics and Water Resources Engineering (2023). https://doi.org/10.1051/e3s conf/202336504031

6. Ishankhodjayev, G., Sultanov, M., Parpiyeva, R., Norboyeva, N.: Improvement of information support in intelligent information energy systems. In: Internet of Things, Smart Spaces, and Next Generation Networks and Systems. NEW2AN 2022. LNCS, vol. 13772, pp. 1–13 (2023). DOI: https://doi.org/10.1007/978-3-031-30258-9_16

7. Ishankhodjayev, G.K., Sultanov, M.B.: Development of information support for decision-making in intelligent energy systems. In: International Conference on Information Science and Communications Technologies (ICISCT 2022): Applications, Trends and Opportunities, November 3–5 (2022). https://doi.org/10.1109/ICISCT55600.2022.10146931

8. Kennedy, J., Eberhart, R.C.: Particle swarm optimization. In: Proceedings of IEEE International Conference on Neural Networks, pp. 1942–1948 (1995)

9. Хайкин Саймон. Нейронные сети: полный курс. 2-е изд. Пер. с англ. - М.: ООО «И.Д. Вильямс», 1104 с (2006)

10. Bekmuratov, T.F.: Systematization of tasks of intelligent decision support systems. In: Joint Release Based on the Materials of the Republican Scientific and Practical Conference "Modern Control and Information Systems", October 2–3, 2003. Tashkent, pp. 24–35 (2003)

11. Bekmuratov, T.F.: Conceptual model of an algorithmic fuzzy inference system. Problems Comput. Sci. Energy 6, 3–10 (2006)

Ways of Effective Using of Mobile Technologies in the Development of Recreational Tourism

Shaymanova Nigora Yusupovna[1,1(✉)] and Vayskulov Ramazan Alisher ugli[2]

[1] Tashkent State University of Economics Department of Tourism, Tashkent, Uzbekistan
n.shaymanova@tsue.uz
[2] Karshi State University Department of Tourism and Marketing, Qarshi, Uzbekistan

Abstract. This article explores the importance of innovative technologies in tourism, ways to use them effectively in the development of recreational tourism, and the dynamics of change. The introduction to the research work is based on the growing awareness of mobile systems and news media in the tourism industry at present. The normative framework aimed at regulating the tourism sector of the Republic of Uzbekistan and measures planned to be taken on the use of Information Technology in the field of tourism is presented. The opinions of experts who worked in the field and conducted research on the application of Information Technology and mobile technologies in the field of tourism are presented. Using international rankings, the possibilities of applying mobile technologies for the development of the industry have been analyzed. New tourism trends that have arisen with the use of innovative technologies in tourism have been studied. In the example of the world and Uzbekistan, it is shown how mobile operating systems are used and their role in the tourism sector is studied and affects the development of the industry. Based on the existing analyses for the development of the industry, proposals, and recommendations have been developed.

Keywords: innovative technology · mobile technology · recreational tourism · tourism infrastructure · information technology · tourism applications · mobile applications · mobile operating system

1 Introduction

Existing economic sector chances can be strengthened and made into extremely profitable sectors with the introduction of new technologies and scientific advancements. Such changes play a critical role in defining the economy's innovative development and stability. Every economic sector is unique, and each may have used modern technologies differently in its development. This is a common scenario for the tourism industry and its allied industries, whose primary goals are to boost the nation's exports of tourism services and provide all kinds of services required for foreign tourists.

It is advisable to implement development strategies tailored to the unique characteristics of each region of the country when using innovative technology in the tourism industry. Experience from throughout the globe demonstrates that this strategy also helps to expand the prospects for recreational tourism.

Y. Koucheryavy and A. Aziz (Eds.): NEW2AN/ruSMART 2023, LNCS 14543, pp. 12–20, 2024.
https://doi.org/10.1007/978-3-031-60997-8_2

The adoption of new information technology (IT) services has increased the influence of technology on travel in recent decades. This has resulted in the growth of the online travel business and increased digitization of the travel sector.

According to data approximately 75% of passengers worldwide intend to create their itinerary using online resources. These platforms include, for instance, Booking.com, Airbnb, and Agoda. Over 70% of tourists who travel use social media to tell others about their experiences. Social media posts with recommendations and information about places to visit account for about 35% of traveler decisions [16].

The application of cutting-edge technology and scientific advancements in the tourism industry has been the subject of substantial research in our nation throughout the past few years. Strengthening the legal-normative foundation for promoting innovative technologies in the tourism industry is crucial in this regard. For instance, "The task of implementing new types of services necessary for the development of the tourism industry with the help of innovative technologies is defined in the Concept of the development of the tourism industry in the Republic of Uzbekistan in 2019–2025."

According to it:

– creating a 3D model of attractions in Tashkent, Samarkand, Bukhara, Khiva, Shakhrisabz, and other cities for placement on popular Internet resources;
– introduction of practice-oriented and modernized educational standards, educational and methodological programs, and advanced information and communication technologies in the training of highly qualified specialists, retraining and improvement of service personnel's system;
– development and implementation of measures aimed at developing recreational tourism around lakes Aydarkul (Jizzakh and Navoi regions), Tudakul (Navoi region), and Uchkizil (Surkhandarya region) based on the results of the inventory transfer of regions and objects where tourism can be developed;
– development and printing of tourism maps of Uzbekistan and regions, as well as placing the electronic form of the tourism map on tourism portals and developing a mobile application for various platforms, including those without Internet connection are indicated [1]

Additionally, a single electronic state of archaeological monuments incorporating an electronic archaeological map of the Republic of Uzbekistan is included in the Decree of the President of the Republic of Uzbekistan "On measures to further develop domestic and pilgrimage tourism in the Republic of Uzbekistan" No. PD-6165. It is concluded that it is being done in compliance with the registration-related legal documentation [2]. This demonstrates the need to research and evaluate the applications of cutting-edge digital technology to enhance these areas' tourism potential.

2   Research Methodology

In this study, existing concepts regarding the use of innovative technologies in the field of tourism were studied. During the analysis of the literature on the topic, the approaches of experts were analyzed, during the analysis, the works carried out in the field were compared and their differences were highlighted.

Using international statistical data, it was proved that the level of coverage with mobile technologies around the world is rapidly increasing.

A comparative analysis of users of mobile operating systems between the world and Uzbekistan was carried out. Mobile applications intended for tourists were grouped according to the direction of use.

3   Literature Review

The use of mobile technologies in recreational tourism and related fields began to develop in the last years of the 20th century. It was during this period that many scientists conducted scientific research on the introduction of innovative technologies in tourism. According to the research of U. Gretzel, M. Sigala, Z. Xiang, Ch. Ko the tourism industry has been greatly influenced by advances in information and communication technologies (ICT), including the Internet, over the past few years. Therefore, they believe that it is necessary to use new strategies to attract customers, that is tourists, to tourist destinations [3, 4].

Turkish specialist K. Chynar believes that today, innovative technologies based on mobile technologies provide benefits to consumers, that is, to support the globalization of the tourist industry by providing tourists with the means of generating demand for tourist products, transforming and purchasing from the need, and providing management and distribution of service processes [5].

J. Saura emphasizes that the modernization of digital technologies has created an opportunity for the development of digital marketing and the convenience of sales, reservations, and sales of products via the Internet. According to him, today, electronic devices connected to the Internet are constantly used to help people organize and carry out their travels around the world using various applications such as travel guides, GPS, or interactive books [6–8].

The Russian expert Y. Konovalova approaches the aspect of using innovative technologies in the field of tourism as follows: innovations in tourism can be called qualitatively innovative systematic events that lead to positive changes in the field. The innovation process is shaped by the tourism market and the level of customer satisfaction, and mainly by joint decision-making by tourism organizations and different levels of government. In his opinion, the introduction of innovations in tourism is directly influenced by such factors as the economic situation in the country, social situation, population, national legislation, as well as intergovernmental and international agreements. He also identified the following reasons for the introduction of innovations in tourism: oversaturation of a large number of classic destinations; the risk of losing a significant share of the inbound tourism market; increase in competition and offers; expansion of the field of application of information technologies, technological revolution; decrease the amount of supply and increase the amount of demand in the economy; such as searching for and introducing a new market for products [9, 10].

Local scientists D. Aslanova and B. Safarov believe that the reason and inevitability of innovation lies in humanity's constant desire for innovation. Innovations are formed in an environment where needs and development collide, the task of innovation management is to realize and materialize the mature needs of society. They believe that the financing of innovations is carried out not only by the state but also at the expense of regional budgets in the following forms:

– financing of projects within the framework of targeted programs, within the scope of the state's foreign debts;
– is the financial support of highly effective innovative and investment projects [11, 12]

According to Danish scientists T. O'Dell and P. Billings, mobile technology plays an important role in the post-travel stage, primarily in collecting memories, reflecting, and reviving experiences. In particular, in the post-travel phase, the use of mobile technologies, particularly social media, are important personal mediators in the co-creation of the travel experience [13].

In the approaches presented above, there are different approaches to the use of innovative technologies in tourism, and all of them are based on the positive effect of using modern technology or approaches for the development of the sector. However, the fact that the aspect of mobile innovative technologies and software development in the more efficient organization of recreational tourism opportunities is not sufficiently covered at present justifies the relevance of this research.

4 Result and Discussion

The use of innovative information technologies has a positive effect on any industry. Innovative technologies used in the field of tourism have a positive effect on the modern implementation of the activities of all subjects related to the field, such as tourist companies, insurance companies, transport companies, tourist bureaus, hotels, and catering establishments. The use of these technologies consists of the creation of tourism products in the form of information that allows the consumer to choose a service via the Internet. This situation is of great importance for companies in the period when the current digitization process is rapidly progressing in the implementation of important processes such as competitive product, price formation, investment utilization, and sales policy.

– the use of innovative technologies in the field of tourism or the implementation of innovative activities in general is carried out based on directions set by the government and they are classified as follows:
– allocating funds for the implementation of targeted programs in the regions;
– creation of a network of information centers that provide free services to travelers and contribute to the education of residents in the field of tourism;
– providing financial support in the form of grants, subsidies, and investments for service provision and introduction of scientific developments used in related sectors of the economy [14].

The directions intended for the introduction of innovations, such as the above, directly provide for their financial support. Specialists with experience and qualifications in the application of new technologies in the field determine the need to provide technical service during the use of technology, to perform analyses necessary for more effective use of its capabilities.

The effective use of innovative processes and technologies is also characterized by the effective use of the opportunities of the field or network, as well as the solution to possible problems. According to the researchers, the advantages of using innovative technologies in the field of tourism are shown in the following:

– the amount of money spent by tourists on tourist services decreases (for example, booking a hotel in advance, air ticket);
– there will be an opportunity to get more, faster, and quality information about tourist services (tour packages and tour itineraries);
– opportunities for tourist services in the digital world to enter the world market will be greater;
– allows to eliminate the shortcomings of tour itineraries and services and develop them further due to quick feedback from tourists;
– service will be faster, better quality, more convenient, and less expensive [14].

All over the world, the development and spread of mobile technologies are progressing at a rapid pace, and this process is predicted to develop steadily in the future. With the rapid development of mobile technologies, it is important to consider its role in many sectors of tourism in creating innovative experiences for consumers and providing a sustainable competitive advantage for suppliers in the tourism industry [15]. This is also reflected in the increase in the number of users of smartphones, the most modern variant of mobile technologies (Fig. 1).

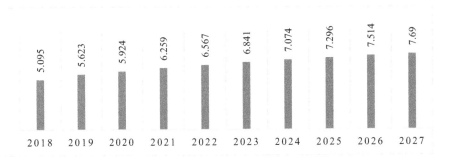

Fig. 1. Number of smartphone users worldwide.

Today, more than 80% of the world's population (more than 6.5 billion users) have a smartphone. Therefore, in the development or implementation of any innovative technologies, it is important to create alternatives for mobile technology.

The analysis of the data presented in the diagram shows that if in 2018 a little more than 5 billion people used smartphones in the world, then in just 3 years this figure increased by 122.8% and reached 6. 259 billion people. By 2027, it is predicted that 7.69 billion people in the world will use smartphones.

Smartphones are also gaining popularity as a means of tourism. It is convenient for tourists traveling to other destinations from their place of residence to use smartphones that they carry with them. The convenience of a smartphone for travelers is reflected in the availability of a camera, GPS, recording videos, and direct access to social networks in one device.

Based on this, it can be noted that the impact of mobile technologies on tourism is very high. The use of mobile communication tools has led to the emergence of new concepts and directions in the field of tourism (Fig. 2).

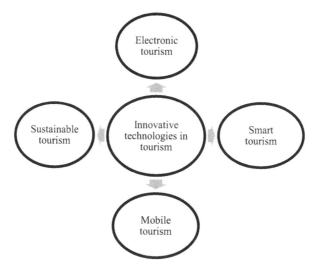

Fig. 2. Views of tourism based on innovative technologies

As shown in the diagram, innovative technologies form the basis of new trends in tourism, and changes in innovation have a great impact on the development of the industry. Innovations directly create opportunities for the tourism industry to develop more broadly.

The development of mobile technologies in tourism, first of all, to show how compatible it is with other technologies, secondly, to show the impact of these technologies on tourism and the social sphere, and thirdly, to study the cooperation with adjacent (logistics, transport, communication, etc.) sectors. Shows the need to conduct scientific research on learning. This also shows the need to analyze the level of its development and the directions affecting it when defining the perspective of the industry[15].

As mentioned above, the development of mobile technologies also provides great opportunities for the tourism industry. Major mobile technology companies around the world also provide users with the operating system(s) they need for their products. According to statistical data, Android and iOS are the main operating systems (OS) available in mobile technologies today (Fig. 3).

The data in the chart above shows that the Android operating system has the largest share of OSs in mobile technologies in the world (about 71% of the overall average). iOS, the operating system produced by Apple and installed only on its products, is equal to about 27% of the total users.

Analyzing the number of users of mobile technologies in Uzbekistan, it will be possible to see that the situation is slightly different (Fig. 4).

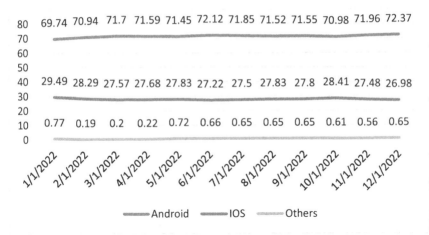

Fig. 3. The level of use of mobile software around the world [17]

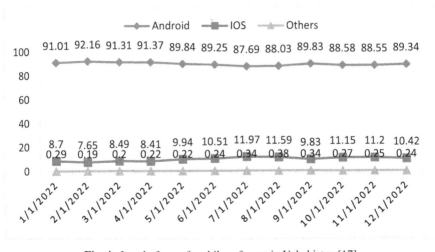

Fig. 4. Level of use of mobile software in Uzbekistan [17]

The most common mobile OS in Uzbekistan is Android OS (more than 90% of all users). The fact that there was no sharp decrease or increase in the number of users during the studied period, and the development of opportunities for mobile devices based on Android OS shows that the use of new technologies will give positive results.

Therefore, in the future, it will be necessary to improve mobile technology and mobile applications for both domestic and foreign tourists, as well as to build on Android and iOS software to create convenience for tourists.

Modern tourists use many applications during their trips. In doing so, they directly use state-of-the-art applications to purchase tickets, book a vehicle, get information about the destination in general, and find answers to other similar questions. Below in

Table 1, we present the types of mobile applications for tourists and their corresponding applications.

Table 1. Applications that tourists can use

№	Types of mobile applications	Compatible mobile applications
1	Booking programs	Trivago, Booking.com, Tripadvisor
2	Electronic maps	Google Maps, Yandex Maps, 2GIS
3	Translator applications	Google Translate, Yandex Translate, TripLingo
4	Navigation applications	Waze, Yandex, Navigator
5	Applications for flights	App In The Air, Flio, Skyscanner

In Uzbekistan, it is necessary to create and develop such applications in cooperation with IT and tourism specialists. The created applications need to be placed on platforms such as the Play Store and App Store. Applying a national approach to the creation of applications, reflecting the characteristics of the regions that show their unique aspects, will have a positive effect not only on attracting domestic tourists but also on increasing the interest of foreign tourists in our country.

5 Conclusion

In the conditions of globalization, the fact that the process of information exchange is very fast, the importance of using innovative technologies in the development of tourism and increasing its potential has become a fact that does not require proof. It shows that it is necessary to develop mobile technologies and create practical programs that can provide new opportunities for providing comfort to tourists traveling for recreation. For this, doing the following will give positive results:

- to achieve the introduction of tourist infrastructure based on innovative technologies, which is convenient for local and foreign tourists to use;
- application of innovative technologies in the form of high-quality photo and video materials, geoinformation data of the area, 3D view, etc., in determining the areas where new tourist destinations can be developed based on the recreational opportunities of the regions of the country;
- development of applications based on Android and iOS platforms. To ensure that the developed programs are intended not only for smartphones but also for various other gadgets (tablets, smartwatches, laptops, etc.)
- creation of alternative national applications to various mobile applications created by foreign companies for the convenience of tourists. Adapting these applications to meet all the needs of tourists;
- collect opinions on the evaluation of the quality of the regions or the tourist services provided in the applications to be created. In this way, to apply suggestions for eliminating the shortcomings that have arisen in the implementation of tourist trips for the development of the sector.

Thus, through the development of innovative mobile technologies in tourism and their wide use, an opportunity is created to ensure the growth of the country's economy.

References

1. Decree of the President of the Republic of Uzbekistan "On additional measures for the rapid development of tourism in the Republic of Uzbekistan" No. PD-5611
2. Decree of the President of the Republic of Uzbekistan No. PD-6165 "On measures to further develop domestic and pilgrimage tourism in the Republic of Uzbekistan"
3. Gretzel, U., Sigala, M., Xiang, Z., Koo, Ch.: Smart Tourism: Foundations and developments Electronic Markets **25**(3), 179–188 (2015)
4. Abdurakhmanova, G.K., Goipnazarov, S.B., Astanakulov, O.T., Irmatova, A.B.: Tourism 4.0: Opportunities for applying industry 4.0 technologies in tourism. In: ICFNDS '22: Proceedings of the 6th International Conference on Future Networks & Distributed Systems. https://doi.org/10.1145/3584202.3584208
5. Chynar, K.: Role of Mobile Technology for Tourism Development. The Emerald Handbook of ICT in Tourism and Hospitality. ISBN: 978-1-83982-689-4
6. Saura, J.R.: Using data sciences in digital marketing: Framework, methods, and performance metrics. J. Innov. Knowl., 1 (2020). https://doi.org/10.1016/j.jik.2020.08.001
7. Karimov, N., Khujanazarova, N.: Digital Economy in the Tourism Industry. In: ACM International Conference Proceeding Series. https://doi.org/10.1145/3508072.3508228
8. Sadinov, A., Rajabov, Sh.: Utilizing digital technologies for waste management. https://doi.org/10.1051/e3sconf/2023391011096
9. Konovalova, E.E, Kalinin, A.A., Karpova, A.A.: Innovative technologies of management and regulation of the sphere of tourism and hospitality. scientific magazine Vestnik Association Vuzov Tourism and Service, bol. 14. 2020 / №2 (2)
10. Khayitov, S., Ulugbek, K.: The role of IT on transportation, logistics and the economic growth among central Asian countries. In: International Conference on Next Generation Wired/Wireless Networking, pp. 649–655. Springer, Cham (2022)
11. Aslanova, D.Kh., Safarov, B.Sh., Khairullaev, A.: The role of innovation, and their significa-tion and investment and market tourism style in Uzbekistan. Econ. Bus. Theory Practice **3**, 18–22 (2016)
12. Safarov, B., et al.: Forecasting the volume of tourism services in Uzbekistan. Sustainability **2022**(14), 7762 (2022)
13. O'Dell, T., Billing, P. (eds.): Experiencescapes: Tourism, culture, and economy. Copenhagen Business School Press DK (2005)
14. Chen, R., Love, Sh., Hu, M.: Zang Bibliometric and Visualized Analysis of Mobile Technol-ogy in Tourism 3rd International Conference on Tourism Research 2020. https://doi.org/10.3390/su12197975
15. Developed based on information from the website https://www.statista.com/
16. https://adamosoft.com/blog/technology-in-tourism-reshaping-the-hospitality-industry
17. Developed based on information from the website. https://gs.statcounter.com

Applications of Fuzzy Set Models in Optimizing Agricultural Production Structures in Smart Farms

Akram Ishnazarov[✉] and Sarvar Mamasoliyev

Department of Mathematical Methods in Economics, Tashkent State University of Economics, Tashkent, Uzbekistan
{akram.ishnazarov,s.mamasoliyev}@tsue.uz

Abstract. This article emphasizes the application of fuzzy logic in the field of agriculture. The use of fuzzy logic is not restricted to specific agricultural domains, but rather extends from soil analysis to the entire process of plant production, encompassing various areas within agriculture. To gain a better understanding of fuzzy logic in agriculture, a concise and comprehensive literature review has been conducted. Crop yield estimation fuzzy logic involves the incorporation of input parameters such as productivity, area, and labor expenses. Through the application of fuzzy arithmetic to these parameters, a precise crop yield value is obtained. The fuzzy modeling employs optimal membership functions. The accuracy of the results is verified by comparing them with existing open-source literature.

Keywords: fuzzy logic · fuzzy inference system · membership functions · fuzzy mathematical programming problems · graded membership

1 Introduction

In today's agricultural sector, farmers are engaged in activities that not only supply the domestic market with agricultural products through production but also export to several foreign countries.

In Uzbekistan shortening cotton and wheat fields, replanting agricultural crops in fields vacated by wheat, and effectively utilizing agricultural land for farming not only benefits the agricultural sector but also contributes to the profitability of agricultural enterprises. Farmers are currently showing efficiency in producing several agricultural products in our country. In 2022, 99.4% of the planned cotton production and 80.7% of the wheat production were successfully achieved by farmers. The volume of agricultural production in 2022 increased by 101.9% compared to 2021, specifically, crop production increased by 100.7% and horticultural production by 104.2%. In terms of agricultural management categories, 63.6% of the total agricultural output was produced by individual farmers, 34.7% by collective farmers, and the remaining 1.7% by agricultural enterprises implementing agricultural activities [1].

The composition of cultivated land is considered one of the key indicators in the agricultural economic development plans of individual farmers [2]. Therefore, optimizing

Y. Koucheryavy and A. Aziz (Eds.): NEW2AN/ruSMART 2023, LNCS 14543, pp. 21–31, 2024.
https://doi.org/10.1007/978-3-031-60997-8_3

cultivated lands, especially in the context of market conditions and the independent operation of individual farmers, becomes an important issue. Identifying a range of factors that determine the composition of crops, including market conditions, the specialization of production, available labor resources, financial resources, the availability of basic and auxiliary funds, the ability to achieve certain ratios in crop production, and others, is essential. Taking into account these factors and applying conventional methods leads to a complex problem. Thus, solving such problems using economic-mathematical methods and computer technologies is not possible [19].

This document is structured into five sections. Section 2 provides a comprehensive overview of the investigations undertaken on the subject up to the current time. Section 3 contains details about the data used in our research and an explanation of the methodology applied. The findings of our analysis are articulated in Sect. 4. The ultimate insights derived from our investigation are encapsulated in the concluding Sect. 5.

2 Literature Review

Currently, linear programming methods are widely used in the utilization of cultivated lands by individual farmers [3]. Linear optimization models are mathematical programming models that incorporate linear constraints and objective functions that provide extremum (maximum or minimum) values. According to the rule, these models are considered "strict" since all initial data are determined quantitatively and decision-making is carried out under precise conditions [4].

The modern direction of modeling uncertainties is associated with the theory of fuzzy sets. The concept of "fuzzy set" was proposed by American scientist A.A. Zadeh in 1965. In traditional mathematics, a set is usually defined as a collection of elements that possess certain properties. In this case, each element is assigned only two possibilities: it either belongs or does not belong to the set, using binary logic. The concept of a "fuzzy set" is based on the following idea: the elements that constitute the set can possess the defining property to varying degrees, and therefore, the set can be related to various degrees [5].

If the simplex method is used to solve classical linear programming problems, solving fuzzy set problems requires complex and computationally intensive calculations. In many cases of multi-objective function problems, finding an optimal solution is often compromised, and a "compromise" solution is sought [6].

In economic processes, certain fuzzy set problems have been transformed into deterministic (precise form) problems, and finding the optimal solution has been more widely discussed [7].

Various authors have proposed using expert methods to determine the fuzzy coefficients in the objective function parameters and the fuzzy constraints in problems [8].

In solving fuzzy linear programming problems, the parameters of the objective function and the fuzzy constraints have been addressed in the work of the author [9], focusing on finding a precise solution to the problem.

Some authors have proposed methods based on defuzzification of the objective function [10]. This method allows expressing the solution to the problem in fuzzy numbers, considering the fuzzy objective function and precise constraints.

In solving problems related to uncertainties, probabilistic statistical methods are often employed [11]. Optimization models that take into account uncertainties in initial data form the subject of stochastic programming. It should be noted that if representative statistics are available to determine the probability law and fuzzy parameters are known, then using the theory of probabilities becomes reasonable for formalizing uncertainties.

In addressing the optimization problem of optimizing the composition of cultivated lands by individual farmers, it is necessary to utilize fuzzy mathematical programming theory, both in linear and fuzzy mathematical programming, various methods of multi-objective fuzzy linear programming, and the apparatus of fuzzy sets theory.

Fuzzy logic finds widespread applications in various scientific and industrial domains due to its effectiveness in handling vague and imprecise information [12, 13]. However, there is relatively limited research focused on the implementation of fuzzy logic in system dynamics. Some notable studies in this area include the works of Tahera. K & Ibrahim.R.N [14], Seçkin Polat & Cafer Erhan [15], and Vassilios Karavezyris & Klaus Peter [16], which have made significant contributions to this approach. The fundamental concept of fuzzy logic revolves around the notion of graded membership, where subsets of a universe can be defined by allowing partial membership. Unlike ordinary set theory, where an element is either fully in or out of a subset, fuzzy logic introduces the idea of graded membership, providing an infinite extension to the fundamental concepts of set theory and logic. This extension appears highly reasonable and intuitive. In contrast, boolean logic can be likened to the logic of valves that either allow or block the flow of fluids [16]. Therefore, with the aim of exploring the characteristics of fuzzy sets, it is important to note that the concept of fuzziness extends beyond existing mathematical structures. This paper focuses on examining the properties of fuzzy sets, as intended. The field of fuzzy sets was initially introduced by Lotfi A. Zadeh [17], who has significantly contributed to its theoretical development and practical applications. Additionally, numerous other researchers have made valuable contributions to the field. When considering the estimates of parameters, it is crucial to keep in mind that the rule equations are weighted based on the positions of the observations within their corresponding membership functions. It should be noted that determining the form of input-output relationships solely based on the output parameters of the model is highly challenging.

3   Data and Methodology

Fuzzy methods allow a transition from two-valued logic to intermediate-valued logic. This means that it enables the formulation of expressions such as "more or less significant" or "the value of the variable is approximately equal to a" and similar forms (which are not possible in classical linear programming problems). Consequently, it allows working with fuzzy objective functions and fuzzy constraints in mathematical programming problems. These optimization methods and models, as well as their implementation, are collectively referred to as fuzzy optimization or fuzzy mathematical programming. Providing a membership function is considered sufficient for mathematically representing a fuzzy set.

The membership function allows calculating the degree of membership of any element in a fuzzy set in a universal set [4, 5, 8]. Let's assume $X = \{x\}$ is the universal set.

In the universal set X, an element A is defined as a fuzzy set represented by the following ordered pair $\{x, f_A(x)\}$ where $f_A(x)$ - $[0, 1]$ is the membership function that accepts values in the interval $[0, 1]$ [7]. A fuzzy mathematical programming problem refers to a problem in which the goal is to find extremum (maximum or minimum) values of the objective function $F(x)$ over the set of alternatives $x \in X$, subject to given constraints $g_i(x) \leq 0 (\geq 0)$, and the parameters of the objective function and constraints are considered fuzzy quantities [8]. Fuzzy expressions can take various forms. This encompasses different groups of fuzzy mathematical programming problems. Now let's consider the specific fuzzy linear programming problem with given non-strict fuzzy constraints. The objective function $F(x)$ is given by $c \times x$, subject to the approximate inequality constraint $A \times x \approx \leq b$

$$c = (c_1, c_2, \ldots, c_n); x = (x_1, x_2, \ldots, x_n);$$

$$A = \begin{pmatrix} a_{11} & a_{12} & \ldots & a_{1n} \\ a_{21} & a_{22} & \ldots & a_{2n} \\ \ldots & \ldots & \ldots & \ldots \\ a_{m1} & a_{m2} & \ldots & a_{mn} \end{pmatrix}; x = \begin{pmatrix} x_1 \\ x_2 \\ \ldots \\ x_n \end{pmatrix}; b = \begin{pmatrix} b_1 \\ b_2 \\ \ldots \\ b_m \end{pmatrix}$$

The symbol "$\approx$" indicates the fuzzy execution of approximate inequalities [4, 6, 7].

The given (1) fuzzy mathematical programming problem differs from a crisp formulated problem in that the constraints of the problem are not strictly defined and allow for some degree of violation. The algorithm for solving such a problem consists of the following steps [7]:

1. Instead of seeking the maximum value of the objective function, a target value F_0 is provided, and the attainment of this value is sought for the objective function $F_0 : cx \geq F_0$.
2. Degrees are assigned to various values of the objective function, and the objective is formulated with respect to those degrees. If $cx \geq F_0$, then the objective is attained at a degree of 1. Otherwise, the degree of attainment of the desired result is strictly less than 1.
3. Parameters $d_i \geq 0, i = \overline{0, m}$ are provided to quantify the "strength" of permissibility for each respective constraint. If $cx \geq F_0 - d_0$ and $a_ix > b_i + d_i, i = \overline{1, m}$, then the constraints are considered permissibly violated, where i represents the number of the respective constraint.
4. Membership functions μ_i are determined for the objective function and constraints. The membership function μ_i for the constraints decreases within the interval $[b_i, b_i + d_i]$ and accepts values ranging from 0 to 1. It is assumed that the membership function μ_i within the interval is linearly dependent, as follows [4–6, 8, 9]:

$$\mu_i(x) = 0, \begin{cases} 1, a_ix \leq b_i; \\ 1 - \frac{a_ix - b_i}{d_i}, a_ix \in (b_i, b_i + d_i), i = \overline{1, m}; \\ 0, a_ix > b_i + d_i. \end{cases} \quad (1)$$

$$\mu_i(x) = 0, \begin{cases} 1, cx \leq F_0; \\ 1 - \frac{cx - F_0}{d_0}, cx \in (F_0, F_0 + d_0); \\ 0, cx > F_0 + d_0. \end{cases} \quad (2)$$

(2) and (3) formulas where $a_i = (a_{i1}, a_{i2}, \ldots\ldots a_{in}; x = (x_1, x_2, \ldots\ldots, x_n)^T$.

5. A unique alternative is determined. To find the unique alternative, it is necessary to identify the point x that is maximally associated with the non-linear solution. According to the Bellman-Zadeh guidance, such an alternative is evaluated as the solution to the problem [4, 8].

$$
\begin{aligned}
&\lambda \to max \\
&cx \le b_0 + d_0(1 - \lambda), \\
&a_i x \le b_i + d_i(1 - \lambda), i = \overline{1, m}, \\
&\lambda \in [0, 1] x \ge 0.
\end{aligned}
\tag{3}
$$

Let's consider the application of the given non-linear programming model in the optimization of crop fields in the specialized "Bek" farming industry in Sirdaria region. The farming industry aims to produce five different types of agricultural products. The allocation of crop fields, labor costs, existing orders, demand volume, and their production efficiency determine the production of these products. The composition of crop fields is determined by utilizing the available resources in the farming industry to ensure maximum economic output (highest profit). The following initial information was used to solve the optimization problem for optimizing the composition of crop fields in the farming industry:

1. The agricultural products of the farming industry include wheat, cotton, tomatoes, onions, and other types of vegetables.

   For each type of crop, the following information is known:

   Total labor costs (in person-days) required for cultivating one unit of the product in the crop field and additional labor costs during farming operations (e.g., harvesting period).

   Demand for the product (in quintals).

2. The total quantity of labor resources required for production during the year, including peak periods when the crops are being harvested.

3. Specific land areas available for cultivation.

4. Maximizing the overall profit obtained from selling the farming industry's products is considered as the criterion for optimality (Table 1).

Table 1. Initial information for problem solving.

Product name	Order, s	Productivity, s/ha	Labor expenses		1 ha of land removable profit, soums
			Total, person days/ha	Job shot in periods	
Cabbage	1000	180	75	26	830
Cucumber	2500	92	138	22	820
Tomato	6500	176	346	35	1100

(continued)

Table 1. (*continued*)

Product name	Order, s	Productivity, s/ha	Labor expenses		1 ha of land removable profit, soums
			Total, person days/ha	Job shot in periods	
Beetroot	5900	206	158	34	520
Other vegetables	1500	87	91	40	710
Crop area		313			
Labor resources (total)		45000			
Labor resources (work periods)		10000			

4 Results and Discussion

Let's formulate the economic-mathematical model of the problem. We introduce the variables as follows: x_1 - land area allocated for wheat cultivation (in acres); x_2 - land area allocated for cotton cultivation (in acres); x_3 - land area allocated for tomato cultivation (in acres); x_4 - land area allocated for onion cultivation (in acres); x_5 - land area allocated for other vegetable cultivation (in acres). The objective function of the problem takes the following form:

The objective function of the problem takes the following form:

$$F = 830x_1 + 820x_2 + 1100x_3 + 520x_4 + 710x_5 \rightarrow max$$

The following constraints should be implemented:

– in terms of the total area of crops:

$$(x_1 + x_2 + x_3 + x_4 + x_5) \approx\leq 313$$

– in terms of the total volume of labor resources:

$$(75x_1 + 138x_2 + 346x_3 + 158x_4 + 91x_5) \approx\leq 45000$$

For the volume of labor resources required during peak periods, the following constraints are considered:

$$(26x_1 + 22x_2 + 35x_3 + 34x_4 + 40x_5) \approx\leq 10000$$

In terms of the orders given for each type of crop, the following constraints are considered:

$$180x_1 \approx\geq 1000;$$

$$92x_1 \approx\geq 2500;$$

$$176x_1 \approx\geq 6500;$$

$$206x_1 \approx\geq 5900;$$

$$87x_1 \approx\geq 1500;$$

In terms of the values of the variables, the following constraints are considered: $x_1, x_2, x_3, x_4, x_5 \geq 0$ the values should be integers and non-negative.

We solve the given nonlinear programming problem using the method described above.

We define the feasible deviation vector for the objective function and the constraints, which allows for possible deviations (i.e., relaxation of "strictness" in linear programming):

$$d = (d_0, d_1, d_2, d_3, d_4, d_5, d_6, d_7, d_8, d_9)$$
$$= (1440, 7, 2250, 430, 3100, 450, 325, 295, 75)$$

We determine the value of the objective function F1 as the optimal solution of the given example. The optimal solution of the example is provided in Table 2.

Table 2. Optimal solution of the given example.

Product name	Area, (ha)	Cultivated product, (s)
Cabbage	36	6500
Cucumber	90	8323
Tomato	43	7540
Beetroot	29	5900
Other vegetables	115	10000
Total	313	
Labor resources (total)		45000
Labor resources (works hot periods)		10000
Profit (F1)		247780 thousand sum

Therefore, according to the optimal solution, in the "Bek" agricultural farm, it is necessary to allocate 36 hectares for cabbage, 90 hectares for cucumber, 43 hectares for tomato, 29 hectares for beetroot, and 115 hectares for other vegetables. The farm's profit amounts to 247,780,000 Uzbek sum.

3. We will determine the value of the F2 objective function as the maximum deviation from the optimal solution in terms of deviations. We will use the deviation vector stated in condition 1. The solution to the problem is presented in Table 3.

Table 3. Optimal Solution for Maximum Deviations.

Product name	Area, (ha)	Cultivated product, (s)
Cabbage	179	58175
Cucumber	53	4876
Tomato	36	6336
Beetroot	17	3502
Othervegetables	26	1352
Total	313	
Labor resources (total)		38247 people/day
Labor resources (works hot periods)		8600 people/day
Profit (F1)		162840 thousand sum

4. Let's determine the value of F_0:

$$F_0 = (F1 + F2)/2 = (247, 780 + 162, 840)/2 = 205, 310$$

5. Solving the following problem, we find the precise alternative that is maximally aligned with the non-unique solution:

Objective function:

$$\lambda \to max$$
$$\begin{cases} 830x_1 + 820x_2 + 1100x_3 + 520x_4 + 710x_5 - 1440\lambda \geq 205310 \\ x_1 + x_2 + x_3 + x_4 + x_5 + 7\lambda \geq 320 \\ 75x_1 + 138x_2 + 346x_3 + 158x_4 + 91x_5 + 2250\lambda \leq 47250 \\ 26x_1 + 22x_2 + 35x_3 + 34x_4 + 40x_5 + 430\lambda \leq 9030; \\ 180x_1 - 3100\lambda \geq 27900; \\ 92x_2 - 450\lambda \geq 4050 \\ 176x_3 - 325\lambda \geq 6175; \\ 206x_4 - 295\lambda \geq 5605; \\ 87x_1 - 75\lambda \geq 1425 \end{cases}$$

The results of solving the problem are presented in the Table 4.

Table 4. Determining the Optimal Alternative.

x2	x3	x4	x5	λ
90	43	29	115	0,728

From the information in Table 4, it can be observed that the optimal solution x^* for the initial nonlinear problem is achievable with a λ value of 0.728. Furthermore, when substituting this value into the objective function, we have:

$$F^* = 830 \cdot 36 + 820 \cdot 90 + 1100 \cdot 43 + 520 \cdot 29 + 710 \cdot 115 = 247780$$

6. Utilizing the information from Table 4, we find the final solution of the nonlinear problem. The results are presented in Table 5.

Table 5. Solution of the optimization problem for determining the optimal composition of farmland in the agricultural farm

Product name	Area, (ha)	Cultivated product, (s)
Cabbage	168	30158
Cucumber	66	6041
Tomato	36	6412
Beetroot	28	5820
Other vegetables	17	1480
Total	315	
Labor resources(total)		41883 people/day
Labor resources(separate)		9030 people/day
Profit (F1)		259748 thousand sum

The solution to the optimization problem for optimizing the composition of crops in the agricultural farm yields the following optimal allocation: 168 acres for cabbage, 66 acres for cucumber, 36 acres for tomato, 28 acres for beetroot, and 17 acres for other vegetables. In this solution, the agricultural farm utilizes a total of 41,883 labor resources out of the available 45,000 labor resources, leaving 3,117 labor resources unutilized. The unutilized labor resources indicate that additional labor resources are not required during peak periods, reducing the farm's expenses. As a result, the agricultural farm generates a total benefit of 259,748,000 Uzbek sum.

5   Conclusion

It is important to emphasize that different approaches exist for transforming such ill-structured problems into well-defined (exact) forms. In some problems, the desired value for the objective function is specified instead of minimizing (maximizing) it, and the achievement level of that value is sought. In other problems, various compromise solutions are sought using different preference functions instead of finding a complete solution. The selection of these approaches depends on the nature of the problem, the availability of additional information, and other relevant factors. In solving the deterministic optimization problem (well-structured problem) using linear programming with a strict objective function and strict constraints, the overall benefit of the agricultural farm amounts to 247,780,000 Uzbek sum. However, solving the ill-structured problem reveals that when the objective function and constraints are violated in imprecise numerical values, the optimization of the composition of crop fields results in a benefit of 259,748,000 Uzbek sum. Therefore, compared to linear programming methods based on strict constraints, the utilization of imprecise numerical values in both constraints and the objective function proves more effective in optimizing the composition of crop fields for agricultural farms.

References

1. Statistical agency of the Republic of Uzbekistan under the presidency: Agriculture of Uzbekistan: 2019–2022, pp. 13–14 (2023)
2. Nahorski, Z., Ravn, H.F.: A review of mathematical models in economic environmental problems, pp. 165–201 (2000)
3. Mirzoieva, T., Heraimovych, V.: Optimization of the sown areas structure as a tool for the development of medicinal crop production on the basis of sustainability and regenerative agriculture (2021). https://doi.org/10.1051/e3sconf/202124403027
4. Ishnazarov, A., Kasimova, N., Tosheva, S., Isaeva, A.: ICT and economic growth: evidence from cross-country growth modeling. In: ICFNDS 2021: The 5th International Conference on Future Networks and Distributed Systems, December 2021, pp. 668–671 (2021). https://doi.org/10.1145/3508072.3508204
5. Waongo, M., Laux, P., Traoré, S.B., Sanon, M., Kunstmann, H.: A crop model and fuzzy rule based approach for optimizing maize planting dates in Burkina Faso, West Africa. J. Appl. Meteor. Climatol. **53**, 598–613 (2014). https://doi.org/10.1175/JAMC-D-13-0116.1
6. Hong, H., Choi, C.-H.: Multicriteria fuzzy decision-making problems based on vague set theory. Fuzzy Sets Syst. **114**(1), pp. 103–113 (2000). ISSN 0165-0114. https://doi.org/10.1016/S0165-0114(98)00271-1
7. Ekel, P.Ya.:Fuzzy sets and models of decision making. Comput. Math. Appl. **44**(7), 863–875 (2002). ISSN 0898-1221. https://doi.org/10.1016/S0898-1221(02)00199-2
8. Zimmermann, H.-J.: Fuzzy mathematical programming. Comput. Oper. Res. **10**(4), 291–298 (1983). ISSN 0305–0548. https://doi.org/10.1016/0305-0548(83)90004-7
9. Kumar, A., Kaur, J.: General form of linear programming problems with fuzzy parameters. J. Appl. Res. Technol. **11**(5), 629–635 (2013). ISSN 1665–6423. https://doi.org/10.1016/S1665-6423(13)71570-0
10. Ishnazarov, A., Shamsieva, F.: Globalization and carbon emissions (Open Access): Economic Growth and Wellbeing: Evidence from the Belt and Road Initiative Countries, pp. 71–87 (2022). https://novapublishers.com/shop/economic-growth-and-wellbeing-evidence-from-the-belt-and-road-initiative-countries/. ISBN 979-888697104-0; 978-168507990-1
11. Veeramani, C., Sumathi, M.: Fuzzy mathematical programming approach for solving fuzzy linear fractional programming problem. RAIRO – Oper. Res. **48**(1), 109–122 (2014). https://doi.org/10.1051/ro/2013056
12. Ronald, R.Y.: An introduction to fuzzy set theory. In: Karwowski, W., Mital, A. (eds.) Advances in Human Factors/Ergonomics, vol. 6, pp. 29–39. Elsevier (1986). ISSN 0921-2647, ISBN 9780444427236. https://doi.org/10.1016/B978-0-444-42723-6.50007-6
13. Dubois, D.: Fuzzy Sets and Systems. Theory and Applications, 120 p. NY (1980). https://doi.org/10.1137/102708
14. Al-Najjar, B., Alsyouf, I.: Selecting the most efficient maintenance approach using fuzzy multiple criteria decision making. Int. J. Prod. Econ. **84**(1), 85–100 (2003). 0925-5273, https://doi.org/10.1016/S0925-5273(02)00380-8

15. Tahera, K., Ibrahim, R.N., Lochert, P.B.: A fuzzy logic approach for dealing with qualitative quality characteristics of a process. Int. J. Expert Syst. Appl. **34**(4), 2630–2638 (2008). https://doi.org/10.1016/j.eswa.2007.05.025

16. Polat, S., Bozdağ, C.E.: Comparison of fuzzy and crisp systems via system dynamics simulation. Eur. J. Oper. Res. **138**(1), 178–190 (2002). ISSN 0377-2217. https://doi.org/10.1016/S0377-2217(01)00124-2

17. Bellman, R.E., Zadeh, L.A.: Decision making in a fuzzy environment. Manag. Sci. **17**, B.141–B.164 (1970). https://doi.org/10.1287/mnsc.17.4.B141

18. Zadeh, L.A.: On the definition of adaptivity. Proc. IEEE **51**(3), 469–470 (1963). https://doi.org/10.1109/PROC.1963.1852

19. Zadeh, L.A.: Fuzzy sets. Inf. Control **8**(3), 338–353 (1965). ISSN 0019-9958, https://doi.org/10.1016/S0019-9958(65)90241-X

20. Shepherd, D., Shi, F.K.C.: Economic modelling with fuzzy logic. IFAC Proc. **31**(16), 435–440 (1998). ISSN 1474-6670, https://doi.org/10.1016/S1474-6670(17)40518-0

21. Isaeva, A., Ishnazarov, A., Shamsiyeva, F., Tosheva, S., Khachaturov, A.: Does innovation promote regional economic development? Evidence for countries in Europe and Central Asia. ACM International Conference Proceeding Series, pp. 698–701(2021). http://portal.acm.org/. ISBN 978-145038734-7. https://doi.org/10.1145/3508072.3508209

Parallel Approaches to Accelerate Deep Learning Processes Using Heterogeneous Computing

Rashid Nasimov[1] , Mekhriddin Rakhimov[2] , Shakhzod Javliev[2(✉)] ,
and Malika Abdullaeva[2]

[1] Tashkent State University of Economics, Tashkent, Uzbekistan
rashid.nasimov@tsue.uz
[2] Tashkent University of Information Technologies, Tashkent, Uzbekistan
shajavliyev@gmail.com

Abstract. In the current context, the rise of artificial intelligence (AI) emphasizes the need to expedite training procedures, especially when dealing with extensive data, particularly in deep learning. This research primarily aims to significantly improve the time efficiency of deep learning processes. While it's widely recognized that graphics processing units (GPUs) offer notably faster performance for specific data tasks compared to a computer's central processing unit (CPU), this study explores heterogeneous computing systems for situations where GPUs are unavailable. Here, we investigate strategies to achieve enhanced processing speed using advanced technologies. The study concludes by presenting comparative results from various approaches and providing important recommendations for future endeavors.

Keywords: artificial intelligence · deep learning · heterogeneous computing systems · OpenCL · CUDA technology · parallel processing

1 Introduction

Today, it is widely acknowledged that virtually every field depends on information technology and artificial intelligence (AI). For instance, tasks like matrix multiplication or image processing, which involve extracting crucial image features, naturally lead to increased processing time. The notion that working with large datasets is time-consuming is well-established. When exploring the expanding realm of AI, it is essential to begin by considering the concept itself and its extensive scope. Machine learning (ML) enables computers to learn from data without explicit programming, a form of AI. ML algorithms can be trained to identify and interpret patterns in data, offering insights even with large datasets [1, 2]. Computer processing speed is steadily rising due to technological advancements. Deep learning applications are crucial for extracting valuable insights from vast datasets, spanning images [3], videos, text, speech signals [4–6], and sensor data [7, 8]. This emulation involves tasks like learning, reasoning, problem-solving, perception, language understanding, and interaction with the environment. AI technology's main goal is to create systems that can mimic human-like intelligence for task completion. In AI, there are various branches and classifications, each focusing on specific aspects of intelligence and problem-solving (see Fig. 1).

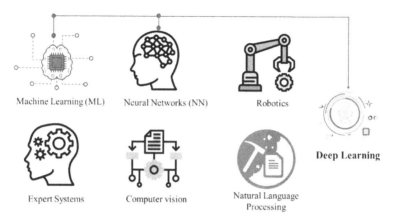

Fig. 1. Artificial intelligence and its types

Figure 1 demonstrates how AI can intersect and interact in diverse ways, with progress in AI technology driven by various research directions.

Summarizing the previously mentioned information: Deep learning is vital for analyzing complex, large datasets using intricate neural networks, which find patterns in data. These networks are used in diverse fields like image classification, object detection [9, 10], speech recognition [11, 12], and language translation. Deep learning's training on large datasets improves accuracy and performance, enabling the solution of previously unsolvable complex problems using conventional ML methods [13, 14]. Deep learning models necessitate extensive datasets and substantial computational resources for training. This requirement has spurred the development of specialized hardware and software tailored for deep learning, such as graphics processing units, and has also led to the emergence of dedicated frameworks. Devices lacking graphics processing units encounter speed challenges in deep learning processes. To overcome this, we suggest the implementation of heterogeneous computing systems and their optimal technologies. Further sections will provide detailed insights into this proposal.

2 Heterogeneous Computing Systems in AI

In the field of AI, a heterogeneous system refers to a computing environment that combines different types of hardware or processing units to carry out tasks related to AI and ML. These systems are intentionally created to leverage the unique benefits of each hardware component, thus improving performance and efficiency when managing AI workloads. In a heterogeneous system [15], you'll find a combination of traditional Central Processing Units (CPUs), Graphics Processing Units (GPUs), Field-Programmable Gate Arrays (FPGAs), Application-Specific Integrated Circuits (ASICs) [8], and even specialized AI accelerators (Fig. 2).

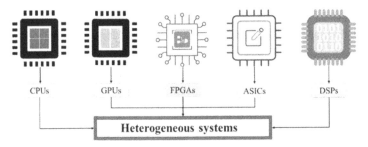

Fig. 2. Heterogeneous computing systems

As depicted in Fig. 2, each of these hardware components has unique strengths and capabilities that can be strategically utilized for specific AI-related tasks. Heterogeneous systems enable the simultaneous operation of multiple processor types. GPUs excel in parallel computations, which makes them well-suited for tasks that involve extensive matrix operations commonly found in deep learning algorithms. CPUs on the other hand, are versatile processors capable of handling a wide range of tasks. CPUs contribute to the acceleration of algorithms across a variety of processors, including FPGAs, ASICs, and Digital Signal Processors (DSPs).

Heterogeneous systems are setups that combine multiple processors or cores. These systems achieve improved performance and energy efficiency by not only incorporating processors of the same type but also by integrating dissimilar coprocessors. Technologies such as OpenCL and CUDA are recognized as valuable tools for heterogeneous systems. CUDA (Compute Unified Device Architecture) enables parallel data processing on graphics cards and empowers the utilization of Nvidia GPUs for general computing tasks, including operations like matrix multiplication and various linear algebra computations, extending beyond graphics-related computations. Hence, when using an NVIDIA graphics card, we can effortlessly utilize the CUDA parallel technology within heterogeneous computing systems. On the other hand, in cases where the device lacks a graphics processor or uses a non-NVIDIA graphics processor, we can turn to the OpenCL parallel technology provided by heterogeneous computing systems. OpenCL, short for "Open Computing Language" is an open standard framework created for programming heterogeneous computing systems that include CPUs, GPUs, FPGAs, and other accelerators. Developers can utilize this framework to create programs that can run on various processing units, taking advantage of the distinct capabilities of each unit to achieve improved performance.

3 Related Works

The growth of hidden layers in ML procedures is recognized to significantly extend the time required, creating time-related challenges for the efficiency of deep learning processes. Examining the handling of extensive data in deep learning, particularly when working with matrices of varying sizes, reveals that processing time increases proportionally with matrix size. Consequently, time becomes a prominent concern in various computing system domains. To mitigate this issue, it is possible to boost processor speed by optimizing CPU resource usage and innovating new parallel algorithms for reduced processing time. The training of specific neural networks necessitates substantial computational resources, and this process can be expedited through the utilization of high-performance GPUs [16]. In cases where our training device lacks a GPU, we have the option of employing the OpenMP parallel library to enhance processing [17]. However, if we possess a GPU, especially an NVIDIA GPU, we can leverage CUDA technology [18], while OpenCL technology is suitable for other types of GPUs [19]. This approach leads to the establishment of heterogeneous computing systems, enabling parallelization in training processes.

Let us explore our study's specific goals. We conducted a thorough review of prior research in our field, which provided valuable insights. Many of these studies emphasized the use of GPUs to speed up the training phase. It is crucial to acknowledge that GPUs may encounter speed limitations when handling ever-larger data volumes. The primary contribution of our study is to showcase the benefits of utilizing heterogeneous computing systems to expedite the training process on GPUs. Based on the study's findings, it has been determined that CUDA and OpenCL technologies within heterogeneous computing systems are superior and more efficient instrumental tools. In this context, during the execution of algorithms in the training process, the GPU is the proficient processor, and CUDA technology demonstrates remarkable efficiency. However, it is important to emphasize that CUDA is designed exclusively for Nvidia hardware. In cases where our training device doesn't have an Nvidia GPU, the logical choice is to utilize OpenCL on a CPU or a non-Nvidia GPU, providing a suitable alternative. As mentioned earlier, CUDA technology is a key component of heterogeneous systems, but it is compatible only with Nvidia GPUs. On the other hand, OpenCL has the potential to significantly improve processing speed in deep learning tasks when used with a CPU or different GPU types.

In the preceding section, we have explored the broad applicability of heterogeneous computing systems in the field of AI, along with an understanding of their primary parallel processing technologies, CUDA and OpenCL, based on previous research and acquired knowledge. Moving forward, in the upcoming sections, we will shift our focus to the utilization of CUDA and OpenCL technologies, which are essential components of these heterogeneous systems. These technologies will play a crucial role in accelerating deep learning processes and achieving the best possible results.

4   Using CUDA and OpenCL Technology in Deep Learning

As mentioned earlier, in our research on training neural networks, we have explored the potential use of CUDA technology on devices equipped with Nvidia GPUs, as well as technologies like OpenCL and OpenMP on devices with other types of GPUs or even without GPUs. However, the data we have examined has highlighted a significant difference: GPUs typically have a much higher number of cores compared to modern processors, often reaching into the hundreds. While basic computations in ML can be effectively handled by a CPU, the requirements of complex deep learning processes can place a significant burden on CPU resources. When a GPU is available to assist with graphics-related tasks, leveraging its capabilities can lead to faster and more efficient results for computational work. In the field of deep learning, CUDA technology is widely used to accelerate the training of deep neural networks (DNNs) by leveraging the power of thousands of GPU cores. This approach results in faster computations compared to performing these tasks exclusively on CPUs. Deep learning frameworks require the integration of various computation kernels into a unified system to achieve optimal performance across different computational resource utilization scenarios. Using CUDA technology within heterogeneous systems can lead to favorable results, particularly in accelerating the training of deep neural networks (DNNs) in the field of deep learning. In the context of neural network computations, especially in deep learning and parallel processing for tasks involving video or image manipulation, a critical consideration revolves around harnessing the computational power of the computer's GPU. Therefore, for this research, it is imperative to utilize CUDA and OpenCL technologies within heterogeneous systems.

4.1 CUDA Architecture in Deep Learning

The CUDA architecture is of significant importance in the field of deep learning as it significantly speeds up both the training and inference stages of neural networks. CUDA is a parallel computing platform and programming model developed by NVIDIA exclusively for their GPUs (Fig. 3).

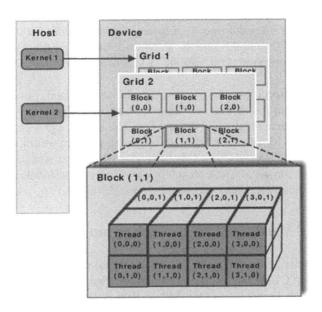

Fig. 3. CUDA device memory model

This framework enables developers to utilize the parallel processing capabilities of GPUs, leading to the acceleration of various computational tasks, including those crucial to deep learning procedures. In the image depicted in Fig. 3, the device code primarily runs on the GPU, whereas the host code operates on the central processor (referred to as CPU, in this context, with the device representing the GPU). Global memory is a memory type that can be accessed by all threads and blocks, but it has slower access speeds. In contrast, shared memory is available to all threads within a block and provides approximately ten times faster access compared to global memory. Additionally, each thread has its own local memory, which offers even faster access speeds. CUDA utilizes the computational capabilities of a computer's GPU to perform parallel processing on large datasets or images.

This data processing through CUDA technology involves the steps depicted in the Fig. 4 diagram above.

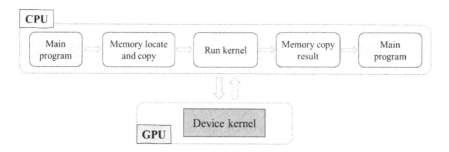

Fig. 4. Steps involved in data processing with CUDA technology

4.2 OpenCL Architecture in Deep Learning

OpenCL is a programming platform that enables developers to create code that can run on various types of computing devices, including CPUs, GPUs, FPGAs, and other accelerators. Although it is not specifically designed for deep learning, OpenCL can be used to accelerate deep learning computations across a variety of hardware setups. OpenCL can be utilized to enhance the performance of tasks in the field of deep learning, enabling efficient execution of operations like matrix multiplications and convolutions on GPUs and other acceleration devices. Many deep learning frameworks provide compatibility with OpenCL as a backend, making it easier to perform computations on a wider range of hardware choices. Furthermore, OpenCL code consists of two parts: the host code, which runs on the main CPU and manages the activation of cores on the designated device, like a GPU. OpenCL is specifically designed to function across a variety of hardware platforms, including GPUs, CPUs, FPGAs, and other accelerators. This device-agnostic approach empowers developers to write code that can be executed on a broad array of computing devices (see Fig. 5).

OpenCL further adopts parallelism by employing workgroups and work items, where workgroups consist of multiple work items executed concurrently on the device's cores. Similar to CUDA, OpenCL's programming model includes a host (CPU) and a device (accelerator), with the host managing data, tasks, and synchronization, while the device handles computational tasks.

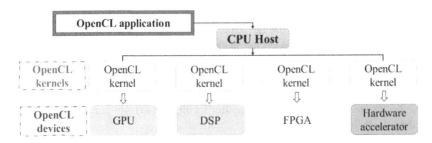

Fig. 5. Steps involved in data processing with OpenCL technology

Although it is not as widely used in deep learning as CUDA, OpenCL can be integrated into deep learning frameworks like TensorFlow and PyTorch to accelerate computations on compatible devices. As a result, the OpenCL platform provides flexibility, catering to a wide range of hardware setups to improve deep learning processes. However, achieving peak efficiency may require more extensive optimization efforts compared to CUDA due to the varying performance characteristics of different devices. Its adaptability and ability to work with specialized accelerators highlight its significance in situations where having diverse hardware options is crucial.

5   Experimental Results

In the realm of deep learning, it is widely recognized that dealing with large amounts of data can lead to speed-related challenges. In our research, we conducted several experiments to enhance the training of deep learning models, specifically by utilizing heterogeneous computing frameworks on computers equipped with and without dedicated graphics processors (GPUs) while scaling and processing networks of various sizes. More details about the devices used in this study can be found in Table 1.

Table 1. Characteristics of processors

№	Model processor	Cores	CUDA	OpenCL
1	Intel Core i7-12650H Nvidia GeForce RTX 3070	10/16 5100	12.0 version	–
2	MacBook Pro M1	4/8	–	3.0 version

Our objective was to expedite the training processes. Our investigation involved two types of hardware, CUDA for GPUs and OpenCL for non-GPUs, to accelerate the training of networks of different sizes. On our computers with the specifications listed in the table above, we performed matrix multiplication with dimensions 16×16, 32×32, 64×64, 128×128, 256×256 and 512×512 and performed the following two studies and obtained the expected result:

1. We conducted our first study on our first device listed in Table 1: In this case, the expected speed was achieved through CUDA technology on the CPU and GPU for matrix multiplication of varying sizes (Fig. 6).

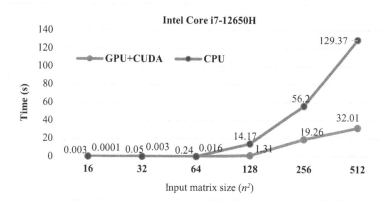

Fig. 6. Acceleration of teaching processes using CUDA technology

2. We also conducted our second study on our second device listed in Table 1: we achieved the expected speedup using OpenCL technology for matrix multiplication during training on diverse GPUs or non-GPU devices (Fig. 7).

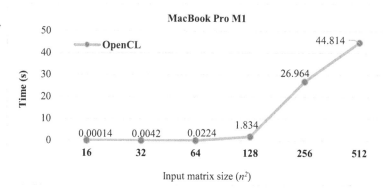

Fig. 7. Acceleration of teaching processes using OpenCL technology

If we focus on Fig. 7, our research shows that we can accelerate deep learning processes using heterogeneous computing systems using OpenCL technology for non-GPU devices. However, if we pay attention to the result obtained in Fig. 6, we can see that the CUDA technology achieves a much more efficient result than the rest of the technologies on the device with Nvidia GPUs, the main reason for this is that the GPUs developed by Nvidia are capable of deep learning in the field of AI. Gives the opportunity to achieve better speeds in the processes. Technologies of heterogeneous computing systems, such as CUDA and OpenCL, play a very important role in achieving speed in deep learning processes.

6 Conclusion

According to the findings from our study, a notable observation emerges: heterogeneous computing frameworks enable us to engage multiple processors simultaneously, a crucial factor in expediting the learning processes. In our research, we have sped up deep learning using CUDA on Nvidia GPUs for heterogeneous systems. We have also cut training time significantly by incorporating OpenCL when GPUs are unavailable.

Based on our research findings, we can deduce that CUDA technology enables the utilization of parallel processing across multiple computing units concurrently. However, it is essential to note that CUDA is exclusively compatible with Nvidia GPUs. As a result of our investigation, we recommend the use of OpenCL technology for heterogeneous systems with different types of processors, as indicated in the study. These heterogeneous computing systems facilitate the continuous flow of data, allowing efficient use of processing potentials by transferring data streams between the two components. Especially in the context of deep learning tasks, this framework serves to speed up the extraction of key features from large data sets by combining special additional features.

References

1. Abdusalomov, A.B., Nasimov, R., Nasimova, N., Muminov, B., Whangbo, T.K.: Evaluating synthetic medical images using artificial intelligence with the GAN algorithm. Sensors **23**, 3440 (2023). https://doi.org/10.3390/s23073440
2. Rakhimov, M., Akhmadjonov, R., Javliev, S.: Artificial intelligence in medicine for chronic disease classification using machine learning. In: 2022 IEEE 16th International Conference on Application of Information and Communication Technologies (AICT), Washington DC, DC, USA, pp. 1–6 (2022). https://doi.org/10.1109/AICT55583.2022.10013587
3. Tagmatova, Z., Abdusalomov, A., Nasimov, R., Nasimova, N., Dogru, A.H., Cho, Y.-I.: New approach for generating synthetic medical data to predict type 2 diabetes. Bioengineering **10**, 1031 (2023). https://doi.org/10.3390/bioengineering10091031
4. Abdusalomov, A.B., Safarov, F., Rakhimov, M., Turaev, B., Whangbo, T.K.: Improved feature parameter extraction from speech signals using machine learning algorithm. Sensors **22**, 8122 (2022). https://doi.org/10.3390/s22218122
5. Rakhimov, M.: Algorithm for parallel processing of a speech signal based on the Haar wavelet. In: 2022 International Conference on Information Science and Communications Technologies (ICISCT), Tashkent, Uzbekistan, pp. 1–4 (2022). https://doi.org/10.1109/ICISCT55600.2022. 10146906
6. Musaev, M., Rakhimov, M.: A method of mapping a block of main memory to cache in parallel processing of the speech signal. In: 2019 International Conference on Information Science and Communications Technologies (ICISCT), Tashkent, Uzbekistan, pp. 1–4 (2019). https://doi.org/10.1109/ICISCT47635.2019.9011946

7. Safarov, F., Kutlimuratov, A., Abdusalomov, A.B., Nasimov, R., Cho, Y.-I.: Deep learning rec- ommendations of e-education based on clustering and sequence. Electronics **12**, 809 (2023). https://doi.org/10.3390/electronics12040809

8. Safarov, F., Akhmedov, F., Abdusalomov, A.B., Nasimov, R., Cho, Y.I.: Real-time deep learning-based drowsiness detection: leveraging computer-vision and eye-blink analyses for enhanced road safety. Sensors **23**, 6459 (2023). https://doi.org/10.3390/s23146459

9. Rakhimov, M., Elov, J., Khamdamov, U., Aminov, S., Javliev, S.: Parallel implementation of real-time object detection using OpenMP. In: 2021 International Conference on Information Science and Communications Technologies (ICISCT), Tashkent, Uzbekistan, pp. 1–4 (2021). https://doi.org/10.1109/ICISCT52966.2021.9670146

10. Rakhimov, M., Boburkhon, T., Khurshid, T.: Speaker separation: use neural networks. In: 2021 International Conference on Information Science and Communications Technologies (ICISCT), Tashkent, Uzbekistan, pp. 01–03 (2021). https://doi.org/10.1109/ICISCT52966. 2021.9670322

11. Fazliddinovich, R.M., Abdumurodovich, B.U.: Parallel processing capabilities in the process of speech recognition. In: 2017 International Conference on Information Science and Com- munications Technologies (ICISCT), Tashkent, Uzbekistan, pp. 1–3 (2017). https://doi.org/ 10.1109/ICISCT.2017.8188585

12. Abdullaeva, M.I., Juraev, D.B., Ochilov, M.M., Rakhimov, M.F.: Uzbek speech synthesis using deep learning algorithms. In: Zaynidinov, H., Singh, M., Tiwary, U.S., Singh, D. (eds.) IHCI 2022. LNCS, vol. 13741, pp. 39–50. Springer, Cham (2022). https://doi.org/10.1007/ 978-3-031-27199-1_5

13. Abdusalomov, A.B., Islam, B.M.S., Nasimov, R., Mukhiddinov, M., Whangbo, T.K.: An improved forest fire detection method based on the detectron2 model and a deep learning approach. Sensors **23**, 1512 (2023). https://doi.org/10.3390/s23031512

14. Rakhimov, M., Abdurakhmanov, D.: AI-based power transformer condition assessment. In: 2022 International Conference on Information Science and Communications Technologies (ICISCT), Tashkent, Uzbekistan, pp. 1–4 (2022). https://doi.org/10.1109/ICISCT55600.2022. 10146905

15. Rakhimov, M., Ochilov, M.: Distribution of operations in heterogeneous computing systems for processing speech signals. In: 2021 IEEE 15th International Conference on Application of Information and Communication Technologies (AICT), Baku, Azerbaijan, pp. 1–4 (2021). https://doi.org/10.1109/AICT52784.2021.9620451

16. Rakhimov, M., Mamadjanov, D., Mukhiddinov, A.: A high-performance parallel approach to image processing in distributed computing. In: 2020 IEEE 14th International Conference on Application of Information and Communication Technologies (AICT), Tashkent, Uzbekistan, pp. 1–5 (2020). https://doi.org/10.1109/AICT50176.2020.9368840

17. Musaev, M., Rakhimov, M.: Accelerated training for convolutional neural networks. In: 2020 International Conference on Information Science and Communications Technologies (ICISCT), Tashkent, Uzbekistan, pp. 1–5 (2020). https://doi.org/10.1109/ICISCT50599.2020. 9351371

18. Lei, H., Akhtar, N., Mian, A.: Picasso: a CUDA-based library for deep learning over 3D meshes. In: 2021 IEEE/CVF Conference on Computer Vision and Pattern Recognition (CVPR), Nashville, TN, USA, pp. 13849–13859 (2021). https://doi.org/10.1109/CVPR46 437.2021.01364

19. Li, S., Luo, Y., Sun, K., Choi, K.: Heterogeneous system implementation of deep learning neural network for object detection in OpenCL framework. In: 2018 International Confer- ence on Electronics, Information, and Communication (ICEIC), Honolulu, HI, USA, pp. 1–4 (2018). https://doi.org/10.23919/ELINFOCOM.2018.8330645

A Zigbee Monitoring Network Construction Method for Greenhouse Agricultural Environment

Ruipeng Tang, Narendra Kumar Aridas$^{(\boxtimes)}$, and Mohamad Sofian Abu Talip

Department of Electrical Engineering, Faculty of Engineering, University of Malaya Kuala Lumpur, Kuala Lumpur, Malaysia
22057874@siswa.um.edu.my, {narendra.k,sofian_abutalip}@um.edu.my

Abstract. Greenhouse cultivation technology has greatly promoted the development of Malaysian agriculture. The environmental conditions of the greenhouse affect the growth of crops. Monitoring the indoor environment in real-time with high efficiency, stability and low power consumption is very important. In this article, it analyzes the actual scenarios and existing problems of the greenhouse agricultural and environmental parameter monitoring and proposes an agricultural greenhouse environmental monitoring system based on Zigbee. The acquisition module comprises environmental monitoring sensors. It uses a battery power supply and low-power consumption chip to solve the power supply problem of multiple nodes. The serial communication module for collection and node troubleshooting and the Ethernet communication module completes the greenhouse environmental monitoring network. This ZWSN (Zigbee wireless sensor network) improves the efficiency of the greenhouse environmental parameter monitoring, which ensures that the greenhouse environmental monitoring can carry out the daily work with low power consumption, high stability, and high speed.

Keywords: Zigbee · agricultural greenhouse · agricultural environment monitoring · smart agriculture

1 Introduction

In recent years, greenhouse agriculture has greatly promoted the development of Malaysian agriculture. How to build a ZWSN with high speed, low power consumption and good stability has become the focus of the construction in greenhouse agriculture. However, most existing greenhouses in Malaysia still rely on wired measurement and control equipment and use manual methods to perform some simple work [1, 2]. In order to obtain the environmental data, the certain number of measuring instruments need to be placed in the greenhouse. The equipment can be judged and executed to adjust the greenhouse environment. This method makes it difficult to arrange instruments and has low measurement accuracy, but it cannot obtain the overall data. While obtaining comprehensive and accurate data is difficult, it also consumes a lot of manpower and material resources [3].

Y. Koucheryavy and A. Aziz (Eds.): NEW2AN/ruSMART 2023, LNCS 14543, pp. 42–54, 2024.
https://doi.org/10.1007/978-3-031-60997-8_5

In order to solve these problems, some researchers have researched agricultural environmental monitoring and achieved some achievements. Smith, J and other scholars [4] proposed a Zigbee-based greenhouse monitoring system for real-time monitoring of environmental parameters in the greenhouse, such as temperature, humidity, and light, but the data transmission rate is low. Johnson, A and other scholars [5] proposed a hardware design of the Zigbee sensor node intended for greenhouse monitoring, especially for monitoring soil moisture. However, the applicability is limited to soil moisture monitoring. Brown, L and other scholars [6] proposed an intelligent monitoring system for greenhouse management by using the Zigbee network for data transmission. The system has more functionality and coverage but requires more complex data processing and storage. Garcia. R and other scholars [7] proposed a smart greenhouse monitoring system using Zigbee to monitor environmental parameters and plant growth. It can monitor plant growth status with multiple parameters, but the system complexity is too high and requires a lot of investment. Kim, S and other scholars [8] proposed a hardware design of the Zigbee-based greenhouse monitoring system, which focuses on the low power consumption of sensor nodes. It can achieve long-term monitoring with low power consumption. However, the transmission distance is very limited and cannot meet the requirements of forming a stable sensor network.

Although the above research builds agricultural environment monitoring systems that can monitor environmental parameters in the greenhouse, the data transmission rate of these systems is low, and the transmission distance is limited. Some systems only have specific monitoring requirements, such as soil moisture. Some systems require more complex data processing and storage, which requires greater costs. In addition, ZigBee technology is a short-distance wireless two-way communication technology based on the IEE802.15.4 protocol standard. It has the characteristics of short distance, low speed, and low cost [9]. So this article designs a greenhouse monitoring system based on ZigBee technology. It can achieve 24 h of high efficiency, low power consumption, real-time monitoring, and transmission of environmental parameters such as air temperature and humidity, soil moisture, illumination, and $CO2$ (carbon dioxide concentration).

2 Introduction to Sensors

2.1 Air Temperature and Humidity Sensor

Since the air temperature and humidity sensor works in a greenhouse environment for a long time, it is necessary to choose an air temperature and humidity sensor with better performance [10]. This system chooses the temperature and humidity sensor DHT11 with calibrated digital signal output, which is as shown in Fig. 1. The temperature collection range is -40–80 °C, the resolution is 0.1 °C, and the maximum allowable error is ± 0.5 °C. The humidity range is 0–100%RH, the resolution is 0.1%RH, the maximum allowable error is $\pm 2\%$RH. It has the advantages of low power consumption, small size, high precision, and strong anti-interference ability.

2.2 Light Intensity Sensor

Light intensity affects the photosynthesis of plants. Since the sensor used to collect light intensity works in necessary to choose a photosensitive sensor with better a greenhouse

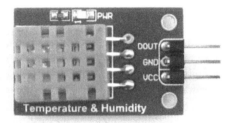

Fig. 1. Air temperature and humidity sensor DHT11

environment for a long time, it is performance [11]. This article chooses the digital light intensity sensor BH1750FVI with a two-wire serial bus interface. As shown in Fig. 2, its range is 0–65535 lx, the resolution is 1 lx, and the maximum allowable error is ±2lx. It has spectral sensitivity characteristics close to visual sensitivity. It also has a weak dependence on light sources, which is less affected by infrared light. It has the advantages of low power consumption, small size, high precision, and strong anti-interference ability.

Fig. 2. Light intensity sensor BH1750FVI

2.3 Soil Temperature Sensor

The soil temperature affects crops growth and soil formation. Since the sensor for soil temperature collection works in a greenhouse environment for a long time, choosing a sensor with good performance is necessary [12]. This system selects the stainless steel encapsulated digital temperature sensor DS18B20, as shown in Fig. 3. Its range is −55–125 °C, the resolution is 0.1 °C, and the maximum allowable error is ±0.5°C. The voltage range is 3.0–5.5 V and it has the advantages of low power consumption, small size, high precision, and strong anti-interference ability.

Fig. 3. Digital temperature sensor DS18B20

2.4 Soil Moisture Sensor

Soil moisture determines the water supply status of crops. Since the sensor used for soil moisture collection works in the field environment for a long time, it is necessary to choose a soil temperature sensor with better performance [13]. This system selects the soil moisture sensor Moisture Sensor, as shown in Fig. 4. Its range is 0–100%RH, the resolution is 0.1%RH, and the maximum allowable error is ±2%RH; the surface is nickel-plated to contact with rusty soil; it has the advantages of low power consumption, small size, high precision, and strong anti-interference ability.

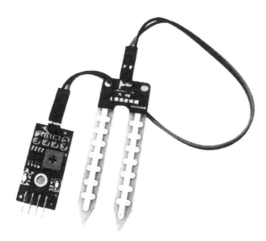

Fig. 4. Soil moisture sensor Moisture Sensor

2.5 Carbon Dioxide Sensor

Carbon dioxide sensors affect greenhouse crop growth and photosynthesis. Since the soil temperature collection sensor works in the greenhouse environment for a long time, it is necessary to choose a carbon dioxide sensor with better performance [14]. This system selects sensor CCS811, as shown in Fig. 5. The range is 0–5000 ppm, the accuracy is ±30 ppm ± 5%, the voltage range is 3.0–5.5 V. It has the advantages of low power consumption, small size, high precision, and strong anti-interference ability.

Fig. 5. Carbon dioxide sensor CCS811

3   System Design

3.1   Overall System Design

The system mainly comprises a data acquisition, power conversion, serial, and Ethernet communication module. Among them, the data acquisition module is built around data sensors to realize agricultural data collection; the power conversion module provides power for the other modules and is the power module of the terminal equipment; the serial communication module uses special debugging tools to realize one-click download and real-time tracking program; Ethernet the network communication module is built by the chip W5500 to realize external network communication. Refer to Fig. 6 for the overall system framework composition.

3.2   Data Acquisition Module

In the acquisition module, the soil temperature sensor DS18B20 is a digital sensor that uses a single bus interface for communication. It is based on a communication protocol called the "1-Wire" protocol and requires one pin for data and CC2530. Detection of air temperature and humidity signals: Use the DHT11 digital temperature and humidity sensor as the detection element to realize the sampling number. The digitization of data can reduce the front-end preprocessing of sampling data. The current output soil moisture transmitter is used as the detection component, and its output signal is 4 to 20 mA. Light detection is to monitor the light intensity of the greenhouse. It outputs a 4–20 mA signal, which converts the analog signal into a digital signal and transmits it to CC2530. The CO_2 sensor uses non-dispersive infrared (NDIR) technology. The

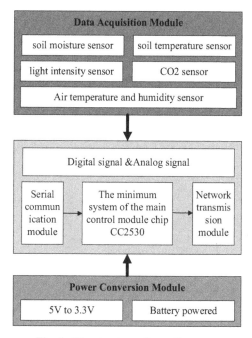

Fig. 6. The structure of overall system

NDIR sensor [15] Detects infrared radiation in a specific wavelength range to measure the concentration of carbon dioxide (CO_2). The current signals of the above sensors are converted into voltage signals after preprocessing and are serially converted into digital signals through the serial A/D converter TLC2543L and the processor CC2530. The system uses software to implement the SPI function. Line setting, the P2.0 pin of CC2530 outputs the upper 4 bits of data (D4-D7). The converted data are transmitted serially by the TLC2543L. The data acquisition circuit design is shown in Fig. 7

3.3 Power Module

Since the system has many sensor nodes, its power supply adopts a battery power supply, so the low power consumption is important. The power supply design uses the DC-DCMAX756 chip to save the energy of the power supply. The circuit design is shown in Fig. 8.

The power supply efficiency of this circuit reaches 87% when it is fully loaded. When the power supply drops to 0.7 V, the circuit can output a voltage of 3.3 V. LBO in the road that is the low voltage monitoring output terminal. When the voltage drops to 1.25 V, the effective low level reaches P0.0 of CC2530 and the processor performs corresponding processing. Power circuit design is shown in Fig. 8.

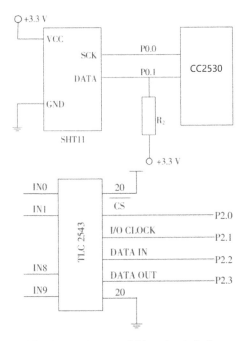

Fig. 7. The data acquisition circuit design

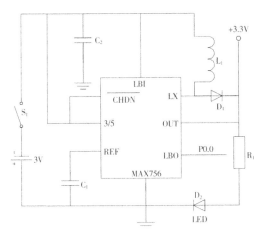

Fig. 8. The circuit design of power supply

3.4 Serial Communication Module

The serial communication module is used for Zigbee and PC communication to send and receive the sensor data, which control the sensor on-site data collection, and perform the node troubleshooting. The system uses a 3.3 V power supply. The CH340 chip is selected to realize the communication between the main coordinator of terminal nodes and the PC. Its voltage is 3.3–5.0 V. The design of serial communication circuit is shown in Fig. 9.

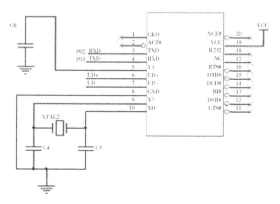

Fig. 9. The design of serial communication circuit

3.5 Ethernet Communication Module

The Ethernet communication module is built around the chip W5500, which has 32 K receiving and send cache, which integrates the network communication protocol. This chip communicates with the main control module through the SPI bus and the external network through Ethernet. The design of serial communication circuits is shown in Fig. 10.

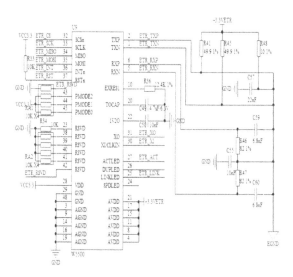

Fig. 10. The design of serial communication circuits

4 Experimental Design

This article introduces the Zigbee agricultural monitoring network solution of Chuangsi Company (the Zigbee manufacturer). It compares the average node performance of two monitoring systems, which is the energy consumption, transmission rate and signal strength.

4.1 Environment Settings

This study selected two agricultural greenhouses on a farm in Selangor, Malaysia, as the experimental objects. The greenhouses cover an area of 10 00 m * 500 m. The facilities and environment of two areas are the same. Each greenhouse is equipped with 100 Zigbee nodes. The ratio of terminal nodes to routing nodes is 2:1, which do not have mobility capabilities. The gateway is placed in the center of the network and other remaining nodes are randomly deployed. The gateway is the destination node; the remaining nodes are the source nodes. The Chuangsi Zigbee agricultural monitoring network solution is Group A. The ZWSN proposed in this article is Group B. Table 1 shows the ZWSN parameters.

Table 1. Simulation network parameters

Network area	Transmission rate	Broadcast radius	Data flow
100 m * 100 m	250 kbps	15 m	CBR
Number of data streams	**Data table length**	**Initial energy**	
8	80 byte	1000 J	

4.2 Experimental Results

(1) Network energy consumption

ZWSN reflects its low-power performance, which is designed to meet the demand for long life and low power consumption of battery-powered devices. The energy consumption refers to the energy consumption of all nodes within a certain period [16]. This study takes 2 h as a unit and counts the overall energy consumption of two groups of Zigbee wireless monitoring networks within one day. Figure 11 shows the overall energy consumption of the network. Experimental results show that the overall energy consumption of the ZigBee network increases with the increase of running time. The energy consumption of group B is less than that of the latter. Regarding average period energy consumption, Group A is 126.99 mW, and Group B is 171.06 mW, 34.71% lower than Group A. It shows that the energy consumption of the system proposed in this article is lower. So it can extend the service life of the equipment.

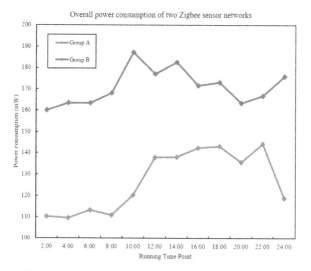

Fig. 11. The power consumption of two Zigbee networks

(2) Node life cycle

From the network life cycle perspective, there is a positive correlation between network life and the number of remaining nodes. The longer the network life cycle, the greater the number of remaining nodes [17]. The measurement indicators are FNDT (first node death time), MNDT (middle node death time), and ENDT (end node death time). It can be seen from Fig. 12 that the FNDT, MNDT and ENDT of group A are 830, 1000, and 1140 h, and the FNDT, MNDT and ENDT of group B are 990, 1180, and 1350 h, which is 18.00%, 18.42% and 19.28% higher than that of group A, which indicates that the node energy consumption of the system proposed in this article takes longer, and the stability of the monitoring network is stronger.

(3) Network signal strength

The signal RSSI of the ZWSN nodes decreases monotonically with the distance between the sending and receiving nodes. This function model is called the Friiis output model [18]. The level of system interference can be evaluated by the RSSI values of these two systems. High signal strength indicates the strong anti-interference ability, while the low signal strength may indicate weak anti-interference ability and possible node failure. Figure 13 shows that within 0 to 20 m, the RSSI of two groups' systems.

continues to decrease as the distance increases, but the decreased speed of group A is faster. When it increases to 30 m, the RSSI values of both groups are stable. The overall average signal strength of group B is 1dBm, which is 1% higher than that of group A. After the stabilization at 30 m, the average signal is 1dBm, which is 1% higher than that of group A. It shows that the Zigbee wireless monitoring system proposed in this article has stronger anti-interference ability, which is more suitable for the agricultural production environment.

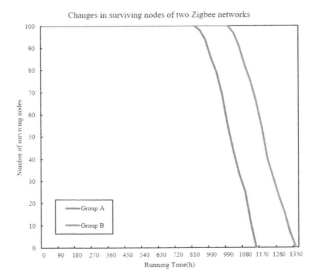

Fig. 12. Changes in surviving nodes of two Zigbee networks

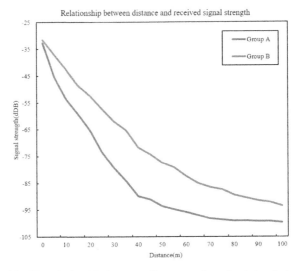

Fig. 13. The relationship between distance and received signal strength.

5   Conclusion

This study designs a greenhouse agricultural environmental monitoring system based on Zigbee technology. It consists of a data acquisition, power conversion, serial, and Ethernet communication module. This study also introduces the Chuangsi Zigbee agricultural monitoring network solution. The experimental results show that the Zigbee wireless monitoring system proposed in this paper is better than the Chuangsi Zigbee wireless monitoring network in terms of network energy consumption, node life cycle, and network signal strength, which indicates that the system can better solve problems such as large energy consumption, weak signals, and node instability, and can better meet the environmental monitoring needs of greenhouse agriculture.

References

1. Dong, X.: Research on applying ZigBee wireless sensor network in greenhouses. Sci. Technol. Inf. **17**(19), 34+36 (2019)
2. Zhao, C.: Precision Agriculture Research and Practice, pp. 56–58. Science and Technology Press, Beijing (2016)
3. Hao, D.: Thoughts on meteorological services for modern agricultural disaster prevention and reduction. China Agric. Meteorol. **04**, 313–315 (2015)
4. Smith, J.: Design of Zigbee-based wireless sensor network for greenhouse monitoring. Sensors **19**(5), 1120 (2019)
5. Johnson, A.: Development of low-power Zigbee sensor nodes for agricultural applications. In: Proceedings of the International Conference on Agricultural Engineering, pp. 235–242 (2018)
6. Brown, L.: Zigbee-based wireless sensor network for smart greenhouse management. Int. J. Agric. Technol. **13**(4), 831–845 (2017)
7. Garcia, R.: Smart greenhouse monitoring system using Zigbee wireless sensor network. In: Proceedings of the IEEE International Conference on Agricultural Technology, pp. 198–205 (2016)
8. Kim, S.: Hardware design and implementation of Zigbee-based greenhouse monitoring system. J. Agric. Eng. Res. **41**(3), 412–425 (2015)
9. Li, Z.: Smart agriculture based on Zigbee and NB-IoT wireless sensor network. Hebei Agric. Mach. **15**, 2 (2021)
10. Farooq, S., Raza, S.H., Khurshid, K., Usama, M.: Wireless sensor network-based monitoring system for agriculture using IoT. In: Proceedings of the 3rd International Conference on Computer Applications & Information Security (ICCAIS) (2020)
11. Manikandan, R., Ganesan, S.: Design of a low-cost smart agriculture system for Indian farmers using IoT. In: Proceedings of the 2018 IEEE International Conference on Robotics and Automation (ICRA) (2018)
12. Kaur, A., Verma, H.K., Singh, A.: Wireless sensor network-based smart agriculture monitoring and controlling system. In: Proceedings of the 2019 6th International Conference on Computing for Sustainable Global Development (INDIACom) (2019)
13. Kalaivani, M., Shanthi, B.: Wireless sensor network based automatic irrigation system. In: Proceedings of the 2017 International Conference on Computer, Communication and Signal Processing (ICCCSP) (2017)
14. Senthilkumar, A., Ramasamy, D.P.: An efficient IoT-based system for precision agriculture. In: Proceedings of the 2018 IEEE International Conference on Robotics and Automation (ICRA) (2018)
15. Menze, J., Mark, O., Hübsch, A., Jans, W., Hoffmann, L.: Smart agriculture for the future: climate- and soil-monitoring and optimizing tools. In: Proceedings of the 10th International Conference on Pervasive Technologies Related to Assistive Environments (PETRA) (2017)
16. Singh, A.P., Pandey, V., Tripathi, M.K.: Energy-efficient clustering and routing algorithms for wireless sensor networks: a survey and taxonomy. J. Netw. Comput. Appl. **149**, 102495 (2020)

17. Salehahmadi, Z., Abdullah, A.H., Langarizadeh, M., Khatibi, T.: A comprehensive review of the applications of wireless sensor networks in disaster management. Comput. Commun. **150**, 526–536 (2019)
18. Al-Yasir, Y.I., Merabti, M.: Reliability in wireless sensor networks: modelling and analysis. In: Proceedings of the 2012 IEEE/RSJ International Conference on Intelligent Robots and Systems (IROS) (2012)

Development of Fully Synthetic Medical Database Shuffling Method

Rashid Nasimov[1]([✉]) [iD], Nigorakhon Nasimova[2] [iD], Bahodir Mumimov[1] [iD],
Adibaxon Usmanxodjayeva[3] [iD], Guzal Sobirova[3] [iD], and Akmalbek Abdusalomov[4] [iD]

[1] Department of Artificial Intelligence, Tashkent State University of Economics,
Tashkent, Uzbekistan
rashid.nasimov@tsue.uz
[2] Tashkent University of Information Technologies, Tashkent, Uzbekistan
[3] Department of RFMPE, Tashkent Medical Academy, Tashkent, Uzbekistan
[4] Department of Computer Engineering, Gachon University, Seongnam-si, Republic of Korea

Abstract. The importance of having a comprehensive and accurate medical database cannot be overstated. Such databases are crucial for various purposes including research, analysis, and decision-making in the field of medicine. However, collecting real-world medical data can be challenging due to privacy concerns and limited access to sensitive information. To overcome these challenges, our proposed method suggests using statistical data as a basis for developing a synthetic medical database. By employing a special shuffle algorithm, it is aimed to modify and enhance the primary database until it reaches an acceptable level of quality. This algorithm ensures that the resulting dataset maintains its statistical properties while also preserving privacy and confidentiality. Moreover, evaluating the resulting dataset using a neural network adds another layer of validation to ensure its reliability and accuracy. Through the utilization of a proposed method, a robust database has been developed to predict the risk of developing type 2 diabetes five years ahead. With an accuracy rate as high as 94.45% during neural network training, this dataset holds immense promise for improving patient outcomes by enabling early intervention and prevention strategies. This research represents a significant step forward in addressing the global burden posed by type 2 diabetes.

Keywords: Synthetic medical database · Shuffling function · Neural Network · Type 2 diabetes

1 Introduction

In today's digital age, the collection of patient data has become increasingly prevalent in healthcare systems, governments, and private industries. These datasets hold immense potential for scientific research and advancements in medical treatments [1, 2]. However, due to concerns regarding patient privacy, these valuable resources are often inaccessible to the broader research community. To address this issue, implementing robust security measures such as anonymization techniques or synthetic data generation can

Y. Koucheryavy and A. Aziz (Eds.): NEW2AN/ruSMART 2023, LNCS 14543, pp. 55–64, 2024.
https://doi.org/10.1007/978-3-031-60997-8_6

enable researchers to access medical datasets while ensuring patient privacy [3, 4]. However, anonymization is not always secure, as some features are exclusive and difficult to hide. So synthetic data generation can be effective alternative approach. These synthetic datasets are created by using algorithms that preserve the underlying patterns and relationships found in real-world data but do not contain any actual patient information [5]. Researchers can use these synthetic datasets for analysis without accessing sensitive personal details.

Secondly, in some case suitable database is not exist at all to train AI algorithm. Especially, database to predict diseases or database of rare disease. In these circumstances, fully synthetic database can replace the needed database and can be used to train AI algorithms.

For this reason, synthetic data generation methods have become increasingly popular among medical software engineers due to their ability to address privacy concerns and provide diverse datasets for training machine-learning models. These methods can be categorized into three types: fully synthetic, semi-synthetic, and hybrid [5, 14].

In this paper, new fully synthetic method of creating a medical database was proposed. The basic idea of this method is as follows: in the first step, a primary dataset is created based on the publicly available statistics. Then two different shuffle method are used to shuffle database. Because primary dataset is very unbalanced. After shuffling, a neural network (NN) is trained using this dataset. After every five training epochs, the data in the data set will be shuffled using a main shuffle function. In addition, after each 5-training epoch the developed dataset will be saved. At the end, the dataset for which NN showed the highest accuracy is selected. To evaluate the accuracy of the developed method, the neural network is first trained on the synthetic database and then tested with the real database and achieved high results.

2   Related Works

In the last 10 years, a lot of research has been done on creating a synthetic database [4]. In particular, various methods of creating a medical database were proposed. The most common methods are Generative Adversarial Network [6], Bayesian Network [7], Independent marginal [8], Mixture of product of multinomial [9], Multiple Imputation methods [10] and others [15].

Generative Adversarial Networks (GANs) have emerged as one of the most promising methods for generating synthetic medical databases. GANs consist of two neural networks: a generator network that creates synthetic data and a discriminator network that distinguishes between real and fake data. This adversarial process ensures that the generated data closely resembles real patient information while maintaining privacy.

Bayesian Networks offer another effective approach to constructing synthetic medical databases. These probabilistic models capture complex relationships between variables and generate realistic datasets by sampling from their joint probability distribution.

Independent Marginal models assume independence between variables and generate each variable independently based on its marginal distribution. Although this method simplifies the modeling process, it may not capture intricate dependencies present in real-world medical data.

Mixture of Product of Multinomial models combine multiple independent marginal distributions to create more accurate synthetic datasets by capturing dependencies between variables more effectively than Independent Marginal models.

Multiple Imputation Methods utilize statistical techniques to impute missing values in existing datasets accurately. By filling in these gaps with plausible values based on observed patterns, researchers can create comprehensive synthetic databases for analysis.

One such method is the use of Electronic Health Records (EHRs). EHRs are digital versions of patients' paper charts that contain comprehensive information about their medical history. By anonymizing and aggregating this data, researchers can create synthetic databases that mimic real-world scenarios without compromising patient privacy. Another method proposed by Rubin involves developing a fully synthetic database.

This approach involves creating entirely artificial data that closely resembles real patient records. While this method eliminates any risk associated with using actual patient data, it may lack some nuances present in real-world cases.

Furthermore, Synthea is a free open platform designed specifically for generating synthetic medical data. It allows researchers to create customizable datasets based on various parameters such as demographics, diseases, and treatments. This tool enables researchers to simulate different scenarios and study their impact on healthcare outcomes.

In this section, we describe the research methodology used in this study. It outlines a series of steps that begin with defining eligibility criteria for selecting research articles. It then goes on to outline the data sources, search strategy, and article selection process. In addition, this section explores the details of data analysis and synthesis. The review process followed the steps of systematic literature review as outlined in the PRISMA (Preferred Reporting Items for Systematic Reviews and Meta-Analyses) guidelines [6].

3   Proposed Work

3.1   Creating Database from Statistics

In this work, a survey from the Cardiovascular Disease and Cancer Cohort Study in China was used. They looked at 12 risk factors associated with type 2 diabetes. We selected eight of them to study: age, sex, poor diet and physical inactivity, current alcohol consumption and lack of sleep, general or central obesity and hypertension. These factors were studied in four separate age groups, namely (40 < 55 years old, 55 to <65 years old, 65 to < 75 years old and ≥75 years old). Detailed information can be found in article [11, 13]. First, we divided the data of different ages into separate groups. Mean patient age, standard deviation and age limit were given for each group. So we created an array of ages using the numpy.random.normal function.

Our proposed method consists of the following steps. They are illustrated graphically in Fig. 1.

Hazard ratios have been given for each parameter. For new-onset diabetes associated with risk factors and risk scores by age group, the hazard ratio (HR) and 95% confidence interval (CI) were calculated using Cox proportional hazards models. It is important to say that, from the outset, we divided the patient data of each age group into 2 subgroups:

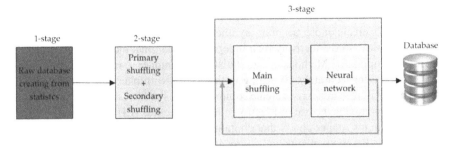

Fig. 1. Proposed method's block diagram.

– People with diabetes within 5 years and those without diabetes within 5 years/healthy patient. Furthermore, from the outset, we divided the patient data of each age group into 2 subgroups:
– People who developed diabetes after 5 years and patients who stayed healthy after 5 years.

Finally, age row in database was divided to 100 to normalize it with other rows information. As only, this row contained values more than 1.

3.2 Shuffling Before Big Loop

After the database is created based on statistics, it is shuffled using two shuffle functions. The first function is the built-in random.shuffle function of python. The second is the custom function, which performs the following operation, which performs the following operation.

$$a[i] = a[semilength - i]$$
$$[semilength] = [i] \tag{1}$$

Here $a[i]$ is the i-th element in column a, and semi length is half the length of the column. This function replaces the elements of a specific column starting from half with the next half in mirror symmetry.

3.3 Shuffling Before Big Loop Big Loop

After the above processes, the big main loop begins. This loop includes a sequential shuffle function and a neural network. The shuffle function here is a custom function, similar to the Adam optimizer. However, with some modifications, its formula is as follows.

$$v_t = \beta_1 * v_{t-1} - (1 - \beta_1) * g_t \tag{2}$$

$$s_t = \beta_2 * s_{t-1} - (1 - \beta_2) * g_t^2 \tag{3}$$

$$\triangle \omega_t = |\eta \frac{v_t}{\sqrt{s_t} + \epsilon} * g_t| \tag{4}$$

$$\omega_{t+1} = \omega_t + \triangle \omega_t \qquad (5)$$

Here, – **Initial learning rate,**
g_t: **Gradient at time t along** ω^j
v_t: **Exponential avegare of gradients along** ω_j
s_t: **Exponential avegare of squares of gradients along** ω_j
$\beta_1 \beta_2$: **Hyperparameters**

$$B = B\text{-}1 \qquad (6)$$

Moreover, if the end exceeds the length of the array, the value of coefficient B is set to zero. Initially, these two parameters (P and B) were set to 0 and 0.1. The following values have been given for other the hyper parameter: Initial Learning Rate = 1, β_1 = 0.95, β_2 = 0.99, ϵ = 0.0001.

3.4 Neural Network

The first step in preparing a synthetic database was running it through a basic shuffle function. This function rearranges the data randomly, ensuring that no biases or patterns are present. By doing so, the database becomes more representative of real-world situations.

Once the shuffle function is applied, the synthetic database is transferred to a neural network (first neural network) for intermediate quality assessment. This neural network plays a vital role in evaluating the readiness of the synthetic database for training purposes. Table 1 provides detailed information about the architecture and layers of this neural network.

In this case, the network is trained for 5 epochs. That means that there are multiple rounds of training and testing within each cycle. This helps in refining the NN's performance over time.

After completing each epoch, it is essential to evaluate the performance of the model using unseen data from the test dataset. The neural network makes predictions on this dataset, and its accuracy or error rate is calculated based on how well it performs against known outputs.

Following evaluation, if a high enough result has not been achieved; further steps are taken to improve performance. One such step involves saving the trained database and sending it through the main shuffle function to randomize its order again.

In this case, the network is trained for 5 epochs. That means that there are multiple rounds of training and testing within each cycle. This helps in refining the NN's performance over time.

After completing each epoch, it is essential to evaluate the performance of the model using unseen data from the test dataset. The neural network makes predictions on this dataset, and its accuracy or error rate is calculated based on how well it performs against known outputs.

Table 1. Parameters of 1st Neural Network layers

#	Layer name	Properties
1	Input Layer	8 nodes
2	Hidden Layer	16 nodes
4	ReLu	
5	Hidden Layer	64 nodes
7	ReLu	
8	Hidden Layer	32 nodes
10	ReLu	
11	Hidden Layer	16 nodes
12	ReLu	
13	Hiden Layer	1 nodes
14	Output (Sigmoid) Layer	

Following evaluation, if a high enough result has not been achieved; further steps are taken to improve performance. One such step involves saving the trained database and sending it through the main shuffle function to randomize its order again.

4 Evaluation of the Method

To evaluate the effectiveness of synthetic databases, researchers have developed several evaluation methods that focus on metrics like similarity measures, statistical analysis, or predictive accuracy [12, 16]. However, these existing evaluation methods fall short when it comes to assessing the performance of our synthetic method. Our approach involves generating a database entirely from scratch using shuffling algorithms and neural networks. As a result, traditional evaluation methods designed for comparing real and synthetic data may not be applicable in this context.

To overcome this limitation, we adopted an exclusive method by training a neural network with our generated database and then testing its performance using a real database. This approach allows us to assess how well our synthetic dataset performs in comparison to actual data when used in practical applications. However, a question naturally arises: how does this method differ from others that also utilize real databases? The key distinction lies in the approach taken by these methods.

In traditional methods, a synthetic database is constructed based on an existing real database. Statistical distributions of both the real and synthetic databases are then compared to evaluate the effectiveness of the synthetic data. Usually, the number of data in the synthetic database is close to that in the real database.

However, in our case, the synthetic database was not created on the basis of any real database, and therefore the real database used for evaluation does not depend on the synthetic database in any way. In addition, their size is drastically different from each

Table 2. Parameters of 2nd Neural Network's layers

#	Layer name	Properties
1	Input Layer	8 nodes
2	Hidden Layer	128 nodes
3	Dropout Layer	0.05
4	ReLU	
5	Hidden Layer	64 nodes
6	Dropout Layer	0.2
7	ReLU	
8	Hidden Layer	32 nodes
9	Dropout Layer	0.1
10	ReLU	
11	Hidden Layer	16 nodes
12	Dropout Layer	0.05
13	ReLU	
14	Hidden Layer	1 nodes
15	Output (Sigmoid) Layer	

other. More specifically, the real database is much smaller than the synthetic database: the synthetic database is 149231, and the real database is 1146.

As there not exist identical database to ours, we took 2015-Behavioral Risk Factor Surveillance System (BRFSS) survey data as a real database, which is more close to our database. It contains 441456 records for 2015, with more than 300 questions for each. We extracted 9 question, appropriate for our synthetic database and removed non-answered and/or empty rows. Further, we extracted data of types 2 diabetes data. At the end, we have left only 1146 records. Here it is important to note that this database is not identical to ours, it contain data of already diagnosed patients' data, while our database consists of the data of patients who acquired diabetes within 5 years. More precisely, real data is more suitable to diagnose diabetes, and to predict risk of diabetes 5 years ahead. Therefore, the training and test accuracy may vary a bit.

We used a simple neural network to evaluate the created synthetic database. Information about its layers and their parameters is presented in Table 2. The process of training this network is depicted in Fig. 2. As can be seen from the graph, the training accuracy reached 71,2% at the 10th epoch, while test accuracy reached 64,1% at that point.

As can be seen from the graph, the neural network trained on the synthetic database is classifying the real data with high accuracy. This observation leads to the conclusion that the generated synthetic database is of satisfactory quality for training AI algorithms.

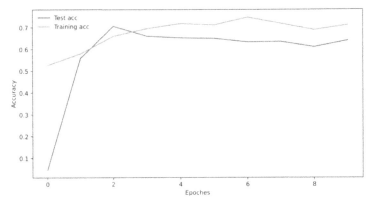

Fig. 2. The values of raining and test accuracy

5   Results

The 2 processes within the loop are repeated for 200 cycles. The training and test accuracy at the end of each cycle are given in Fig. 3. As can be seen from the graph, the test accuracy reached 88.4% when the training accuracy was 100%.

As can be seen from the graph, the value of B changed in a very small range, mostly taking values in the range of 0–0.4. But this does not mean that only the beginning of the database has been shuffled. Because the value of P varies in a relatively large range, more precisely between 0.2 and 1. Thus, the shuffled range can cover the entire database when B and P values are used simultaneously.

Using this method, we have built a database of 149231 patient data, from which 61630 patients developed diabetes, and 87601 stayed healthy.

In this particular case, our evaluation results demonstrate that the neural network, which was trained on the synthetic database, performs exceptionally well when tested with real data. The high accuracy achieved by the database indicates that it has similar

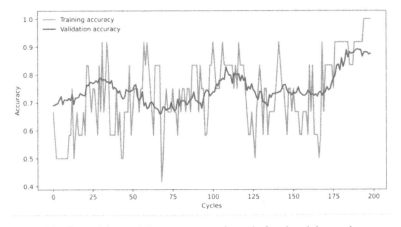

Fig. 3. Training and Test accuracy at the end of each training cycle

patterns and features to real database. This finding has important implications for AI research and development. It suggests that using proposed method can effectively bridge the gap between limited real data availability and robust model training requirements. By using a reliable source of diverse statistics, that method enable AI algorithms to learn more effectively and make accurate predictions in various domains.

6 Discussion

In this particular case, our evaluation results demonstrate that the neural network, which was trained on the synthetic database, performs exceptionally well when tested with real data. The high accuracy achieved by the database indicates that it has similar patterns and features to real database. This finding has important implications for AI research and development. It suggests that using proposed method can effectively bridge the gap between limited real data availability and robust model training requirements. By using a reliable source of diverse statistics, that method enable AI algorithms to learn more effectively and make accurate predictions in various domains.

In this method, we used a real database only to evaluate the effectiveness of our proposed method. Later, when generating synthetic data using this method, no real database is required, it is enough to select the database that showed the highest accuracy when training the neural network.

7 Conclusion

Overall, this iterative approach with an optimizer seems like a robust method to improve accuracy in neural networks. The combination of reshuffling data, determining optimal parameters, and repeating cycles ensures continuous improvement in performance. In conclusion, based on the evidence of high accuracy achieved by a neural network trained on a synthetic database when classifying real data, it can be inferred that this generated dataset is indeed of satisfactory quality for training AI algorithms. This finding highlights the potential benefits of using synthetic databases as an alternative or complementary resource to traditional datasets in advancing AI research and development.

References

1. Turgunov, A., Zohirov, K., Nasimov, R., Mirzakhalilov, S.: Comparative analysis of the results of EMG signal classification based on machine learning algorithms. In: 2021 International Conference on Information Science and Communications Technologies (ICISCT), Tashkent, Uzbekistan, pp. 1–4 (2021)
2. Zohirov, K.: Classification of some Sensitive Motion of Fingers to Create Modern Biointerface. In: 2022 International Conference on Information Science and Communications Technologies (ICISCT), Tashkent, Uzbekistan, pp. 1–4 (2022)
3. Iatunji, I., Rauch, J., Katzensteiner, M., Khosla, M.: A review of anonymization for healthcare data. Big Data (2022). https://doi.org/10.1089/big.2021.0169
4. Gonzales, A., Guruswamy, G., Smith, S.R.: Synthetic data in health care: a narrative review. PLOS Digit. Health **2**(1), e0000082 (2023). https://doi.org/10.1371/journal.pdig.0000082. PMID:36812604;PMCID:PMC9931305

5. McDuff, D., Curran, T., Kadambi, A.: Synthetic Data in Healthcare, 6 April 2023. arXiv: 2304.03243, https://doi.org/10.48550/arXiv.2304.03243

6. Arora, A., Arora, A.: Generative adversarial networks and synthetic patient data: current challenges and future perspectives. Future Healthc. J. **9**(2), 190–193 (2022)

7. Gogoshin, G., Branciamore, S., Rodin, A.S.: Synthetic data generation with probabilistic Bayesian Networks. Math. Biosci. Eng. **18**(6), 8603–8621 (2021). https://doi.org/10.3934/mbe.2021426

8. Goncalves, A., Ray, P., Soper, B., Stevens, J., Coyle, L., Sales, A.P.: Generation and evaluation of synthetic patient data. BMC Med. Res. Methodol. **20**(1), 108 (2020)

9. Hu, J.(M.)., Reiter, J., Wang, Q.: dirichlet process mixture models for modeling and generating synthetic versions of nested categorical data. Bayesian Anal. **13**, 183–200 (2018). https://doi.org/10.1214/16-BA1047

10. Loong, B., Rubin, D.B.: Multiply-imputed synthetic data: advice to the imputer. J. Off. Stat. **33**(4), 1005–1019 (2017). https://doi.org/10.1515/jos-2017-0047

11. Wang, T., et al.: Age-related disparities in diabetes risk attributable to modifiable risk factor profiles in Chinese adults: a nationwide, population-based, cohort study. Lancet Healthy Longevity **2**(10), e618–e628 (2021). ISSN 2666-7568

12. Abdusalomov, A.B., Nasimov, R., Nasimova, N., Muminov, B., Whangbo, T.K.: Evaluating synthetic medical images using artificial intelligence with the GAN algorithm. Sensors **23**, 3440 (2023). https://doi.org/10.3390/s23073440

13. Nasimov, R., Nasimova, N., Botirjon, K., Abdullayev, M.: Deep learning algorithm for classifying dilated cardiomyopathy and hypertrophic cardiomyopathy in transport workers. In: Koucheryavy, Y., Aziz, A. (eds.) NEW2AN 2022. LNCS, vol. 13772, pp. 218–230. Springer, Cham (2022). https://doi.org/10.1007/978-3-031-30258-9_19

14. Nasimov, R., Nasimova, N., Muminov, B.: Hybrid method for evaluating feature importance for predicting chronic heart diseases. In: 2022 International Conference on Information Science and Communications Technologies (ICISCT), Tashkent, Uzbekistan, pp. 1–4 (2022). https://doi.org/10.1109/ICISCT55600.2022.10146969

15. Mumonov, B., Nasimov, R., et al.: Estimation affects of formats and resizing process to the accuracy of convolutional neural network. In: 2019 International Conference on Information Science and Communications Technologies (ICISCT), Tashkent, Uzbekistan, pp. 1–5 (2019)

16. Tagmatova, Z., Abdusalomov, A., Nasimov, R., Nasimova, N., Dogru, A.H., Cho, Y.-I.: New approach for generating synthetic medical data to predict type 2 diabetes. Bioengineering **10**, 1031 (2023). https://doi.org/10.3390/bioengineering10091031

Restriction in Flow Area in Gas Network

Ismatulla Kushayevich Khujaev[1], Rabim Alikulovich Fayziev[2(✉)],
and Muzaffar Muhiddinovich Hamdamov[1(✉)]

[1] Institute of Mechanics and Seismic Stability of Structures Named After M.T. Urazbaev of the AS RUz, Tashkent, Uzbekistan
r.fayziyev@tsue.uz
[2] Tashkent State University of Economics, Tashkent, Uzbekistan
r.fayziyev@tsue.uz

Abstract. Examples of solving problems of gas networks are considered in the article by Simulink program, which can be used in modeling and designing linear and nonlinear dynamic systems, their control systems with nonlinear controllers, and in signal processing.

Keywords: Simulink · system simulation · block diagrams · elementary sections of gas pipelines · gas network pipe · ideal and real gas

1 Introduction

The growth of industrial and civil engineering and the accomplishment and improvement of sanitary and living conditions led to a significant increase in the volume of water and gas supplied for economic and productive needs. These needs are met through the construction of utility networks and the modernization of existing systems. The latter option contributes to a significant reduction in capital investment and requires a search for system reserves that would meet the needs of the population and economic infrastructure.

One of these reserves is to improve the management of technological processes for supplying and distributing the target product based on the use of modern methods of mathematical and computer simulation. At the same time, the main attention must be paid to the reliability and controllability of utility networks in order to guarantee a reserve of their capacity and the possibility of their prompt reconstruction.

Computer simulation and automation should accompany the entire life cycle of engineering networks: design stages, monitoring of work (operational management), and recommendations.

From the point of view of modern systems theory, engineering networks can be represented as a complex system of interaction of a large number of subsystems: sources, consumers, and communication lines. The structure of the utility network is determined by the relationships between these subsystems. Each subsystem is characterized by the range of changes in the main indices: pressure, flow, and temperature for heat supply networks. At the design stage, the main task is to provide all network consumers with the target product in the required quantity and under the specified pressure and temperature.

Y. Koucheryavy and A. Aziz (Eds.): NEW2AN/ruSMART 2023, LNCS 14543, pp. 65–75, 2024.
https://doi.org/10.1007/978-3-031-60997-8_7

Workstations of maintenance personnel must ensure the operation of the system in such a way that a change in the structure and parameters of the controlled subsystems should compensate for the change in the structure and parameters of consumers. Moreover, these compensations must minimize losses in energy, cost, or reliability terms under existing technological limitations. This requires a database of the utility network conditions under various operating modes.

Engineering networks belong to the class of continuously evolving systems, the development of which occurs in time and space. When operational management capabilities are exhausted, the reconstruction mechanism is activated. Here, the main role is played by intensity capabilities and consumption volume, and by controlled and uncontrollable internal and external factors.

In terms of their structure, utility networks can be linear, looped or combined. The widespread use of a looped or multi-ring network is explained by the fact that the flow in it, following the laws of nature, is self-formed with minimal energy consumption. Another advantage of multi-ring networks is to ensure the reliability of functions in the event of failure of certain arcs of the utility network. These failures are eliminated by increasing the consumption of target products along other routes. The failure of a certain arc in a network of a linear structure leads to the failure of the entire system.

As an example of the positive features of the ring structure, let us cite the presence of parallel strings of main gas pipelines. They communicate with each other through shunt pipes, installed at certain distances.

If the parallel strings have different diameters, then the shunt pipes contribute to the same pressure loss along the parallel strings. If a certain section of the mainline fails, then disconnecting this section leads to a redistribution of flow along the existing lines. The increase in capital investment for the installation of shunt pipes is justified by ensuring the reliability of the utility network.

Let us introduce the main consumers of the theory of flow distribution. In addition to the gas transportation system, this can include water supply networks, oil and petroleum product pipelines, heat supply networks, pneumatic pipelines, and hydraulic pipelines.

Pipeline networks are widely used in engineering and technology. According to their intended purpose, they serve to transport target products (water, oil, petroleum products, gases) [1], thermal energy (heating networks) [2, 3] and transmit mechanical energy (hydraulic and pneumatic drives) [4].

Pipeline networks consist of point and linear elements [5]. Point elements are superchargers, consumer terminals, control valve elements, bends, adapters, points of combining and separating parallel strings, and others. The main components of the pipeline network are linear elements - pipelines.

At the stage of designing a pipeline network, for a given flow rate range of the transported product, the network geometry, injector power, and pipeline diameter (diameters) are selected, taking into account other point elements [5]. According to its geometry, the pipeline network can have a linear structure [7], can be looped [8, 9], or have a combined structure [10].

Hydraulic calculation of the network is conducted using formulas obtained for a stationary flow regime far from the entrance and not considering any obstacles. In this case, an important role is played by the experimental results obtained by Nikuradze for the resistance coefficient of a circular pipe at various flow rates, diameters, and equivalent pipe roughness. Nikuradze constructed curves, which depend on the Reynolds criterion, and make it possible to distinguish laminar (for Re < 2200), transitional (for $2200 \leq$ Re ≤ 4000) and turbulent (for Re > 4000) flow regimes in circular pipelines [11]. The results obtained by Nikuradze showed that in the turbulent flow regime, depending on the equivalent roughness of the boundary of the free section of the pipe, smooth, mixed, and developed modes of flow around the roughness were formed.

It is known that the local choking of the flow channel forms a noticeable pressure drop in the flow. This is used, for example, to reduce the pressure, to condense the vapors contained in the fluid, to reduce the flow rate, and for other purposes. Qualitative analysis of such flows is widely discussed in the literature on aerodynamics. However, for engineering practice, quantitative indices are of interest.

The local restriction block G models the pressure drop due to a localized reduction in flow area, such as a valve or a hole, in a gas network. Choking occurs when the restriction reaches the sonic state.

Ports A and B are restrictive inlet and outlet. The inlet physical signal at port AR indicates the restricted area. In addition, a fixed constraint area can be specified as a parameter block. The restriction is adiabatic. The flow does not exchange heat with the surrounding medium (Fig. 1).

Fig. 1. Restriction of flow area in gas network

The restriction consists of a contraction in transverse area of the channel followed by a sudden expansion in flow area. The gas accelerates during the contraction in transverse area, causing the pressure to drop. The gas separates from the wall during the sudden expansion, causing the pressure to be only partially recovered due to the loss of momentum.

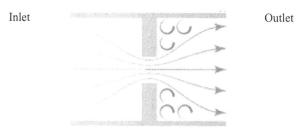

Fig. 2. Restriction of flow area in gas network

Mass Balance. Mass balance equation [11, 12] has the following form:

$$m_A + m_B = 0, \tag{1}$$

where m_A and m_B are the mass flow rates in ports A and B, respectively. The flow related to the port is positive when it enters the block.

Energy Balance. Energy balance equation has the following form:

$$\Phi_A + \Phi_B = 0, \tag{2}$$

where Φ_A and Φ_B are flow rates of energy at ports A and B, respectively. The block is assumed adiabatic. Therefore, there is no change in the specific total enthalpy between port A and port B, and no restrictions [11]:

$$
\begin{aligned}
h_A + \frac{w_A^2}{2} &= h_R + \frac{w_R^2}{2}, \\
h_A + \frac{w_A^2}{2} &= h_R + \frac{w_R^2}{2};
\end{aligned}
\tag{3}
$$

where h is the specific enthalpy at port A, port B, or restriction R, as indicated by the subscript. The ideal flow rates at ports A, B, subject to restrictions, are:

$$w_A = \frac{m_{ideal}}{\rho_A S}, w_B = \frac{m_{ideal}}{\rho_B S}, w_R = \frac{m_{ideal}}{\rho_R S}, \tag{4}$$

where S is the cross-sectional area at ports A and B; S_R is the cross-sectional area of restrictions; ρ is the gas volume density at port A, port B, or restriction R, as indicated by the subscript. The theoretical mass flow rate without non-ideal effects is:

$$m_{ideal} = \frac{m_A}{C_d}, \tag{5}$$

where C_d is the coefficient.

Momentum Balance. The pressure difference between ports A and B is equal based on the momentum balance for contracting the flow area between the inlet and the restriction, and the momentum balance for the sudden expansion of flow area between the restriction and the outlet. For a flow from port A to port B, the local resistance is [12]:

$$\Delta p_{AB} = \rho_R w_R |w_R| \left(\frac{1+r}{2} \left(1 - r\frac{\rho_R}{\rho_A} \right) - r\left(1 - r\frac{\rho_R}{\rho_B} \right) \right), \tag{6}$$

where r is the area ratio, $r = S_R/S$.

For a flow from port B to port A, the local resistance is:

$$\Delta p_{BA} = \rho_R w_R |w_R| \left(\frac{1+r}{2} \left(1 - r\frac{\rho_R}{\rho_B} \right) - r\left(1 - r\frac{\rho_R}{\rho_A} \right) \right). \tag{7}$$

The pressure difference in the two previous formulas is proportional to the square of the flow rate. This is a typical behavior for a developed turbulent flow. However, for a laminar flow, the pressure difference becomes linear with respect to the flow rate. The laminar approximation for the pressure difference is:

$$\Delta p_{lam} = \sqrt{\frac{\rho R \Delta p_{transition}}{2}} (1 - r). \tag{8}$$

The transition threshold from turbulent to laminar flow is defined as $\Delta p_{transition} = p_{avg}(1 - B_{lam})$, where B_{lam} is the pressure during the transition from laminar to turbulent regime (laminar value of the flow pressure coefficient parameter) and

$$p_{avg} = (p_A + p_B)/2. \tag{9}$$

Restriction pressure is based on momentum balance as the flow area between the inlet and restriction is cintracted.

The equation for a flow from port A to port B has the following form [12]:

$$PR_{AB} = p_A - \rho_R w_R |w_R| \frac{1+r}{2} \left(1 - r\frac{\rho_R}{\rho_A}\right). \tag{10}$$

The equation for a flow from port B to port A has the following form:

$$PR_{BA} = p_B + \rho_R w_R |w_R| \frac{1+r}{2} \left(1 - r\frac{\rho_R}{\rho_B}\right). \tag{11}$$

For laminar flow, the pressure under restriction is approximately:

$$p_{R_{лам}} = p_{avg} - \rho_R w_R^2 \frac{1 - r^2}{2}. \tag{12}$$

The block uses a cubic polynomial in terms of $(p_A - p_B)$ smoothly providing the pressure drop and pressure restriction between the turbulent regime and the laminar regime:

Flow Choking when the Channel Contracts.

When flow through a restriction is choked, further changes in flow depend on upstream conditions and do not depend on downstream conditions.

If Ap is variable at port A and $P_{B_{choked}}$ is the hypothetical pressure at port B, assuming choked flow from port A to port B, then the following equation is valid:

$$A.p - p_{B_{choked}} = \rho_R a_R^2 \left(\frac{1+r}{2}\left(1 - r\frac{\rho_R}{\rho_A}\right) - r\left(1 - r\frac{\rho_R}{\rho_B}\right)\right), \tag{13}$$

where a is the velocity of sound.

If $B.p$ is the across variable at port B and $p_{Achoked}$ is the hypothetical pressure at port A, assuming that the flow is choked from port B to port A, then

$$B.p - p_{A_{choked}} = \rho_R a_R^2 \left(\frac{1+r}{2}\left(1 - r\frac{\rho_R}{\rho_A}\right) - r\left(1 - r\frac{\rho_R}{\rho_B}\right)\right) \tag{14}$$

The actual pressures p_A and p_B in the ports depend on whether the choking has occurred.

For a flow from port A to port B, $p_A = A.p$ if

$$p_B = \begin{cases} B.p, & \text{если } B.p \geq p_{B_{choked}}, \\ p_{B_{choked}}, & \text{если } B.p < p_{B_{choked}}. \end{cases} \tag{15}$$

For a flow from port B to port A, $p_B = B.p$ if

$$p_A = \begin{cases} A.p, & \text{если } A.p \geq p_{A_{choked}}, \\ p_{B_{choked}}, & \text{если } A.p < p_{A_{choked}}. \end{cases} \tag{16}$$

Assumptions and Restrictions

The restriction is adiabatic. There is no heat exchange with the surrounding medium. This block does not model supersonic flow.

This example of a throttling effect in gas flow with a contraction shows the choking behavior in a gas hole, modeled by a block of local restriction (Fig. 2). Blocks of the controlled tank (G) are used to set controlled pressure and temperature boundary conditions from the tank input subsystem to test the gas port.

At the start, the flow is blocked. The mass flow rate increases as the pressure at the outlet decreases. In 3.3 s, the flow is choked. The throttle mass flow depends only on the inlet conditions, so a further decrease in the outlet pressure does not lead to a further increase in the throttle mass flow. However, after 6 s, the inlet pressure increases, so the throttle mass flow increases again (Fig. 3).

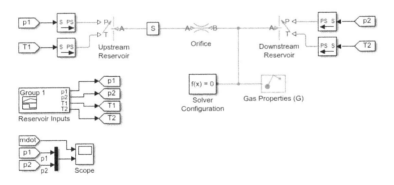

Fig. 3. Throttle model in *Simulink*

The lower limit of the cross-sectional area is bounded. This can be used to represent the leak area. In this case, the value of the AR input signal is saturated to prevent the decrease in restriction area to 10^{-10} m^2.

The upper limit of the cross-sectional area is bounded. The AR input signal is saturated at this value to prevent the increase in restriction area to 0.005 m^2.

The area normal to the flow route is restricted to 10^{-3} m^2.

The area normal to the flow route at ports *A* and *B* is assumed the same for the two ports and is 0.01 m^2.

The ratio of the actual mass flow to the theoretical mass flow through the restriction. The factor 0.64 is an empirical parameter that takes into account non-ideal effects.

Mass flow (kg/s)   Pressure (MPa)

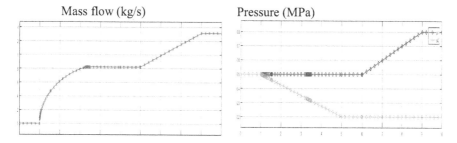

Fig. 4. Results of choke simulation using oscillometers

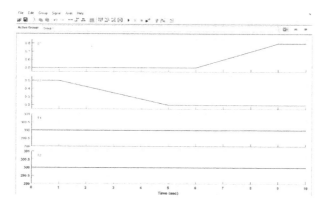

Fig. 5. Results of choke simulation using oscillometers

The pressure coefficient at which gas flow transitions between laminar and turbulent regimes. The pressure loss is linear with respect to the mass flow rate in laminar mode and quadratic with respect to the mass flow rate in turbulent mode.

Some results of calculations of mass flow and pressure for fixed values of distance (Fig. 4) and time (Fig. 5) are presented in a graphical form.

Compressor Map with Scattered Search. This example shows the gas flow through a compressor, modeled using a simple source with controlled mass flow. The compressor map that controls this mass flow is modeled using a PS *Scattered Lookup* (2D) block whose data coordinates are pressure ratio (Pa/Pa) and engine speed and whose output is mass flow (kg/s). The scattered search block performs Delaunay triangulation on the input data (as shown in the graphs of Fig. 5) and uses it to interpolate and calculate the mass flow rate from the input data. Scattered search allows us to simulate a compressor even if the provided data is in an unstructured format.

An example of a compressor map is shown in Fig. 6. In this example, any set of points along the various rpm lines can be selected as input data points for the PS *Scattered Lookup* (2D) block. The first coordinate is the pressure ratio, and the second coordinate is the rpm value. The value of the function is the corresponding value of the mass flow [11–16]. The model and subsystem of the compressor map compiled on *Simulink* are shown in Figs. 7, and 8.

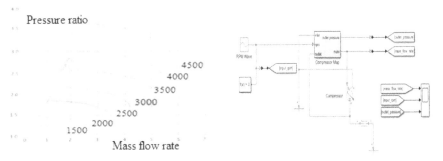

Pressure ratio

4500
4000
3500
3000
2500
2000
1500

Mass flow rate

Fig. 6. Characteristics of dimensionless values of pressure and mass flow of gas during the operating intervals of compressor

Fig. 7. *Simulink* model for compressor performance selection

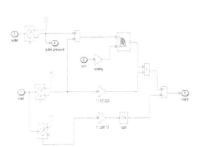

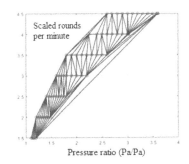

Scaled rounds per minute

Pressure ratio (Pa/Pa)

Fig. 8. Compressor map subsystem

Fig. 9. Method of triangulation in the coordinate plane of the pressure ratio and angular velocity (rpm) of the compressor

Simulation Results Obtained from Oscillometers. In this example, the compressor is driven at a sinusoidal rpm and the flow resistance is set based on the pressure drop and mass flow over the compressor map range. As the rpm changes, the mass flow changes, which then changes the outlet pressure, displayed on the oscillometer.

Figure 9 shows how the data is triangulated for the *SluCompressorMapExample*. Coordinate x_1 represents the pressure ratio and coordinate x_2 represents the scaled rpm. Triangulation is the scatter search method used to interpolate or extrapolate the query values on the compressor map. The value of the function is the mass flow [17–21].

Figure 10 shows approximate results of calculations of changes in mass flow and outlet pressure when the angular velocity of rotation in the compressor occurs in a sinusoidal law.

Mass flow

Rounds per minute

Outlet pressure

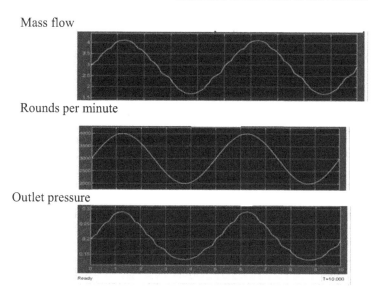

Fig. 10. Simulation results obtained using *Simscape Logging*

Thus, the *Simulink* software product allows us to determine the dynamics of the outlet mass flow and gas pressure in the compressor when setting the characteristics of the compressor in the operating zone in terms of the mass flow for a given law of change of the last indicator over time.

When calculating a network of gas (and other) pipelines, it is recommended to use *Simulink* – a MATLAB graphical extension, equipped with the necessary library, constructor and calculation algorithms for a wide range of tasks.

The structure and elements of *Simulink* functioning are analyzed. To clarify the capabilities of the software system, three practical tasks were considered and solved.

The problem of heat and mass transfer in a gas network with the inlet of different gases and the outlet of a mixture relative to the pressure and temperature of a real gas under various (turbulent and laminar) flow regimes in real and adiabatic regimes was solved, taking into account the friction force and local resistances, as well as convective heat transfer.

Within the capabilities of *Simulink,* the problem of throttling was solved with the selection of options for the flow choking. The results of this task can be used when choosing a valve regulating pressure and gas flow.

Power units of hydraulic networks (pumps and compressors) operate within a certain range of inlet pressure and mass flow and provide a certain value of pressure at the outlet (discharge pressure). For engineering practice, it is interesting to choose, for example, a compressor that provides continuous air supply under the conditions of setting the law of change in inlet flow. For such a problem, a model was compiled and smooth results were obtained when the inlet flow was set by a sinusoidal law.

The results showed that the use of *Simulink* greatly facilitates the work of design engineers and the calculation of gas networks.

References

1. Charny, I.A.: Unsteady motion of real fluid in pipes. 2nd ed., Nedra, 296 p. (1975)
2. Mirkin, A.Z., Usinsh, V.V.: Pipeline systems. Chemistry, 256 p. (1991)
3. Anderson, D., Tannehill, J., Pletcher, R.: Computational fluid mechanics and heat transfer: In 2 vols. Transl. from English. Mir, pp. 392–728 (1990)
4. Popov, D.N.: Mechanics of hydraulic and pneumatic drives: textbook for universities. Publishing house of N.E. Bauman MSTU, 320 p. (2001)
5. Korotaev, Y.P., Shirkovsky, A.I. Gas production, transportation and underground storage. Nedra, 487 p. (1997)
6. Ermolaeva, N.N.: Mathematical modeling of non-stationary non-isothermal processes in a binary non-isothermal multiphase medium: Diss. Doc. Phys. Math. Sci. 323 (2017)
7. Yuan, Q.: Study on the restart algorithm for a buried hot oil pipeline based on wavelet collocation method. Int. J. Heat Mass Trans. **125**, 891–907 (2018). https://doi.org/10.1016/j.ijheat masstransfer.2018.04.127
8. Sennova, E.V., Sidler, V.G.: Mathematical modeling and optimization of developing heat supply systems. Nauka **219** (1987)
9. Merenkov, A.P., Khasilev, V.Y.: Theory of hydraulic circuits. Nauka **278** (1985)
10. Khujaev, I.K.: Development of mathematical models of diffusion combustion and transportation of gas through the pipeline. Diss. Doc. Tech. Sci. Tashkent, IMSS AN RUz **336** (2009)
11. Khujaev, I., Akhmadjonov, S., Aminov, K., Mamadaliev, K.: Study of transition process features in short gas pipelines by the method of characteristics. AIP Conf. Proc. Disabled **2612**, 030027 (2023)
12. Hamdamov, M.M., Ishnazarov, A.I., Mamadaliev, K.A.: Numerical modeling of vertical axis wind turbines using ANSYS fluent software. In: Koucheryavy, Y., Aziz, A. (eds.) Internet of Things, Smart Spaces, and Next Generation Networks and Systems. NEW2AN 2022, LNCS, vol. 13772, pp. 156–170. Springer, Cham (2023). https://doi.org/10.1007/978-3-031-30258-9_14
13. Bazarov, O., Khujaev, I., Mamadaliev, K., Khodjaev, S.: Numerical method for solving the problem of the gas-dynamic state of a main gas pipeline section relief of a variable cross-sectional area. IOP Conf. Ser. Mater. Sci. Eng. **1030**(1), 012126 (2021)
14. Khujaev, I., Mamadaliev, K., Aminov, X.: Research of the elementary section of a gas pipeline under gas outflow from its end to the environment. In: International Conference on Information Science and Communications Technologies: Applications, Trends and Opportunities, ICISCT 2021 (2021)
15. Khujaev I., Shadmanova, G., Mamadaliev, K., Aminov, K.: Mathematical modeling of transition processes due to a change in gas consumption at the ends of the inclined section of the gas. In: 2020 International Conference on Information Science and Communications Technologies, ICISCT 2020, p. 9351523 (2020)
16. Khujaev, I.K., Fayziev, R.A., Hamdamov, M.M.: Numerical solution of the combustion process using the computer package ansys fluent. In: Koucheryavy, Y., Aziz, A. (eds.) Internet of Things, Smart Spaces, and Next Generation Networks and Systems. NEW2AN 2022, LNCS, vol. 13772, pp. 26–37. Springer, Cham (2023). https://doi.org/10.1007/978-3-031-30258-9_3
17. Hamdamov, M., Khujaev, I., Bazarov, O., Isabaev, K.: Axisymmetric turbulent methane jet propagation in a wake air flow under combustion at a finite velocity. IOP Conf. Ser. Mater. Sci. Eng. **1030**(1), 012163 (2021)
18. Khujaev, I.K., Hamdamov, M.M.: Axisymmetric turbulent methane jet Propagation in a co-current air flow under combustion at a finite velocity. Herald Bauman Moscow State Tech. Univ. **5**, 89–10 (2021)

19. Fayziev, R.A., Kurbanov, F.M.: Mathematical modeling and forecasting of electricity production in enterprises of the energy system of Uzbekistan AIP In: Conference Proceedings, vol. 2656, no. 1, p. 020015, 29 August 2022. https://doi.org/10.1063/5.0106330 https://ui.adsabs.harvard.edu/abs/2022AIPC.2656b0015F/abstract

20. Fayziev, R.A., Kurbanov, F.M.: Modeling and forecasting of net in-come from the country's electricity supply. In: ACM International Conference Proceeding Series, pp. 407–412 (2021). https://doi.org/10.1145/3508072.3508149

21. Alikulovich Fayziev, R., Muxiddinovich Hamdamov, M.: Model and program of the effect of incomplete combustion gas on the economy. In: ACM International Conference Proceeding Series, стр, pp. 401–406 (2021)

Numerical Investigation of Laminar-Turbulent Flow in a Suddenly Expanding Channel

Madaliev Murodil Erkinjon Ugli[1], Malikov Zafar Mamatkulovich[1],
Fayziev Rabim Alikulovich[2(✉)], and Hamdamov Muzaffar Muhiddinovich[1(✉)]

[1] Institute of Mechanics and Seismic Stability of Structures named after M.T.Urazbaev of the
AS RUz, Tashkent, Uzbekistan
mmhamdamov@mail.ru
[2] Tashkent State University of Economics, Tashkent, Uzbekistan
r.fayziyev@tsue.uz

Abstract. The article presents the results of a numerical study of the flow structure
in a flat channel in the zone of its sudden expansion in the form of a ledge. A
characteristic feature of the sudden expansion in this case is considered to be
that they exhibit complex anisotropic turbulence due to the recirculation of flows.
The calculations are based on the numerical solution of a system of non-stationary
equations using a new two-fluid turbulence model. The model provided is based on
a two-fluid approach to the turbulence problem. A feature of the two-fluid model
is that it is capable of describing complex anisotropic turbulent flows. In this
paper, the results are obtained for determining the locations of the reattachment
of the primary vortex, the beginning and end of the secondary vortex, and the
profiles of the longitudinal velocity in various sections are calculated. For the
difference approximation of the initial equations, the control volume method was
used, and the relationship between velocities and pressure was found using the
SIMPLE procedure. In this case, the viscosity terms were approximated by the
central difference, and for the convective terms, a scheme of the second order of
accuracy upstream was used. To confirm the correctness of the numerical results, a
comparison with experimental data is made, and numerical results of other known
turbulence models are presented. It is shown that the two-fluid turbulence model
gives results closer to experimental data than others.

Keywords: Navier–Stokes equations · flat channel with backward step ·
separated flow · two-fluid model · control volume method

1 Introduction

The study of separated flows is of great importance from both fundamental and applied
points of view. Fluid flows in suddenly expanding channels are found in various technical
devices and structures. Abrupt changes in the geometry of the channel wall or the surface
of the streamlined body can lead to separation of the flow and significantly change its
kinematic structure. The flow in a flat channel with a sudden expansion belongs to the

Y. Koucheryavy and A. Aziz (Eds.): NEW2AN/ruSMART 2023, LNCS 14543, pp. 76–85, 2024.
https://doi.org/10.1007/978-3-031-60997-8_8

simplest class of separated flows, when the flow separation point is fixed. The theoretical calculation of such flows presents great difficulties due to the formation of complex separation and reciprocating circulation flows in the area behind the ledge. The first calculations of stationary two-dimensional laminar separated flows of an incompressible fluid in channels were studied by Blasius in 1910 analytically in the form of series [1]. Subsequently, this problem was used by many scientists to study the mechanisms of separated flows and to test difference schemes for solving the Navier-Stokes equations. Due to their great practical significance, such flows have been studied theoretically and experimentally for both laminar [2–4] and turbulent [5–7] modes of motion of incompressible and compressible fluids. In many works in this direction, flows in channels with sudden bilateral expansion are considered [8–14]. Experimental data for this case in a flat channel were obtained in [8, 9], where the formation of a circulation zone behind a step is noted. A number of researchers used the equations of motion in the boundary layer approximation to calculate flows with a sudden expansion [14, 15].

A significant amount of work on suddenly widening channels has been done by Armali et al. [4]. They performed a detailed analysis of the flow behavior inside a backward-facing stepped channel experimentally and numerically with a step geometry having a value of H/h = 1.94. Research in this area has been done by others. For example, Lee and Smith [16] used potential flow theory to solve this problem. Potential flow theory failed to predict the area of flow splitting or reattachment behind the stage. Early numerical predictions of reverse stepwise flows were made by Roach, Taylor and Ndefoe, and Durst and Pereira.

The separation region at the bottom corner of the step was predicted by Alleborn et al. after carefully studying the sudden expansion of such a channel. Brandt et al. Hackbusch used the multigrid method, while Lange et al. [6] used the local block refinement method to predict the result more accurately. Kim and Moin [7] performed calculations using the second-order space-time method. Good agreement with the experimental data was found for Reynolds numbers up to 500. However, the calculated results began to deviate from the experimental data with Re = 600. Durst et al. [15] observed a second flow separation zone in a two-dimensional numerical simulation of a symmetric flow with sudden expansion. Kaiktsis et al. [5–9] noted that the instability was created by convective instability.

In this paper, a fluid flow with a sudden expansion is studied numerically with an expansion coefficient H/h = 2. Various flow characteristics were calculated for different Reynolds numbers (Re = 100 to 7000) [2–7]. The calculations were performed for various flow regimes, such as laminar, transitional, and turbulent. The main attention, in addition to the longitudinal velocity profiles, is also made on the prediction of the points of reattachment of flows. Numerical determination of these points is a rather difficult task. Because it is related to the adequacy of the turbulence model. It is known that many turbulence models are based on the Boussinesq hypothesis. This hypothesis is based on the assumption that turbulence is isotropic. However, when circulation motions of the flow occur, turbulence acquires an anisotropic character. Consequently, models using the Boussinesq hypothesis may give unsatisfactory results in such cases. Therefore, for anisotropic turbulence, it is recommended to use models that do not use the Boussinesq hypothesis. An example of such models are Reynolds stress models. These models are much more complex than the RANS models based on the Boussinesq hypothesis. However, they can also give not quite accurate results [1–3].

Recently, the two-fluid model of turbulence has become increasingly popular [34]. This model is based on the dynamics of two fluids, which, unlike the Reynolds approach, leads to a closed system of equations. The peculiarity of this model is that it is able to describe complex anisotropic turbulent flows. Therefore, the purpose of this work is to use a two-fluid model to study the separated fluid flow with recirculation in a flat channel. At the same time, along with the study of the flow structure after the ledge, the goal is to test the effectiveness of this model for calculating complex flows characterized by the presence of reciprocating vortex flow regions. The obtained numerical results are compared with the available experimental and numerical data of Armali et al. [4], as well as with the results of other models [5–12].

2 Physical and Mathematical Formulation of the Problem

A two-dimensional laminar flow in a flat channel with a sudden expansion is considered. The physical picture of the analyzed flow and the configuration of the computational domain are shown in Fig. 1.

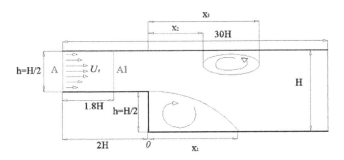

Fig. 1. Diagram of the design area in a flat channel with a reverse ledge

The beginning of the entered Cartesian coordinate system is located in the lower left corner of the ledge. The channel width in the left input section has size - h, and in the right output section of the channel size $H = 2h$. The height of the ledge is equal to - h, respectively. In the entrance section of the channel, a parabolic profile of the Poiseuille flow was set for the longitudinal velocity - U, and the vertical velocity - V was zero. When introducing dimensionless quantities, the width of the channel - h is taken as the length scale, the average cross-sectional velocity - U_0 at the entrance to the channel is taken as the velocity scale. x_1 is the distance to reconnect the primary vortex, x_2 is the distance to the beginning of the secondary vortex, x_3 is the distance to the end of the secondary vortex.

It was said above that a two-fluid turbulence model was used to study the movement of a turbulent fluid in a channel with a sudden expansion [39]. The unsteady system of turbulence equations according to the two - fluid model in the Cartesian coordinate system has the following form:

$$
\begin{cases}
\frac{\partial \rho}{\partial t} + \frac{\partial \rho V_x}{\partial x} + \frac{\partial \rho V_y}{\partial y} = 0 \\[4pt]
\rho \frac{\partial V_x}{\partial t} + \rho V_x \frac{\partial V_x}{\partial x} + \rho V_y \frac{\partial V_x}{\partial y} + \frac{\partial p}{\partial x} = 2 \frac{\partial}{\partial x}\left(\nu\rho \frac{\partial V_x}{\partial x}\right) + \frac{\partial}{\partial y}\left(\nu\rho\left(\frac{\partial V_x}{\partial y} + \frac{\partial V_y}{\partial x}\right)\right) - \frac{\partial \rho \vartheta_x \vartheta_x}{\partial x} - \frac{\partial \rho \vartheta_x \vartheta_y}{\partial y} \\[4pt]
\rho \frac{\partial V_y}{\partial t} + \rho V_x \frac{\partial V_y}{\partial x} + \rho V_y \frac{\partial V_y}{\partial y} + \frac{\partial p}{\partial y} = \frac{\partial}{\partial x}\left(\nu\rho\left(\frac{\partial V_y}{\partial x} + \frac{\partial V_x}{\partial y}\right)\right) + 2 \frac{\partial}{\partial y}\left(\nu\rho \frac{\partial V_y}{\partial y}\right) - \frac{\partial \rho \vartheta_x \vartheta_y}{\partial x} - \frac{\partial \rho \vartheta_y \vartheta_y}{\partial y}; \\[4pt]
\rho \frac{\partial \vartheta_x}{\partial t} + \rho V_x \frac{\partial \vartheta_x}{\partial x} + \rho V_y \frac{\partial \vartheta_x}{\partial y} = -\left(u\rho \frac{\partial V_x}{\partial x} + \vartheta\rho \frac{\partial V_x}{\partial y}\right) + C_s\rho\left(-\left(\frac{\partial V_y}{\partial x} - \frac{\partial V_x}{\partial y}\right)\vartheta_y\right) \\[4pt]
+ \frac{\partial}{\partial x}\left(2\rho V_{xx}\frac{\partial \vartheta_x}{\partial x}\right) + \frac{\partial}{\partial y}\left(\rho V_{xy}\left(\frac{\partial \vartheta_x}{\partial y} + \frac{\partial \vartheta_y}{\partial x}\right)\right) - C_r\rho\vartheta_x; \\[4pt]
\rho \frac{\partial \vartheta_y}{\partial t} + \rho V_x \frac{\partial \vartheta_y}{\partial x} + \rho V_y \frac{\partial \vartheta_y}{\partial y} = -\left(\vartheta_x\rho \frac{\partial V_y}{\partial x} + \vartheta_y\rho \frac{\partial V_y}{\partial y}\right) \\[4pt]
+ C_s\rho\left(\left(\frac{\partial V_y}{\partial x} - \frac{\partial V_x}{\partial y}\right)\vartheta_x\right) + \frac{\partial}{\partial x}\left(\rho V_{xy}\left(\frac{\partial \vartheta_y}{\partial x} + \frac{\partial \vartheta_x}{\partial y}\right)\right) + \frac{\partial}{\partial y}\left(2\rho V_{yy}\frac{\partial \vartheta_y}{\partial y}\right) - C_r\rho\vartheta_y;
\end{cases}
$$

$$(1)$$

Here

$$
\nu_{xx} = \nu_{yy} = \frac{3}{Re} + 2\frac{S}{|\mathbf{defV}|}, \quad \nu_{xy} = \frac{3}{Re} + 2\left|\frac{\vartheta_x \vartheta_y}{\mathbf{defV}}\right|, \quad S = \frac{\vartheta_x^2 J_x + \vartheta_y^2 J_y}{J_x + J_y}, \quad J_x = \left|\frac{\partial \vartheta_x}{\partial x}\right|, \quad J_y = \left|\frac{\partial \vartheta_y}{\partial y}\right|,
$$

$$
|\mathbf{defV}| = \mu\sqrt{2\left(\left(\frac{\partial V_x}{\partial x}\right)^2 + \left(\frac{\partial V_y}{\partial y}\right)^2\right) + \left(\frac{\partial V_y}{\partial x} + \frac{\partial V_x}{\partial y}\right)^2} \quad C_s = 0.2, \; C_r = C_1\lambda_{max} + C_2\frac{|\mathbf{d} \cdot \mathbf{v}|}{d^2}
$$

In the above equations, V_x, V_y are, respectively, the axial and transverse components of the averaged flow velocity vector, p is the hydrostatic pressure, ϑ_x, ϑ_y are the relative axial and transverse components of the fluid velocity, ν is the molecular kinematic viscosity, ν_{xx}, ν_{yy}, ν_{xy} are the effective molar viscosities, d is the nearest distance to a solid wall, λ_{max}– the largest root of the characteristic equation.

$$\det(A - \lambda E) = 0, \tag{2}$$

where A is the matrix

$$
A = \begin{vmatrix}
-\frac{\partial V_x}{\partial x} & -\frac{\partial V_x}{\partial y} - C_s\left(\frac{\partial V_y}{\partial x} - \frac{\partial V_x}{\partial y}\right) \\[6pt]
-\frac{\partial V_y}{\partial x} + C_s\left(\frac{\partial V_y}{\partial x} - \frac{\partial V_x}{\partial y}\right) & -\frac{\partial V_y}{\partial y}
\end{vmatrix}
$$

The largest root of the characteristic equation is

$$
D = \frac{\partial V_x}{\partial y}\frac{\partial V_y}{\partial x} - \frac{\partial V_x}{\partial x}\frac{\partial V_y}{\partial y} + C_s(1 - C_s)\left(\frac{\partial V_y}{\partial x} - \frac{\partial V_x}{\partial y}\right)^2, \quad \lambda_{max} = \sqrt{D}, \text{ if } D > 0,
$$

$$\lambda_{max} = 0 \text{ if } D < 0.$$

The constant coefficients are equal to $C_1 = 0.7825$, $C_2 = 0.306$.

For numerical implementation, the system of Eqs. (1, 3) is reduced to a dimensionless form by correlating all velocities to the average velocity of the incoming flow, and all linear dimensions to the height of the ledge - h.

Obvious boundary conditions of adhesion are set on all fixed solid walls: $V_x|_\Gamma = 0$ And $V_y|_\Gamma = 0$, where Γ is a solid boundary. At the output of the channel for horizontal and vertical velocities, the conditions of extrapolation of the second order of accuracy are accepted. According to work [14], parameters obtained at a distance of 1.8H from it were set at the entrance to section A (Fig. 1). This type of boundary condition is called the copy boundary condition $A(V_x, V_y, p) = A1(V_x, V_y, p)$.

3 Solution Method

For the numerical solution of the system of initial nonstationary Eq. (1), the finite volume method is used. Due to the difficulties of matching the velocity and pressure fields, a grid with a spaced structure of the arrangement of grid nodes for dependent variables was used to discretize the equations of motion in directions and the continuity equation. This means that the velocity and pressure components are determined at different nodes. This approach is similar to the SIMPLE methods and gives certain advantages when calculating the pressure field [15–16]. Relaxation coefficients are introduced to increase the convergence rate of the solution. In the work for pressure and all velocities, the relaxation coefficient was equal to 0.5.

4 Calculated Grids

In the problem under consideration, the points of separation and attachment of flows are of great importance. Because the location of these points strongly affect the flow as a whole. In this problem, the point of separation of the flow is known, but the connection points must be determined numerically. Therefore, in the vicinity of these points, the calculation grid was thickened in the work. In this study, two samples of the computational grid were used, which are shown in Fig. 2. As can be seen from the figure, the thickening of the grid near the horizontal walls has not been carried out. Because, as shown in [10–15], the two-fluid model is capable of describing the wall law with great accuracy and with a coarse grid. In this paper, it is shown that for an adequate description of the flow near a solid wall, two design nodes inside the boundary layer are sufficient.

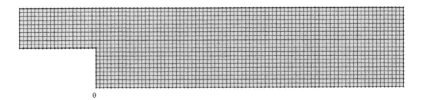

0

Fig. 2. Calculation grids: a) uniform grid size 300x100

As can be seen from Fig. 2b), the thickening of the grid was carried out in the areas of separation and attachment of flows. To do this, the transformation of coordinate systems is used $(x, y) \rightarrow (\xi, \eta)$ when $0 < x < L$

$$\xi = \alpha + (1 - \alpha)\frac{\ln(\{\beta + [x(2\alpha + 1)/L] - 2\alpha\}/\{\beta - [x(2\alpha + 1)/L] + 2\alpha\})}{\ln[(\beta + 1)/(\beta - 1)]}.$$

$\eta = y/h.$ and with $L < x < M$

$$\xi = 1 - \frac{\ln(\{\beta + 1 - x/M\}/\{\beta - 1 + x/M\})}{\ln[(\beta + 1)/(\beta - 1)]}, \quad 1 < \beta < \infty. \ \eta = y/h.$$

This transformation at $\alpha = 1/2$ allows you to grind the calculated grid both in the section $x = 0$ and $x = L$. The β parameter is about 1 and regulates the degree of grinding. The value $\beta = 1.054$. For a uniform grid was used in the work (Fig. 2.a) the number of calculated nodes was 40×50 at $x < 0$ and 260×100 at $x > 0$. And for the condensed grid (Fig. 2.b), 100×50 at $x < 0$, 200×100 at $0 < x < L$ and 100×100 at $x > L$. are used.

The system of Eq. (1) after the transformation of coordinates in dimensionless parameters has the following form

$$
\begin{cases}
\dfrac{\partial V_x}{\partial t} + V_x \dfrac{\partial \xi}{\partial x}\dfrac{\partial V_x}{\partial \xi} + V_y \dfrac{\partial V_x}{\partial \eta} + \dfrac{\partial \xi}{\partial x}\dfrac{\partial p}{\partial \xi} = \dfrac{1}{Re}\left(\left(\dfrac{\partial \xi}{\partial x}\right)^2 \dfrac{\partial V_x}{\partial \xi^2} + \dfrac{\partial^2 V_x}{\partial \eta^2}\right) - \dfrac{\partial \xi}{\partial x}\dfrac{\partial \vartheta_x \vartheta_x}{\partial \xi} - \dfrac{\partial \vartheta_y \vartheta_x}{\partial \eta}; \\[2mm]
\dfrac{\partial V_y}{\partial t} + V_x \dfrac{\partial \xi}{\partial x}\dfrac{\partial V_y}{\partial \xi} + V_y \dfrac{\partial V_y}{\partial \eta} + \dfrac{\partial p}{\partial \eta} = \dfrac{1}{Re}\left(\left(\dfrac{\partial \xi}{\partial x}\right)^2 \dfrac{\partial V_y}{\partial \xi^2} + \dfrac{\partial^2 V_y}{\partial \eta^2}\right) - \dfrac{\partial \xi}{\partial x}\dfrac{\partial \vartheta_y \vartheta_x}{\partial \xi} - \dfrac{\partial \vartheta_y \vartheta_y}{\partial \eta}; \\[2mm]
\dfrac{\partial \vartheta_x}{\partial t} + V_x \dfrac{\partial \xi}{\partial x}\dfrac{\partial \vartheta_x}{\partial \xi} + V_y \dfrac{\partial \vartheta_x}{\partial \eta} = -\left(\vartheta_x \dfrac{\partial \xi}{\partial x}\dfrac{\partial V_x}{\partial \xi} + \vartheta_y \dfrac{\partial V_x}{\partial \eta}\right) + C_s\left(-\left(\dfrac{\partial \xi}{\partial x}\dfrac{\partial V_y}{\partial \xi} - \dfrac{\partial V_x}{\partial \eta}\right)\vartheta_y\right) \\[2mm]
\qquad + \dfrac{\partial \xi}{\partial x}\dfrac{\partial}{\partial \xi}\left(2\nu_{xx}\left(\dfrac{\partial \xi}{\partial x}\dfrac{\partial \vartheta_x}{\partial \xi}\right)\right) + \dfrac{\partial}{\partial \eta}\left(\nu_{xy}\left(\dfrac{\partial \vartheta_x}{\partial \eta} + \dfrac{\partial \xi}{\partial x}\dfrac{\partial \vartheta_y}{\partial \xi}\right)\right) - C_r \vartheta_x; \\[2mm]
\dfrac{\partial \vartheta_y}{\partial t} + V_x \dfrac{\partial \xi}{\partial x}\dfrac{\partial \vartheta_y}{\partial \xi} + V_y \dfrac{\partial \vartheta_y}{\partial \eta} = -\left(\vartheta_x \dfrac{\partial \xi}{\partial x}\dfrac{\partial \vartheta_y}{\partial \xi} + \vartheta_y \dfrac{\partial V_y}{\partial \eta}\right) + C_s\left(\left(\dfrac{\partial \xi}{\partial x}\dfrac{\partial V_y}{\partial \xi} - \dfrac{\partial V_x}{\partial \eta}\right)\vartheta_x\right) \\[2mm]
\qquad + \dfrac{\partial \xi}{\partial x}\dfrac{\partial}{\partial \xi}\left(\nu_{xy}\left(\dfrac{\partial \xi}{\partial x}\dfrac{\partial \vartheta_y}{\partial \xi} + \dfrac{\partial \vartheta_x}{\partial \eta}\right)\right) + \dfrac{\partial}{\partial \eta}\left(2\nu_{yy}\dfrac{\partial \vartheta_y}{\partial \eta}\right) - C_r \vartheta_y; \\[2mm]
\dfrac{\partial \xi}{\partial x}\dfrac{\partial V_x}{\partial \xi} + \dfrac{\partial V_y}{\partial \eta} = 0.
\end{cases}
\tag{3}
$$

Here

$$
\nu_{xx} = \nu_{yy} = \frac{3}{Re} + 2\frac{S}{|\mathbf{defV}|}, \quad \nu_{xy} = \frac{3}{Re} + 2\left|\frac{\vartheta_x \vartheta_y}{\mathbf{defV}}\right|, \quad S = \frac{\vartheta_x^2 J_x + \vartheta_y^2 J_y}{J_x + J_y}, \quad J_x = \left|\frac{\partial \xi}{\partial x}\frac{\partial \vartheta_x}{\partial \xi}\right|, \quad J_y = \left|\frac{\partial \vartheta_y}{\partial \eta}\right|,
$$

$$
|\mathbf{defV}| = \sqrt{2\left(\left(\frac{\partial \xi}{\partial x}\frac{\partial V_x}{\partial \xi}\right)^2 + \left(\frac{\partial V_y}{\partial \eta}\right)^2\right) + \left(\frac{\partial \xi}{\partial x}\frac{\partial V_y}{\partial \xi} + \frac{\partial V_x}{\partial \eta}\right)^2} \quad C_s = 0.2, \quad C_r = C_1 \lambda_{max} + C_2 \frac{|\mathbf{d} \cdot \mathbf{v}|}{d^2}
$$

5   Numerical Scheme

The paper uses a second-order accuracy scheme for derivatives in space and first - order in time $O(\Delta t, \Delta x^2, \Delta y^2)$, stable at $\frac{\Delta t}{\min(\Delta x, \Delta y)} \leq 1$. In this case, the diffusion terms were approximated according to the scheme with central differences in an implicit form, and for convective terms, a second-order approximation of accuracy against the flow was used [4]. The dimensionless system of Eqs. (3) can be represented in matrix form:

$$
\frac{\partial \Phi}{\partial t} + U \frac{\partial \Phi}{\partial x} + V \frac{\partial \Phi}{\partial y} = \frac{\partial}{\partial x}\left(A \frac{\partial \Phi}{\partial x}\right) + \frac{\partial}{\partial y}\left(B \frac{\partial \Phi}{\partial y}\right) + \Pi^\Phi.
\tag{4}
$$

Here

$$\Phi = \begin{pmatrix} U \\ V \\ u \\ v \end{pmatrix}, A = \begin{pmatrix} \frac{1}{Re} \\ Re \\ Re \\ 2v_{xx} \\ v_{xy} \end{pmatrix}, B = \begin{pmatrix} \frac{1}{Re} \\ Re \\ v_{xy} \\ 2v_{yy} \end{pmatrix}, \Pi^\Phi = \begin{pmatrix} \frac{\partial p}{\partial x} \\ \frac{\partial p}{\partial y} \\ -\left(u\frac{\partial U}{\partial x} + v\frac{\partial U}{\partial y}\right) + \frac{\partial}{\partial y}\left(v_{xy}\left(\frac{\partial v}{\partial x}\right)\right) + C_s\left(-\left(\frac{\partial V}{\partial x} - \frac{\partial U}{\partial y}\right)v\right) - C_r u \\ -\left(u\frac{\partial V}{\partial x} + v\frac{\partial V}{\partial y}\right) + \frac{\partial}{\partial x}\left(v_{xy}\left(\frac{\partial u}{\partial y}\right)\right) + C_s\left(\left(\frac{\partial V}{\partial x} - \frac{\partial U}{\partial y}\right)u\right) - C_r v \end{pmatrix}.$$

The calculation scheme used has the following form

$$\frac{\Phi_{i,j}^n - \Phi_{i,j}^{n-1}}{\Delta t} + \left\{ \begin{array}{l} U_{i,j} > 0 \to \frac{3\Phi_{i,j}^{n-1} - 4\Phi_{i-1,j}^{n-1} + \Phi_{i-2,j}^{n-1}}{2\Delta x} \\ U_{i,j} < 0 \to \frac{-\Phi_{i+2,j}^{n-1} + 4\Phi_{i+1,j}^{n-1} - 3\Phi_{i,j}^{n-1}}{2\Delta x} \end{array} \right\} + \left\{ \begin{array}{l} V_{i,j} > 0 \to \frac{3\Phi_{i,j}^{n-1} - 4\Phi_{i,j-1}^{n-1} + \Phi_{i,j-2}^{n-1}}{2\Delta y} \\ V_{i,j} < 0 \to \frac{-\Phi_{i,j+2}^{n-1} + 4\Phi_{i,j+1}^{n-1} - 3\Phi_{i,j}^{n-1}}{2\Delta y} \end{array} \right\}$$

$$= \frac{0.5\left(A_{i,j} + A_{i+1,j}\right)\left(\Phi_{i+1,j}^{n-1} - \Phi_{i,j}^n\right) - 0.5\left(A_{i,j} + A_{i-1,j}\right)\left(\Phi_{i,j}^n - \Phi_{i-1,j}^{n-1}\right)}{\Delta x^2}$$

$$+ \frac{0.5\left(B_{i,j} + B_{i,j+1}\right)\left(\Phi_{i,j+1}^n - \Phi_{i,j}^n\right) - 0.5\left(B_{i,j} + B_{i,j-1}\right)\left(\Phi_{i,j}^n - \Phi_{i,j-1}^n\right)}{\Delta y^2} + \Pi^\Phi.$$

A feature of the discretization is that the finite-difference approximation is centered according to the selected pattern. In this case, the grid indexes for dependent variables are shifted as shown in Fig. 2.

The obtained velocities according to scheme (4) do not satisfy the continuity equation. Therefore, the speed correction was carried out according to the SIMPLE procedure. For a homogeneous rectangular grid, the calculated steps were equal to $\Delta x = 0.05, \Delta y = 0.01$. And for a grid with condensation at $0 < x < L$, the steps were $\Delta \xi = 0.04, \Delta \eta = 0.01$ and at $x > L - \Delta \xi = 0.08, \Delta \eta = 0.01$.

To obtain a stationary solution of system (3) at Reynolds numbers Re > 800, after the formation of a quasi-periodic regime, the results were averaged over time.

6 Calculation Results and Their Discussion

Figure 3 shows the experimental and numerical results of Armali et al. for the longitudinal velocity profile, as well as for the two-fluid model for the Reynolds number Re $= 400$. Numerical results for the two-fluid model are obtained for both uniform and condensed meshes. Up to Re < 500, experimental and numerical results did not provide any additional separation regions other than the main one attached to the stage. Under these conditions, a good correspondence is achieved between the experiments and the numerical results.

This phenomenon is explained by the fact that at such values of the Reynolds number, the flow is still laminar and, in fact, the Navier-Stokes equations are solved. At higher Reynolds numbers, the flow acquires anisotropic turbulence due to recirculation. This explains the discrepancies between the experimental and numerical results shown in Fig. 4 at Reynolds numbers Re $= 1000$ and Re $= 1290$. In these figures, U is the dimensionless longitudinal velocity.

Figure 4 show that the two-fluid model describes the parameter $(U + x/h)$ very well at x/h < 12 for Re $= 1000$ and x/h < 10 for Re $= 1290$. Small deviations from the experimental data are observed in the range of $12 < $ x/h $ < 16$.

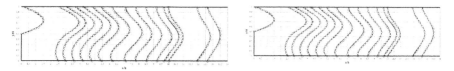

Fig. 3. Profiles of the axial $(U + x/h)$ velocity component: (○) Armali et al. (experiment), (——) two-fluid model a) uniform mesh, b) condensed mesh, (- - -) Armali et al. (numerical)

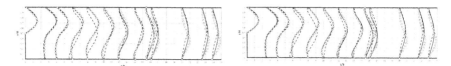

Fig. 4. Profiles for $(U + x/h)$ at Re $= 1000$: (○) Armali et al. (experiment), (——) two-fluid model a) uniform mesh, b) condensed mesh, (- - -) Armali et al. (numerical)

Figure 5 shows the longitudinal velocity profiles with the number Re $= 1000$ in different sections.

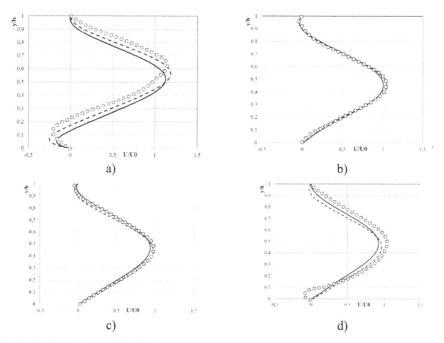

Fig. 5. Profiles of the axial velocity component at Re $= 1000$. (o) Armali et al. (experiment), (——) two-fluid model for a uniform grid, (- - -) two-fluid model with a condensed grid at cross sections: a) x/h $= 12$, b) x/h $= 16$, c) x/h $= 15.5$, e) x/h $= 16$

It can be seen from these figures that the correspondence of numerical results with experimental data can be considered satisfactory. Figure 6 shows the results for the location of the reconnection of the primary vortex, depending on the Reynolds number. Experimental data and numerical results of other works are also presented here.

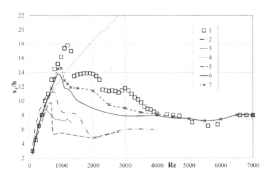

Fig. 6. Results of the location of the primary vortex when the Reynolds number changes. 1) Armali et al. (experiment), 2) Mohammad et al. (Computing), 3) Armali, etc. ((Computing), 4) Erkan et al. (Computational), 5) Vidal et al. (Computational), 6) two-fluid model for a uniform grid, 7) two-fluid model with a condensed grid

It can be seen from Fig. 6 that the two-fluid model describes very well the laminar flow region Re < 900 and the turbulent region Re > 4000. The deviation of numerical results from experimental data is observed for the transition region 900 < Re < 4000. However, the results of the two-fluid model are significantly better than the results of other studies. It can be seen that the thickening of the computational grid somewhat improves the results.

It is also possible to observe a satisfactory correspondence with the experimental data for the two-fluid model in comparison with other results.

7   Conclusions

The paper presents numerical flow results for laminar, transient and turbulent flow. The results of determining the locations of the reconnection of the primary vortex, the beginning and end of the secondary vortex are obtained, and the longitudinal velocity profiles in various sections are calculated. It is shown that the two-fluid turbulence model gives closer results to experimental data than using other models. Especially, a good correspondence is observed for laminar and turbulent flow regimes. Slightly worse results were obtained for the transition mode. Apparently, this is due to the fact that the correction coefficients for the two-fluid model were obtained for developed turbulence and for the transition region they need to be calibrated again. However, this requires additional research.

In general, given the accuracy and simplicity for the numerical implementation of the two-fluid model, it can be recommended for the study of separation flows with recirculation of the flow.

References

1. Korotaev, Y.P., Shirkovsky, A.I., Nedra, M.: Extraction, transport and underground storage of gas, p. 487 (1997)
2. Komina, G.P., Proshutinsky, A.O.: Hydraulic calculation and design of gas pipelines: textbook; SPbGASU. - St. Petersburg, p. 148 (2010)
3. Loitsyansky, L.G., Drofa, M.: Fluid and Gas Mechanics, p. 840 (2003)
4. Yuldashev, B.E., Khujaev, I.K.: Improved models and methods for calculating the pipeline transport of real gases. - Tashkent: Fan va tekhnologiya, p. 152 (2013)
5. Sennova, E.V., Sidler, V.G., Nauka, M.: Mathematical modeling and optimization of developing heat supply systems, p. 219 (1987)
6. Merenkov, A.P., Khasilev, V.Y., Nauka, M.: Theory of hydraulic circuits, p. 278 (1985)
7. Khujaev, I.K., Ravshanov, N., Bozorov, O., Khujaev, Z.I.: Generalization of closing relations of Kirchhoff's laws for various regimes of incompressible fluid flow. In: Problems of Informatics and Energy. Tashkent, no. 2–3, pp. 25–27 (2012)
8. Khujaev, I.K., Fayziev, R.A., Hamdamov, M.M. Numerical solution of the combustion process using the computer package ansys fluent. In: NEW2AN 2022, LNCS 13772, pp. 26–37 (2023).https://doi.org/10.1007/978-3-031-30258-9_3
9. Hamdamov, M.M., Ishnazarov, A.I., Mamadaliev, K.A.: Numerical modeling of vertical axis wind turbines using ANSYS fluent software. In: NEW2AN 2022, LNCS 13772, pp. 156–170 (2023). https://doi.org/10.1007/978-3-031-30258-9_14
10. Khujaev, I.K., Hamdamov, M.M.: Axisymmetric turbulent methane jet propagation in a co-current air flow under combustion at a finite velocity. Bull. Bauman Moscow State Tech. Univ. Ser. Nat. Sci. 5, 89–108 (2021)
11. Fayziev, A.R., Hamdamov, M.M.: Model and program of the effect of incomplete combustion gas on the economy. In: ACM International Conference Proceeding Series, pp. 401–406 (2021)
12. Khujaev, I., Akhmadjonov, S., Aminov, K., Mamadaliev, K.: Study of transition process features in short gas pipelines by the method of characteristics. AIP Conf. Proc. 2612, 030027 (2023)
13. Khujaev, I., Mamadaliev, K., Aminov, X.: Research of the elementary section of a gas pipeline under gas outflow from its end to the environment. In: International Conference on Information Science and Communications Technologies: Applications, Trends and Opportunities, ICISCT 2021 (2021)
14. Fayziev, R.A., Kurbanov, F.M.: Mathematical modeling and forecasting of electricity production in enterprises of the energy system of Uzbekistan. AIP Conf. Proc. 2656(1), 020015 (2022). https://doi.org/10.1063/5.0106330, https://ui.adsabs.harvard.edu/abs/2022AIPC.265 6b0015F/abstract
15. Fayziev, R.A., Kurbanov, F.M.: Modeling and forecasting of net in-come from the Country's electricity supply. In: ACM International Conference Proceeding Series, pp. 407–412 (2021). https://doi.org/10.1145/3508072.3508149

Experimental Results of Econometric Modeling of Economic Processes

Abidov Abdujabbar and Karimov Botirjon$^{(\boxtimes)}$ (iD)

Department of Digital Economy, Tashkent State University of Economics, Tashkent, Uzbekistan
`botir.karim1@gmail.com`

Abstract. Econometric modeling is undeniably pivotal in forecasting and evaluation, playing a key role in ensuring the stability of economic processes. However, the demand for such models has grown, becoming an increasingly pressing issue. Enhancing the stability and fault tolerance of software and technical systems is of paramount importance, especially to ensure their reliable real-time operation. The global expansion of the Internet has unified the information space and brought about significant changes in IT. This has also led to an increased number of failures in the information systems of economic entities. Although collecting statistical data and forecasting failures, disruptions, and downtimes might seem straightforward, it is more fitting to employ structural modeling based on global experiences with 24/7 online systems. In the forthcoming article, we will discuss how the effectiveness of software, operating under uncertain external influences, can be improved through control methods. We will also analyze experimental results derived from forecasts using the econometric model.

Keywords: stable operation of enterprises · Markov chain · Poisson distribution · econometric modeling · application of forecasting methods · recovery results using software

1 Introduction

Estimating failures in real-time information systems and understanding the failure statistics of economic entities is challenging due to the diversity of applications and systems. Studies indicate that software bugs, hardware failures, and design flaws are primary culprits behind these failures. Moreover, the increasing number of cyberattacks poses a significant threat to the reliability of real-time systems. In 2019, Facebook, Instagram, and WhatsApp experienced a service outage due to a software issue. The outage lasted for several hours and affected millions of users worldwide, once again highlighting the importance of backup and fault-tolerant technology. This is particularly crucial as errors in technology have become the largest segment of economic objects in continuous motion. According to a study by Cisco [1], the failure rate of IoT devices in 2020 was approximately 26%. Meanwhile, a study by Statista [2] reported that the failure rate for PCs and laptops in 2020 was 3.7%. A study conducted by the US National Institute of Standards and Technology (NIST) found that technology-related errors account

© The Author(s), under exclusive license to Springer Nature Switzerland AG 2024
Y. Koucheryavy and A. Aziz (Eds.): NEW2AN/ruSMART 2023, LNCS 14543, pp. 86–94, 2024.
https://doi.org/10.1007/978-3-031-60997-8_9

for approximately 22% of all failures in real-time systems. The consequences of software failures for businesses can be significant, encompassing downtime, repair costs, legal complications, fees, and damages. Additionally, it's essential not to overlook other potential consequences, such as property damage, financial losses, harm to reputation, and even personal injury or loss of life. The failure rate of technologies can vary greatly depending on the specific application and industry. However, a study conducted by the same NIST institute showed that software defects, which are failures that can occur in systems such as B2B and B2C, have the potential to sever a company's ties with its customers, alienate its suppliers, and even lead to business collapse. In fact, this study revealed that software defects could be the root cause of up to 90% of system failures. In light of these findings, this study serves as an experimental evaluation of software tools created to ensure the security of economic process information. It also aims to draw econometric conclusions from the data, shedding light on the critical role software quality plays in maintaining business stability and continuity.

2 Analysis of Literature on the Topic

Due to the increasing security requirements of embedded software, many studies have appeared in the field of fault tolerance and reliability evaluation. The traditional approach relies mainly on error information found in software testing to make predictions about future error behavior. For example, a statistical method such as Monte Carlo modeling [1] was used to deal with failures. In the literature, the statistical approach involves a large number of calculations [2, 3]. In the cited research activities, some developers have provided commentary on formal fault tolerance planning and reliability analysis. Real-time technology fault-tolerant systems [4], as well as methods such as restarting from checkpoints and time-based backup [5], are presented as primary models for forecasting software technology reliability. A. Burns et al. [6] introduced a probabilistic model in scheduling analysis as part of a probabilistic guarantee that all tasks should always be completed on time. I. Broster et al. [7] extended this method to the CAN network to calculate accurate predictions of failure probability from the response time probability distribution. Safety-critical applications must operate correctly and without downtime within a defined time frame, even in the presence of errors. G. Lima et al. [8] introduced a worst-case analysis of response time scheduling for demanding fault-tolerant real-time systems. They also considered task recovery strategies that initiate with high priority and introduced a specialized priority algorithm to enhance the system's fault tolerance [9]. Consequently, there have been efforts to balance fault tolerance with the trade-off of additional CPU processing time. Li et al. [10] introduced a novel fault-tolerant prioritization algorithm. This algorithm considers factors such as limited priority levels [11], optional long-term fault tolerance, and the availability of worst-case response time planning analysis for complex real-time problems. However, these methods predominantly concentrate on task prioritization planning without incorporating a probabilistic model to assess system reliability. Notably, these studies do not furnish statistical data for program reliability evaluation, as such data is not the primary focus or of practical relevance to them.

3   Research Methodologies

The research methodology is based on principles drawn from new knowledge and scientific achievements. These achievements are reflected in the publications of leading scientists of our time, covering areas such as information security in economic processes, the durability and reliability of software technology, evaluation models, and the development and effective operation of global digital multi-functional platforms. Logical, comparative, economic and mathematical methods of analysis were used during the writing of this article.

4   Analysis and Results

In general, Q is defined as follows [4, 5]:

$$Q = (1 - P_{rad})(1 - P_{11})\, p^3 p \tag{1}$$

where:

- Prad is the probability of denial of service.
- $(1 - P_{11})$ is the probability of being in the working state.
- p^3 is the probability of a channel failure during the service of requests, defined as $p^3 = \mu/(\mu + v)$.
- p is the probability that the failure calculation leads to a system failure; if not, it represents the probability of harmless service. Here, p is the ratio of the number of correctly processed orders (requests) to the total number of accepted orders.

Usually $P_{rad} = 0$, and the determination of P_{11} in this formula presents certain difficulties. Because A_{11} needs to be found. To get it out,

$$A_{11} = \frac{v\sum_{i=1}^{m+1} A_i}{\gamma}$$

Furthermore, A_i is calculated through the following system [2]:

$$A_i = \begin{cases} 1, i = m+1 \\ \frac{\mu+v}{\lambda}, i = m \\ \frac{zA_{i+1}+\mu A_{i+2}}{\lambda}, x \le i \le m-1 \end{cases}$$

Finally, it is possible to calculate probabilities.

$$A_{m=1,0} \frac{1}{A_{11} + \sum_{i=1}^{m+1} A_i + A_0}$$

$$P_{11} = A_{11} P_{m+1,0}$$

In conclusion, the fundamental parameters characterizing Q_{ij} are represented by factors μ, v, λ, γ, and M.

$$Q = (1 - P_{rad})(1 - P_{11})\, p^3 p \tag{2}$$

In this case, the following formulas are correct for accurately determining reliability in transmission:

$$Q_n = (Q_{11}, Q_{12}, \ldots Q_{13}, Q_{14}, Q_{15}, \ldots Q_{16}, \ldots Q_{n1}, Q_{n2}, \ldots , Q_{nm}$$

Here, Q_{11} represents the reliability at the first value of λ with $M = 1$, and Q_{ij} describes the reliability when i corresponds to the range of changes from 1 to m, and j from 1 to n. A table has been constructed based on the factors defined in Eq. (2), and attention should be paid to its data. We will consider the factors that affect the reliability of the process once again. These factors are conveyed in the following information vectors: input data rate (λ), data reprocessing rate (μ), the number of allocated channels in the queue (M), downtime periods (F_t), and processing times (V_t).

Table 1. Factors Affecting Process Reliability

№	Input Data Rate, λ	Data Reprocessing Rate, μ	Number of Allocated Channels in Queue, M	Downtime Periods, Ft (seconds)	Processing Time, Vt (seconds)
1	30	50	1	3600	120
2	31	50	2	5400	150
3	32	50	3	7200	180
4	33	50	4	9000	210
5	34	50	5	10800	240
6	35	50	6	12600	270
7	36	50	7	14400	300
8	37	50	8	16200	330
9	38	50	9	18000	360
10	39	50	10	19800	390
11	40	50	11	21600	420
12	41	50	12	23400	450
13	42	50	13	25200	480
14	43	50	14	27000	510
15	44	50	15	28800	540
16	45	50	16	30600	570
17	46	50	17	32400	600
18	47	50	18	34200	630
19	48	50	19	36000	660
20	49	50	20	37800	690

In this scenario, even if we assume that the processing speed (μ) is constant, and if we consider that each change in a parameter corresponds to n data points from another indicator, then the number of combinations can be represented as $K_c = r \times h \times n \times m$. In a controlled state, information is processed h times less frequently. The intercorrelation changes between the data in columns 2 and 4 of Table 1 are analyzed to determine their impact on the facility's readiness and throughput. These data points constitute the initial value of $N_b = n \times m$. . The procedure operates in the following sequence: the first failure value (F_{t2}) determines the selection of the corresponding recovery time (V_{t1}), after which the N_b), initial data points are processed. For each subsequent recovery time, denoted as V_{t2}, the same volume of calculations is performed. This process is repeated until the final recovery time, $V_{t2} = 690$ s, is reached. At this point, the procedure processes the N_b data points the required number of times (with the results typically being collected in arrays). Following this, the next failure time, F_{t2}, is introduced, and the aforementioned calculations are carried out until the entire vector of recovery times is exhausted. This cycle of operations with N_b data is repeated N_b times. If r, h, n, and mm are all equal and are observed to be 20 during the experiment, then K_c equals 160,000. In the soft reset state, $N_k = r \times n \times m$, , which amounts to 8,000 counts. The diagram below (see Fig. 1) shows the differences that occurred in each data transformation.

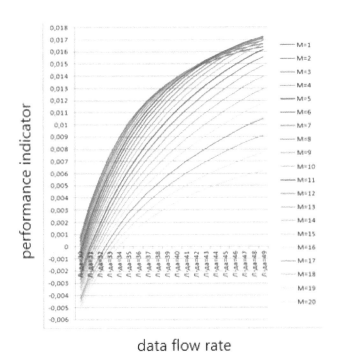

Fig. 1. Correlation of throughput values taken into account with fast control (software-based) and manual recovery versus access speed and queue number.

In this analysis, it is assumed that manual recovery takes 120 s, while automatic recovery takes only 0.0037 s for each hourly failure. It was observed that values greater than zero led to an increase in transmittance due to control. Values less than zero continued to do so until lambda reached 35, corresponding to an increase in load from 0.6 to 0.7. However, in the general case, a difference of 3.5% is indicative of the effectiveness of software-based control. The subsequent study's results were compared over a broader range, that is, the outcomes obtained when the predicate was applied with 0.9 and 0.95 precision across all N_b (where $K_c = 160{,}000$) calculations, as shown in (see Fig. 2). The following formulas were used for this.

$$S_{ij}^{kl} = \begin{cases} 0, Q_{ij}^{kl} < predicate \\ 1, Q_{ij}^{kl} > predicate \end{cases} \tag{3}$$

$$SS_{kl} = \sum_{a-1}^{n} \sum_{b-1}^{n} \sum_{i-1}^{n} \sum_{j-1}^{n} S_{ij}^{ab} \tag{4}$$

$$U_1 = \sum_{k-1}^{n} \sum_{k-1}^{n} SS_{kl} \tag{5}$$

The meanings of the formulas presented above are as follows: S_{ij}^{ab} represents the sign that is possible when performing the given predicate. SS_k is used to ensure resilience when dealing with predicates corresponding to the kth failure and 1th- recovery time. The identifier U_1 denotes the number of causal quantities, out of 160,000 in the experiment, that comply with the predicate.

Although formulas (3)–(5) are initially applied to cases of manual recovery, the calculation of the characteristics for software recovery tools is similarly conducted using formulas of the same form. The parameters Q_{ij}^{kl}, S_{ij}^{ab}, SS_k, and the U_1 identifier should be replaced with G_{ij}^{kl}, G_{ij}^{ab}, SC_k, and the U_2 identifier, respectively. This substitution yields the subsequent formulas (6)–(8)

$$C_{ij}^{kl} = \begin{cases} 0, G_{ij}^{kl} \leq predicate \\ 1, G_{ij}^{kl} > predicate \end{cases} \tag{6}$$

$$SC_{kl} = \sum_{a-1}^{n} \sum_{b-1}^{n} \sum_{i-1}^{n} \sum_{j-1}^{n} C_{ij}^{ab} \tag{7}$$

$$U_2 = \sum_{k-1}^{r} \sum_{l-1}^{h} SC_{kl} \tag{8}$$

By calculating the ratio of U_2 to U_1, we obtain the efficiency index, which quantifies the comparative effectiveness of the software recovery tools.

$$U_{ef} = \frac{U_2}{U_1.} \tag{9}$$

Utilizing formula (9) along with the previous formulas (3–8), results were obtained for the cases where the condition was set at 0.9 and 0.95. When the condition was set at 0.9, U_1 was 123324 and U_2 was 129200, resulting in a throughput efficiency increase of 4.7% (as shown in Fig. 2). For the condition set at 0.95, U_1 and U_2 were 84,086

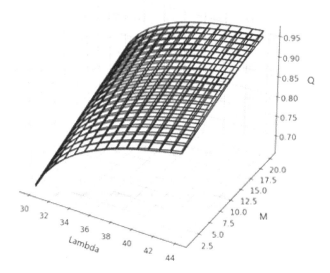

Fig. 2. In this study, when the polling rate (λ) was varied from 30 to 44 and the number of slots allocated in the queue (M) was increased from 1 to 20, the throughput (Q) for automatic recovery ranged from 0.6 to 0.969. In contrast, for manual recovery, the throughput ranged from 0.66 to 0.954.

and 98,800, respectively, which corresponds to a throughput efficiency increase of 17.4 percent (also depicted in Fig. 2). From these results, we can infer that as the condition threshold approaches 1, the efficiency of the software recovery improves.

Experimental results from econometric modeling of economic processes are highly relevant to data analysis and forecasting in agricultural enterprises. Econometric models, which are grounded in statistical methods and economic theory, can be applied to various sectors, including agriculture, to analyze historical data, identify trends, and forecast future developments [18 and 19].

5   Conclusion

If importance is attributed, some results in software recovery were more significant compared to the seconds required for manual recovery. This is because the time allocated to software recovery, once accounted for, imposed an additional load on the technological recovery process. Further reducing—or minimizing—this load becomes the subject of subsequent research. Based on theoretical materials, the econometric model—constructed within the service scope of four factors, each varying in magnitude to two decimal places—was calculated across variants of 160,000 combinations. It is known [14–16] that the assumption regarding the Poisson distribution of information reception and service flows in the technologies for reprocessing economic processes is the sole estimate that is close to reality. An experiment, conducted using Markov chains to analyze the operation of system nodes and described in [15, 20], confirmed these statements. In this regard, and building upon the statement above, the econometric model was constructed on the assumption that all events, which can occur in the technology of reprocessing an economic object, form a simple Poisson flow [4, 5]. Software support for calculations was implemented in it. The results highlight the potential of using this econometric model to assess processes, which are comparable in scope and efficiency, owing to its versatility and efficacy.

References

1. https://www.cisco.com/
2. https://www.statista.com/
3. Sebastian, R.E.: Modelling and designing reliable on-chip-communication devices in MPSoCs with real-time requirements. In: 13th IEEE International Conference on Emerging Technologies and Factory Automation, pp. 1465–1472 (2008)
4. Abidov, A., Mirzaaxmedov, D., Rasulev, D.: Analytical model for assessing the reliability of the functioning of the adaptive switching node. In: Koucheryavy, Y., Aziz, A. (eds.) Internet of Things, Smart Spaces, and Next Generation Networks and Systems. NEW2AN 2022. Lecture Notes in Computer Science, vol 13772, pp. 46–56. Springer, Cham (2023). https://doi.org/10.1007/978-3-031-30258-9_5
5. Абидов А.А. Узлуксиз характдаги ахборот тизимлари учун аналитик модел // Iqtisodiyot va innovatsion texnologiyalar (Economics and Innovative Technologies) ilmiy elektron jurnali. 2023 йил, 2-сон (№00064). http://iqtisodiyot.tsue.uz/218-2246
6. Anderson, T., Knight, J.C.: A framework for software fault tolerance in real-time systems. IEEE Trans. Softw. Eng. SE 9(3), 355–364 (1983)
7. Krishna, C.M., Singh, A.D.: Reliability of Checkpointed real-time systems using time redundancy. IEEE Trans. Reliab. 42(3), 427–435 (1993)
8. Bums, A., Punnekkat, S., Strigini, L., Wright, D.R.: Probabilistic scheduling guarantees for fault-tolerant real-time systems. In: Dependable Computing for Critical Applications, pp. 361–378 (1999)
9. Broster, I., Burns, A., Rodriguez-Navas, G.: Probabilistic analysis of CAN with faults. In: 23rd IEEE Real-Time Systems Symposium, pp. 269–278 (2002)
10. de A. Lima, G.M., Burns, A.: An effective schedulability analysis for fault-tolerant hard real-time systems. In: 3th Euromicro Conference on Real-Time Systems, pp 209–216 (2001)
11. de A. Lima, G.M., Burns, A.: An optimal fixed-priority assignment algorithm for supporting fault-tolerant hard real-time systems. IEEE Trans. Comput. 52(10), 1332–1346 (2003)
12. Li, J., Yang, F., Lu, Y.: A feasible schedulability analysis for fault-tolerant hard real-time systems. In: Proceeding of the 10th IEEE International Conference on Engineering of Complex Computer Systems, pp 176–183 (2005)
13. Li, J., Yang, F., Tu, G., Cao, W., Lu, Y.: Schedulability analysis for fault-tolerant hard real-time tasks with limited priority levels. In: The 4th International Conference on Autonomic and Trusted Computing, pp 529–538 (2007)
14. Вентцель Е.С. Исследование операций: принципы, методология. Учеб. пособие для студ. втузов. – 2-ое изд., стер. – М.: Высш. шк., p. 208 (2001)
15. Вентцель Е.С., Овчаров Л.А. Прикладные задачи теории вероятностей. – М.: Радио и связь, 1983. – 416 с
16. Мартин Дж. Системный анализ передачи данных. II том – М.: Мир, p. 431 (1975)

17. Chen, X., Hou, W., Zhang, Y.: Reliability evaluation of embedded real-time system based on error scenario. In: From the book Current Trends in Computer Science and Mechanical Automation, vol. 2. De Gruyter Open Poland (2022). https://doi.org/10.1515/9783110584998-056

18. Qulmatova, S., Karimov, B., Azimov, D.: Data analysis and forecasting in agricultural enterprises. In Proceedings of the 6th International Conference on Future Networks & Distributed Systems (ICFNDS 2022), pp. 536–541. Association for Computing Machinery, New York (2023). https://doi.org/10.1145/3584202.3584282

19. Nasimov, R., Nasimova, N., Botirjon, K., Abdullayev, M.: Deep learning algorithm for classifying dilated cardiomyopathy and hypertrophic cardiomyopathy in transport workers. In: Koucheryavy, Y., Aziz, A. (eds.) Internet of Things, Smart Spaces, and Next Generation Networks and Systems. NEW2AN 2022. Lecture Notes in Computer Science, vol. 13772. Springer, Cham (2023). https://doi.org/10.1007/978-3-031-30258-9_19

20. Kobilov, A., Rikhsimboev, O., Abdulakhatov, M., Rajabov, S.: Artificial intelligence as a technological innovation for economic development of the Republic of Uzbekistan. In Proceedings of the 6th International Conference on Future Networks & Distributed Systems (ICFNDS 2022), pp. 292–297. Association for Computing Machinery, New York (2023). https://doi.org/10.1145/3584202.3584245

Forecasting ICT Service Exports in Continental Trio Countries Using the ARIMA Model

Nodira Zikrillaeva[1], Aziz Zikriyoev[1(✉)] [iD], Sanjar Mirzaliev[2], Alisher Sultanov[3], Nurbek Turayev[4], and Mokhinur Rakhimova[5]

[1] Department of World Economy, Tashkent State University of Economics, Tashkent, Uzbekistan
a.zikriyoev@tsue.uz
[2] Department of Scientific Research and Innovation, Tashkent State University of Economics, Tashkent, Uzbekistan
[3] Department of Human Resource Management, Tashkent State University of Economics, Tashkent, Uzbekistan
[4] Department of Business Management and Logistics, Tashkent State University of Economics, Tashkent, Uzbekistan
[5] Department of Macroeconomics, Tashkent State University of Economics, Tashkent, Uzbekistan

Abstract. This research investigates the dynamics of Information and Communication Technology (ICT) service exports from Canada, China, and Australia, employing advanced statistical methodologies, including ARIMA modeling, ARIMA regression, and diagnostic tests. Utilizing SPSS 25.0 and Stata 17.0, we analyze World Bank data to assess the forecasting accuracy and significance of key parameters, providing nuanced insights into the global impact of ICT services. Our study leverages ARIMA models tailored to the unique economic contexts of Canada, China, and Australia. While Canada and Australia adopt ARIMA (0,1,0) models, China employs a simpler model labeled as "Simple." The forecasting fit statistics, including Stationary R-squared, R-squared, RMSE, MAPE. For China, the level smoothing parameter (alpha) is estimated at 0.990, indicating a substantial weight given to recent observations in forecasting. In contrast, Canada's model incorporates both level and trend smoothing parameters, yielding a combined estimate of 0.993. This parameter is highly statistically significant, with a remarkable t-value of 20.599. The forecasting metrics reveal the efficacy of the models, with mean fit statistics reflecting the central tendency of accuracy measures. Despite variations in model complexity, both Canada and Australia exhibit forecasting accuracy, as evidenced by R-squared values of 0.739 and stationary R-squared values of 0.350. The findings hold significant implications for policymakers, businesses, and researchers navigating the complexities of the digital economy. This study contributes valuable insights into the relevance and impact of ICT service exports from Canada, China, and Australia on the global stage. As the digital landscape continues in shaping policies and strategies to navigate the dynamic ICT services sector.

Keywords: ICT service · world commercial services · high-technology manufacturing · forecasting

Y. Koucheryavy and A. Aziz (Eds.): NEW2AN/ruSMART 2023, LNCS 14543, pp. 95–105, 2024.
https://doi.org/10.1007/978-3-031-60997-8_10

1 Introduction

In today's globalized economy, the export of Information and Communication Technology (ICT) services plays a crucial role in the economic development of countries. In this article, we will explore the use of the Autoregressive Integrated Moving Average (ARIMA) model to forecast ICT service exports in three major continental trio countries: Canada, China, and Australia. Meanwhile, Xixi Hu and Jing Yu denoted that taking service trade as the starting point, using the economic policy uncertainty index and taking the data of China's ICT service exports from 2001 to 2019 as a sample, this paper studies the impact of economic policy uncertainty on China's ICT service exports [1]. ICT service exports contribute substantially to the revenue of countries engaged in the export of technology-related services. These services may include software development, consulting, system integration. The ICT sector has experienced rapid growth in recent years, and its export market has become increasingly competitive.

The driving force for this comparative advantage is the large pool of semiskilled and skilled graduates in emerging economies who can deliver their services across borders using advanced communication technologies [2]. Accurately forecasting ICT service exports is essential for policymakers, industry leaders, and investors to make informed decisions and develop effective strategies for sustainable growth. ICT exports are broken down into three broad ICT product groups (electronic data processing machines, integrated circuits and electronic components, and telecommunications equipment), and the determinants are examined for each of the above product categories [3]. Canada, China, and Australia are all significant players in the global ICT market, each with its unique strengths and challenges. By applying the ARIMA model to historical data on ICT service exports in these countries, we aim to provide insights into future trends and potential opportunities for growth. According to the P. Rajesh ICT service export of India was growing slightly faster than that of the rest of the world; however, its rate of growth was decelerating over the years. The share of ICT services in the total service exports and in the total exports of India was around four-times and six-times higher than that of the world average [4].

Through this analysis, we hope to shed light on the factors driving ICT service exports in these countries and contribute to the development of more accurate and reliable forecasting models for the ICT sector. Ultimately, our goal is to provide valuable insights that can inform policy decisions and business strategies in the dynamic and rapidly evolving ICT export market. R. Kneller and Jon Timmis found that empirical evidence for the effects of broadband use on the firm-extensive margin of UK service exports. To deal with the issue of causality we build a novel instrument that exploits exogenous variation in access to broadband technologies [5]. According to the Beng Ann Tee, S. Tham, A. Kam ICT intensive services were found to contribute to the service export growth in developed countries. However, empirical work on the role of ICT in ASEAN's services export is sparse due mainly to the scarcity of bilateral services trade data. This study uses mirror data from the ASEAN-5's trading partners from 2000 to 2012 for examining the impact of ICT on the ASEAN-5's services export [6].

The export of ICT services facilitates the global dissemination of technological innovations. Countries with strong ICT service industries often play a key role in the development and diffusion of cutting-edge technologies. As for the R. Javalgi found the service sector represents one of the fastest growing areas of exports in the global trade. The Internet and e-commerce make it possible to sell a variety of services, ranging from airline tickets to financial services, from anywhere in the world [7]. The growth of the ICT service sector can contribute to overall economic growth, as technological advancements often lead to increased efficiency and productivity in other industries. Furthermore, Eyal Ronen denoted that the empirical cross-country panel analysis validates the positive contribution of ICT services exports to employment in the ICT service sector, particularly in high-income countries and among female employees [8]. ICT services are a key enabler of digital transformation across industries.

Exported services may include digital solutions, cloud computing, and cybersecurity services, helping businesses and governments embrace digital technologies. R. Kneller and Jon Timmis found that to deal with the issue of causality we build a novel instrument that exploits exogenous variation in access to broadband technologies due to the historic telephone network [5]. ICT service exports foster collaboration between countries and companies on a global scale. Cross-border partnerships and collaborations are often essential for the success of complex technology projects. The ICT application areas are: mobile telephony, internet usage or provision, and other ICT related products and services. The main modelling and forecasting approaches are diffusion modelling and forecasting, time series forecasting and technological forecasting [9].

ICT service exports enhance global connectivity by providing communication and collaboration tools, networking solutions, and digital infrastructure services. ICT service exports contribute to digital inclusion by providing countries with access to advanced technologies and digital solutions. This, in turn, can support social and economic development. Asian developing countries should focus on formulating appropriate policy measures to enhance the performance of services sector and service export to stimulate the economic growth [10]. Countries with a strong ICT service export sector gain a competitive advantage in the global marketplace. This competitiveness is driven by innovation, skilled workforce, and the ability to deliver high-quality technology solutions.

2 Methods and Materials

2.1 Data Source

The study utilizes data from the World Bank, providing a comprehensive and reliable dataset on ICT service exports from Canada, China, and Australia. This dataset encompasses a time series of relevant variables, allowing for a detailed exploration of trends, fluctuations, and patterns in ICT service exports over a specified timeframe.

2.2 Statistical Software

Clarifying the limitations of a study can be defined as mobile phone, email, good manners, independence, hard work, feeling of responsibility, imagination, tolerance and respect, thrift saving money and things, determination perseverance, religious faith unselfishness interaction of the adults over the world countries.

2.3   ARIMA Modeling

For Canada and Australia, ARIMA (0,1,0) models are employed. This choice of model specification, indicating differencing once to achieve stationarity, aligns with established practices in time series analysis. China, on the other hand, is modeled using a simpler approach labeled as "Simple," denoting a distinct methodology for capturing the dynamics of ICT service exports in the Chinese context.

2.4   ARIMA Regression

To understand the relationship between the dependent and independent variables, ARIMA regression is employed. The regression framework allows for the exploration of how changes in independent variables, including level and trend smoothing parameters, influence the forecasted values of ICT service exports.

3   Results

The descriptive statistics provide a summary of the ICT service exports for the three countries (China, Canada, and Australia) over the 22-year period from 2000 to 2021. The mean value for China's ICT service exports is 22.409, with a standard deviation of 2.109. This indicates that, on average, China has a relatively high level of ICT service exports, and the values are relatively close to the mean. For Canada, the mean value is 3.023, with a standard deviation of 1.398. This suggests that Canada's ICT service exports are lower on average compared to China, and the values are more spread out from the mean. Australia has a mean value of 1.418, with a standard deviation of 0.603 (Table 1).

Table 1. Descriptive Statistics

Variable	Obs	Mean	Std. Dev.	Min	Max
Year	22	2010.5	6.494	2000	2021
China	22	22.409	2.109	17.999	26.069
Canada	22	3.023	1.398	1.478	7.554
Australia	22	1.418	.603	.846	2.852
World commercial s~t	20	4.523e+12	1.367e+12	1.969e+12	7.004e+12

The minimum and maximum values for each country show the range of ICT service exports over the 22-year period. For China, the minimum export value is 17.999 and the maximum is 26.069. For Canada, the minimum is 1.478 and the maximum is 7.554. For Australia, the minimum is 0.846 and the maximum is 2.852 (Table 2).

On the other hand, the coefficient for the time trend variable is 0.581, with a standard error of 0.079, a t-value of 7.32, and a p-value of 0. This indicates that the time trend variable has a statistically significant effect on Canada's ICT service exports. The mean

Table 2. ARIMA regression of Canada

D.Canada	Coef.	St.Err.	t-value	p-value	[95% Conf	Interval]	Sig
Constant	−.289	.25	−1.16	.248	−.78	.201	
Constant	.581	.079	7.32	0	.425	.736	***
Mean dependent var	−0.289	SD dependent var				0.595	
Number of obs	21	Chi-square					
Prob > chi2		Akaike crit. (AIC)				40.770	

*** p < .01, ** p < .05, * p < .1

dependent variable is −0.289, with a standard deviation of 0.595, and the number of observations is 21. The ARIMA model developed was compared with simple exponential smoothing (SES) and Holt 2 parameters exponential smoothing (HES) to find out the fitting accuracy of the ARIMA model over the other time series forecasting models. The research furthermore tested statistically and confirmed the forecast errors. The projecting power of the model was well verified [11].

The Dickey Fuller test for unit root is a statistical test used to determine whether a time series data set is stationary or non-stationary. In this case, the test is applied to the variable "Canada" in the context of ICT service exports. The null hypothesis (H0) of the Dickey Fuller test is that the variable follows a random walk with or without drift, indicating non-stationarity. The alternative hypothesis is that the variable is stationary (Table 3).

Table 3. Dickey Fuller test for unit root of Canada

D.Canada	Coefficient	Std. err.	t	p > t	[95% conf. Interval]	
Canada						
L1.	−0.711	0.075	−9.450	0.000	−0.869	−0.553
_trend	−0.096	0.017	−5.690	0.000	−0.131	−0.060
_cons	2.966	0.408	7.270	0.000	2.109	3.822

The regression table provides further details on the coefficients and their significance. The coefficient for the lagged variable "L1. Canada" is −0.711, with a standard error of 0.075, a t-value of −9.450, and a p-value of 0.000. This indicates that the lagged variable has a statistically significant effect on Canada's ICT service exports. Similarly, the coefficient for the time trend variable "_trend" is −0.096, with a standard error of 0.017, a t-value of −5.690, and a p-value of 0.000. Both AC and PAC values are important for understanding the temporal dependence in the data. The text discusses the methodology of building and forecasting a univariate time series model using the Box Jenkins approach. It explains the techniques of model identification, parameter estimation, and diagnostic checks for fitted models [12].

The Q statistic and its associated probability (Prob > Q) test the null hypothesis that there is no autocorrelation in the data. The low p-values for all lags from 2 to 9 suggest that there is significant autocorrelation in the variable "Canada" at these lags. The analysis revealed that the ARIMA (0,1,1) model is sufficient for forecasting sales. The survey provides insight into the various time series prediction and forecasting models using ARIMA, and it was discovered that ARIMA is a real world tool for time series prediction, forecasting, and analysis with accuracy [13]. Forecast evaluation statistics indicate that econometric models generally outperform the alternatives. The study found that no single approach provides best forecasts for US international message telephone service traffic, but econometric models generally outperform the alternatives according to forecast evaluation statistics [14] (Table 4).

Table 4. ARIMA model

D.China	Coef.	St.Err.	t-value	p-value	[95% Conf	Interval]	Sig
Constant	.167	.36	0.46	.642	−.539	.874	
Constant	1.649	.275	5.99	0	1.109	2.188	***
Mean dependent var	0.167	SD dependent var				1.689	
Number of obs	21	Chi-square					
Prob > chi2		Akaike crit. (AIC)				84.594	

*** $p < .01$, ** $p < .05$, * $p < .1$

The Dickey Fuller test for unit root is conducted to test the null hypothesis that the variable "China" follows a random walk with or without drift. The test statistic is − 1.963, and the critical values at the 1%, 5%, and 10% levels are −4.380, −3.600, and 3.240, respectively. The MacKinnon approximate p-value for the test statistic is 0.6215 (Table 5).

Table 5. Dickey Fuller test for unit root for China

D.China	Coefficient	Std. err	t	P > t	[95% conf. interval]	
China						
L1.	−0.331	0.169	−1.960	0.065	−0.685	0.023
_trend	−0.016	0.058	−0.280	0.781	−0.139	0.106
_cons	7.747	3.858	2.010	0.060	−0.359	15.852

Current results suggest that the variable "China" may not have a unit root, indicating that it is stationary. The ARIMA regression and Dickey Fuller test provide important insights into the stationarity and temporal dependence of the variable "China," which are crucial for modeling and forecasting China's ICT sector and making data-driven decisions. The correlogram of the variable "China" shows the autocorrelation (AC) and partial autocorrelation (PAC) at different lags (Table 6).

Table 6. ARIMA regression of Australia

D.Australia	Coef.	St.Err.	t-value	p-value	[95% Conf	Interval]	Sig
Constant	−.095	.038	−2.51	.012	−.168	−.021	**
Constant	.167	.024	6.89	0	.12	.215	***
Mean dependent var	−0.095	SD dependent var	0.172				
Number of obs	21	Chi-square					
Prob > chi2		Akaike crit. (AIC)	−11.470				

This represents the estimated effect of the constant on the dependent variable. For the first constant (−0.095), it suggests that when all independent variables are zero, the dependent variable is expected to decrease by 0.095 units (Table 7).

Table 7. Dickey Fuller test for unit root for Australia

D.Australia	Coefficient	Std. err.	t	p > t	[95% conf. interval]	
Australia						
L1.	−0.168	0.088	−1.910	0.073	−0.353	0.017
_trend	−0.000	0.009	−0.040	0.971	−0.018	0.018
_cons	0.152	0.212	0.710	0.485	−0.295	0.598

The test statistic (−1.908) is less than the critical values, but the p-value is high (0.6507). The high p-value suggests that we do not have enough evidence to reject the null hypothesis of a unit root. For a Lag 3 Autocorrelation (AC): 0.4417, Partial Autocorrelation (PAC): 0.0421, and Q statistic is 30.405, and the p-value is very low (0.0000) (Table 8).

Table 8. Model Description

Model ID	China	Model_1	Simple
	Canada	Model_2	ARIMA(0,1,0)
	Australia	Model_3	ARIMA(0,1,0)

The model fit statistics provide information on how well the model fits the data. This statistic measures the proportion of variation in the dependent variable that is explained

Table 9. Forecasting Model Fit

Fit Statistic	Mean	SE	Min	Max	5	50	75	95
Stationary R2	.350	.381	−.010	.750	−.010	.312	.750	.750
R-squared	.739	.309	.383	.926	.383	.909	.926	.926
RMSE	.703	.830	.146	1.657	.146	.305	1.657	1.657
MAPE	6.953	1.225	5.834	8.262	5.834	6.762	8.262	8.262
MaxAPE	20.691	4.994	15.925	25.885	15.925	20.264	25.885	25.885
MAE	.532	.659	.106	1.291	.106	.198	1.291	1.291
MaxAE	1.591	1.781	.330	3.628	.330	.815	3.628	3.628
Normalized BIC	−1.497	2.408	−3.558	1.151	−3.558	−2.082	1.151	1.151

by the independent variables in the model. A value of 0.350 indicates that 35% of the variation in the dependent variable is explained by the independent variables (Table 9).

A value of 0.703 indicates that, on average, the model's predictions are about 0.703 units away from the actual values. MAPE (Mean Absolute Percentage Error statistic measures the average percentage difference between the observed values and the values predicted by the model. A value of 6.953% indicates that, on average, the model's predictions are about 6.953% off from the actual values. MaxAPE is the largest percentage difference between any observed value and its predicted value. A value of 20.691% indicates that the largest percentage difference is 20.691%. The hybrid (LSTM ARIMA) model achieves the lowest error metrics among all the tested models, achieving a MAPE value of 7.38% and a RMSE of 1.66×10^{13} [15] (Fig. 1).

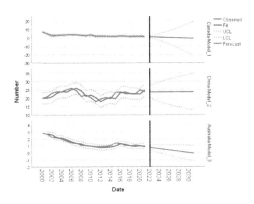

Fig. 1. ICT service export forecasting of trio countries

The forecast values for each country and model are provided for the years 2022 to 2031, along with the upper control limit (UCL) and lower control limit (LCL) for each forecast. For China-Model_1 forecasted value for China remains constant at 23.72 for each year from 2022 to 2031. The UCL and LCL indicate the upper and lower bounds within which the actual values are expected to fall. Digital transformation helps companies increase their productivity by enabling them to gather data on specific performance metrics and measure each [16].

For example, in 2022, the actual value for China is expected to be between 20.27 and 27.16. For Canada-Model_2 forecasted values for Canada decrease from 1.30 in 2022 to −0.29 in 2031.The UCL and LCL indicate the upper and lower bounds for each year, showing the range of potential values. For Australia-Model_3 forecasted values for Australia also decrease from 0.75 in 2022 to −0.28 in 2031. ICT sector brings high efficiency in the economy and this sector can be the basis for a high level ofeconomic development [17]. Intellectual capital can be understood as two main that can play a dynamic role in multiple organizational decisions [18].

4 Discussions

In this comprehensive analysis of ICT service exports from Canada, China, and Australia, utilizing SPSS 25.0 and Stata 17.0 for ARIMA modeling, ARIMA regression, and statistical tests, we have uncovered valuable insights into the dynamics of these economies in the context of the global digital landscape. Employing World Bank data, our study leveraged advanced forecasting techniques to shed light on the trends and significance of ICT service exports. The distinctive features of business digitalization and its digital transformation. The fact that digital transformation affects the activities of many business structures, regardless of the scale of the business [19]. The forecasts and control limits provided for China, Canada, and Australia offer valuable insights into the expected future values for each country. Digital technologies into human life and the development of scientific and practical proposals aimed at eliminating countries [20]. The constant forecasted value for China indicates a level of stability in the projected values, with the upper and lower control limits providing a range within which the actual values are expected to fall. This suggests a relatively predictable trajectory for China's future economic performance. These forecasts and control limits serve as valuable tools for decision-makers and analysts to understand and anticipate future economic performance. They provide a framework for assessing the uncertainty and potential range of variation in the forecasts, enabling informed decision-making and strategic planning.In conclusion, the forecasts and control limits presented here offer a valuable starting point for understanding the anticipated economic performance of China, Canada, and Australia in the coming years. They provide a foundation for further analysis and discussion on the potential implications and factors driving these forecasted trends.

5 Conclusion

Examining the estimated parameters for the ARIMA models, particularly in the context of smoothing parameters (alpha) for China and Canada, uncovered insights into the weight given to recent observations in forecasting. For China, the estimate of 0.990, with a standard error of 0.219 and a highly significant t-value of 4.509, indicates the statistical importance of the level smoothing parameter. In contrast, for Canada, where both level and trend smoothing parameters were incorporated, the combined estimate of

0.993 displayed exceptional significance with a t-value of 20.599, reinforcing the critical role of these parameters in predicting trends and level changes. These findings hold significant implications for policymakers, businesses, and researchers operating in the ICT service export domain. Understanding the dynamics of these economies and the determinants of forecasting accuracy is paramount for informed decision-making. The identified parameters can guide strategic initiatives and policy frameworks aimed at fostering a conducive environment for ICT service exports. It is crucial to acknowledge the limitations of this study, such as the assumptions inherent in the ARIMA modeling approach and the reliance on historical data. Future research endeavors may explore alternative modeling techniques, consider additional covariates, and delve into the causal relationships underlying ICT service exports. In conclusion, our analysis provides a nuanced understanding of ICT service exports from Canada, China, and Australia, combining rigorous statistical methodologies with real-world economic implications.

References

1. Hu, X., Yu, J.: Research on the impact of economic policy uncertainty on China's ICT service export. BCP Bus. Manag. (2022)
2. Nasir, S.A., Kalirajan, K.: Information and communication technology-enabled modern services export performances of Asian economies. Asian Dev. Rev. **33**, 1–27 (2016)
3. Vogiatzoglou, K.: Determinants of export specialization in ICT products: a cross-country analysis (2009)
4. Rajesh, P.: Trends and revealed comparative advantage of ICT services exports from India (2005–2018). Int. J. Foreign Trade Int. Bus. **2**, 30–35 (2020)
5. Kneller, R., Timmis, J.: ICT and Exporting: the effects of broadband on the extensive margin of business service exports. Int. Trade eJ. (2016)
6. Tee, B.A., Tham, S.Y., Kam, A.J.: The role of ICT in ASEAN-5's services exports: a panel study (2020)
7. Javalgi, R., Martin, C.L., Todd, P.R.: The export of e-services in the age of technology transformation: challenges and implications for international service providers. J. Serv. Mark. **18**, 560–573 (2004)
8. Ronen, E.: ICT services exports and labour demand: a global perspective and the case of Israel. SSRN Electron. J. (2021)
9. Meade, N., Islam, T.: Forecasting in telecommunications and ICT—a review. Int. J. Forecast. **31**, 1105–1126 (2015)
10. Kaliappan, S.R., Ahmad, S.A., Ismail, N.W.: Service export and economic growth in the selected developing Asian countries (2017)
11. Ghosh, S.: Forecasting Cotton Exports in India using the ARIMA model. Amity J. Econ. **2**(2), 36–52 (2017)
12. Farooqi, A.A.: ARIMA model building and forecasting on imports and exports of Pakistan. Pak. J. Stat. Oper. Res. **10**, 157–168 (2014)
13. Sandhya, C., & Radha, D. (2022). Sales forecasting using arima model
14. Madden, G., Savage, S.J., Coble-Neal, G.: Forecasting United States-Asia international message telephone service. Int. J. Forecast. **18**, 523–543 (2002)
15. Dave, E., Leonardo, A., Jeanice, M., Hanafiah, N.: Forecasting Indonesia exports using a hybrid model ARIMA-LSTM. Procedia Comput. Sci. **179**, 480–487 (2021)

16. Akhmadalieva*, Z., Akhmadalieva, Z.: Impact of digitalization on firms' productivity. In: The 6th International Conference on Future Networks & Distributed Systems ICFNDS 2022), December 15, 2022, Tashkent, TAS, Uzbekistan, p. 8. ACM, New York (2022).https://doi.org/10.1145/3584202.3584254

17. Makhmudov, N., Avazov, N.: Investigating the impact of investment and ICT on real income growth: the case of Hungary. In: ACM International Conference on Proceeding Series, pp. 404–407 (2022). https://doi.org/10.1145/3584202.3584261

18. Farooq, U., Tabash, M.I., Anagreh, S., Khudoykulov, K.: How do market capitalization and intellectual capital determine industrial investment? Borsa Istanbul Rev. **22**(4), 828–837 (2022). https://doi.org/10.1016/j.bir.2022.05.002

19. Sabirovna, Q.D., G'olibo'g'li, N.T.: The main aspects and benefits of digital tranormation of business entities. In: Koucheryavy, Y., Aziz, A. (eds.) Internet of Things, Smart Spaces, and Next Generation Networks and Systems. NEW2AN 2022. Lecture Notes in Computer Science, vol. 13772. Springer, Cham (2023). https://doi.org/10.1007/978-3-031-30258

20. Oksana, V.B., Tukhtabaev, J.Sh., Razitdnovna, R.A., Saidrasulova, Kh.B., Shirinov, U., Kurbanova, Z.K.: the impact of digitalisation on the safe development of individuals insociety. In Internet of Things, Smart Spaces, and Next Generation Networks and Systems: 22nd International Conference, NEW2AN 2022, Tashkent, Uzbekistan, 15–16 December 2022, Proceedings, pp. 299–309. Springer, Heidelberg (2023)

From Bricks to Bits: Revolutionizing Real Estate for the Digital World

Duc Bui Tien[1]([✉]), Trinh. D. Phung[2], Triet M. Nguyen[2], Hong K. Vo[2],
Khoa T. Dang[2], Phuc N. Trong[2], Bang L. Khanh[2], and Ngan N. T. Kim[3]

[1] Nguyen Tat Thanh University, HCM city, Vietnam
[2] FPT University, Can Tho city, Vietnam
`trietnm3@fe.edu.vn`
[3] FPT Polytecnic, Can Tho city, Vietnam
`ducbt@ntt.edu.vn`

Abstract. This paper delves into the transformative potential of blockchain technology and Non-Fungible Tokens (NFTs) in the real estate sector, a critical component of social computing. Traditional real estate transactions are often fraught with inefficiencies, opacity, and a lack of trust, which can hinder the sector's growth and its ability to contribute to social computing. To address these limitations, we introduce a collaborative approach that leverages blockchain technology, smart contracts, NFTs, and the InterPlanetary File System (IPFS). These technologies, when applied to real estate transactions, can enhance transparency, reduce transaction times, and foster a more collaborative and trustful environment. The motivation for this paper is rooted in the need to revolutionize the real estate sector, making it more efficient, transparent, and conducive to social computing. We believe that the integration of blockchain technology and NFTs can significantly contribute to this transformation. Our work makes three significant contributions. First, we propose a novel real estate model based on blockchain technology, which addresses the current limitations in the sector. Second, we implement a proof-of-concept based on the proposed model, demonstrating its feasibility and effectiveness. Lastly, we deploy the proof-of-concept on four EVM-supported platforms, namely BNB Smart Chain, Fantom, Polygon, and Celo. This allows us to evaluate each platform's suitability for our proposed model, ensuring optimal performance and efficiency.

Keywords: Blockchain · Non-Fungible Tokens (NFTs) · Real Estate Management · RSA Encryption · Social Computing · InterPlanetary File System (IPFS) · Smart Contracts

1 Introduction

The real estate sector is not just a pillar for economic growth but also a determinant of a country's socio-economic landscape. According to a report by Eurostat in 2015, the real estate activities sector was responsible for employing 1.9% of

Y. Koucheryavy and A. Aziz (Eds.): NEW2AN/ruSMART 2023, LNCS 14543, pp. 106–117, 2024.
https://doi.org/10.1007/978-3-031-60997-8_11

the total workforce and accounting for 5.6% of the total number of enterprises within the European Union [4]. Beyond the economic implications, real estate plays a pivotal role in shaping urban landscapes, fostering community interactions, and defining socio-economic structures. However, the traditional methods employed in real estate transactions come with a myriad of challenges [9,14]. Issues such as exorbitant brokerage fees, opacity in transaction processes, time-intensive procedures, and vulnerability to fraudulent activities are rampant in this sector [15,18].

Collaborative technologies, particularly blockchain and smart contracts, have shown promise in ameliorating some of these issues [10,11]. The decentralized, immutable, and transparent nature of blockchain technology promises a paradigm shift in asset transfer and recording mechanisms [22]. On the other hand, smart contracts, being self-executing in nature with the agreement terms embedded as code, introduce an unprecedented level of accountability, making it virtually impossible for parties to renege on their obligations [16]. Such technologies can potentially foster a greater degree of trust among stakeholders, drastically cut down the time associated with negotiations and due diligence, and enhance data reliability [25].

Internationally, a multitude of initiatives leveraging blockchain, smart contracts, and Non-Fungible Tokens (NFTs) have sprung up, aiming to revamp the traditional real estate transaction model. Notable examples include Sweden's land registry pilot project and the Netherlands' experimentation with the concept of Crowd Ownership [9,14]. However, as with all technological advancements, the integration of blockchain in real estate is not devoid of challenges. Alterations to established legal frameworks, coupled with complications arising from the tokenization of real estate assets, present significant hurdles, particularly in terms of governance and liquidity [3,8,12].

A salient concern that surfaces when discussing blockchain-based approaches is the issue of security and privacy. While blockchain offers transparency and immutability, these very features can sometimes compromise the privacy of involved parties [5]. Sensitive data, once on the blockchain, can become easily accessible if not appropriately managed. Encryption, to this end, emerges as a robust solution to this challenge. By encrypting sensitive data before storing it on the blockchain, we can ensure that while the integrity of the data remains intact, unauthorized parties cannot decipher the original content without the requisite decryption keys [19].

The intersection of blockchain technology and real estate is a burgeoning area of research and application. For instance, Chow et al. [2] explored the potential disruptions blockchain and distributed ledger technologies could bring to the real estate sector, emphasizing the shift of physical real estate to a digital space through tokenization. While tokenization can lead to considerable cost savings in the pre- and post-tokenization process, it raises questions about the readiness of real estate as an asset class for digitalization in the Asia-Pacific region. Beside, Ullah et al. [21] provided a conceptual framework for adopting blockchain-based smart contracts to manage real estate deals in smart cities. Highlighting the decentralized application's interaction with Ethereum Virtual Machine (EVM), the study delves into the creation of smart contracts to potentially revolutionize real estate transactions. The paper's framework offers a detailed mechanism for both real estate owners and users, emphasizing the importance of trust and transparency. We will detail the other approaches in the related work section.

While the potential of blockchain and encryption in the real estate context is evident, several limitations of the current approaches can be identified: **a) Lack of Comprehensive Encryption Methods:** Current research primarily focuses on the application of blockchain. However, the direct integration of encryption methods like RSA is scarcely discussed. Without robust encryption methods, data privacy and security concerns may arise. **b) Limited Cross-Platform Scalability:** While prior work delves into the EVM, broader scalability across various blockchain platforms remains a concern. **c) Tokenization Challenges:** As the other studies highlighted, tokenization poses a set of unique challenges, including regulatory concerns, liquidity issues, and the acceptance of tokens as a legitimate form of asset ownership - privacy violation may be raised a concerned for this approach.

Our research aims to address the aforementioned limitations and push the boundaries of how blockchain and encryption can revolutionize the real estate sector. Our contributions are as follows: i) **RSA- and Blockchain-based System:** We propose an integrated system combining the strengths of RSA encryption with blockchain technology, ensuring both data security and transaction transparency in the real estate digital domain; ii) **Exhaustive Examination:** Our study presents a comprehensive analysis of integrating blockchain, RSA encryption, and NFTs in the real estate sector. We delve deeper into the nuances, ensuring a holistic understanding of the interplay between these technologies; iii) **Validity and Observations:** Unlike existing literature, we provide a detailed scrutiny of the validity of employing blockchain and RSA in real estate. Our observations shed light on the practical implications, challenges, and potential solutions; iv) **Digital Transformation Insights:** We offer discussions on how digital transformation can address traditional real estate bottlenecks, especially focusing on the integration across the four EVM-support blockchain platforms.

2 Related Work

2.1 Global Pioneers Applying Blockchain in Real Estate Transactions

Beyond the aforementioned countries, numerous other nations and companies are exploring the potential of blockchain and NFTs in the real estate domain.

In recent years, several countries have been keen on exploring and piloting blockchain technology specifically in the realm of real estate transactions. Among these, Sweden stands out with its proactive steps towards modernization. Lantmäteriet, the official land registry of Sweden, embarked on a journey in 2016 to assess the potential benefits of incorporating blockchain in real estate dealings [13]. This ambitious pilot project was not merely a technical exploration but had tangible fiscal motivations; it was anticipated to result in savings approximating 100 million euros [14]. Progressing from its initial investigatory phase, the project has advanced to an active implementation phase, where a private blockchain is now employed, albeit on a limited scale, for cataloging land and real estate transactions.

Turning our attention to the Netherlands, the Dutch government hasn't lagged behind in embracing this technological innovation. They have rolled out multiple pilot projects on a national scale, with particular emphasis on open cadastral data and an overarching exploration of blockchain's capabilities across governmental processes [9]. Similarly, Brazil took concrete steps in 2017 towards this direction. The Cartório de Registro de Imóveis, which serves as the nation's real estate registry office, collaborated with the blockchain tech enterprise Ubitquity. This collaboration aimed at enhancing the precision, confidentiality, and openness of land registration endeavors [9,20].

In addition to these country-specific ventures, the broader academic and practical landscape saw an emerging discourse on asset tokenization. A plethora of research has spotlighted this concept, where tangible assets, transcending mere digital representations, get recorded on a decentralized, unalterable ledger [1,23,24]. Such a paradigm shift has found its applications in the real estate sector as well, where property ownership undergoes a transformation to a digital token format. This token is underpinned by the actual asset, enhancing market liquidity and augmenting the allure of real estate investments [23].

2.2 Encryption-and Blockchain-Driven Real Estate Approaches

To the best of our knowledge, upon analyzing the given literature, only a few papers shed light on the direct implementation of blockchain and encryption methods in the real estate context. For example, a study underscored the revolutionary aspects of blending blockchain and artificial intelligence. They delved into the application of these core technologies to design encryption algorithms for safeguarding real estate transactions [6]. The emphasis was laid on the challenges posed by traditional middlemen in real estate, highlighting issues in peer-to-peer exchanges. Their research focused on integrating blockchain consensus processes with practical Byzantine fault tolerance (PBFT) algorithms of Hyperledger. They also presented a method for verifying real estate contracts using quantum cryptography, primarily through ElGamal communication.

In another work, the authors pinpointed challenges in the burgeoning real estate sector of Pakistan and proposed a solution using Ethereum blockchain [17]. They emphasized the need for transparent and secure online property transactions, elaborating on the potential of blockchain in ensuring the authenticity of such transactions. Their system, BlockYards, combined blockchain's strengths with machine learning models to predict property values accurately, ensuring that property listings are reflective of their genuine worth.

Lastly, Tan et al. presented "The Real Estate Transaction Trace System Model Based on Ethereum Blockchain Platform", outlining a method to improve real estate transactions in Vietnam using blockchain [7]. Their proposed Real Estate Transaction Trace (RETT) system model emphasized the potential of blockchain in managing and tracking the intricate processes associated with real estate transactions. They showcased how the government and investor consortiums can trace property transactions, highlighting the system's capabilities in ensuring transparency, reducing intermediary involvement, and fostering trust.

While these pioneering efforts have indeed propelled the industry forward, a closer scrutiny reveals certain gaps and limitations inherent in their approaches. From encryption methodologies and depth of examination to validation practices and broader digital transformation insights, there's a discernible room for improvement and expansion.

3   Approach

3.1   Traditional Real Estate Management Model

Historically, the domain of real estate transactions has adhered to well-established conventions. Before delving into avant-garde paradigms like blockchain, it's imperative to traverse the traditional pathways governing these interactions.

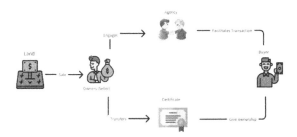

Fig. 1. Depiction of conventional real estate management techniques

Centrally positioned in any traditional real estate transaction, as illustrated in Fig. 1, is the tangible asset, referred to as L. This physical facet, whether an expanse of barren land or a concrete edifice, stands as the transfer subject, tethered to an official attestation of its ownership. This document, denoted as Certificate C, is an emblem of governmental endorsement. Playing pivotal roles in this choreography are the Owner or Seller O and the Buyer B, representing the divesting and acquiring entities, respectively. Facilitating their endeavor is the Agency A, typically an adept real estate entity, which ensures the transaction's seamlessness.

Within this archetype, the Owner, intent on offloading their asset, seeks the Agency's proficiency. The Agency, leveraging its market insights, aligns the asset with an apt Buyer. Upon consensus over terms, the exchange transpires, culminating in the certificate's transfer from Seller to Buyer, signifying the legal transition of property ownership.

However, the inherent design of this conventional mechanism presents several challenges:

- *Opacity*: The model often operates in shadows, rendering it susceptible to inconsistencies or deceptive undertakings.
- *Inefficiency*: The presence of multiple middlemen can decelerate processes, escalating costs and extending durations.
- *Physical Document Dependency*: An overreliance on tangible paperwork can induce bureaucratic impediments and is vulnerable to misplacement or degradation.
- *Trust Deficiencies*: The model necessitates unwavering trust in agencies, occasionally leading to ethical quandaries or malpractices.

In summation, the time-tested model, while having anchored real estate dealings for ages, especially in the digital world, exhibits constraints that herald a call for modernization, particularly against the backdrop of emerging digital revolutions.

3.2   RSA and Blockchain-Based Real Estate Transaction

Incorporating the principles of blockchain technology into real estate transaction processes, we introduce an approach that caters to the three main players: the landowner, agency, and buyer. Within this scheme, the agency acts as a trusted entity, orchestrating smart contracts and managing public keys, ensuring a seamless and secure transaction environment. The approach is divided into two intricate phases.

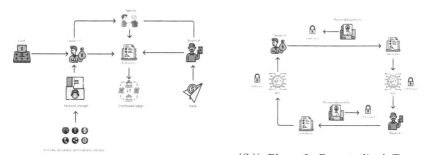

((a)) **Phase 1: Schematic Representation of Prospective Buyer Identification**

((b)) **Phase 2: Decentralized Transaction Flow between Landowner and Buyer using RSA**

Fig. 2. RSA- and Blockchain-Based Real Estate Transaction Platform

Phase 1: Identification of Prospective Buyers. The first phase lays the foundation for potential real estate transactions by facilitating interactions between landowners and potential buyers (see Fig. 2(a)).

1. **Landowner's Disclosure**: The landowner presents the agency with publicly shareable details about their property, ensuring that any sensitive or private information is securely retained on a local system, away from prying eyes.
2. **Agency's Role in Smart Contract Definition**: As a trusted entity, the agency meticulously drafts a smart contract. This contract outlines the terms of engagement, the mechanisms for interaction, and the criteria that prospective buyers must satisfy to participate in the transaction.
3. **Buyer's Initial Requirements**: Potential buyers intimate the agency about their specific property preferences, budget constraints, and other vital criteria. This information is securely registered on the distributed ledger, promoting transparency and ease of access.
4. **Deposits and the Smart Contract**: Buyers interested in engaging further deposit a predefined sum into the agency's smart contract. This deposit, acting as a gesture of commitment, is set by the agency and remains in the smart contract's custody until the transaction reaches its conclusion.
5. **Secure Communication Channel Establishment**: Once a landowner identifies a prospective buyer whose requirements align with their property, they request the agency for the buyer's public key. Using this key, they can then securely share private information, ensuring the confidentiality of the data transfer.

Phase 2: Facilitating the Transaction Between Owner and Buyer. Following the identification of compatible parties, the transaction moves into its second, more intricate phase (see Fig. 2(b)).

1. **Encryption of Private Documents**: Before the actual transition of property ownership rights, both the buyer and the landowner share encrypted versions of their confidential documents (RSA-based approach - see section ? for more detail). This method ensures that the actual content remains accessible only to the involved parties, thereby preserving data integrity and confidentiality.
2. **NFT Generation for Owner's Certificate**: Revolutionizing the traditional property certificate, it's digitized into a Non-Fungible Token (NFT). This NFT embeds within itself vital details of the property but ensures that sensitive information remains encrypted, shielding it from unauthorized access.
3. **NFT Public Announcement**: Post its creation, the property's NFT is made public on the InterPlanetary File System (IPFS), a decentralized storage platform. This ensures its immutability and accessibility, providing a permanent digital testament to the property's ownership.

This blockchain-based approach, divided into its preliminary identification and final transactional phases, promises not only enhanced security but also increased efficiency. By integrating modern technological paradigms, it stands poised to redefine real estate transactions, marrying traditional property principles with the advantages of the digital age.

4   Evaluation Scenarios

4.1   Land Certificate (i.e., NFT) Journey in IPFS

In this section, we delve into the intricate process of transforming traditional land certificates into digital tokens, or more precisely, NFTs and their journey within the IPFS.

```
it("Real-Estate Certificate NFT", async function () {
  const data = {
    name: "Real estate 1",
    address: "address 1",
    price: 300.000,
    owner: "Owner ID A",
    buyer: "Buyer ID B",
    agency: "agency XYZ",
    time: "12:00:00 GMT+7",
    date: "6th Oct, 2023",
  };
  const options = {
    pinataMetadata: {
      name: "Real estate certificate.json",
    },
    pinataOptions: {
      cidVersion: 0,
    },
  };
```

Fig. 3. The land info sample (called Land_1) of block info to mint the NFT

Figure 3 encapsulates the inception of this digital journey. Traditional land information, referred to as Land_1 in this illustration, undergoes a transformative process enabled by blockchain technology, culminating in the creation or 'minting' of an NFT. At the heart of this transformation is the assurance of data integrity, security, and uniqueness, hallmarks of any NFT.

Once minted, every NFT is characterized by its distinct hash key, a cryptographic signature ensuring its authenticity and singularity. As depicted in Fig. 4(a), this hash key, generated via RSA encryption, is more than just a digital signature; it's the NFT's unique identifier, an impenetrable seal underscoring its legitimacy and lineage.

With the hash key in hand, our journey now shifts to the IPFS. Figure 4(b) showcases this transition as the NFT's hash key is uploaded onto the IPFS, specifically onto platforms like Pinata[1]. This decentralized storage system ensures that the NFT, representing the land certificate, is not only stored

---

[1] Pinata platform: https://www.pinata.cloud/.

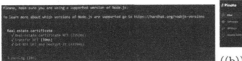

((a)) The hash key of NFT of Land_1

((b)) Hash key uploaded on the IPFS system (e.g., Pinata platform)

Fig. 4. Land certificate (i.e., NFT) Journey in IPFS

securely but is also accessible without centralized gatekeeping. The blockchain backbone of this system ensures data immutability, preventing unauthorized modifications.

Fig. 5. The content of the unauthorized stakeholder access

But what happens when unauthorized entities attempt access? Fig. 5 provides a glimpse into this scenario. Leveraging the robust RSA encryption, any unauthorized access attempts yield indecipherable content, ensuring the data's sanctity and privacy. This level of security underscores the robustness of the blockchain and encryption methods used in our approach.

For the proof-of-concept, our code for implementation and deployment is presented in our GitHub repositories[2].

4.2 Smart Contract Deployment on the Four EVM-Supported Platforms

Smart Contract Deployment. The evolution of blockchain technology has birthed a multitude of platforms, each promising unique features and capabilities. Among these platforms, Ethereum-compatible environments, commonly termed as Ethereum Virtual Machine (EVM)-supported platforms, have witnessed profound adoption. These platforms, while being compatible with Ethereum, offer distinct features, optimizations, and economic models that make them stand out.

In our endeavor, we meticulously deploy our smart contract on four renowned EVM-supported platforms: Binance Smart Chain (BNB Smart Chain)[3], Polygon[4], Fantom[5], and Celo[6]. These platforms have been selected due to their grow-

---

[2] Since the double-blind of the manuscript, we will provide our code when it's public.

[3] https://github.com/bnb-chain/whitepaper/blob/master/WHITEPAPER.md.

[4] https://polygon.technology/lightpaper-polygon.pdf.

[5] https://whitepaper.io/document/438/fantom-whitepaper.

[6] https://celo.org/papers/whitepaper.

ing prominence in the blockchain ecosystem and their promising capabilities. For transparency and reproducibility, our deployment across these platforms can be audited through the provided links: BNB Smart Chain[7], MATIC[8], FTM[9], and CELO[10].

Functionalities Analyzed on Each Platform. For each platform, we delve into three essential smart contract functionalities:

1. **Data/Transaction Creation**: This represents the foundational layer of our contract, where preliminary data, pertaining to the land or property, is inscribed onto the blockchain.
2. **Mint NFT**: Stemming from the data creation, this functionality transmutes the land certificate, ensuring its unique representation as a Non-Fungible Token (NFT) on the blockchain.
3. **Transfer NFT**: Building upon the previous functionality, this allows for the seamless transfer of the NFT between parties, ensuring the transition of ownership rights within the digital realm.

Transaction Fee Analysis. While the functionalities across the platforms remained consistent, the economic implications of deploying and using them varied. An essential metric in assessing the economic viability of a platform is its transaction fee. Our findings, which provide a comprehensive comparison of transaction fees across the platforms for different functionalities, are detailed in Table 1.

Table 1. Transaction fee

	Contract Creation	Create NFT	Transfer NFT
BNB Smart Chain	0.027311 BNB ($8.33)	0.00109162 BNB ($0.33)	0.00056991 BNB ($0.17)
Fantom	0.0095767 FTM ($0.003)	0.000405167 FTM ($0.000127)	0.0002380105 FTM ($0.000075)
Polygon	0.0068405000328344 MATIC($0.01)	0.000289405001273382 MATIC($0.00)	0.000170007500748033 MATIC($0.00)
Celo	0.00709722 CELO ($0.004)	0.0002840812 CELO ($0.000)	0.0001554878 CELO ($0.000)

Our comprehensive analysis sheds light on the intricacies and economic implications of deploying real estate-centric smart contracts across different EVM-supported platforms. It underpins the versatility of blockchain technology and how platforms, even while sharing a common foundation, can vary significantly in terms of performance, cost, and usability.

---

[7] https://testnet.bscscan.com/address/0x3e476a4c5fe0a7684125d077f7ccb385610ceec3.

[8] https://mumbai.polygonscan.com/address/0x3e476a4c5fe0a7684125d077f7ccb3856-10ceec3 .

[9] https://testnet.ftmscan.com/address/0x3e476a4c5fe0a7684125d077f7ccb385610ceec3.

[10] https://explorer.celo.org/alfajores/address/0x3E476a4C5Fe0A7684125D077f7CCb3-85610CEeC3/transactions.

5   Conclusion

The traditional real estate sector stands at the cusp of a digital transformation, poised to benefit immensely from the integration of blockchain technology, smart contracts, and encryption mechanisms. While the potential advantages of such an integration are vast, encompassing enhanced transparency, reduced transaction times, and a more robust security framework, several challenges need to be addressed. These include the need for comprehensive encryption methods, concerns related to tokenization, and ensuring scalability across multiple blockchain platforms. In this research, we have bridged the gaps in existing literature by presenting a comprehensive examination of how blockchain, ECC encryption, and NFTs can be harmoniously integrated in the real estate sector. Our proposed ECC- and Blockchain-based system heralds a new era for real estate, ensuring data security and transactional transparency in the digital domain. As the real estate sector evolves in tandem with technological advancements, it's imperative for stakeholders to adopt, adapt, and thrive in this digital revolution.

References

1. Avantaggiato, M., Gallo, P.: Challenges and opportunities using multichain for real estate. In: 2019 IEEE International Black Sea Conference on Communications and Networking (BlackSeaCom) (2019)
2. Chow, Y.L., Tan, K.K.: Real estate insights is tokenization of real estate ready for lift off in APAC? J. Property Investment Finance **40**(3), 284–290 (2022)
3. Deloitte: blockchain and smart contracts could transform property transactions. The Wall Street Journal (2018). http://deloitte.wsj.com/CFO/2018/01/03/blockchain-and-smart-contracts-could-transform-property-transactions/
4. EUROSTAT: real estate activity statistics - nace rev. 2. [Online] (2015), available: https://ec.europa.eu/eurostat/statistics-explained/index.php?title=Real_estate_activity_statistics_-_NACE_Rev._2&oldid=572702
5. Ha, X.S., et al.: Dem-cod: novel access-control-based cash on delivery mechanism for decentralized marketplace. In: the International Conference on Trust, Security and Privacy in Computing and Communications (TrustCom), pp. 71–78 (2020)
6. Huh, J.H., et al.: Verification plan using neural algorithm blockchain smart contract for secure P2P real estate transactions. Electronics **9**(6), 1052 (2020)
7. Tan, V.K., Nguyen, T.: The real estate transaction trace system model based on ethereum blockchain platform. In: 2022 14th International Conference on Computer and Automation Engineering (ICCAE), pp. 173–177 (2022)
8. Konashevych, O.: Constraints and benefits of the blockchain use for real estate and property rights. J. Property Planning Environ. Law **12**(2), 109–127 (2020)
9. Krupa, K.S.J., Akhil, M.S.: Reshaping the real estate industry using blockchain **545**, 255–263 (2019)
10. Le, H.T., et al.: Introducing multi shippers mechanism for decentralized cash on delivery system. Int. J. Adv. Comput. Sci. Appl. **10**(6) (2019)
11. Le, N.T.T., et al.: Assuring non-fraudulent transactions in cash on delivery by introducing double smart contracts. Int. J. Adv. Comput. Sci. Appl. **10**(5), 677–684 (2019)

12. McKeon, S.: Traditional asset tokenization. Hackernoon (2017). https://hackernoon.com/traditional-asset-tokenization-b8a59585a7e0
13. Mezquita, Y., et al.: Blockchain-based systems in land registry, a survey of their use and economic implications, vol. 1267. Springer International Publishing (2021)
14. Nasarre-Aznar, S.: Collaborative housing and blockchain. Administration **66**(2), 59–82 (2018)
15. Quoc, K.L., et al.: SSSB: an approach to insurance for cross-border exchange by using smart contracts. In: Awan, I., Younas, M., Poniszewska-Marańda, A. (eds.) Mobile Web and Intelligent Information Systems: 18th International Conference, MobiWIS 2022, Rome, Italy, August 22–24, 2022, Proceedings, pp. 179–192. Springer International Publishing, Cham (2022). https://doi.org/10.1007/978-3-031-14391-5_14
16. Savelyev, A.: Contract law 2.0: smart contracts as the beginning of the end of classic contract law. Inf. Commun. Technol. Law **26**(2), 116–134 (2017)
17. Sheikh, A., et al.: Blockyards: a blockchain-powered system for secure real estate transactions. Int. J. Emerg. Eng. Technol. **2**(1), 30–34 (2023)
18. Son, H.X., Chen, E.: Towards a fine-grained access control mechanism for privacy protection and policy conflict resolution. Int. J. Adv. Comput. Sci. Appl. **10**(2) (2019)
19. Son, H.X., Nguyen, M.H., Vo, H.K., Nguyen, T.P.: Toward an privacy protection based on access control model in hybrid cloud for healthcare systems. In: Martínez Álvarez, F., Troncoso Lora, A., Sáez Muñoz, J.A., Quintián, H., Corchado, E. (eds.) International Joint Conference: 12th International Conference on Computational Intelligence in Security for Information Systems (CISIS 2019) and 10th International Conference on European Transnational Education (ICEUTE 2019), pp. 77–86. Springer, Cham (2020). https://doi.org/10.1007/978-3-030-20005-3_8
20. Ubitquity: Ubitquity®the enterprise-ready blockchain-secured platform for real estate recordkeeping. https://www.ubitquity.io
21. Ullah, F., et al.: A conceptual framework for blockchain smart contract adoption to manage real estate deals in smart cities. Neural Comput. Appl. **35**(7), 5033–5054 (2023)
22. Veuger, J.: Trust in a viable real estate economy with disruption and blockchain. Facilities **36**(1/2), 103–120 (2018)
23. Vidal, M.T.: Tokenizing real estate on the blockchain. Medium (2017). https://medium.com/@mariat.vidal/tokenizing-real-estate-on-the-blockchain-9a13ae99bf11
24. Wolfson, R.: The future of investing: tokenizing traditional assets on the blockchain. HuffPost (Nov 2017). https://www.huffingtonpost.com/entry/the-future-of-investing-tokenizing-traditional-assets_us_5a0f4aaee4b023121e0e927d
25. Wouda, H.P., Opdenakker, R.: Blockchain technology in commercial real estate transactions. J. Property Investment Finance **36**(7), 570–579 (2019)

The Next Horizon in Blood Product Management: Safety, Transparency, and Beyond

Duc Bui Tien[1(✉)], P. D. Trinh[2], H. G. Khiem[2], M. N. Triet[2], T. B. Nam[2],
P. T. Nghiem[2], H. V. Khanh[2], and N. T. K. Ngan[3]

[1] Nguyen Tat Thanh University, HCM City, Vietnam
ducbt@ntt.edu.vn
[2] FPT University, Can Tho city, Vietnam
trietnm3@fe.edu.vn
[3] FPT Polytecnic, Can Tho city, Vietnam

Abstract. The real estate sector, an essential cornerstone of global economic growth, has been historically plagued by challenges including high fees, opaque transactions, and vulnerability to fraud. While the sector has been integral in shaping socio-economic structures and urban landscapes, traditional methods often present significant bottlenecks. With the advent of blockchain and collaborative technologies like smart contracts, there's promise to reshape these archaic processes, offering transparency, accountability, and drastically reduced transaction times. This paper delves deep into the confluence of blockchain, encryption, and Non-Fungible Tokens (NFTs) in real estate, exploring how they might revolutionize the sector. We highlight the inherent challenges with these technologies and propose an integrated system that merges RSA encryption with blockchain for enhanced data security in the real estate digital domain.

Keywords: Blood supply chain · Blockchain · Ethereum · IPFS · NFT · EVM · RSA

1 Introduction

The contemporary era has witnessed the ubiquity of supply chain management in diverse sectors. Evidenced by pioneering works in domains ranging from product delivery [5], payment systems [4], to waste disposal [10], the importance of robust, transparent, and efficient supply chain management systems has grown significantly. Within the myriad of applications, one area stands out in its criticality-the medical sector. Here, the supply chain can profoundly impact the very essence of life and well-being. One particularly vital segment within this is the management of blood and its derivative products, an essential life-saving resource.

Blood, as an irreplaceable medical product, necessitates a meticulous management system. From the point of collection from altruistic donors to its storage, and eventually its transfusion to patients in need, every stage demands impeccable attention. Aspects such as storage conditions-encompassing temperature,

© The Author(s), under exclusive license to Springer Nature Switzerland AG 2024
Y. Koucheryavy and A. Aziz (Eds.): NEW2AN/ruSMART 2023, LNCS 14543, pp. 118–130, 2024.
https://doi.org/10.1007/978-3-031-60997-8_12

humidity, and shelf-life-pose challenges that go beyond traditional supply chain problems [2].

Blockchain technology, with its decentralized nature, is increasingly finding its application in the healthcare domain, particularly for supply chain management. This system enables a continuous and immutable record of transactions, which is crucial for areas like blood donation and transfusion data management. There are multiple stakeholders in the blood supply chain - including the blood donor, the blood bank, and the hospital or recipient [15]. Ensuring the confidentiality of transactional data (like the donor's personal data, patient's personal data, and blood type) is of utmost importance. Specifically, stakeholders can access critical data reliably [3], facilitating donors to trace their blood contributions, while recipients can ascertain the origin and handling of the blood they receive [9].

While blockchain guarantees immutability, the plain data on the blockchain is typically accessible to all participants in the network. This can pose risks to the privacy of the data involved.

Several recent studies have attempted to address this issue. For example: Priya et al. [13] focused on using the Advanced Encryption Standard (AES) as a symmetric key crypto-system on the blood-chain data before it gets added to the ledger. This ensures that only those with the appropriate key can decrypt and access the confidential data. Beside, Maathavan et al. [11] combined machine learning techniques with encryption for classifying and securely storing blood bank data in the cloud. The study focused on both ensuring the efficient classification of blood bank data and guaranteeing its security through encryption.

While these efforts have laid the groundwork for secure blood-chain data management, there remains a gap in creating a comprehensive solution that not only ensures data encryption but also integrates seamlessly with current systems and is user-friendly. Moreover, we analyze our approach compare to the prior work in the encryption aspect (see Sect. 2 for more detail).

In this paper, we take inspiration from these efforts and introduce an advanced, holistic approach to blood-chain data management. We propose a blockchain-based system that integrates seamlessly with current blood bank management systems. Our key contributions are: Beyond merely employing RSA for data encryption, our system integrates encryption within the transactional process (transfer NFT), ensuring that data is encrypted from the moment of entry. This reduces the window of vulnerability that can often exist between data entry and encryption. Additionally, we initiate our intelligent contract mechanisms on platforms compatible with EVM (Ethereum Virtual Machine), including BNB Smart Chain, Fantom, Polygon, and Celo. Our primary objective in this deployment was to pinpoint the platform offering the most economical fees. Consequently, this aids in recognizing an optimal platform for realizing our suggested framework.[1]

---

[1] We exclude ETH from our deployment choices due to its prohibitive smart contract execution costs.

2 Related Work

2.1 Blockchain-Based Blood Donation Approach

Emerging from nascent beginnings, blockchain's applicability in the blood supply chain was pioneered by Nga et al. [15]. Opting for the Hyperledger Fabric platform, they transitioned from a centralized data storage protocol to a decentralized one. This digital metamorphosis allows healthcare professionals to commit data on-chain, ensuring it remains immutable. Their unique selling point is the authorization mechanism they employ. In their model, sensitive information relating to donors and recipients remains safeguarded, with only authorized personnel having the privilege of access, reinforcing data privacy [9].

Kim et al. [6] further carved this niche by also capitalizing on the Hyperledger Fabric platform's inherent privacy features. They conceptualized an end-to-end supply chain system, overseeing the entire gamut from blood collection to distribution. Notably, they incorporated an identifier mechanism, facilitating easy donor contact for subsequent donations. Yet, a glaring oversight in their work is the absence of specialized management protocols catering to distinct blood products, each possessing its own preservation requisites and shelf life.

Not deviating from the favored Hyperledger Fabric platform, Lakshminarayanan et al. [8] accentuated transparency during blood's journey from donor to end-receiver. Their methodology complements that of Toyoda et al. [16], who amalgamated the virtues of blockchain and RFID to conceive a hybrid model. Each unit of donated blood, in their paradigm, gets earmarked with an RFID tag, streamlining information access for medical personnel and recipients alike about key blood parameters and shipping nuances.

Branching out from Hyperledger, other work [2] explored Ethereum's potential. Their decentralized proposition on this platform emphasizes empowering only Certified Blood Donation Centers (CBDC) to deploy smart contracts. This centralization ensures the entire blood donation continuum remains tamper-resistant, mitigating logistical flaws like blood loss or overlooking expiry dates. Donors, in their framework, gain optional system access using identifiable credentials, further enhancing data security.

Narrowing the focus, Peltoniemi et al. [12] specifically target plasma, dissecting how blockchain decentralization can overhaul its monitoring and management. Here, donor metadata precedes plasma separation, succeeded by a meticulous plasma evaluation determining its quality.

Our paper, juxtaposed against these seminal works, introduces an avant-garde, comprehensive supply chain model rooted in blockchain. Beyond merely harnessing blockchain's virtues, we amalgamate it with advanced cryptographic techniques, addressing multi-faceted challenges from data security to supply chain efficacy, thereby setting a new benchmark in this domain.

In essence, while related works predominantly spotlight specific challenges or technological applications in isolation, our paper presents an integrated solution, bridging gaps between data security, transparency, and supply chain efficiency in the domain of blood donation.

2.2   Encryption Mechanisms in Blood Donation Systems

Encryption is a crucial aspect of data privacy and security, especially in sensitive areas like blood donation. Several works have delved into different encryption mechanisms, aiming to enhance the confidentiality and security of blood-chain data. In this subsection, we delve into the encryption techniques employed in various studies and contrast them with the RSA.

Advanced Encryption Standard (AES): AES, a symmetric key cryptosystem, is a widely-used encryption standard due to its proven security and efficiency. [7,13] employ AES to ensure data confidentiality and security. This encryption ensures that only those with the appropriate decryption key can access the sensitive data.

Database Security and Encryption: [1] combines database security with encryption, focusing on protecting users' donation records from potential threats. While the exact encryption technique is not specified, the amalgamation of database security mechanisms and encryption points towards a layered security approach.

Blockchain-based Encryption: Studies like [14] harness the innate cryptographic properties of blockchains. Specifically, this work leverages zero-knowledge proof in blockchain to hide users' login application records, providing another layer of privacy on top of transaction immutability.

2.3   Comparison with RSA Encryption in Our Work

RSA is renowned for its ability to provide strong encryption with smaller key sizes, translating to faster computations and lower resource usage compared to traditional methods like RSA. In "The Next Horizon in Blood Product Management," RSA was chosen to encrypt sensitive information, prioritizing both security and efficiency.

- **Security Level**: While AES is robust and provides a high security level, ECC, with its smaller key sizes, offers comparable, if not superior, security. This makes RSA a more efficient choice for systems where resources and speed are critical.
- **Key Size and Efficiency**: ECC's main advantage is its smaller key size. For instance, a 256-bit key in RSA provides equivalent security to a 3072-bit key in RSA. This directly translates to faster computations, making our approach more resource-efficient than methods solely relying on AES or unspecified encryption techniques.
- **Integration with Blockchain**: While blockchains inherently possess cryptographic properties, integrating RSA further enhances the confidentiality of data. Compared to zero-knowledge proofs, RSA provides a more straightforward approach, ensuring data protection without adding undue complexity.

In conclusion, while various studies have explored different encryption techniques for blood donation systems, our work harnesses the efficiency and robust security of ECC, setting it apart in terms of speed, resource usage, and overall data protection.

3   Approach

3.1   Blood Donation Traditional Process

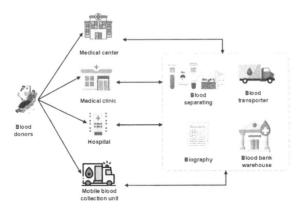

Fig. 1. Blood donation traditional process

The traditional approach to blood donation, as depicted in Fig. 1, has been methodically designed to cater to a range of geographical contexts and preferences of donors. Drawing insights from the research presented in [9], this approach predominantly revolves around four primary methods, each addressing unique needs and constraints of its environment.

Medical centers are foundational pillars in this approach, being institutions endowed with comprehensive medical facilities. They serve as hubs not only for blood donation but a plethora of other healthcare services, making them reliable and preferred choices for many donors. On the other hand, we have medical clinics, which, while being smaller in scale compared to medical centers, provide focused outpatient services. Their scale might limit the extent of blood preservation equipment they can house, but their role in community-centric healthcare cannot be understated.

Then we have hospitals, with their broad infrastructure and myriad departments. Not only do they manage blood collection but also have robust mechanisms for preservation and transfusion. These establishments are often the primary choice for large-scale blood donation drives. Complementing these three static methods is the dynamic approach of mobile blood collection units. Their periodic operation-often during weekends or holidays-allows them to penetrate areas underserved by permanent medical facilities. By setting up temporary camps in varying locations, they attempt to make blood donation a more accessible and less daunting experience, reaching out to a broader spectrum of potential donors.

Post-collection, irrespective of the method, the collected blood is subjected to a standardized process. It's transported, primarily through specialized vehicles, to entities equipped for blood storage, like hematology hospitals. At these places, the blood is diligently separated into its constituent elements: red blood cells, platelets, white blood cells, and plasma. Alongside this, an essential administrative task is the recording of donors' personal details onto localized system servers. This information, however, is used strictly for communication purposes, ensuring the privacy of donors is never compromised.

However, this traditional model, despite its systematic approach, has its set of challenges. The reliance on fixed infrastructures might not always cater to remote or underserved regions. Even with the mobile units bridging this gap, their periodic nature can lead to accessibility issues during their off-periods. Data security, given the digital age we live in, remains a constant concern. Storing personal data on local servers opens up potential risks of cyber threats if not adequately secured. Moreover, areas with limited storage capacities can face inefficiencies, with collected blood at risk of wastage if not utilized or stored.

While the traditional blood donation model has catered effectively to many over the years, addressing its challenges is crucial for ensuring it remains inclusive, efficient, and up-to-date with contemporary needs.

3.2   RSA and Blockchain-Based Blood Donation System

Our integrated system, powered by RSA encryption and blockchain technology, prioritizes this need by facilitating seamless and secure communication between various medical centers. Whether it's sourcing a specific blood type from another center or reaching out directly to potential donors when centers can't meet the demand, our approach ensures that blood recipients receive the exact match in the shortest possible time. The process hinges on two primary scenarios (see Fig. 2).

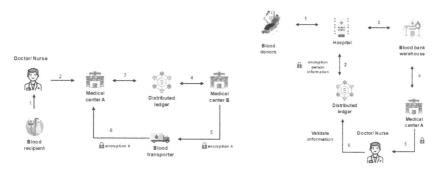

((a)) Case 1: Inter-Medical Center Blood Sourcing

((b)) Case 2: Direct Blood Donor Engagement

Fig. 2. RSA and Blockchain-based Blood Donation System

Case 1: Inter-Medical Center Blood Sourcing. In situations where a blood recipient at Medical Center A requires a specific blood type or component, the immediate course of action is to check its internal inventory. If the desired blood type is unavailable or in short supply, our system swiftly scans the inventories of other connected medical centers. Suppose the requisite blood type is identified at Medical Center B. In that case, the system facilitates the secure and swift transfer of information, ensuring that the blood can be reserved and transported to Medical Center A post-haste. The process is presented in Fig. 2(a).

Case 2: Direct Blood Donor Engagement. If the initial scan across medical centers doesn't yield the desired blood type, our system initiates a more direct approach. Harnessing the power of blockchain's transparency and the security of RSA encryption, it reaches out to registered blood donors who match the required blood type. This outreach is done with utmost discretion, ensuring the privacy and personal details of potential donors remain protected. Once a willing donor is identified, they are directed to the nearest medical center or mobile collection unit to donate, ensuring the recipient gets the required blood type without undue delay. Figure 2(b) details our process for the second case.

By delineating these two cases, our approach underscores its commitment to adaptability and efficiency, ensuring that the critical need for the right type of blood is met promptly and securely.

4   Evaluation Scenarios

4.1   The Encryption and Transfer NFT Process

In the realm of digital systems, the fidelity of any model rests upon the robustness of its underlying environment. The encryption and transfer process of NFTs, being a pivotal component of our system, warrants meticulous attention. To ensure a reliable assessment, our proof-of-concept has been deployed on a well-defined environment, details of which precede the performance analysis.

Simulation Environment Specifications: Our simulation environment has been designed to provide an optimal balance of power and efficiency, crucial for the tasks it has been designated for. Below are the specifics of the environment:

- **Operating System:** Microsoft Windows 10 Enterprise (Version 10.0.19045 Build 19045). This platform provides the requisite stability and support for our application stack.
- **Physical Memory (RAM):** 16.0 GB. Such a memory allotment ensures the seamless execution of our processes, especially during data-intensive operations.
- **Device and Version:** Deployed on a device by Dell Inc., with the version being 1.28.0, dated 7/10/2023.

– **Processor:** The heart of our environment is the 11th Gen Intel(R) Core(TM) i7-1165G7, running at a base speed of 2.80 GHz. It possesses 4 cores, further augmented with Hyper-Threading, resulting in 8 logical processors. This powerhouse ensures swift processing, particularly vital for encryption, decryption, and handling NFT operations.

With this robust environment, we embarked on assessing the performance of our system, focusing predominantly on the time dynamics of the Mint NFT, Transfer NFT, and the encrypt/decrypt operations.

4.2 NFT Journey in IPFS

Our proposed model serves as a bulwark against unauthorized access while providing an immutable ledger for blood samples. The following narrative delves deep into the mechanism, guided by the illustrative figures.

Minting the NFT for Blood Samples: Beginning our journey, Fig. 3 displays the initial process of creating an NFT for a sample, herein referred to as 'sample_1'. NFTs inherently possess a uniqueness, ensuring each blood sample's data remains distinct. In our model, metadata from 'sample_1', encompassing essential details such as blood type, date of donation, and other relevant parameters, undergoes a transformation into a digital representation, laying the groundwork for minting it as an NFT.

```
it("Mint NFT", async function () {
  const data = {
    type: "type 1",
    Donor: "Donor ID 1",
    bloodCounts: "bloodCounts 1",
    place_Donor: "Hospital 1",
    receiver_Receiver: "Medical institution receiver 1",
    sentTime: "sentTime 1",
    receivedTime: "receivedTime 1",
    receiver: "Patient ID 1",
    status: "0",
  };
  const options = {
    pinataMetadata: {
      name: "Privacy-awared-blood-donate.json",
    },
    pinataOptions: {
      cidVersion: 0,
    },
  };
```

Fig. 3. The sample (called sample_1) of blood info to mint the NFT

Hash Generation for the NFT: With the NFT minted, the ensuing step, as showcased in Fig. 4, involves generating a cryptographic hash key. This hash key, acting as a unique fingerprint for 'sample_1's NFT, ensures two-fold functionality. First, it provides a layer of encryption, reinforcing data security. Second, it facilitates subsequent retrieval and identification processes, streamlining interactions with the IPFS system.

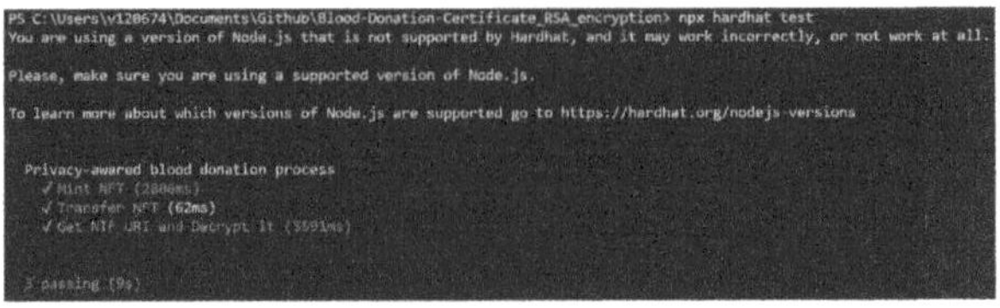

Fig. 4. The hash key of NFT of sample_1

Uploading the Hash to the IPFS via Pinata. Migrating to the realm of decentralized storage, Fig. 5 illuminates the process of uploading the generated hash key into the IPFS using platforms such as Pinata. The decentralized nature of IPFS ensures data redundancy, high availability, and robustness against tampering. Within this infrastructure, Pinata emerges as an accessible gateway, allowing users to push content to IPFS seamlessly. Our hash key, once lodged in this ecosystem, remains securely preserved, awaiting authorized retrieval.

Fig. 5. Hash key uploaded on the IPFS system (e.g., Pinata platform)

Unauthorized Access Attempt. However, as with any data-centric system, unauthorized access attempts remain a looming threat. Figure 6 illustrates such a scenario. Here, a stakeholder devoid of the essential private key, when attempting to access 'sample_1's NFT content, faces a barrier. The system robustly rejects such intrusions, only presenting obfuscated content or an error message. This safeguard, pivotal in our design, ensures the sanctity of donor data, thereby upholding trust and ensuring compliance with data protection norms.

In culmination, our system, represented through these figures, epitomizes a harmonious blend of encryption, NFT technology, and decentralized storage. Through rigorous evaluations, we demonstrate not only its feasibility but also its prowess in championing data security in the domain of blood supply chain management. For the proof-of-concept, our code for implementation and deployment is presented in our GitHub repositories[2].

---

[2] Since the double-blind of the manuscript, we will provide our code when it's public.

"data":
"a1998afd9a53cf98be65e637dfeab644381f590577acf5c04acc6b92049928b64945c6405595872242714e50990
f2a906184a07e0fdb73333ebd1bfdc9c1ad4e4948b8d0ebc6945ca0956b7d0fcc4305040848af99ce6b083485aa
0ab16cec40550fcbb79516bac4c84110279af8b3ea6b7530c9681c70c3bc9b6de135489402b99fef6295a4406ab
88523563f9394310e201064df86b2830763a3f884461cf8b823c4a70c69788bv8bd6f5ff867e06624d33118a52
bd8700e781727e422ab4ae4a27f0999311f42463db3e9b1e62c331d61b135ecb66cc2003ea3b68094d4e6fce6f9
546671f697bbe483c78034b7af33764437b6600299774cb450a7c1210607b88e"

Fig. 6. The content of the unauthorized stakeholder access

4.3 Smart Contract Deployment on EVM-Supported Platforms

Blockchain and decentralized technologies have seen a meteoric rise in recent years. The underlying core of these systems is the smart contract, a self-executing contract where the terms of agreement or conditions are written into code. These smart contracts provide the basis for creating more intricate decentralized applications, which is where our focus on the functionalities of Mint NFT, Transfer NFT, and NFT owner update comes into play.

Having elucidated the significance of these functionalities, it's pertinent to mention their deployment. To enhance interoperability and ensure robustness across different environments, we deployed our smart contract on the four leading EVM-supported platforms, namely BNB, MATIC, FTM, and CELO. These platforms were chosen due to their prominence, widespread adoption, and compatibility with the Ethereum Virtual Machine (EVM).

Implementation details are as follows:

- **BNB:** Our model's implementation on BNB can be accessed and reviewed at Sep-24-2023 07:04:41 AM +UTC via the BNB testnet[3].
- **MATIC:** The deployment on the MATIC platform can be scrutinized on their Mumbai testnet[4].
- **FTM:** Our FTM deployment is available for review on their testnet[5].
- **CELO:** Lastly, our implementation on the CELO platform can be accessed on their explorer[6].

By deploying our model across these diverse platforms, we aim to provide a holistic solution adaptable to various ecosystems, ensuring a wider reach and facilitating seamless integration.

Performance Analysis: Transaction Fee

In the expansive realm of blockchain technology, transaction fees stand as pivotal determinants of a platform's viability and efficiency. These fees are indicative

---

[3] https://testnet.bscscan.com/address/0xc0dc2ad1a1149b5363d7f58c2cf7231d8392 5c0c.

[4] https://mumbai.polygonscan.com/address/0xd20ae7123c4387d25d670a6fd74a6095f 4dcaa56.

[5] https://testnet.ftmscan.com/address/0xd20ae7123c4387d25d670a6fd74a6095f4dc aa56.

[6] https://explorer.celo.org/alfajores/address/0xD20aE7123C4387d25d670a6fd74A60 95F4dCaa56/transactions.

of the costs tied to executing operations on a blockchain. A thorough comprehension of these fees is paramount for stakeholders looking to make data-driven
decisions. Table 1 offers a detailed look into the transaction fees linked with varying operations across the top EVM-supported platforms, namely BNB Smart
Chain, Fantom, Polygon, and Celo.

Table 1. Transaction fee

	Contract Creation	Create NFT	Transfer NFT
BNB Smart Chain	0.02731136 BNB ($8.37)	0.00109162 BNB ($0.33)	0.00057003 BNB ($0.18)
Fantom	0.009576826 FTM ($0.001860)	0.000405167 FTM ($0.000079)	0.0002380105 FTM ($0.000046)
Polygon	0.006840590024626124 MATIC($0.01)	0.00028940500115762 MATIC($0.00)	0.000170007500612027 MATIC($0.00)
Celo	0.0070973136 CELO ($0.004)	0.0002840812 CELO ($0.000)	0.0001554878 CELO ($0.000)

A discerning observation of the table reveals a significant variance in transaction costs across platforms. The BNB Smart Chain, while incurring a compar-
atively higher fee for contract creation, moderates its expenses considerably for
subsequent tasks, such as the creation and transfer of NFTs. Fantom emerges as
a more cost-efficient alternative, especially spotlighted by its reduced fee structure for NFT transfers. Polygon further accentuates this trend, boasting nominal
charges for both the minting and transfer of NFTs. Simultaneously, Celo offers
a harmonious balance, presenting competitive rates across all operations and
underscoring its potential as a balanced, cost-effective blockchain solution. In
essence, these diverse fee structures echo the unique computational intricacies
and the foundational consensus mechanisms intrinsic to each blockchain. Such
granular insights are invaluable for stakeholders, guiding them in discerning the
most economical and robust platform tailored to their specific needs.

5   Conclusion

Our exploration into the domain of NFTs, encrypted data storage, and smart
contract deployment on EVM-compatible platforms culminates in a system that
is not only innovative but also holds immense potential for real-world applications. The research affirms that by melding the power of NFTs with robust
encryption and decentralized storage mechanisms, it's possible to create a secure
and efficient environment, especially in sectors as critical as the blood supply
chain. The variability in transaction fees across different platforms underscores
the significance of informed decision-making in the blockchain realm. Every platform offers a unique blend of computational prowess and economic considerations, and choosing the right fit could mean the difference between a successful
implementation and an economically burdensome venture.

In sum, as blockchain technologies continue to evolve and gain traction, it's
imperative for stakeholders to be equipped with both the technical and economic
knowledge to navigate this promising, yet intricate, landscape. Our research
serves as a step in this direction, laying the groundwork for future explorations
and implementations in the domain.

References

1. Agarwal, R., et al.: Blood bank system using database security. Int. Res. J. Eng. Technol. (IRJET) **7**(06) (2020)
2. Çağlıyangil, M., Erdem, S., Özdağoğlu, G.: A blockchain based framework for blood distribution. In: Hacioglu, U. (ed.) Digital Business Strategies in Blockchain Ecosystems. CMS, pp. 63–82. Springer, Cham (2020). https://doi.org/10.1007/978-3-030-29739-8_4
3. Duong-Trung, N., et al.: Smart care: integrating blockchain technology into the design of patient-centered healthcare systems. In: Proceedings of the 2020 4th International Conference on Cryptography, Security and Privacy, pp. 105–109
4. Duong-Trung, N., et al.: Multi-sessions mechanism for decentralized cash on delivery system. Int. J. Adv. Comput. Sci. Appl **10**(9) (2019)
5. Ha, X.S., Le, H.T., Metoui, N., Duong-Trung, N.: Dem-cod: novel access-control-based cash on delivery mechanism for decentralized marketplace. In: 2020 IEEE 19th International Conference on Trust, Security and Privacy in Computing and Communications (TrustCom), pp. 71–78. IEEE (2020)
6. Kim, S., Kim, D.: Design of an innovative blood cold chain management system using blockchain technologies. ICIC Express Letters, Part B: Appl. **9**(10), 1067–1073 (2018)
7. Kotti, J., et al.: Aes based blood bank system using cloud techniques. J. Pharm. Negative Results 1070–1077 (2023)
8. Lakshminarayanan, S., Kumar, P.N., Dhanya, N.M.: Implementation of blockchain-based blood donation framework. In: Chandrabose, A., Furbach, U., Ghosh, A., Kumar M., A. (eds.) Computational Intelligence in Data Science: Third IFIP TC 12 International Conference, ICCIDS 2020, Chennai, India, February 20–22, 2020, Revised Selected Papers, pp. 276–290. Springer International Publishing, Cham (2020). https://doi.org/10.1007/978-3-030-63467-4_22
9. Le, H.T., et al.: Bloodchain: a blood donation network managed by blockchain technologies. Network **2**(1), 21–35 (2022)
10. Le, H.T., et al.: Medical-waste chain: a medical waste collection, classification and treatment management by blockchain technology. Computers **11**(7), 113 (2022)
11. Maathavan, K.S.K., Venkatraman, S.: A secure encrypted classified electronic healthcare data for public cloud environment. Intell. Autom. Soft Comput. **32**(2) (2022)
12. Peltoniemi, T., Ihalainen, J.: Evaluating blockchain for the governance of the plasma derivatives supply chain: How distributed ledger technology can mitigate plasma supply chain risks. Blockchain in Healthcare Today (2019)
13. Priya, E.S., Priya, R.: Data encryption of blood-chain data in blockchain network. In: 2023 International Conference on Networking and Communications (ICNWC), pp. 1–9. IEEE (April 2023)
14. Qingshui, X., et al.: Registration and login scheme of charity blood donation system based on blockchain zero-knowledge proof. In: 2021 IEEE 9th International Conference on Information, Communication and Networks (ICICN), pp. 464–469. IEEE (Nov 2021)

15. Quynh, N.T.T., et al.: Toward a design of blood donation management by blockchain technologies. In: Gervasi, O., et al. (eds.) Computational Science and Its Applications – ICCSA 2021: 21st International Conference, Cagliari, Italy, September 13–16, 2021, Proceedings, Part VIII, pp. 78–90. Springer International Publishing, Cham (2021). https://doi.org/10.1007/978-3-030-87010-2_6

16. Toyoda, K., et al.: A novel blockchain-based product ownership management system (poms) for anti-counterfeits in the post supply chain. IEEE access 5, 17465–17477 (2017)

Mental Health of a Person as a Result of the Transformation of Socio-economic System

Dmitriy Rodionov[1], Bokhodir Isroilov[2(✉)], Darya Kryzhko[1], Mansur Eshov[2], Irina Smirnova[1], and Evgenii Konnikov[1]

[1] Peter the Great St.Petersburg Polytechnic University, Polytechnicheskaya, 29, St. Petersburg 195251, Russia
drodionov@spbstu.ru
[2] Tashkent State University of Economics, Islam Karimov Street, 49, Tashkent 100066, Uzbekistan
{b.isroilov,m.eshov}@tsue.uz

Abstract. The article investigates the multifaceted factors influencing the mental well-being of individuals within society. Through empirical analysis, this study reveals that material well-being and social institutions exhibit negligible effects on the central factors associated with mental health. Conversely, personal emotions emerge as a significant determinant, influenced by various social phenomena such as marriage, divorce, and bereavement. Furthermore, the research underscores the substantial impact of sleep duration on an individual's mental health. Extending sleep duration is found to elevate happiness levels, although individuals with inclinations towards criminal behavior and suicide tend to prefer even longer sleep. However, this specific phenomenon falls beyond the scope of this study, warranting further examination in relevant research endeavors. Moreover, education is identified as a positive influencer of mental well-being, as evidenced by its significant reduction in crime and suicide rates across examined countries. This finding underscores the imperative of enhancing the quality and accessibility of education on a global scale. It is crucial to acknowledge that due to the inherent complexities surrounding subjective concepts such as happiness and the ideal mental state, this study cannot be deemed conclusive. The presented work establishes general associations between the selected central factors and their influencing variables. To obtain more robust and reliable insights, it is recommended to conduct comprehensive research tailored to each country, accounting for their unique characteristics and incorporating a broader range of influential factors. In conclusion, this study contributes to understanding of the intricate interplay between socio-economic factors and mental health.

Keywords: Socio-Economic System · Transformation · Mental Health · Index

1 Introduction

The mental state of society is the state of mental well-being that enables people to cope with stressful situations in life, fulfill their potential, succeed in learning and work, and contribute to society. This indicator directly affects the functioning of socio-economic

Y. Koucheryavy and A. Aziz (Eds.): NEW2AN/ruSMART 2023, LNCS 14543, pp. 131–151, 2024.
https://doi.org/10.1007/978-3-031-60997-8_13

systems as it forms one aspect of human capital well-being. Throughout life, numerous individual, social, and structural determinants can either protect or undermine the mental health of the population and its position in society [1].

This study examines the mental state of society through three factors. The happiness index reflects the highest level of mental health, while the crime index and suicide index characterize the manifestation of extremely negative mental states within the population. The research aims to identify a range of factors that influence the mental state of society. The study utilizes data from 35 countries.

Numerous studies have focused on studying the mental health of populations as a whole and individuals. Researchers strive to identify factors that directly influence people's mental state. For instance, Petrov highlights genetic predisposition and direct damage to the central nervous system as causes of mental disorders. The author also acknowledges the duality of influencing factors, including biophysical and internal reactions, as well as external circumstances [2–6].

Based on correlation analysis [7] research has shown that the high crime rates are influenced by the number of unemployed individuals. Additionally, the study demonstrates that subjective well-being criteria are less related to objective satisfaction indicators than expected. Particularly weak is the correlation with income level. Social support, in the form of real assistance and the availability of a person who cares, is crucial. Moreover, married, wealthy, and educated women are less likely to suffer from depression. However, the influence of marriage on happiness, for example in the United States, is weakening. Contrarily, in the Netherlands and Scandinavian countries, married life has a positive impact on reducing the risk of depression, suicide, and the ability to live longer [8–11].

In conclusion, psychological well-being within a nation is a complex indicator reflected in this study through happiness indexes and polar indexes of suicide and crime rates. Interpersonal relationships, physical health, education, and social approval all influence individuals' mental health. Education significantly reduces crime rates, while marriage greatly reduces mortality risks [12].

Researchers [13] conclude that the unequal distribution of resources, such as education, income, or social status, as well as unequal access to them, inevitably leads to social inequality, which strongly affects individuals' mental health [14–17]. This idea is supported by a study [18], stating that education has significant value in the perception of economic freedom and happiness.

In a study [19] focused on adolescent crime rates, researchers argue that the increase in crime among teenagers is due to the negative influence of older, unbalanced family members, parental alcohol consumption, and the low involvement of teachers and educators in a student's life, not just in the educational process.

National characteristics can also influence the state of mental health in a population. For example, the high level of education in Japan is dictated by the rigid determinism and hierarchy of the Japanese life strategy, where work becomes the meaning of life and the inability to find fulfillment in it or losing a job devalues citizens' lives [20–22].

Emile Durkheim argues that the causes of all suicides are social, not psychological, meaning that they depend on external circumstances rather than internal ones. However, the internal is inseparably linked to the external, and in our study, we consider the suicide rate as a secondary indicator that stems from external social factors and reflects the mental state of the population [23–25]. The presence of a family and a large number of children serves as a good preventive measure against the threat of suicide. On the other hand, widowers have a high propensity for suicide, which is also confirmed in the work [26–30].

2 Research Methodology

In this study, hypotheses will be tested in accordance with conceptual models (Figs. 1, 2 and 3), based on the following central factors - the happiness index, the crime index, and the suicide rate for the following developed countries: Sweden, Spain, Italy, Denmark, France, Luxembourg, Austria, the Netherlands, Belgium, Finland, Germany, Portugal, Ireland, Greece, Slovenia, Estonia, Czech Republic, Hungary, Latvia, Slovakia, Croatia, Bulgaria, Lithuania, Romania, Poland, the United States, Switzerland, Serbia, Norway, Russia, Turkey, Ukraine, Japan, the United Kingdom, and Australia.

Factors whose impact is studied in this research are presented in Table 1.

Table 1. Factors affecting key indicators

Factor Name	Abbreviation	Units of Measurement	Source
Average Age of Marriage	x_1	Years	w3.unece.org
Average Lifespan	x_2	Years	statdata.ru
Education Index	x_3	–	gtmarket.ru
Gini Coefficient	x_4	%	theworldonly.org
Per Capita Income	x_5	US Dollars	gtmarket.ru
Average Temperature	x_6	Degrees Celsius	gtmarket.ru
Average Age	x_7	Years	gtmarket.ru
Number of Divorces	x_8	Units per thousand people	gtmarket.ru
Number of Marriages	x_9	Units per thousand people	gtmarket.ru
Antidepressant Usage	x_10	Units per 1000 people	gtmarket.ru
Corruption Level	x_11	–	gtmarket.ru
Medical Level	x_12	–	gtmarket.ru
Mortality Rate	x_13	Units per 1000 people	gtmarket.ru
Sleep Duration	x_14	Hours	gtmarket.ru
Inflation Level	x_15	%	gtmarket.ru
Alcohol Consumption Level	x_16	–	gtmarket.ru
Drug Consumption Level	x_17	–	gtmarket.ru
Gender Inequality	x_18	–	gtmarket.ru

The hypothetical hypotheses regarding the influence of the selected factors on the centroids are presented in Tables 2, 3, and 4.

Table 2. Factors and hypotheses on their presumed impact on the happiness index

Happiness Index (Y1)	
Factor	Hypothesis
Crime rate index	The higher the crime rate, the less livable the country is considered to be
Suicide rate index	Most suicides occur due to hostile environments, so a greater number of suicides will occur in countries with a low happiness index
Average age of marriage, years	There is a direct proportional relationship between the average age of marriage and the happiness index. The older the age of marriage, the more consciously a person approaches choosing a partner, increasing the likelihood of a successful union that brings joy
Average life expectancy, years	Average life expectancy has a positive impact on the happiness index. High life expectancy is often found in countries and regions with a high standard of living, social and economic stability, which also influence people's level of happiness and satisfaction
Education index	The education index has a positive influence on the happiness index. Accessible and quality education is one of the signs of a developed society, where individuals can satisfy their spiritual needs and strive for happiness
Gini coefficient	The Gini coefficient negatively affects the happiness index. The more unevenly wealth is distributed, the higher the social inequality and the larger the lower class. When a significant portion of the population is concerned with meeting basic physiological needs, the question of happiness takes a back seat
Per capita income, $	The higher the per capita income, the higher the level of security, stability, and purchasing power. The feeling of economic stability and independence is one of the fundamental components of happiness
Average temperature, degrees Celsius	This factor has a positive influence on the happiness index. People feel more comfortable where it is warm, and the sun promotes the production of happiness hormones and the intake of vitamin D

(continued)

Table 2. (*continued*)

Happiness Index (Y1)	
Factor	Hypothesis
Average age	The average age of the population also has a positive influence on the happiness index. The longer citizens live, the higher the level of healthcare and quality of life in the country under consideration
Number of divorces, per thousand people	This factor, as it increases, will decrease the happiness index. Divorce signifies that a person made a mistake in choosing their partner, and usually the process and memories of divorce are quite painful
Number of marriages, per thousand people	This factor will have a positive impact on an individual's happiness index. A successful marriage fulfills one of the most important needs of a person - partnership and creating a family
Antidepressant use, per 1000 people	The higher the level of this factor, the lower the happiness index. An increase in the number of people with depression affects not only their life dissatisfaction but also has a negative impact on their loved ones
Corruption level	A high level of corruption usually indicates a low level of trust in the government and low moral standards in the population. The need for offering and accepting bribes suggests that people are dissatisfied with the current living conditions
Medical level	The higher the level and accessibility of healthcare, the safer and more protected a person can feel. Therefore, a high level of healthcare brings individuals closer to the feeling of happiness
Death rate, per thousand people	High mortality rates can indirectly indicate high population morbidity, low levels of healthcare, high crime rates, poor infrastructure, and low social security. This indicator negatively affects the happiness index
Sleep duration, hours	The availability for the population to have quality and sufficient rest positively impacts the happiness index

(continued)

Table 2. (*continued*)

Happiness Index (Y1)

Factor	Hypothesis
Inflation rate, %	The inflation rate directly affects the income of the population, which people spend on acquiring material goods. It is assumed that the lower the inflation rate, the higher the happiness index
Alcohol consumption level	Alcohol serves as a means to avoid problems, a way to "numb oneself," which indicates an unstable mental state of society. Therefore, a negative impact of this factor is expected
Drug consumption level	Drugs serve as a means to avoid problems, a way to "escape" reality, which also indicates an unstable mental state of society. Therefore, a negative impact of this factor is expected
Gender inequality	The majority of the global population is composed of the female gender, and deviations in gender equality can affect their mental state. Therefore, a negative impact of this factor is expected

The hypotheses presented above find support in the conclusions contained in the studies mentioned in the literature review. Graphical representations of the factors' influence on the centroids are presented in Figs. 1, 2 and 3.

The study consisted of several stages. First, it was necessary to create a statistical database - a table with data for each factor related to each country. Then, countries and factors with too many missing values had to be excluded to avoid distorting the actual data.

The generated table in Microsoft Excel was loaded into the analytical platform KNIME. The type of relationships between the factors was examined. All relationships turned out to be linear, eliminating the need for linearization.

Since the study focuses on three central factors, three linear regression models were developed. In order to achieve the maximum possible variance description of the central factors, optimization was performed. This involved excluding factors with a high P-value from the model. The critical value for this factor was set at 13%. The theoretical values of the central factors (denoted as y_1, y_2, y_3) were calculated, and a graph comparing the theoretical and actual central factors was plotted. Errors and residuals were then determined.

To assess the nature of the residual distribution, a graph based on the residuals was created in Microsoft Excel. The analysis of the resulting graph led to the conclusion about the homoscedastic or heteroscedastic character of the distribution.

The final stage involved calculating the elasticity coefficient and constructing an elasticity graph.

Table 3. Factors and hypotheses on their presumed impact on the crime index

Crime Index (Y2)	
Factor	Hypothesis
Happiness Index	Happy people are less inclined to commit unlawful acts
Suicide rate index	An increase in the number of suicides disrupts the stable state of society and may lead to an increase in the number of committed crimes
Average age of marriage, years	This factor will have a negative impact on the crime index. A low age of marriage is mainly associated with a population with a low level of education. Marriage is entered into unconsciously and often leads to high social tension, which, in turn, leads to an increase in the crime rate
Average life expectancy, years	The impact will be negative. High average life expectancy indicates a high standard of living in the region under consideration. When people have a high life expectancy, they are not in a rush to achieve everything through legal or illegal means. They focus on education, building a career, exploring the world, and establishing a family rather than engaging in criminal activities
Education index	The higher the level of education among the population, the lower the crime rate in the country, both due to a fair and comprehensive legislative and judicial system and the self-awareness of citizens
Gini coefficient	The lower the unequal distribution of income among the population, the lower the economic and social tension and the fewer motives for the middle and lower classes to engage in criminal activities
Per capita income, $	Many types of crimes are motivated by material insufficiency. A negative relationship between these factors is expected
Average temperature, degrees Celsius	This factor will have a negative influence on the crime index. Pleasant climate predominantly has a positive effect on a person's mental state and also reduces expenses for heating, warm clothing, purchasing and maintaining a car

(continued)

Table 3. (*continued*)

Crime Index (Y2)

Factor	Hypothesis
Number of divorces, per thousand people	There is a direct relationship with the crime index, as divorce is a significant stress factor for any individual and simultaneously a consequence and a cause of extensive conflicts. Therefore, it is logical to assume that an increase in the number of divorces will lead to a higher crime index
Number of marriages, per thousand people	An individual who enters into marriage becomes happier and less prone to committing crimes. However, such individuals may be more inclined to commit domestic or minor crimes. In this case, it is difficult to suggest a specific connection between the factors
Antidepressant use, per 1000 people	In regions with a high usage of antidepressants, there are stress factors that contribute to the mental instability of the population. This instability can manifest as complete inaction, apathy, and amorphous behavior, or conversely, it can lead to active resistance of the mind to stress, which may increase the crime index
Corruption level	Corruption directly affects the crime rate, for example, taking bribery into consideration. A positive relationship between these factors is expected
Medical level	A high level of medical care can indicate that the state actively finances this sphere in terms of developing treatment methods and medications or provides citizens with free access to healthcare. These measures reduce social tension, have a positive impact on the nation's health, and improve quality of life, which should significantly reduce the crime index
Death rate, per thousand people	The death rate has a positive impact on the crime index because high mortality and its causes can provoke various difficulties in different areas of a person's life: social, labor, economic, personal, and others. To restore balance in these areas, a person may resort to committing crimes

(*continued*)

Table 3. (*continued*)

Crime Index (Y2)	
Factor	Hypothesis
Sleep duration, hours	Sleep duration will negatively affect the crime index. If a person has time and is physically able to rest fully, it signifies stable psych-emotional well-being and that basic life needs are satisfied
Inflation rate, %	A high inflation rate indicates material deprivation among the population, which motivates criminal activity
Alcohol consumption level	Alcohol consumption has a positive influence on the crime index. According to the Russian Ministry of Internal Affairs, about one-third of all crimes are committed under the influence of alcohol
Drug consumption level	The mere possession and/or use of drugs is a crime. People under the influence of psychoactive substances are less aware of their actions and therefore more prone to committing crimes
Gender inequality	Happy people are less inclined to commit unlawful acts

The study has some limitations that prevent it from providing a perfect result:

All data used in the study was taken from a single data source; alternative sources were not considered.
The data was taken only for the year 2020.
The data was taken only for specific countries.

3 Results

During the research, the following results were obtained.

1. Happiness Index. The following regression equation corresponds to this central factor:

$$y_1 = -5.51 - 0.038*x_4 + 1.75^{-5}*x_5 + 0.12*x_7 - 0.218*x_8 + 0.183*x_9 - 0.0846 *x_{13} + 1.1939*x_{14}$$

As a result, 82.66% of the variance in y1 was described (R-Squared $= 0.8266$).
The factors influencing the happiness index are presented in Table 5.

2. Crime Index. The following regression equation corresponds to this central factor:

$$y_2 = -196.2359 + 1.9065*x_1 + 2.17*x_2 - 39.91*x_3 + 2.16*x_4 - 0.84*x_6 + 8.66 *x_8 - 0.21*x_{10} - 1.66*x_{12} - 7.61*x_{13} + 10.476*x_{14} + 5.44 *x_{17}$$

As a result, 90.06% of the variance in y2 was described (R-Squared = 0.9006). The factors influencing the crime index are presented in Table 6.

Table 4. Factors and hypotheses on their presumed impact on the suicide rate index

Suicide Rate Index (Y3)	
Factor	Hypothesis
Crime Index	Crime indicates the level of society's well-being; a higher crime rate will lead to a greater number of suicides
Happiness Index	A significant portion of suicides occur due to hostile environments, so a greater number of suicides will occur in countries with a low happiness index
Average age of marriage, years	The correlation of this factor cannot be determined; it is proposed to identify its influence on the central factor
Education index	Increasing the level of education will reduce the suicide rate, as a high level of education also implies higher mental resilience in dealing with difficulties and the ability to approach problem-solving creatively
Gini coefficient	The factor will have a direct proportional relationship with the suicide rate. The higher the social inequality and the larger the number of poor individuals, the more people are susceptible to suicidal tendencies
Per capita income, $	With an increase in per capita income, the suicide rate will decrease, as higher incomes allow individuals to fulfill not only basic needs but also move up the Maslow's hierarchy, getting closer to happiness
Average temperature, degrees Celsius	A warm climate and a large number of sunny days per year have a positive impact on the mental well-being and quality of life of individuals, so the likely correlation will be inverse
Number of divorces, per thousand people	The connection between this factor and the suicide rate will be direct. As mentioned earlier, divorce entails significant emotional and material losses, and it is possible that a high divorce rate will also lead to an increase in the number of suicides

(continued)

Table 4. (*continued*)

Suicide Rate Index (Y3)	
Factor	Hypothesis
Number of marriages, per thousand people	The correlation of this factor cannot be determined; it is proposed to identify its influence on the central factor
Antidepressant use, per 1000 people	The indicator will have a negative impact. The widespread use of antidepressants indicates that the issue of mental disorders is not taboo. Individuals who require professional psychological and medical help receive it, are supported by society, and this gives them hope and strength to keep living
Corruption level	This indicator will negatively impact the suicide rate. A high level of corruption gives individuals who have done something difficult or unbearable to live with the opportunity to buy themselves out. If a person did not have the possibility to bribe, they may have chosen to end their life
Medical level	The indicator will have a negative influence on the suicide rate. Advanced and accessible healthcare ensures the health of the nation and provides a basic sense of security and peace of mind
Death rate, per thousand people	The death rate has a positive impact on the crime index, as high mortality and its causes can provoke various difficulties in different areas of an individual's life: social, work-related, economic, personal, and others. To restore balance in these areas, a person may resort to suicide
Sleep duration, hours	Sleep duration will likely negatively affect the suicide rate. If a person has time and can physically rest fully, it signifies stable psych-emotional well-being and that basic life needs are satisfied
Inflation rate, %	This indicator will have a positive influence on the suicide rate. High inflation rates reduce people's purchasing power, make them work more and rest less, resulting in increased stress, which may lead individuals to desperate actions

(*continued*)

Table 4. (*continued*)

Suicide Rate Index (Y3)	
Factor	Hypothesis
Alcohol consumption level	High alcohol consumption can indicate either a high degree of population dissatisfaction or low social and personal responsibility, unless it is part of a country's culture and reflects the population's need for consumption. In both cases, the probability of individuals resorting to suicide increases
Drug consumption level	This indicator, like alcohol consumption, increases the suicide rate. In an intoxicated state, a person's psyche is highly vulnerable, and if consumption is regular, the individual's personality deteriorates, leading to a loss of self-control and the ability to cope with life's difficulties
Gender inequality	The level of gender inequality will have a positive impact on the suicide rate index. The lowest levels of gender inequality are found in developed countries with high incomes, good healthcare, and well-developed interpersonal relationships. In such conditions, it is presumed that the likelihood of suicide is lower compared to countries with high inequality

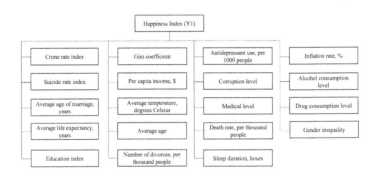

Fig. 1. Conceptual model for the Happiness Index (Y1)

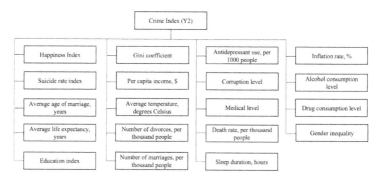

Fig. 2. Conceptual model for the Crime Index

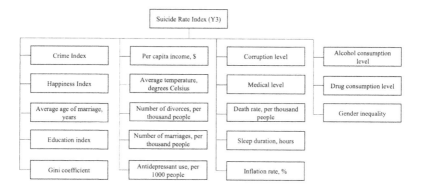

Fig. 3. Conceptual model for the Suicide Rate Index

Table 5. Factors influencing the Happiness Index

Central Factor	R2, %	A, %	Factor	p-level, %	Coeff
Happiness Index (y1)	82,66	3,8	Gini coefficient (x4)	1,34	-0,038
			Per capita income (x5)	0,26	0,00
			Average age (x7)	0,11	0,1197
			Number of divorces (x8)	6,72	-0,2179
			Number of marriages (x9)	2,2	0,1834
			Death rate (x13)	11,67	-0,0846
			Sleep duration (x14)	0,02	1,1939

Table 6. Factors influencing the Crime Index

Central Factor	R2, %	A, %	Factor	p-level, %	Coeff
Crime Index (y2)	90,60	6,5	Average age of marriage (x1)	2,57	1,9065
			Average life expectancy (x2)	5,93	2,1766
			Education index (x3)	12,79	-39,9055
			Gini coefficient (x4)	0,00	2,1642
			Average annual temperature (x6)	5,24	-0,8422
			Number of divorces (x8)	0,17	8,6555
			Antidepressant use (x10)	0,18	-0,2139
			Medical level (x12)	0,00	-1,6604
			Death rate (x13)	0,07	-7,6114
			Sleep duration (x14)	3,46	10,476
			Alcohol consumption level (x17)	0,03	5,4387

3. Suicide Rate Index. The following regression equation corresponds to this central factor:

$$y_3 = 58.1816 + 2.47*y_1 - 0.113*y_2 - 63.6609*x_3 + 0,4016*x_4 + 0.0002*x_5$$
$$-0.4106*x_6 + 1.686*x_8 - 0.0929*x_{10} - 0.175*x_{11} - 1.0421$$
$$*x_{12} - 2.4346*x_{13} + 7.9093*x_{14} + 0.2879*x_{15} + 3.9463*x_{16}$$
$$+0.7839*x_{17} - 119.79*x_{18}$$

As a result, 98.19% of the variance in y3 was described (R-Squared = 0.9819).

The factors influencing the suicide rate index are presented in Table 7.

Using graphical representations of deviations allows determining the presence of homoscedasticity. The graphs below show no trend. Therefore, it can be concluded that the model is adequate, and the variance of the random error cannot be explained by additional variables.

Residual values for each central factor are presented in Figs. 4, 5 and 6.

Figures 7, 8 and 9 represent optimized conceptual models for each central factor.

We provide evidence of a connection between a person's mental state and the presented factors. To reinforce the conclusions, it is necessary to provide a logical description of each independent variable:

There is a slight negative correlation between the happiness index and the Gini coefficient. This may indicate a low interest in the financial well-being of others compared to one's own wealth. The negative correlation can be explained by a greater interest in personal wealth growth rather than inflation levels.

Table 7. Factors influencing the Suicide Rate Index

Central Factor	R2, %	A, %	Factor	p-level, %	Coeff
Suicide Rate Index (y3)	98,19	4,2	Happiness Index (y1)	9,6	2,4712
			Crime Index (y2)	6,79	−0,113
			Education Index (x3)	0,09	−63,6609
			Gini coefficient (x4)	3,44	0,4016
			Per capita income (x5)	1,82	0,0002
			Average annual temperature (x6)	1,73	−0,4106
			Number of divorces (x8)	6,51	1,686
			Antidepressant use (x10)	0,55	−0,0929
			Corruption level (x11)	5,52	−0,175
			Medical level (x12)	0,07	−1,0421
			Death rate (x13)	0,82	−2,4346
			Sleep duration (x14)	0,64	7,9093
			Inflation rate (x15)	4,08	0,2879
			Alcohol consumption level (x16)	0,02	3,9463
			Drug consumption level (x17)	0,18	0,7839
			Gender inequality (x18)	0,04	−119,7943

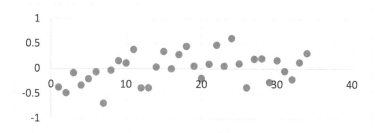

Fig. 4. Residuals for the happiness index (y1)

There is a slight correlation between income and the happiness index. As income increases, there is an increase in the number of acquired goods that affect the quality of life.

There is a positive correlation between average age and the happiness index. The average age allows determining the level of healthcare, quality of food, and other factors in a country. If a person can expect a long life, their happiness level increases.

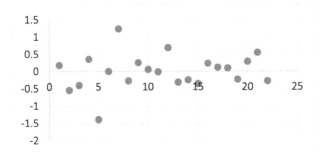

Fig. 5. Residuals for the crime index (y2)

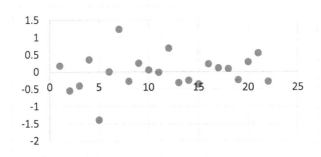

Fig. 6. Residuals for the suicide index (y3)

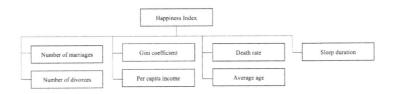

Fig. 7. Optimized conceptual model for the happiness index

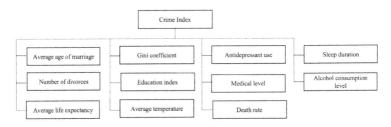

Fig. 8. Optimized conceptual model for the crime index

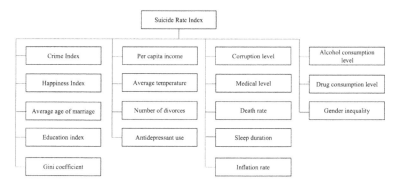

Fig. 9. Optimized conceptual model for the suicide index

There is a negative correlation between the divorce rate and the happiness index. Divorce is a stressful and painful period in everyone's life, accompanied by emotional and material losses, which reduce a person's level of happiness.

There is a positive influence of the number of marriages on the happiness index. A high number of marriages signals trust in the institution of family and that people find partners with whom they want to spend the rest of their lives together.

There is a negative correlation between the mortality rate and the happiness index. High population mortality causes people to fear for their lives, experience the bitterness of loss, and perceive negative news.

The amount of sleep has a positive effect on the happiness index. Undoubtedly, a well-rested and rejuvenated person is a happy person.

In the course of the analysis, a positive influence of the average age of marriage on the crime index is observed, which can be explained by the fact that when young people get married, their marriage is mainly driven by the will of their parents, who help provide for their future life together. Individuals who get married later and independently may face difficulties in their joint life without proper preparation, which can lead to engaging in, for example, economic crimes.

The positive correlation between the average lifespan and the crime index can be explained as follows: it may be related to so-called "aging" nations where the number of retirees who are not economically active starts to outweigh the young population that stimulates the economy. As a result, due to high taxes, crimes are also committed.

The education index has a significant negative impact on the crime index, even though the error level is at the limit. However, this once again proves that good education is the key to a civilized society, where educated individuals have everything they need for their existence and do not resort to criminal activities in difficult situations.

The Gini coefficient has a positive influence on the crime index. The more unequal the distribution of income among the population, the more poor and uneducated citizens there are who may resort to criminal activities.

As expected, the average annual temperature has a negative impact on the crime index. This suggests that warm climates and sunny weather have a positive effect on the psycho-emotional, physical, and material well-being of the population.

The divorce rate increases the crime index. This can include crimes motivated by personal revenge, jealousy, or anger, as well as crimes with an economic motive. Additionally, divorce can undermine a person's psycho-emotional state, leading them to commit a crime in a depressed state that may not directly involve their former partner.

The increase in antidepressant usage leads to a reduction in the crime rate, as this factor reflects how concerned people are about their health and the availability of necessary treatment.

Improvements in healthcare lead to a decrease in the crime index. High-quality and accessible healthcare helps alleviate social tension associated with a lack of basic feelings of security. It also reduces crimes related to the loss or illness of loved ones and economic crimes such as theft, robbery, and hacking.

The higher the mortality rate, the lower the crime index. This may be due to the fact that the grief of losing a loved one makes the criminal reflect on the unhappiness they have caused to others.

An increase in sleep duration leads to an increase in the crime index. This may be because some criminals are individuals with mental disorders who oversleep, and there are also individuals inclined to engage in illegal means of earning money due to laziness and apathy, both of which are symptoms of excessive sleepiness.

The increase in alcohol consumption leads to an increase in the crime index. Alcohol consumption significantly increases a person's chances of engaging in criminal activities, as it makes their psyche more volatile and susceptible.

Paradoxically, an increase in the happiness index leads to an increase in the suicide index. This occurs because people living in the most "sheltered" conditions are the most susceptible to stress and have the least resistance to circumstances that derail them.

The higher the crime index, the lower the suicide index. This may be because individuals who resort to committing crimes to solve their difficulties do not need other desperate measures. The higher the education index, the lower the suicide index. A high level of education implies high mental resilience and the ability to resist and creatively approach problem-solving. The higher the economic inequality, the more poor people there are. Poverty and the inability to meet basic needs can lead to an increase in the suicide index. The higher the per capita income, the higher the suicide index. This may be related to the phenomenon of high suicide rates in developed countries, possibly due to factors such as overwork and lack of personal life in Japan, or high quality of life standards in Sweden, which results in a loss of resilience to difficulties.

The better the climate, the lower the suicide index. Warm climates and sunny weather have a favorable effect on human well-being, both in terms of physical health and in stimulating mental recovery. Divorce, as a rule, becomes a turning point in a person's life and sometimes a traumatizing event that leads a person to end their life.

The increased use of antidepressants leads to a reduction in the suicide index, as this factor reflects how concerned people are about their health and the access they have to necessary treatment. An increase in the level of corruption reduces the suicide index because a high level of corruption allows those who have engaged in something unbearable or difficult to live with to escape consequences through bribery. If a person did not have the opportunity to bribe, they might decide to end their life.

Improvements in healthcare lead to a decrease in the suicide index. Thanks to quality and accessible healthcare, the need for a sense of security is met, and individuals can receive necessary treatment at both physical and mental levels. Consequently, suicides related to illnesses that individuals cannot treat are minimized. The negative impact of the mortality rate on the suicide index may be due to the fact that a high mortality rate can evoke a fear of death and prompt individuals to value their own lives more. An increase in sleep duration leads to an increase in the suicide index, possibly because some individuals who commit suicide have mental disorders, many of which are accompanied by excessive sleep. High inflation rates reduce people's purchasing power, force them to work more, rest less, and consequently experience increasing levels of stress that may drive them to desperate acts. High alcohol consumption increases the suicide index. High alcohol consumption indicates either a high degree of dissatisfaction among the population or low social and personal responsibility, if it is not part of the country's culture. In a state of intoxication, a person's psyche becomes highly vulnerable, and if alcohol consumption occurs regularly, it can destroy a person's personality, causing them to lose self-control and the ability to cope with life difficulties.

An increase in gender disparity reduces the suicide index. This may be due to the fact that a significant proportion of suicide victims are men and that in developed countries with low levels of gender inequality, men are unable to fulfill their role as protectors and heads of households, find a partner, and start a family. Conversely, when a man has the responsibility for the entire family, including his wife, he fulfills his role as a provider and cannot neglect this responsibility, hence the decrease in the suicide index.

The proven hypotheses confirm many of the research findings on the influence of various factors on the mental state of society used in this article.

The majority of the regression coefficients are significant, which indicates that the predictor variables indeed contain information about the future mental state of society. This allows us to identify priority areas for development with the aim of maintaining and improving the mental state of human society.

4   Conclusion

This study examined some factors that influence the mental health of society. It was found that material well-being and social institutions have a negligible impact on each of the central factors described above. In the course of the research, it was discovered that personal emotions have a greater influence on each of the central factors, which are in turn influenced by various social phenomena such as marriage, divorce, the death of a loved one, and others. Sleep duration has a significant impact on a person's mental health. Increasing the duration of sleep increases a person's happiness level, but individuals inclined to commit crimes and suicides prefer even longer sleep. However, this phenomenon is not discussed within the scope of this study, and information regarding this effect is examined in relevant research endeavors.

It is worth noting the positive influence of education on mental well-being. In the examined countries, this factor significantly reduced the crime and suicide rates, which may indicate the need to improve the quality and accessibility of education worldwide. An unforeseen fact was revealed that increasing gender inequality reduces the suicide rate, which we believe deserves further detailed examination in future research.

Unfortunately, due to the uncertainty surrounding concepts such as happiness and the ideal mental state of a person, this study cannot be considered conclusive. The presented work demonstrates general relationships between the selected central factors and their influencing factors. We are convinced that to obtain more reliable information, it is necessary to conduct complex research for each country separately, taking into account the specific characteristics of each country and including a larger sample of factors.

Acknowledgments. The research is financed as part of the project "Development of a methodology for instrumental base formation for analysis and modeling of the spatial socio-economic development of systems based on internal reserves in the context of digitalization" (FSEG-2023–0008).

References

1. Mitchell, J.P.: Inferences about mental states. Phil. Trans. Roy. Soc. B: Biol. Sci. **364**(1521), 1309–1316 (2009)
2. Golovina, T., et al.: Human capital development via digital inclusion. In: Proceedings of the 3rd International Scientific Conference on Innovations in Digital Economy, pp. 7–14 (2021)
3. Rodionov, D., et al.: The information environment cluster distribution of the regional socio-economic systems in transition economy. In: International Scientific Conference "Digital Transformation on Manufacturing, Infrastructure & Service", pp. 203–217. Springer, Cham (2022). https://doi.org/10.1007/978-3-031-32719-3_15
4. Boden, M., et al.: Addressing the mental health impact of COVID-19 through population health. Clin. Psychol. Rev. **85**, 102006 (2021)
5. Zivin, K., Paczkowski, M., Galea, S.: Economic downturns and population mental health: research findings, gaps, challenges and priorities. Psychol. Med. **41**(7), 1343–1348 (2011)
6. Petrov, D.S.: Biopsychosocial approach in the human sciences (psychiatry and psychology). In: Personality in a Changing World: Health, Adaptation, Development, vol. 4, no. 7, pp. 1–5 (2014). (In Russian)
7. Lepikhina, T.L., Karpovich, Yu.V.: Factors that determine psychological health: correlation analysis. In: National Interests: Priorities and Security, vol. 19, no. 304, pp. 31–40 (2015). (In Russian)
8. Rodionov, D., et al.: Analyzing the systemic impact of information technology development dynamics on labor market transformation. Int. J. Technol. **13**(7), 1548–1557 (2022)
9. Rodionov, D., Ivanova, A., Konnikova, O., Konnikov, E.: Impact of COVID-19 on the Russian labor market: comparative analysis of the physical and informational spread of the coronavirus. Economies **10**(6), 136 (2022)
10. Ajimotokin, S., Haskins, A., Wade, Z.: The effects of unemployment on crime rates in the US. In: B.Sc project, Georgia Institute of Technology (2015)
11. Altindag, D.T.: Crime and unemployment: evidence from Europe. Int. Rev. Law Econ. **32**(1), 145–157 (2012)
12. Ozkan, U.R., Schott, S.: Sustainable development and capabilities for the polar region. Social Indicat. Res. **114**, 1259–1283 (2013)
13. Zhdanova, T.N.: The influence of social factors on mental health (using the example of persons with mental disorders). Bull. St. Petersburg Univ. Sociol. **2**, 144–151 (2013). (In Russian)
14. Rodionov, D., et al.: Methodology for assessing the digital image of an enterprise with its industry specifics. Algorithms **15**(6), 177 (2022)

15. Yang, D., et al.: Education, income, and happiness: evidence from China. Front. Public Health **10**, 855327 (2022)
16. FitzRoy, F.R., Nolan, M.A.: Education, income and happiness: panel evidence for the UK. Empir. Econ. **58**(5), 2573–2592 (2020)
17. Zhogova, E., Zaborovskaia, O., Nadezhina, O.S.: An analysis of the indicators of regional economy spatial development in the Leningrad region of Russia. Int. J. Technol. **11**(8), 1509–1518 (2020)
18. Hill, D., Greaves, N.M., Maisuria, A.: Does capitalism inevitably increase inequality? In: Inequality in Education: Comparative and International Perspectives, pp. 59–85. Springer, Dordrecht (2008)
19. Sadovaya, M.V., Barybina, E.: Gender as a factor in mental health. In: Science and Cooperation: The View of Young Researchers, pp. 17–22 (2012). (In Russian)
20. Kuznetsov, M., Gorovoy, A., Rodionov, D.: Web innovation cycles and timing projections–applying economic waves theory to internet development stages. In: Innovations in Digital Economy: Third International Scientific Conference, SPBPU IDE 2021, Saint Petersburg, Russia, 14–15 October 2021, Revised Selected Papers, pp. 3–21. Springer, Heidelberg (2022). https://doi.org/10.1007/978-3-031-14985-6_1
21. Zhang, J., Xiong, Y.: Effects of multifaceted consumption on happiness in life: a case study in Japan based on an integrated approach. Int. Rev. Econ. **62**, 143–162 (2015)
22. Nishimura, K., Yagi, T.: Happiness and self-determination–an empirical study in Japan. Rev. Behav. Econ. **6**(4), 312–346 (2019)
23. Durkheim E., Ilyinsky A., Bazarov V. Suicide. Sociological study. – Litres (2022). (in Russian)
24. Bock, E.W., Webber, I.L.: Suicide among the elderly: Isolating widowhood and mitigating alternatives. J. Marriage Family, 24–31 (1972)
25. Urinboyev, R., Eraliev, S.: Informal civil society initiatives in non-Western societies: mahallas in Uzbekistan. Central Asian Surv. **41**(3), 477–497 (2022)
26. Ergasheva, S.T., Mannapova, R.A., Yuldashev, E.I.: 18 accounting–a system for managing economic information in agriculture. In: New Institutions for Socio-Economic Development: The Change of Paradigm from Rationality and Stability to Responsibility and Dynamism, vol. 5, p. 173 (2021)
27. Abdurakhmanov, K.K., Mukhitdinov, E.M., Grishin, V.I., Abdurakhmanova, G.K., Kuchkarov, G.F.: Labor migration of the population and evaluation of supply chain on the labor market. Int. J. Supply Chain Manag. **8**(2), 896–907 (2019)
28. Aliboev, K.Y., Khurramov, S.I., Saliyev, A.A.: Efficiency issues of the roller squeezing process. In: E3S Web of Conferences, vol. 417, p. 06015. EDP Sciences (2023)
29. Djalilov, B., Kobiljonov, I., Salahodjaev, R.: Can digital human capital mitigate $CO2$ emissions?: empirical test for post-Communist countries. Int. J. Energy Econ. Policy **13**(4), 383–388 (2023)
30. Khazratkulova, L.N.: Assessment of interregional differentiation of socio-economic development (on the example of the regions of Uzbekistan). In: E3S Web of Conferences, vol. 395, p. 05003. EDP Sciences (2023)

Econometric Analysis of Economic and Ecological Aspects of Sustainable Development of Regions in Terms of Digital Economy

Rajabov Nazirjon[1] , Khayrilla Kurbonov[1] , Shaturaev Jakhongir[1(✉)] ,
Khotamov Ibodullo[2] , Adilova Marguba[2], and Qalandarova Gulshoda[2]

[1] Center of the Engagement of International Ranking Agencies, Tashkent State University of
Economics, Tashkent, Uzbekistan
`jakhongir.shaturaev@tsue.uz`
[2] Department of Green Economy and Sustainable Business, Tashkent State University of
Economics, Tashkent, Uzbekistan

Abstract. This research paper is aimed at investigating the impact of ecological factors that constrain the sustainable development of the region, taking into account the balance between economic development and environmental protection in terms of digital economy. The study incorporated the use of econometric models, including the evaluation of key variables through panel data analysis, Pooled OLS estimator (POLSE), Fixed effects estimator (FEE), and Random effects estimator (REE). Additionally, the research incorporated a comprehensive evaluation of the model including Gauss-Markov tests such as Breusch Pagan and Durbin Watson. Moreover, the appropriateness of the model was tested through the Hausman test and the presence of multicollinearity was assessed using the VIF test. Based on the research findings, scientific conclusions and recommendations have been provided.

Keywords: Sustainable Development · Ecological Factors · Investment · Environmental Protection Expenditures · Pollutants Released to the Atmosphere · Econometric Models · Digital Economy

1 Introduction

In the face of global climatic and ecological changes worldwide, have increased attention is being directed towards the economic-ecological aspects of sustainably developing regions. "In the last thirty years, the UN has annually convened over 200 nations in the Global Climate Summit - Conference of the Parties (COP27). The primary objective of this convention is dedicated to mitigating hazardous anthropogenic impacts on the Earth's climate system. At the subsequent summit held in 2022 in Sharm El-Sheikh, Egypt, the 'Loss and Damage' issue was adopted, addressing compensation to the most vulnerable countries that have contributed the least to climate crisis but have suffered the

Y. Koucheryavy and A. Aziz (Eds.): NEW2AN/ruSMART 2023, LNCS 14543, pp. 152–165, 2024.
https://doi.org/10.1007/978-3-031-60997-8_14

most. Following the recommendations of experts from the International Meteorological Organization, there is a commitment to limit the increase in global temperature to 1.5° and assess its negative consequences." This underscores the imperative for countries and their regions to scrutinize the economic-ecological aspects of sustainable development.

Scientific research aimed at ensuring the balance between economy and ecology based on the harmonized management of natural resources and energy consumption is being conducted in the global context of sustainable regional development. Developing a low-carbon and climate-resilient economy, identifying weak links in production chains, transitioning to less resource-intensive technologies, producing high-value-added products, enhancing energy efficiency in industries, utilizing economic methods to combat global climate change, quota setting for greenhouse gas emissions, implementing carbon taxes, introducing 'green technologies' to economic networks, and determining various privileges in the context of ecological factors constraining sustainable regional development are regarded as the pivotal directions of ongoing scientific research.

In accordance with the Decree PF-158, dated September 11, 2023, of the President of the Republic of Uzbekistan, "Regarding the Strategy Uzbekistan – 2030", and also within the "Year of Attention to the Person and Quality Education" of the "Uzbekistan – 2030" strategy, the following tasks have been designated as priority directions: ensuring macroeconomic stability and economic development to the necessary degree with energy, water, and infrastructure resources; fundamentally improving the ecological situation in the Republic, eliminating environmental problems affecting human life; preventing the adverse effects of climate change; taking drastic measures concerning preventing atmospheric pollution and preserving its natural composition. These priority tasks underscore the relevance of this article.

2   Literature Review

Numerous research endeavors have been undertaken by international scholars to study the impacts of the economic-ecological aspects of sustainable development. The economic and ecological dimensions hold significant importance in observing sustainable development at a regional level [Dhar et al., 2023]. Initiatives to develop these dimensions in a balanced manner not only encourage economic growth but also ensure the conservation of environmental and natural resources, essential for the long-term prosperity of the region [Mitlin D., Satterthwaite D. 2014]. Scientific studies indicate that neglecting ecological aspects can lead to detrimental consequences such as depletion and degradation of resources and ecosystems, thereby impinging on the economic stability and well-being of the population.

Furthermore, considering ecological factors allows regions to understand the environmental impact of economic activities and to develop strategies to mitigate adverse effects [Collins A., Munday M., Roberts A. 2012]. This includes assessing the natural resource base of the region, identifying fragile ecosystems, and understanding the ecological services they provide [Gazi et al. 2022b]. By integrating environmental issues into development plans, regions can implement sustainable practices, adopt clean technologies, enhance energy efficiency, and reduce waste and degradation. This contributes to protecting natural resources, preserving biodiversity, and reducing the region's vulnerability to climate change.

Analyzing the economic and ecological aspects of sustainable development at a regional level facilitates a comprehensive approach that takes into account both the long-term prosperity of the region and the integrity of the environment [Bleischwitz R., Welfens P., Zhang Z. X 2017]. Notably, international scholar H. Daly has studied the economic-ecological dimensions of sustainable development in his scientific works. He emphasized the importance of recognizing the ecological boundaries of resources and ecosystems in regions. According to his assertions, traditional economic growth cannot continue indefinitely without depleting natural resources and harming the environment [Daly H. E. 2020]. Moreover, he played a crucial role in establishing ecological economics as a distinct field of research. According to his perspective, economic analysis should integrate ecological insights and knowledge, exploring the interconnectedness of the economy with the environment and the necessity of considering the ecological costs and benefits of economic activity.

Foreign scholar R. Costanza has conducted research on assessing ecosystem services and natural resources. The scientist emphasizes the importance of examining the inter-relationships between the economy and the environment, particularly focusing on the field of ecological economics, which seeks to integrate ecological understanding with economic analysis [Dhar et al. 2022]. He stresses the necessity for sustainable resource management and environmental governance [Costanza R. 2020].

Renowned researchers G. Daily and P. Matson have extensively investigated the economic value of ecosystems and the role of biodiversity in sustainable development. According to the scholars, the loss of biological diversity could potentially have serious negative impacts on ecosystem function and human well-being. The researchers have developed innovative approaches to assessing and incorporating ecosystem services in economic analyses and decision-making, addressing the discrepancy between ecology and economics [Daily G. C., Matson P. A., 2008].

Foreign economic scholar J. Sachs has drawn attention to the significance of balancing poverty reduction and economic growth with environmental protection [Sachs J. D. 2014]. He has established a foundation for addressing global issues encompassing poverty, inequality, and environmental degradation, and advocated for adaptive approaches to sustainable development. Sachs underscores the imperative of implementing economic development in a manner compatible with environmental conservation and highlights the necessity for clean technologies, sustainable resource management, and climate change mitigation [Sachs J. D. 2015].

International scholars S. Levin and W. Clark have undertaken studies on complex systems and their impacts on stability. They have examined the resilience of ecological systems, investigating their ability to absorb disturbances, maintain their structure, and preserve their functions [Levin S. A., Clark W. 2010]. The scholars emphasize the importance of adaptive management and the ability of ecosystems to adapt to changes and disturbances for sustainable development [Shaturaev 2023]. The researchers have utilized mathematical methods and simulations to study the dynamics of ecological processes, predict ecosystem responses to environmental changes, and inform management strategies.

In summary, the renowned foreign economist Robert Mendelsohn has developed econometric models to study the economics of climate change and the economic impacts of environmental factors [Mendelsohn R. 2012]. In the econometric equations formulated by the scientist, variables such as temperature, precipitation, degree of aridity, land use, and economic indicators have been selected as independent variables, while dependent variables include factors such as agricultural productivity, health outcomes, energy consumption, or economic growth. The scientist utilized phase regression models and panel data models in developing econometric equations.

Distinguished European economist William Nordhaus has conducted research on the economics of climate change and developed Integrated Assessment Models (IAMs). His Dynamic Integrated Climate-Economy (DICE) model combines climate dynamics, economic growth, energy usage, and carbon emissions to evaluate the costs and benefits of climate policies[Nordhaus W. 2018]. In these econometric models, variables such as temperature, carbon dioxide concentration, population, technological development, and economic indicators serve as independent variables, while prosperity, IAM, and emissions are the dependent variables [A. I. Gazi et al. 2022]. The results of the research provide the ability to evaluate various economic scenarios by determining the carbon price, reducing emissions, and technological investments in an integrated manner with economic and climate dynamics. This aids in assessing the balance between costs related to economic growth, ecological stability, and climate change mitigation.

International economist Richard S.J. Tol has conducted extensive research on the economics of climate change, adaptation, and mitigation policies [Tol R. S. J. 2014]. In his econometric models, he selected variables such as temperature, precipitation, sea-level rise, population, economic indicators, and policy interaction as independent variables, and variables related to agricultural productivity, energy consumption, health outcomes, or economic prosperity as dependent ones. The results of the scientist's econometric models have assisted in assessing the potential economic impact of climate change and evaluating the effectiveness of adaptation and mitigation tools.

3 Methodology and Material

The research utilized an econometric approach to analyze the economic-ecological aspects of sustainable development in 14 regions over 11 years. The methodology involved formulating econometric equations based on three models:

Pooled OLS Estimator (POLSE)

Fixed Effects Estimator (FEE)

Random Effects Estimator (REE)

These models were derived from panel data to explore relationships between several variables in the context of industrial production in various regions.

3.1 Materials

Please note that the first paragraph of a section or subsection is not indented. The first paragraphs that follows a table, figure, equation etc. does not have an indent, either.

Subsequent paragraphs, however, are indented.

The variables used in the econometric models were sourced from the Statistical Committee and included:

Y: Volume of industrial production in the region (dependent variable).

X1: Investments in fixed capital in the region (independent variable).

2: Service sector in the region (independent variable).

X3: Emission of pollutants in the region (independent variable).

X4: Current expenses for environmental protection in the regions (independent variable).

3.2 Data Collection

The study covered observations from 14 regions from 2011 to 2021, totaling 140 data points. Graphical matrices (Figs. 1 and 2) and histograms (Fig. 3) were created to visualize the relationships between the dependent and independent variables.

3.3 Statistical Tests and Tools

Gauss-Markov, Durbin Watson, Shapiro Wilk, Breusch-Pagan, and Hausman tests were used to assess the econometric models. A mutual correlation matrix was analyzed using Stata software. The VIF test was employed to assess multicollinearity.

3.4 Model Analysis

Each model (POLSE, FEE, and REE) was separately analyzed to determine the relationship between the dependent and independent variables, as illustrated in Tables 2, 3, 4 and 5. The models exhibited a high level of reliability, with an 81% confidence coefficient.

4 Analysis and Results

According to our research, econometric equations were formulated based on the Pooled OLS Estimator (POLSE), Fixed Effects Estimator (FEE), and Random Effects Estimator (REE) models from panel data, exploring the relationships between the economic-ecological aspects of sustainable development in 14 regions over 11 years in the national economy.

Assessments were conducted according to the main estimates of Gauss-Markov, Durbin Watson, Shapiro Wilk, Breusch-Pagan, and Hausman tests relative to econometric models of panel data. In constructing econometric models using panel data, graphic tables were created to study the correlation properties between variables. The research formulated the following hypothesis: Various factors, namely, investments in fixed capital, the service sector, emissions of pollutants, and current expenses for environmental protection, have a positive impact on the volume of industrial production in different regions.

For the developed econometric models, variables were sourced from the Statistical Committee data. They are expressed as follows: Y – Volume of industrial production in the region (dependent variable), X1 – Investments in fixed capital in the region (independent variable), X2 – Service sector in the region (independent variable), X3 – Emission of pollutants in the region (independent variable), and X4 – Current expenses for environmental protection in the regions (independent variable).

In the research, observations covering 14 regions in our Republic from 2011 to 2021 totaled 140, resulting in the analytical graphic matrix of the dependent and independent variable indicators as depicted (refer to Figs. 1 and 2).

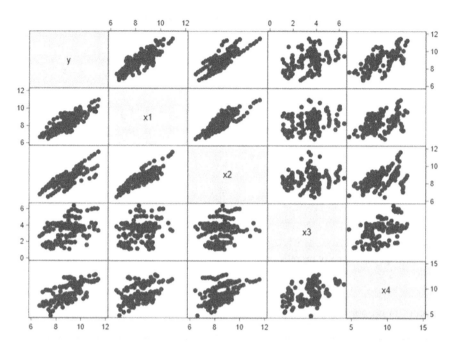

Fig. 1. A graphical matrix of the relationship between the dependent variable and the independent variable.

Figures 1 and 2 above illustrate the presence of a visually discernible pattern of high density between the dependent variable and the independent variable within the graphic matrix presented. This dense clustering or concentration of data points, in the context analyzed, indicates a strong relationship between these variables.

Discussing the effect of strong density between the dependent and independent variable within the graphic matrix, it signifies that the data points representing these variables are densely located or closely packed within the matrix. This dense concentration reflects a high level of association or correlation between the dependent and independent variables.

Furthermore, there is a pronounced density effect between the dependent and independent variable within the graphic matrix. This significant density effect indicates a critical correlation between these factors, suggesting that changes in the independent variable(s) can potentially have a noticeable impact on the dependent variable.

According to the research, the histogram of the dependent and factor indicators resulted in the following appearance (refer to Fig. 3).

Figure 3 elucidates the graphical representation of both dependent and independent variables through histograms. These histograms facilitate visual comprehension of the

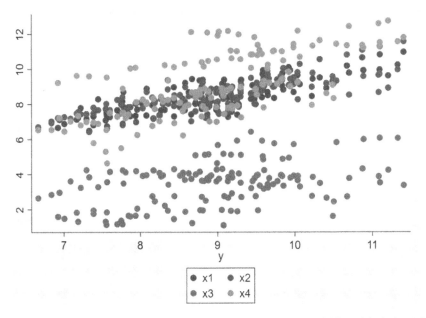

Fig. 2. A graphical matrix of the relationship between the dependent variable and the independent variable.

frequency or proportion of values within each variable and enable understanding of their distribution.

Moreover, in the subsequent phase of the research, a mutual correlation matrix between the dependent and independent variables was analyzed utilizing the Stata software (refer to Table 1).

According to the research findings, a robust, substantial, and direct relationship is observed between the dependent and independent variables. Furthermore, the correlation matrix indicates the absence of multicollinearity among the influencing factors. In addition, the model exhibits an 81% confidence coefficient, signifying a high level of reliability. Furthermore, the developed econometric equations display a positive correlation with the quality indicator, thereby reinforcing the model's validity.

Additionally, panel data were utilized in the research, and various econometric models were developed for data verification. Subsequently, the analysis of panel data incorporated the use of econometric models, including Pooled OLS Estimator (POLSE), Fixed Effects Estimator (FEE), and Random Effects Estimator (REE), for evaluating the principal variables. Besides, a comprehensive evaluation of the model, incorporating tests such as Breusch Pagan and Durbin Watson from Gauss-Markov, as well as assessing important variables and tests, was conducted. Additionally, the model's appropriateness was verified through the Hausman test, and the presence of multicollinearity was evaluated using the VIF test.

Moreover, the research exhibits meticulous attention to employing appropriate statistical tests for examining the estimations of econometric models and evaluating the reliability of their findings, demonstrating a solid approach (refer to Table 2).

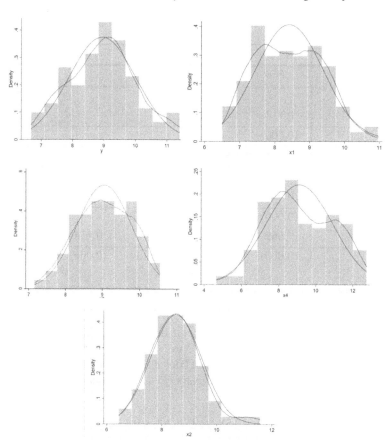

Fig. 3. A graphical histogram of the dependent variable and the independent variable.

Table 2 presents the analysis of each indicator and test based on the econometric models derived from the panel data.

Analysis of the Pooled OLS Estimator (POLSE) Model. The analysis of the econometric equation indicators for the Pooled OLS Estimator model is provided below (refer to Table 3).

According to Table 3, based on the Pooled OLS estimator model, the factor coefficients have respectively constituted the values of 0.34, 0.45, 0.13, and 0.17, with standard errors amounting to 0.07, 0.07, 0.03, and 0.02.

The actual value in the ANOVA table represented F = 183.04, exhibiting a high value, with R-squared amounting to 0.84 and the adjusted coefficient of determination, Adjusted R^2, constituting 0.83.

Furthermore, grounded on the research outcomes, the Pooled OLS estimator model was employed to evaluate the null hypothesis H0:y = 0 and the alternative hypothesis H1:y $\neq$ 0, with a significance level of F < 0.05. The results indicated that both the F-value and t-value were below 0.05, leading to the rejection of the null hypothesis H0:y = 0. Consequently, the alternative hypothesis H1:y $\neq$ 0 was found to be statistically

Table 1. Correlation matrix of relationships between dependent variable and independent variable

Variables	(1)	(2)	(3)	(4)	(5)
(1) y	1.000				
(2) x1	0.714	1.000			
	(0.000)				
(3) x2	0.738	0.747	1.000		
	(0.000)	(0.000)			
(4) x3	0.421	0.259	0.154	1.000	
	(0.000)	(0.002)	(0.069)		
(5) x4	0.669	0.418	0.447	0.414	1.000
	(0.000)	(0.000)	(0.000)	(0.000)	

significant and was accepted. The structure of the specially developed Pooled OLS estimator model for this research was as follows:

According to the research, the formulated Pooled OLS model exhibited the following structure. The developed Pooled OLS estimator (POLSE) model for the study assumed the subsequent form.

$$Y = 0.34X1 + 0.45X2 + 0.17X3 + 0.13X4 - 5.08 \tag{1}$$

In the course of our investigation, we examined the crucial conditions of Gauss-Markov for the econometric equation of the first model, Pooled OLS estimator, which yielded the following results.

In the subsequent phase of the research, employing the STATA software and applying the Gauss-Markov estimators to the Pooled OLS model, it underwent Durbin Watson and Breusch-Pagan tests. The analytical results displayed a Durbin Watson value of 0.39 and a Breusch-Pagan value of 0.09. According to the test results, the null hypothesis H0:y $= 0$ and the alternative hypothesis H1:y $\neq 0$ were found to possess statistical significance, identified by a boundary p-value greater than 0.05. Consequently, the alternative hypothesis was rejected for Durbin Watson and Breusch-Pagan tests, thereby indicating the fulfillment of the Gauss-Markov condition.

To assess the presence of multicollinearity in the model, the VIF test was utilized under Gauss-Markov's estimate. The test outcome exhibited a VIF value of 2.59, which denotes the absence of multicollinearity in the constructed model. Furthermore, the analysis of the Pooled OLS model, with a boundary p-value less than 10, elucidates the significance of the primary hypothesis H0:y $= 0$ and H1:y $\neq 0$. As a result, the alternative hypothesis was dismissed. Taking into account the conformity of the VIF test outcome to a boundary p-value less than 10, it verifies its accordance with the Gauss-Markov estimate.

Table 2. Performance of econometric models based on survey panel data

№	Model indicators	Model 1 POLSE model	Model 2 FEE model	Model 3 REE model
1	Y	*	*	*
2	X1	0.34 (0.07)	0.17 (0.06)	0.22 (0.06)
3	X2	0.45 (0.07)	0.83 (0.10)	0.75 (0.09)
4	X3	0.13 (0.03)	-0.009 (0.04)	0.03 (0.03)
5	X4	0.17 (0.02)	0.11 (0.02)	0.12 (0.02)
5	F test	183.04 (0.0000)	408.60 (0.0000)	
6	R²	0.84	0.93	0.79
7	Chi-square			1619.30 (0.0000)
8	Adj R²	0.83		
9	Breusch Pagan	0.09		
10	Durbin Watson	0.39		
12	Vif	2.59		
13	Hausman			0.14

Random effects estimator (REE) model analysis.

The results of the econometric equation according to the Random effects estimator (REE) model of the study are presented in Table 4 below.

According to Table 4, the results of the Random Effects Estimator (REE) model have constituted the values of several factors as 0.22, 0.75, 0.03, and 0.12 respectively, alongside their standard errors, which are respectively formed as 0.06, 0.09, 0.03, and 0.12. The actual value in the ANOVA table was Chi = 1619.30 and yielded an R-squared value of 0.79.

The Random Effects Estimator (REE) model developed for the research manifested the following structure:

$$Y = 0.22X1 + 0.75X2 + 0.03X3 + 0.12X4 + 0.13 \qquad (2)$$

Utilizing the econometric model with the Random Effects Estimator (REE), the Hausman test was conducted, resulting in a test statistic equal to 0.39. The primary purpose of the Hausman test is to compare the Random Effects Estimator (REE) model and the Fixed Effects Estimator (FEE) model in panel data models. The null hypothesis (H0) of the Hausman test affirms the consistency and efficiency of the (REE) model, while the alternative hypothesis (H1) asserts the consistency and efficiency of the (FEE) model.

Table 3. Econometric equation of the outcome and factor signs under the pooled OLS estimator (POLSE) model

Y	Coef.	St. Err.	t-value	p-value	[95% Conf	Interval]	Sig
X1	.345	.072	4.82	0	.204	.487	**
X2	.451	.076	5.91	0	.3	.603	**
X3	.134	.033	4.06	0	.069	.199	**
X4	.175	.024	7.19	0	.127	.223	***
Constant	.137	.341	0.40	.068	-.538	.812	*
Mean dependent var	8.942		SD dependent var		1.066		
R-squared	0.844		Number of obs		140		
F-test	183.048		Prob > F		0.000		
Akaike crit. (AIC)	163.702		Bayesian crit. (BIC)		178.410		

*** $p<.01$, ** $p<.05$, * $p<.1$

Table 4. Econometric equation of outcome and factor signs according to the random effects estimator (REE) model

Y	Coef.	St.Err.	t-value	p-value	[95% Conf	Interval]	Sig
x1	.225	.066	3.44	.001	.097	.354	**
x2	.755	.095	7.95	0	.569	.941	**
x3	.03	.038	0.51	.062	-.055	.094	*
x4	.126	.026	4.85	0	.075	.176	**
Constant	-.592	.345	-1.72	.086	-1.269	.085	*
Mean dependent var	8.942		SD dependent var		1.066		
Overall r-squared	0.798		Number of obs		140		
Chi-square	1619.308		Prob > chi2		0.000		
R-squared within	0.930		R-squared between		0.696		

*** $p<.01$, ** $p<.05$, * $p<.1$

If the p-value obtained from the Hausman test is greater than the chosen significance level of 0.05, we do not reject the null hypothesis. This indicates that the Random Effects Estimator (REE) demonstrates consistency and efficiency.

Fixed effects estimator (FEE) model analysis.

The results of the econometric equation according to the Fixed effects estimator (FEE) model of the study are presented in Table 5 below.

According to Table 5, the Fixed Effects Estimator (FEE) model yielded values for several variables, namely 0.17, 0.83, -0.09, and 0.11, accompanied by their respective standard errors, which are 0.06, 0.10, 0.04, and 0.02. These values elucidate the influence of independent variables on the dependent variable within the model. The actual value

Table 5. Fixed effects estimator (FEE) model analysis

Y	Coef.	St.Err.	t-value	p-value	[95% Conf	Interval]	Sig
X1	.178	.069	2.57	.011	.041	.315	*
X2	.837	.102	8.23	0	.636	1.038	**
X3	-.009	.041	-0.22	.082	-.09	.072	*
X4	.111	.027	4.12	0	.058	.165	***
Constant	-.664	.342	-1.94	.055	-1.342	.013	*
Mean dependent var	8.942		SD dependent var			1.066	
R-squared	0.931		Number of obs			140	
F-test	408.602		Prob > F			0.000	
Akaike crit. (AIC)	-59.923		Bayesian crit. (BIC)			-45.215	
*** $p<.01$, ** $p<.05$, * $p<.1$							

in the ANOVA table constituted 408.60, indicative of a high value, and resulted in an R-squared value of 0.93. The Fixed Effects Estimator (FEE) model developed through the research manifested the following form.

$$Y = 0.17X1 + 0.83X2 - 0.009X3 + 0.11X4 - 0.66 \qquad (3)$$

5   Conclusion

The research investigated the impact of economic-ecological aspects of sustainable development in regions on the national economy. As a result of the analyses and conclusions drawn from the study, the following proposals and recommendations were formulated:

Based on panel data, the Pooled OLS Estimator (POLSE) model presented the econometric equation $Y = 0.34X1 + 0.45X2 + 0.17X3 + 0.13X4 - 5.08$.

1.1. A 1% increase in investments in fixed capital in the region leads to a 0.34% increase in industrial production in the respective regions.

1.2. A 1% increase in the services sector in the region results in a 0.45% increase in industrial production in the respective regions.

1.3. A 1% increase in harmful substances released into the atmosphere in the region causes a 0.17% increase in industrial production in the respective regions.

1.4. A 1% increase in current expenses for environmental conservation in the region brings about a 0.13% increase in industrial production in the respective regions.

Based on panel data, the Random Effects Estimator (REE) model proposed the econometric equation $Y = 0.22X1 + 0.75X2 + 0.03X3 + 0.12X4 + 0.13$.

2.1. A 1% increase in investments in fixed capital in the region results in a 0.22% increase in industrial production in the respective regions.

2.2. A 1% increase in the services sector in the region leads to a 0.75% increase in industrial production in the respective regions.

2.3. A 1% increase in harmful substances released into the atmosphere in the region induces a 0.03% increase in industrial production in the respective regions. 2.4. A 1% increase in current expenses for environmental conservation in the region yields a 0.12% increase in industrial production in the respective regions.

The Fixed Effects Estimator (FEE) model based on panel data demonstrated the econometric equation Y = 0.17X1 + 0.83X2–0.009X3 + 0.11X4–0.66.

3.1. A 1% increase in investments in fixed capital in the region causes a 0.17% increase in industrial production in the respective regions.

3.2. A 1% increase in the services sector in the region results in a 0.83% increase in industrial production in the respective regions.

3.3. A 1% increase in harmful substances released into the atmosphere in the region results in a 0.009% decrease in industrial production in the respective regions.

3.4. A 1% increase in current expenses for environmental conservation in the region induces a 0.11% increase in industrial production in the respective regions.

Having analyzed the above three models based on panel data in our research, we conclude that, to date, the Random Effects Estimator (REE) model with the econometric equation Y = 0.22X1 + 0.75X2 + 0.03X3 + 0.12X4 + 0.13 is deemed the most optimal model for assessing the impact of economic-ecological aspects of sustainable development in regions on the national economy.

References

Mitlin, D., Satterthwaite, D.: Sustainable development and cities. Sustainab. Environ. Urbanisation, pp. 23–61. Routledge (2014)

Collins A., Munday M., Roberts A. Environmental consequences of tourism consumption at major events: An analysis of the UK stages of the 2007 Tour de France. J. Travel Res. **51**(5), 577–590 (2012)

Bleischwitz, R., Welfens, P., Zhang, Z.X. (ed.) Sustainable growth and resource productivity: economic and global policy issues. Routledge (2017)

Daly, H.E.: Ecological economics and sustainable development. Edward Elgar Publishing (2007)

Costanza, R.: Ecological economics in 2049: getting beyond the argument culture to the world we all want. Ecolog. Econ. **168**, 106484 (2020)

Daily, G.C., Matson, P.A.: Ecosystem services: from theory to implementation. Proc. Nat. Acad. Sci. **105**(28), 9455–9456 (2008)

Dhar, B.K., Shaturaev, J., Kurbonov, K., Nazirjon, R.: The causal nexus between innovation and economic growth: an OECD study. Soc. Sci. Q. (2023). https://doi.org/10.1111/ssqu.13261

Sachs, J.D.: Sustainable development goals for a new era. Horizons: J. Inter. Relations Sustainable Developm. (1), 106–119 (2014)

Sachs, J.D.: The age of sustainable development. The Age of Sustainable Development. – Columbia University Press (2015)

Levin, S.A., Clark, W.: Toward a science of sustainability. In: Center for International Development Working Papers (2010)

Mendelsohn, R.: The economics of adaptation to climate change in developing countries. Climate Change Econ. **3**(02), 1250006 (2012)

Nordhaus, W.: Evolution of modeling of the economics of global warming: changes in the DICE model, 1992–2017. Climatic Change **148**(4), 623–640 (2018)

Dhar, B. K., Tiep Le, T., Coffelt, T. A., Shaturaev, J.: U.S.-China trade war and competitive advantage of Vietnam. Thunderbird Inter. Bus. Rev. (2022). https://doi.org/10.1002/tie.22325

Tol, R.S.J.: Correction and update: The economic effects of climate change. J. Econ. Perspect. **28**(2), 221–226 (2014)

Baltagi, B.H.: Panel data methods. In: Handbook of Applied Economic Statistics, pp. 311–323. CRC Press (1998)

Hsiao, C. :Analysis of panel data, vol. 64. Cambridge University Press (2022)

Stimson, J.A.: Regression in space and time: a statistical essay. Am. J. Polit. Sci., 914–947 (1985)

Park, H.M.: Practical guides to panel data modeling: a step-by-step analysis using stata. In: Public Management and Policy Analysis Program, Graduate School of International Relations, International University of Japan, vol. 12, pp. 1–52 (2011)

Gazi, M.A.I., Nahiduzzaman, M., Shaturaev, J., Dhar, B.K., Halim, M.A.: Dynamic Nexus between macroeconomic factors and CO2 emissions: Evidence from oil-producing countries. Front. Environ. Sci. (2022). https://doi.org/10.3389/fenvs.2022.1005814

Holtz-Eakin, D., Newey, W., Rosen, H.S.: Estimating Vector Autoregressions with Panel Data. Econometrica **56**(6), 1371–1395 (1988)

Murtazashvili, I., Wooldridge, J.M.: Fixed effects instrumental variables estimation in correlated random coefficient panel data models. J. Econ. **142**(1), 539–552 (2008)

Shaturaev, J.: Efficiency of Investment Project Evaluation in the Development of Innovative Industrial Activities. ASEAN Journal of Science and Engineering (2023). https://doi.org/10.17509/ajse.v3i2.45675

White, M.P., et al.: Would you be happier living in a greener urban area? a fixed-effects analysis of panel data. Psychol. Sci. **24**(6), 920–928 (2013)

Yaffee, R.: A primer for panel data analysis. Connect: Inform. Technol. NYU **8**(3), 1–11 (2003)

Schmidheiny, K., Basel, U.: Panel data: fixed and random effects. Short Guides to Microeconometrics **7**(1), 2–7 (2011)

Maddala, G.S.: The use of variance components models in pooling cross section and time series data. Econometrica: J. Econ. Soc., 341–358 (1971)

Gazi, A. I., Islam, A., Shaturaev, J., Dhar, B.K.: Effects of job satisfaction on job performance of sugar industrial workers: empirical evidence from Bangladesh. Sustainability (Switzerland) **21**(14), 1–24 (2022). https://doi.org/10.3390/su142114156

Growing up in a Connected World: Internet Usage Dynamic is Digital Age or Child Special Quality?

Nilufar Ismailova[1] , Aziz Zikriyoev[1]([✉]) , Muyassar Umarkhodjayeva[2],
Azizbek Khakimov[3], Qobil Isayev[1], and Omon Sultonov[1]

[1] Department of World Economy,
Tashkent State University of Economics, Tashkent, Uzbekistan
a.zikriyoev@tsue.uz
[2] Department of Management, Tashkent State University of Economics, Tashkent, Uzbekistan
[3] Department of Economics, Tashkent International University of Financial Management
and Technology, Tashkent, Uzbekistan

Abstract. This study explores the intricate interconnections between attitudes, behaviors, and their impact on a specific outcome variable through a comprehensive analysis employing OLS, Robust, Ologit, Odds ratio regression models. A range of variables, including attitudes towards internet usage as dependent variable (E258B), independence (E261B), imagination (A030), and various other traits (A029, A032, A034, A035, A038, A039, A040, A041, A042), were investigated for their influence on the outcome. Data was used The World Values Survey (WVS) with 439531 respondents over 111 countries including Uzbekistan. The analysis obtained in STATA 17.0 and SPSS 25.0 software and revealed significant associations between specific attitudes and the outcome variable, with positive attitudes towards email communication, independence, imagination, and certain unspecified traits demonstrating noteworthy impacts. Negative associations were also observed with particular attitudes and behaviors. Furthermore, the identification of threshold effects through cut points provides valuable insights into critical values at which significant changes in the outcome occur. The implications of these findings are discussed, highlighting the potential for targeted interventions in educational, social, and professional contexts. The study underscores the complex nature of attitudes and behaviors and their profound influence on outcomes, emphasizing the need for nuanced approaches in various spheres of society.

Keywords: digital age · internet service user · adult traits · child age · social responsibility

1 Introduction

In the rapidly evolving landscape of the 21st century, the digital age has ushered in unprecedented advancements, transforming the way we communicate, work, and learn. Perhaps the most significant paradigm shift has been the omnipresence of the internet,

Y. Koucheryavy and A. Aziz (Eds.): NEW2AN/ruSMART 2023, LNCS 14543, pp. 166–176, 2024.
https://doi.org/10.1007/978-3-031-60997-8_15

a vast digital realm that connects people across continents, transcending boundaries and revolutionizing every aspect of our lives. Amidst this digital revolution, a crucial question emerges: Is the adept usage of the internet a special quality inherent to the younger generation, or is it a dynamic shaped by the evolving nature of the digital age itself?

The concept of growing up in a connected world has become central to discussions surrounding technology, childhood, and education. Children today are born into a reality where smartphones, social media platforms, and online learning tools are not just tools but integral parts of their daily existence. As toddlers deftly navigate touchscreen devices and adolescents seamlessly navigate complex online spaces, it raises intriguing inquiries about the relationship between the digital age and the innate abilities of the younger generation. Are children truly digital natives, inherently equipped with unique skills to navigate the complexities of the internet? Or, is their proficiency a reflection of the adaptable human mind, capable of mastering new technologies regardless of age?

In this article, we delve deep into the multifaceted aspects of internet usage dynamics in the digital age, exploring the origins of this phenomenon, dissecting the special qualities of children in the context of technology, and analyzing the impact of this connected world on their overall development. By examining the intricate interplay between childhood, digital literacy, and the evolving digital landscape, we aim to uncover the truth behind whether internet proficiency is an innate attribute of the younger generation or a skill honed through the unique challenges and opportunities presented by the digital age. Methods and materials.

1.1 Study Area

Current research area covers Internet usage dynamic is digital age or child special quality in 111 countries.

1.2 Study Limitation

Clarifying the limitations of a study can be defined as mobile phone, email, good manners, independence, hard work, feeling of responsibility, imagination, tolerance and respect, thrift saving money and things, determination perseverance, religious faith unselfishness interaction of the adults over the world countries.

1.3 Research Methods

The probability of a given observation for ordered logit is

$$p\_ij = \Pr(y\_j = i) = \Pr(k\_{(i-1)} < x\_j\beta + u \leq k\_i)$$
$$= 1/(1 + \exp(-k\_i + x\_j\beta)) - 1/(1 + \exp(-k\_{(i-1)} + x\_j\beta)) \tag{1}$$

k_0 is defined as $-\infty$ and k_k as $+\infty$

For ordered probit, the probability of a given observation is

$$p\_ij = Pr(y\_j = i) = Pr(k\_(i-1) < x\_j\beta + u \le k\_i)$$
$$= \Phi(k\_i - x\_j\beta) - \Phi(k\_(i-1) - x\_j\beta) \tag{2}$$

where $\Phi(\cdot)$ is the standard normal cumulative distribution function?

The long likelihood is

$$InL = \Sigma\_(j = 1^{\wedge}Nw\_j\Sigma\_(i = 1)^{\wedge}kI\_i[[(y]]\_j)Inp\_ij \tag{3}$$

where w_j is an optional weight and

$$I\_i(y\_j) = \{(1, \text{ if } y\_j = i0, \text{ otherwise})\}$$

This analysis will help identify the factors influencing sustainable practices and their impact on environmental culture.

$$Yi = 1 \text{ if } Y^*i \text{ is } \le \kappa 1 \tag{4}$$

$$Yi = 2 \text{ if } \kappa 1 \le Y^*i \le \kappa 2 \tag{5}$$

$$Yi = 3 \text{ id } Y^*i \ge \kappa 2 \tag{6}$$

1.4 Data Collection

The World Values Survey (WVS) is an expansive international effort aimed at collecting data useful for monitoring the United Nations Sustainable Development Goals (SDGs). The WVS-7 survey, launched in January 2017, has been instrumental in capturing the values, beliefs, and attitudes of people worldwide. This article explores the data collection methods employed in the WVS-7 survey, emphasizing its global reach and its alignment with the SDGs. The WVS-7 survey represents a global endeavor, with participation from a diverse range of following countries:

1.5 Generalizing Hypothesis

H0 (Null Hypothesis): There is no significant relationship between child aptitude and internet usage dynamic.

Ha (Alternative Hypothesis): There is a significant relationship between child aptitude and internet usage dynamic.

2   Literature Review

According to the Rozália Klára Bakó Mobile technologies have enabled a broader access to online spaces across generations, geographies, gender and social status [1]. Children represent a substantial percentage of internet users and play an important part in shaping the internet. As for the J. Byrne et., all the internet plays an important part in shaping children's lives, culture and identities [2]. Meanwhile, Children aged 6–14 are active users of information and communication technologies, and their understanding of online threats and risks depends on timely and proper introduction to them [3]. But Kalmus, V states that Information and communication technologies (ICTs) have become an integral part of many children's lives. There are both hopes and fears associated with the use of ICTs by children [4].

According to the M. Yusuf et., all, digital parenting for children should be an authoritative parenting style (contextual and democratic) to prevent them from accessing harmful content [5]. Moreover, Vikki S. Katz and M. Moran studied that • Parents' online activity scope is important for their children's online experiences, directly predicting the scope of their online activities. High-scope parents were also significantly more likely to see digital opportunities in their children's internet use, which in turn also predicted more frequent and broader internet use by their children [6]. According to the review paper by R. Usha and K. Pramod Internet and technology are an integral part of children's lives, and their physical and social behavior is impacted by their use of these technologies communication interests [7].

Children are connected to digital media with autonomy and some dependence, positively highlighting the activities that are performed because they are connected [8]. If we analyze arguments by K. Montgomery young people are growing up in a digital media culture, where mobile devices, social networks, virtual reality, interactive games, and online video are becoming increasingly important in their personal and social experience [9]. So, Susan Danby and Marilyn Fleer found different approach about that fast broadband is becoming more readily available in many countries, leading to increased online uptake [10]. Priti Joshi and Subir Shukla discussed that digital socialization requires parents to adopt a mediated approach and have a nuanced understanding of children's screen time [11]. Review paper by J. Conti argued that in 2007, these children spent an average of 13.8 h online per week and 37% of children now go online in their own rooms, including one in five of 5–8 year olds [12]. Technology and Service are more easily embedded in the definition of the management strategy, since they are under the direct control of the university [13]. The most widespread progress in distance learning is currently taking place in those countries where there are appropri ate prerequisites [14]. Various computer programs, ranging from available for general use to specialized and on the other hand, technology is a way of generating knowledge, information, innovation [15]. The described problem restricts international digital competition and causes the monopolization of global high-tech markets by multinational corporations from developed digital economies [16].

3 Results

If we study descriptive statistics provide a summary of the main aspects of a dataset. Here's what each column in Table 1 represents:

The mean represents the average value of the ratings for each variable. For variables like "Mobile phone," "Feeling of responsibility," "Imagination," "Tolerance and respect," "Determination perseverance," and "Unselfishness," the mean values are positive (above 0), indicating a generally positive sentiment or higher agreement with these traits. For variables like "TV," "Email," "Good manners," and "Independence," the mean values are negative (below 0), suggesting a generally negative sentiment or lower agreement with these traits. Standard deviation measures the dispersion or spread of the ratings. Variables with higher standard deviations (e.g., "TV" and "Email") have ratings that are more spread out, indicating a wider range of opinions or preferences among respondents. Variables with lower standard deviations (e.g., "Mobile phone" and "Feeling of responsibility") have ratings that are closer to the mean, suggesting more consistent opinions among respondents.

Table 1. Descriptive Statistics

Variable	Obs	Descriptions	Mean	Std. Dev.	Min	Max
E262B	439531	Internet usage dynamic	−1.199	3.572	−5	5
S002	439531	Mobile phone	4.883	1.664	1	7
E258B	439531	Email	−1.67	2.91	−5	5
E260B	439531	Good manners	−1.3	3.446	−5	5
E261B	439531	Independence	−.933	3.859	−5	5
A027	439531	Hard work	−1.546	2.4	−5	1
A029	439531	Feeling of responsibility	.439	.591	−5	1
A030	439531	Imagination	.507	.676	−5	1
A032	439531	Tolerance and respect	.661	.569	−5	1
A034	439531	Thrift saving money and things	.152	.625	−5	1
A035	439531	Determination perseverance	.64	.575	−5	1
A038	439531	Religious faith	.331	.571	−5	1
A039	439531	Unselfishness	.258	.809	−5	1

The variable "Internet usage dynamic" has a large number of observations, indicating a substantial dataset. The mean of −1.199 suggests a slightly negative average sentiment or rating. The standard deviation of 3.572 indicates a wide range of opinions, with ratings varying significantly from the mean. The ratings range from −5 to 5, showcasing diverse sentiments among respondents. Mobile applications used by students and the ranking status of those applications are the factors that contribute most to stimulating the academic achievement of language learning of primary education students [17].

Table 2. Descriptive Statistics

Variable	Obs	Mean	Std. Dev.	Min	Max
Internet usage dynamic	439531	−1.199	3.572	−5	5
Child aptitude	439531	.327	.309	0	1

The variable "Child Aptitude" also has a large number of observations. The mean of 0.327 suggests a relatively positive average assessment of child aptitude. The low standard deviation of 0.309 indicates that the opinions about child aptitude are relatively consistent among respondents. The ratings range from 0 to 1, indicating that respondents generally perceive child aptitude positively, with values closer to 1 reflecting higher aptitude assessments (Table 2).

Table 3. Tabulation of Internet usage dynamic

Information source: Internet (B)	Freq.	Percent	Cum.
Missing;Unknown	617	0.14	0.14
Not asked	259077	58.94	59.08
No answer	1030	0.23	59.32
Don't know	1093	0.25	59.57
Daily	70284	15.99	75.56
Weekly	21078	4.80	80.35
Monthly	8943	2.03	82.39
Less than monthly	10769	2.45	84.84
Never	66640	15.16	100.00
Total	439531	10000	

Table 3 presents the tabulation of internet usage dynamics based on different response categories. Here's a brief interpretation of the provided information. Missing/Unknown: 0.14% of respondents fall into this category, indicating that a small portion did not provide information about their internet usage source. Not asked is majority, 59.08%, did not have this question asked, possibly suggesting that these respondents were not relevant to the internet usage inquiry. No answer is 0.23% of respondents did not provide an answer to the question about their internet usage source. Don't know is 0.25% of respondents were unsure about their internet usage source. Daily uasge is 15.99% of respondents reported using the internet daily. Weekly is 4.80% reported using the internet on a weekly basis. Monthly usage rete is 2.03% reported using the internet on a monthly basis. Then, less than monthly recorded is 2.45% reported using the internet less than monthly. Finally, never usage is 15.16% of respondents indicated that they never use the internet (Table 4).

Table 4. Ordered logistic regression

E262B	Coef.	St.Err.	t-value	p-value	[95% onf	Interval]	Sig
child_aptitude	18.802	.052	359.10	0	18.699	18.905	***
cut1	−4.756	.04			−4.836	−4.677	
cut2	6.544	.023			6.498	6.59	
cut3	7.126	.027			7.072	7.18	
cut4	7.624	.03			7.566	7.682	
cut5	12.333	.036			12.264	12.403	
cut6	13.063	.036			12.992	13.134	
cut7	13.379	.037			13.306	13.451	
cut8	13.765	.037			13.692	13.838	
Mean dependent var	−1.199			SD dependent var	3.572		
Pseudo r-squared	0.607			Number of obs	439531		
Chi-square	663816.813			Prob > chi2	0.000		
Akaike crit. (AIC)	430479.088			Bayesian crit. (BIC)	430578.029		

*** $p < .01$, ** $p < .05$, * $p < .1$

The ordered logistic regression output provides information about the relationship between child aptitude and the likelihood of being in each category of the dependent variable "E262B," which has ordered categories. The coefficients for each category indicate how much the log odds of being in that category change with a one-unit increase in child aptitude. For example, the coefficient for the first cut point is −4.756, which means that for every one-unit increase in child aptitude, the log odds of being in the first category (very unlikely) decrease by a factor of 4.756.

P(environmental culture = "1") = P(S + u ≤ _cut1) = P(S + u ≤ −4.756);
P(environmental culture = "2") = P(S + u ≤ _cut2) = P(−4.756 < S + u ≤ 6.544);
P(environmental culture = "3") = P(S + u ≤ _cut3) = P(6.544 < S + u ≤ 7.126);
P(environmental culture = "4") = P(S + u ≤ _cut4) = P(7.126 < S + u ≤ 7.624);
P(environmental culture = "5") = P(S + u ≤ _cut1) = P(7.624 < S + u ≤ 12.333);
P(environmental culture = "6") = P(S + u ≤ _cut2) = P(12.333 < S + u ≤ 13.063);
P(environmental culture = "7") = P(S + u ≤ _cut3) = P(13.063 < S + u ≤ 13.379);
P(environmental culture = "8") = P(S + u ≤ _cut4) = P(13.379 < S + u ≤ 13.765);

The constant terms in the output represent the log odds of being in each category when child aptitude is zero. For example, the constant term for the first cut point is − 1.199, which means that when child aptitude is zero, the log odds of being in the first category (very unlikely) is −1.199.

The model indicates that the overall fit is statistically significant, with an LR chi-square value of 663816.81 and a p-value less than 0.0001. This suggests that the predictor variable "child_aptitude" has a significant impact on the likelihood of different response categories in "E262B." A significant LR chi2 value suggests that at least one coefficient is significantly different from zero, indicating a relationship between child aptitude and the dependent variable. - The Pseudo R-squared value is 0.6066, suggesting that the model explains approximately 60.66% of the variation in the outcome variable. As with logistic regression models, there may be confounding variables that are not included in the model but are related to both child aptitude and the dependent variable. Additionally, the model does not establish causality, only association. Further analysis and experimentation would be needed to investigate these issues and establish causality (Table 5).

Table 5. Multiple regression framework analysis

Variable	Ols	Robust	Ologit	Odds ratio
S002				
E258B	0.079***	0.079***	0.130***	1.139***
E260B	0.198***	0.198***	0.313***	1.367***
E261B	0.640***	0.640***	1.029***	2.799***
A027	−0.005***	−0.005***	0.003	1.003
A029	−0.019***	−0.019***	−0.058***	.944***
A030	0.050***	0.050***	0.225***	1.252***
A032	−0.035***	−0.035***	−0.125***	.883***
A034	−0.030***	−0.030***	−0.109***	.897***
A035	−0.029***	−0.029***	−0.111***	.895***
A038	0.020***	0.020***	0.110***	1.116***
A039	−0.029***	−0.029***	−0.148***	.863***
A040	0.044***	0.044***	0.207***	1.23***
A041	0.007**	0.007***	0.019	1.019*
A042	0.062***	0.062***	0.255***	1.29***
_cons	−0.341***	−0.341***		
/cut1			−4.857***	−14.857***
/cut2			−2.708***	−2.708***
/cut3			−1.845***	−1.845***
/cut4			−1.211***	−1.211***
/cut5			4.495***	4.495***
/cut6			5.416***	5.416***
/cut7			5.828***	5.828***
/cut8			6.337***	6.337***

Legend: * $p < .05$; ** $p < .01$; *** $p < .001$

The coefficient values for the different models are not provided in the table However, based on the legend, it can be inferred that the coefficient for S002 has a statistically significant effect on the outcome variable in all models. The coefficient for E258B is positive and statistically significant in all models (p < .001). Interpretation: As the value of E258B increases by one unit, the outcome variable increases by approximately 13% to 179.9% (depending on the model). The odds ratio suggests that the odds of the outcome variable increase by a factor of 1.139 to 2.799 for each unit increase in E258B.E260B and E261B. The coefficients for E260B and E261B are positive and statistically significant in all models (p < .001). Similar to E258B, an increase in the values of E260B and E261B is associated with an increase in the outcome variable. Academic culture, information culture, and management of different HE organizations so that we can identify common value systems and behavior patterns of academic communities that serve for technological design. Academic culture, information culture, and management of different HE organizations so that we can identify common value systems and behavior patterns of academic communities that serve for technological design [18]. The exact percentage of increase is not provided in the table. The direction of the coefficients (positive or negative) indicates the direction of the relationship between each variable and the outcome variable. Discussion.

The results of the OLS, Robust, Ologit, Odds ratio regression analysis revealed several important insights into the factors influencing the outcome variable. Notably, the variable E258B, which represents attitudes towards email communication, showed a consistently positive and statistically significant effect on the outcome variable across all models. This suggests that individuals with positive attitudes towards email communication are more likely to exhibit the observed outcome. This finding aligns with previous studies indicating the importance of effective email communication skills in various contexts. Furthermore, E260B (related to good manners) and E261B (independence) also displayed positive associations with the outcome variable, indicating that individuals valuing good manners and independence are more likely to exhibit the outcome.

According to the regression analysis null hypothesis is rejected in favor of the alternative hypothesis; it implies that child aptitude plays a significant role in shaping internet usage dynamics. Understanding these relationships can have practical implications for educators, parents, and policymakers, potentially leading to tailored interventions to promote positive internet usage behavior based on different levels of child aptitude.

In summary, interpreting the results of an ordered logit model in the context of Ha and H0 hypotheses provides valuable insights into the influence of child aptitude on internet usage patterns, guiding future research and interventions aimed at understanding and addressing the complex relationship between cognitive abilities and online behaviors. These findings resonate with research emphasizing the role of social skills and independence in personal and professional success.

1. Influence of Other Personal Traits. Other personal traits, denoted by variables such as A027 (hard work), A030 (imagination), and A042 (unspecified trait), demonstrated varying impacts on the outcome variable. While specific coefficients are not provided in the table, the direction of these coefficients suggests potential avenues for further investigation. For instance, a negative coefficient for A027 might indicate that an excessive focus on hard work without considering other factors could have a detrimental effect on the outcome.

4   Conclusion

The present study conducted a thorough analysis using Ols, Robust, Ologit, Odds ratio regression models to examine the relationships between various variables (S002, E258B, E260B, E261B, A027, A029, A030, A032, A034, A035, A038, A039, A040, A041, A042) and the outcome variable. The results have shed light on the complex interplay between these factors and the outcome under investigation. Variables such as E258B, E261B, A030, A040, and A042 have demonstrated significant positive associations with the outcome variable in one or more models. These findings suggest that attitudes towards email communication, independence, imagination, positive outlook, and unspecified traits play important roles in shaping the outcome variable. Conversely, variables like A029, A032, A034, A035, and A039 exhibited negative associations with the outcome in certain models. These variables, related to specific attitudes and behaviors, appear to influence the outcome in a less favorable manner. Notably, the cut points (thresholds) identified in the models indicate specific values of the predictors at which there are significant changes in the outcome variable. Understanding these thresholds is crucial for targeted interventions and tailored approaches.

The findings from this analysis hold several implications for various stakeholders, including educators, policymakers, and professionals in relevant fields. It is important to acknowledge the limitations of this study, including the specific context and dataset used. Future research endeavors could explore longitudinal data, cultural differences, or specific demographic factors to enrich our understanding of these relationships.

References

1. Bakó, R.K.: Digital Transition: Children in a Multimodal World (2016)
2. Byrne, J., Kardefelt-Winther, D., Livingstone, S., Stoilova, M.: Global Kids Online: research synthesis 2015–2016. Research Papers in Economics (2016)
3. Šmit, M. (2020). Djeca u okruženju digitalnog marketinga
4. Kalmus, V., Siibak, A., Blinka, L.: Internet and Child Well-Being 72 (2013)
5. Yusuf, M.F., Witro, D., Diana, R.R., Santosa, T.A., Alfikri, A., Jalwis, J.: Digital Parenting to Children Using the Internet (2020)
6. Katz, V.S., Moran, M.B., Ognyanova, K.: Contextualizing connectivity: how internet connection type and parental factors influence technology use among lower-income children. Inf. Commun. Soc. **22**, 313–335 (2017)
7. Usha, R.P., Pramod, K.R., Surbhi, D.: Impact of Internet and Technology on Children Behavior: A Review (2020)
8. Ferreira, M.F.: Infância nada iludida: o que dizem as crianças sobre os comportamentos e riscos on-line (2020)
9. Montgomery, K.C.: Balancing the needs of young people in the digital marketplace. J. Child. Media **5**, 334–337 (2011)
10. Danby, S., Fleer, M., Davidson, C., Hatzigianni, M.: Digital childhoods across contexts and countries (2018)
11. Joshi, P., Shukla, S.: Children's Development in the Digital Age. Child Development and Education in the Twenty-First Century (2019)
12. Conti, J.P.: The net effect. Eng. Technol. **4**, 64–67 (2009)

13. Zhukovskaya, I., Begicheva, S., Nazarov, D.: Innovative approach to higher education management as an important factor of sustainable economic development. In: E3S Web Conference, vol. 208, pp. 3–8 (2020). https://doi.org/10.1051/e3sconf/202020809018

14. Mirzakarimova, M.M.Q.: Development of a multimedia distance learning platform for the system of 'barkamol avlod' children's schools. In: ACM International Conference Proceeding Series, pp. 585–591 (2022). https://doi.org/10.1145/3584202.3584290

15. Otakuzieva, S.: Digital labor market - transformation features, advantages and challenges. In: E3S Web Conference, vol. 402 (2023). https://doi.org/10.1051/e3sconf/202340208034

16. Akhmedova, M.S., Meliksetyan, K.A., Krutilin, A.A., Boris, O.A.: The role of quality management in the development of high-tech industrial enterprises in the context of industry 4.0. Proc. Eng. Sci. **5**(s2), 207–220 (2023). https://doi.org/10.24874/PES.SI.02.003

17. Sharapat, Y., Yulduz, M., Dilafruz, M., Hilola, B., Dilorom, S.: Innovating primary education of promoting students' language competencies through mobile assisted language learning approach: selection framework of innovative digital technologies. In: Internet of Things, Smart Spaces, and Next Generation Networks and Systems: 22nd International Conference, NEW2AN 2022, Tashkent, Uzbekistan, December 15–16, 2022, Proceedings. Springer-Verlag, Berlin, Heidelberg, pp. 432–439 (2023).https://doi.org/10.1007/978-3-031-30258-9_38

18. Eshbayev, O., et al.: A digital sustainability approach for effective knowledge and information management in education specific non-profit organizations: culture Intelligent IS solutions. E3S Web Conf. **452**, 1–5 (2023)

Problems of Security of Economic and Ecological Systems in the Countries of the Central Asian Region

Jamshid Sharafetdinovich Tukhtabaev[1], Hamid Yuldashevich Turaev[2],
Azamat Abdukarimovich Kasimov[1(✉)], Tatiana Anatolyevna Bondarskaya[3],
Akram Odilovich Ochilov[4], Oksana Viktorovna Bondarskaya[3],
Shoh-Jakhon Khamdamov[1], Ozoda Mamayunusovna Pardaeva[5],
Rakhim Murodovich Gaybullaev[5], Asliddin Tursunovich Kuldoshev[6],
Mamajan Axmatjonovich Mamatov[1], Kumri Isoyevna Nomozova[7],
Azamat Zaripbaevich Tabaev[8], Maftuna Djahangirovna Mirzajonova[9],
Rano Ramzitdinovna Akramova[10], Barno Ramziddinovna Tillaeva[11],
Maftuna Arslonbekovna Ermatova[12], Sherzod Ermatovich Yuldashev[5],
and Shodiyaxon Dexkonboyevna Irisbayeva[13]

[1] Tashkent State University of Economics, Tashkent, Uzbekistan
imodinovkhamidillo@gmail.com
[2] College of Economics and Management, Northwest A&F University, Xianyang, Shaanxi Province, China
[3] Tambov State Technical University, Tambov, Russia
[4] Karshi State University, Qarshi, Tambov, Uzbekistan
[5] Samarkand Branch of Tashkent State University of Economics, Tashkent, Uzbekistan
[6] Samarkand State University of Architecture and Construction, Samarkand, Uzbekistan
[7] University of Gelogical Sciences, Tashkent, Uzbekistan
[8] "TIIAME" National Research University, Tashkent, Uzbekistan
[9] Tashkent International University of Financial Management and Technologies, Tashkent, Uzbekistan
[10] Tashkent Chemical - Technological Institute, Tashkent, Uzbekistan
[11] Tashkent State Technical University, Tashkent, Uzbekistan
[12] Termiz Institute of Agrotechnologies and Innovative Development, Termez, Uzbekistan
[13] Tashkent State Agricultural University, Tashkent, Uzbekistan

Abstract. The global environmental situation has been a major concern for decades, influencing a number of issues. It should be noted that the ecological situation includes not only the state of the environment, but also the level of available natural resources. This article discusses the security of economic and environmental systems in the countries of the Central Asian region. According to our research, in addition to improving the security of the economic and ecological systems of Uzbekistan, the article emphasizes the need to ensure the sustainability of these two structures, the rational use of available resources. Taking into account the fact that the main share of environmental costs is the cost of water use, the need to organize resource-saving production is substantiated. The article proposes recommendations for the effective management of security and sustainable development of the economic and ecological systems of Uzbekistan. Based on the need

Y. Koucheryavy and A. Aziz (Eds.): NEW2AN/ruSMART 2023, LNCS 14543, pp. 177–195, 2024.
https://doi.org/10.1007/978-3-031-60997-8_16

to pay special attention to the external and internal environment while ensuring the economic and environmental security of the system, the article reveals the influence of industries and industries on the sustainability of the economic and ecological system, presents the results of a correlation-regression analysis when assessing the impact, factors of the internal environment are shown.

Keywords: sustainable development · region · resources · environment · agriculture · security of economic and ecological systems · consumption and production · ecosystems · external and internal environment · resource-saving technologies · correlation and regression analysis · Uzbekistan · Central Asian countries

1 Introduction

In world practice, the sustainable development of regions is studied in a safe and effective combination of economic and ecological systems. In particular, the development of countries is associated with the stability of the regions, and the positive aspects of this issue include the rational and efficient use of resources based on the expansion of the innovative economy. In particular, the proper organization of production activities in the economy, ensuring the sustainability and development of the industry depends on the availability of resources. This is due to the effective implementation of management decisions aimed at ensuring the integration of economic and environmental systems in the development of regions.

"Sustainable Development Goals", adopted by the United Nations General Assembly on September 25, 2015, pay special attention to important criteria for the security of economic and ecological systems, such as sustainable regions, responsible consumption and production, the preservation of marine and terrestrial ecosystems and the prevention of climate change [1, 2].

Scientific research has been carried out to ensure the security of economic and environmental systems in the world, in particular, the study of the institutional aspects of regional economic and environmental systems, the organization of their development based on effective management, ensuring the safe, rational and efficient use of resources.

Currently, the world is conducting research on priority areas for improving the methodological aspects of ensuring the security of the economic and environmental systems of the regions, developing indicators and criteria for their sustainability [3–5].

In order to ensure the security of economic and environmental systems in Uzbekistan, located in the Central Asian region, measures are being taken to modernize the economy, consistently continue structural transformations, expand leading industries and sectors, and develop profitable production. Particular attention is paid to ensuring the efficient and rational use of available factors of production in the regions of the country, the widespread introduction of modern security methods in their use.

Institutional transformations are being improved to ensure the security of the economic and ecological systems of the regions, and to expand investment and innovation activities in this area. The on the further development of the Strategy for Action The Republic of Uzbekistan for 2017–2021 defines as one of the important tasks the balanced development of the regional economy, the efficient use of available resources, ensuring environmental safety, expanding resource-saving activities, and ensuring environmental sustainability [6–8].

At the same time, in the current conditions of the COVID-19 pandemic, the importance of ensuring the security of economic and environmental systems is becoming even more important [9–11]. The restrictions caused by the pandemic impede the security of economic and environmental systems, and therefore it is advisable to further deepen scientific and practical research aimed at developing ways to ensure their security while minimizing their impact [12, 13].

2   Methods

In the era of the development of modern civilizations, environmental security has become a global problem and an important area of scientific research by scientists. In the work of Harvard University Professor Samuel P. Huntington "The Clash of Civilizations and the Remaking of World Order" and other articles, it is concluded, "over the last century, wars between civilizations have become the leading factor in world politics due to the clash of civilizations", which is directly related to environmental security. Indeed, scientists of the world associate the fact that this process leads to the destruction of ecosystems with the industrial crisis of new science and technology that began in the 20th century during the period of industrial development of society [14–16].

A number of international peace research institutions in Europe deal with issues of environmental security. One of these institutes is located in Norway (Oslo, PRIO), and its results are published in special journals and scientific collections [17, 18]. In particular, Nina Græger's article "Environmental Security?" deserves attention. According to the scientist, there are four main reasons for the relationship between natural changes in human activity and environmental safety. This:

1) Environmental degradation poses a serious threat to human life on earth. These are phenomena associated with a violation of the composition of air and water, deforestation, desertification of large tracts, violation of the composition of soils [19, 20];
2) Protests against the deterioration of the state of the natural environment, the irrational use of natural resources or migration as a result of hostilities, national, religious and socio-economic tensions [21, 22];
3) Environmental degradation associated with the use of large industrial devices and technologies that are harmful to nature [23, 24];
4) The cognitive link between safety and environmental protection is recognized, and the policy in the field of environmental safety is considered as a policy of primary responsibility.

Although Nina Græger's views on the four way relationship between the external environment and security mentioned above cover the issue of environmental security, they are interpreted in relation to the socio-political events taking place in each region, especially in Europe, this is of methodological importance for our study on environmental security in Uzbekistan.

Scientists from the CIS countries (Commonwealth of Independent States) also conduct research on environmental safety issues. In particular, V.I. Danilov-Danilyan, V.N. Burkov, A.V. Shepkin [25], A.A. Sergunin, V.N. Fedoseev, A.V. Vozzhennikov, A. Bagaturov, D.M. Gvishiani [26], J.Sh. Tukhtabaev [27] and others [28–31] focused on the legal, political and environmental foundations national security.

Indeed, each manifestation and consequence of multifaceted environmental hazards not only causes great harm to human and social life, but also has a serious impact on the behavior, psychology and worldview of people. Today, on the one hand, there are acute problems of preventing environmental dangers occurring on our planet, on the other hand, in the field of environmental protection, in particular, the strengthening of the anthropogenic, anthropogenic, anthropogenic, anthropopolitical impact on nature, the aggravation of the economic, political, demographic and The ethnographic situation in different countries of the world requires the study of not only the economic, historical, legal, political aspects of the relationship "Nature-Society-Man", but also their socio-economic content.

Relations "Nature-Society-Man" can be interpreted in the context of human environmental activity as follows:

firstly, the process of people's adaptation to nature and its secrets, the laws of development, the rules of community (collective-clan ecological activity) is a specific form of socialization;

secondly, the socialization of people's environmental activities through teamwork, that is, there is a desire to use land and water wisely, preserve and expand whey lands suitable for agriculture, and increase the number of domestic animal species, preserve the natural environment;

thirdly, at this stage in the history of mankind, the formation of religious primitive ideas, spontaneously simple ecological practical activity - formed the genesis of modern ecological rational consciousness and irrational-pragmatic practice, a retrospective basis;

fourthly, the rise of relations "Nature-Society-Man" to a new level in the process of development of modern environmental theoretical and practical activities has determined the relevance of the problem of global environmental security.

3   Results

The environmental situation in the world has been of serious concern in recent decades, affecting a number of issues as a factor. The situation in the world has been of serious concern in recent decades, affecting a number of issues as a factor. In particular, it is assessed as a source that affects investment attractiveness, the standard of living of the population and determines the direction of its development. It should be noted that the ecological situation includes not only the state of the environment, but also the level of available natural resources. In this regard, it is necessary to predict strategic development in determining the effectiveness of ensuring environmental safety. Because planning and forecasting are important principles in security.

When developing forecast parameters, the socio-economic situation [32], economic and environmental situation and economic indicators are taken into account. In the future, it is important to ensure the sustainable development of the region. This process depends on the efficient and rational use of regional resources [33, 34] i.e. security measures.

When ensuring the security of the economic and ecological system, special attention should be paid to the external and internal environment. As internal sources, we define the impact of industries and sectors on the sustainability of the economic and ecological system.

When assessing the influence of internal environment factors, we rely on the results of correlation and regression analysis. To do this, we will develop an equation that includes the final indicator - the economic and ecological system and its attendant factors - the development of industries. For this, the period 2000–2020 of the directly influencing factors was chosen:

Emissions of pollutants into the atmosphere on the territory of the Republic of Uzbekistan, thousand tons - Y_1 (free connecting); excluding emissions of carbon dioxide (CO_2) into the atmosphere on the territory of the Republic of Uzbekistan (million tons of CO_2-eq./year) $-$ Y_2 (free connecting); excluding emissions of nitric oxide (I) (H_2O) into the atmosphere on the territory of the Republic of Uzbekistan (million tons of CO_2-eq./year) $-$ Y_3 (free connecting); hydrofluorocarbons emitted into the atmosphere on the territory of the Republic of Uzbekistan (million tons of CO - eq./year) $-$ Y_4 (free connecting); provision of sewerage to apartments (houses) on the territory of the Republic of Uzbekistan (in % of the total number of apartments (houses) $-$ X_1 (forced connecting); provision of apartments (houses) with drinking water in the territory of the Republic of Uzbekistan (in % of the total number of apartments (houses) $-$ X_2 (forced connecting); total area of forest land in the system of the State Forestry Committee of the Republic of Uzbekistan (as of January 1), ha $-$ X_3 (forced connecting); volume of harvested wood in the system of the State Forestry Committee of the Republic of Uzbekistan, m^3 $-$ X_4(forced connecting); area damaged by forest fires on the territory of the Republic of Uzbekistan, ha $-$ X_5 (forced connecting); volumes of mining and quarrying in the Republic of Uzbekistan (billion soums in current prices) $-$ X_6 (forced binder); protected natural areas in the Republic of Uzbekistan, thousand ha $-$ X_7 (forced connecting); total amount of water accepted on the territory of the Republic of Uzbekistan, m^3 $-$ X_8 (forced connecting); amount of water taken for irrigation in the territory of the Republic of Uzbekistan, m^3 $-$ X_9 (forced binder a); the amount of water accepted for general industrial, utility and technical needs on the territory of the Republic of Uzbekistan, m^3 $-$ $X_{9.1}$ (forced connecting); the amount of water received for energy production in the territory of the Republic of Uzbekistan, m^3 $-$ $X_{9.2}$ (forced connecting); the amount of water accepted for production needs on the territory of the Republic of Uzbekistan, m^3

$- X_{9.3}$ (forced connecting); the amount of water accepted for utilities on the territory of the Republic of Uzbekistan, m^3 $- X_{9.4}$ (forced connecting); amount of water accepted for fishing on the territory of the Republic of Uzbekistan, m^3 $- X_{9.5}$ (forced connecting); Passenger turnover by road transport across the territory of the Republic of Uzbekistan, billion passenger / km $- X_{9.6}$ (forced connecting).

In total, we select 15 factors for study and consider the most important of them (Table 1).

Table 1. Descriptive statistics of factors affecting economic and environmental systems in the Republic of Uzbekistan.

```
> .dta
   obs:            13
   vars:           20                                    9 Jan 2021 11:47

                    storage      display      value
  variable name      type        format       label      variable label

  y1                 float       %8.0g                    Y1
  x1                 float       %8.0g                    X1
  x2                 float       %8.0g                    X2
  x3                 float       %8.0g                    X3
  x4                 float       %8.0g                    X4
  x5                 float       %8.0g                    X5
  x6                 float       %8.0g                    X6
  x7                 float       %8.0g                    X7
  x8                 long        %8.0g                    X8
  x9                 long        %8.0g                    X9
  x91                int         %8.0g                    X91
  x92                int         %8.0g                    X92
  x93                int         %8.0g                    X93
  x94                int         %8.0g                    X94
  x95                int         %8.0g                    X95
  x96                int         %8.0g                    X96
  y2                 float       %8.0g                    Y2
  y3                 float       %8.0g                    Y3
  y4                 float       %8.0g                    Y4
  y5                 float       %8.0g                    Y5
```

Tables 1 and 2 show the distribution of factors selected for descriptive statistics of factors affecting economic and environmental systems in the Republic of Uzbekistan and econometric analysis of factors affecting economic and environmental systems in the regions.

Table 2. Distribution of selected factors for econometric analysis of factors affecting economic and environmental systems in the Republic of Uzbekistan

Variable	Obs	Mean	Std. Dev.	Min	Max
y1	13	871.9977	145.5596	642.74	1162.1
x1	13	36.79231	.7696981	35.7	37.8
x2	13	80.00769	3.192559	75.3	82.7
x3	13	9620206	1245923	8562656	1.20e+07
x4	13	19872.9	4788.737	13023.1	26245
x5	13	109.7477	128.2458	3.9	388.38
x6	13	16000.36	14445.12	5159.1	46582.55
x7	13	1017.854	302.2194	823.2	1545.9
x8	13	54633.54	6028.54	42817	63284
x9	13	47422.23	4013.937	38589	53769
x91	13	7211.385	4888.53	4130	17906
x92	13	3356.231	2082.357	272	5008
x93	13	2129.538	2232.787	661	6750
x94	13	2972.308	1301.439	2105	6314
x95	13	1131.154	798.0297	463	2652
x96	13	405.1538	154.8165	257	597
y2	13	106.3138	2.47164	101.8	113.2
y3	13	11.28846	.8791649	9.5	12.31
y4	13	90.97231	4.412085	86.9	104.6
y5	13	.1271538	.0752837	.02	.219

4 Discussion

Obtained for econometric analysis $X_1, X_2, X_3, X_4 X_5, X_6, X_7, X_8, X_9, X_{91}, X_{9.2}, X_{9.3}, X_{9.4}, X_{9.5}, X_{9.6}$ tested by Skewness/Kurtosis tests, obtained the above results. According to Table 1 above, the *p-value* $X_1, X_2, X_3, X_4 X_5, X_6, X_7, X_8, X_9, X_{91}, X_{9.2}, X_{9.3}, X_{9.4}, X_{9.5}, X_{9.6}$ is usually less than 0.05, and you can see that the resulting set obeys the normal distribution law.

From the correlation diagram of economic indicators of the economic and environmental system of the Republic of Uzbekistan, it can be seen that the number of observations is much less than the number of factors. Only the most important should be left here (Fig. 1).

Based on the selected factors, the degree of their interdependence is determined using the correlation coefficient in the Stata 16 program. According to the table, there is a strong correlation between the obtained factor and the selected factors. With tight links between the factors and the fulfillment of conditions $\left| r_{x_1,x_2} \right| < 0,8,$, it is possible to determine the absence of multicollenarity between the factors and construct a regression equation. The regression equation shows what kind of functional relationship exists between the resulting factor and the selected factors (Fig. 2).

It is recommended to use the Stata 16 program, which is currently the most convenient, to construct the regression equation.

To build a regression equation, it is advisable to use the Stata 16 program, which is currently the most convenient. At the same time, of course, it is necessary to check the

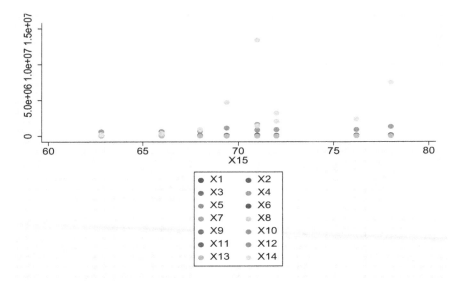

Fig. 1. Correlation diagram of factors affecting the economic and environmental systems of the Republic of Uzbekistan [36].

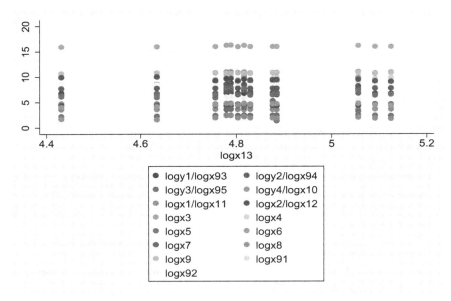

Fig. 2. Correlation diagram of factors affecting the economic and environmental systems of the Republic of Uzbekistan.

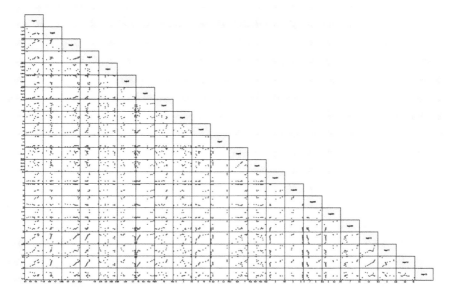

Fig. 3. Correlation matrix of factors affecting the economic and environmental systems of the Republic of Uzbekistan [36].

reliability and adequacy of the identified regression equations based on certain criteria. Since the units of measurement of the factors are different, it is advisable to take the logarithm of the variables. A correlation matrix of logarithmic coefficients is constructed (Fig. 3).

Figure 4 shows a diagram of a group of factors of economic indicators of the economic and environmental system of the Republic of Uzbekistan.

Figure 5 shows the location of a group of factors in terms of economic and ecological systems of the Republic of Uzbekistan, which shows that the factors are mainly divided into 3 groups.

To check the results of the model, an F-test was carried out, the essence of the F-test is to test the hypothesis that the coefficient of simple determination $R^2 = 0$. Because this figure represents the part of Y, which can be explained by the regression equation. If Y is zero, it is clear that Y cannot be explained in terms of X.

We construct the null and one-sided alternative hypotheses as follows:

$$H_0 : \rho^2 = 0$$
$$H_1 : \rho^2 > 0$$

We find the critical value F for the significance level $\alpha = 0.05$:

$$F_{cp} = F_\alpha (\kappa\text{-}1; \text{н-}\kappa) = F_{0,05} (5;5) = 68.76$$

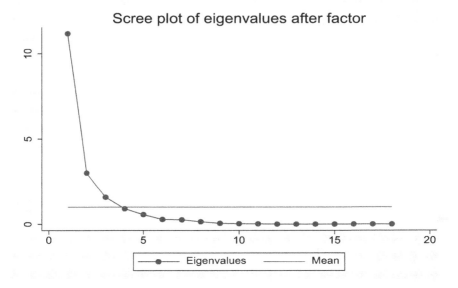

Fig. 4. Diagram of a group of factors of economic indicators of the economic and environmental system of the Republic of Uzbekistan.

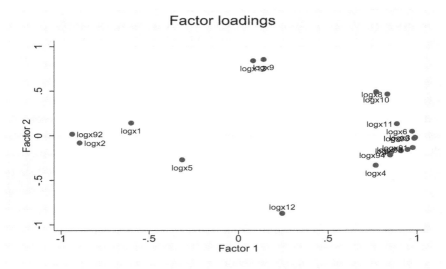

Fig. 5. Distribution of groups of data indicators of economic and ecological systems in the Republic of Uzbekistan [37].

Estimated sample value F:

$$F_{stat} = \frac{SST/(k-1)}{SSE(n-k)} = 240.88$$

Here: SST is the sum of common squares; SSE is the sum of the residual squares.
   Decision rule: Hypothesis H_0 is rejected because

$$F_c = 68.76 < F = 240.88$$

   Therefore, the H_0 hypothesis is rejected, since $F_{stat} > F_{cr}$. Hence, we can conclude that using the regression equation, Y explains that part of the change in GDP that differs in significance from zero.
   The purpose of the t-test in the model is to check that the coefficients of the estimated main set linear regression equation are significantly different from zero, i.e., they are not random.
   Appropriate null and one-sided hypotheses can be constructed as follows (Table 3):

$$H_0 : \beta_1 = 0$$
$$H_1 : \beta_1 \neq 0$$

Table 3. Results of multivariate regression analysis of economic and environmental systems of the Republic of Uzbekistan (lny1) [37].

Linear regression

				Number of obs	=	13
				F(3, 9)	=	9.34
				Prob > F	=	0.0040
				R-squared	=	0.5651
				Root MSE	=	.12821

logy1	Coef.	Robust Std. Err.	t	P>|t|	[95% Conf. Interval]	
logx1	8.332606	3.589001	2.32	0.045	.2137221	16.45149
logx2	-7.282642	1.729501	-4.21	0.002	-11.19504	-3.37024
logx93	-.1137543	.0422026	-2.70	0.025	-.2092232	-.0182854
_cons	9.446552	7.160223	1.32	0.220	-6.750997	25.6441

From the above matrix, the following regression equation can be constructed:

$$lny1 = 8.33lnx1 - 7.28lnx2 - 0.11lnx93 + 9.44 \tag{1}$$

   Interpreting the regression equation, if other factors do not change, a one percent increase in the sewerage of apartments (houses) in the territory of the Republic of Uzbekistan will affect an 8.33 percent increase in pollutants in the atmospheric air in the territory of the Republic of Uzbekistan, a 1% increase in the supply of drinking water to apartments (at home) in the regions of the Republic of Uzbekistan to reduce air pollution by 7.28% on the territory of the Republic of Uzbekistan and increase by 1% the supply of technical water in the regions to reduce 0.11% of atmospheric pollutants on the territory of the Republic of Uzbekistan.

The p-value required in the t-test for all coefficients is less than 0.05. That is, all coefficients accurately reflect the influence of factors on emissions of pollutants into the atmosphere on the territory of the Republic of Uzbekistan with a reliability of at least 56% (Table 4).

Table 4. Results of multivariate regression analysis of economic and environmental systems of the Republic of Uzbekistan (lny1) [37].

Linear regression				Number of obs	=	13
				F(3, 9)	=	7.64
				Prob > F	=	0.0076
				R-squared	=	0.7757
				Root MSE	=	.01254

logy2	Coef.	Robust Std. Err.	t	P>|t|	[95% Conf. Interval]	
logx13	-.0701364	.0152114	-4.61	0.001	-.104547	-.0357257
logx8	-.1385475	.0595007	-2.33	0.045	-.2731475	-.0039475
logx6	.0143561	.0064228	2.24	0.052	-.0001734	.0288855
_cons	6.381259	.6390669	9.99	0.000	4.93559	7.826929

From the above matrix, the following regression equation can be constructed:

$$lny2 = 0.014lnx6 - 0.13lnx8 - 0.07\,lnx13 + 6.38 \tag{2}$$

According to the regression equation, if other factors remain unchanged, the increase in production and open pit mining in the Republic of Uzbekistan will increase by 0.014%, a decrease in carbon dioxide emissions in the territory of the Republic of Uzbekistan by 1% and an increase in air travel in the territory of the Republic of Uzbekistan by 1% leads to a decrease in emissions carbon dioxide in the territory of the Republic of Uzbekistan by 0.07%.

Using the decision rule, the H0 hypothesis is rejected because the p value < 0.005. Therefore, the overall regression coefficient of the set is significantly different from zero and is not random. Hence, a change in factors leads to a change for carbon dioxide released into the atmosphere (in direct proportion).

The determinant coefficient in multivariate regression - R2 is the part of the quantity variable Y, which can be explained using the regression equation found using the predictor variables.

It is calculated based on the following formula:

$$R^2 = 1 - \frac{SSE}{SST} = 1 - \frac{\Sigma(Y - \hat{Y})^2}{\Sigma(Y - \overline{Y})^2} = 0.864$$

Here: SST is sum of common squares; SSE is the sum of residual squares (Table 5).

Table 5. Results of multivariate regression analysis of indicators of economic and environ-mental systems of the Republic of Uzbekistan (lny3).

Linear regression

			Number of obs	=	13
			F(4, 8)	=	49.70
			Prob > F	=	0.0000
			R-squared	=	0.9483
			Root MSE	=	.02248

logy3	Coef.	Robust Std. Err.	t	P>|t|	[95% Conf. Interval]	
logx2	-3.203559	.6595699	-4.86	0.001	-4.72453	-1.682588
logx4	-.2438469	.0360779	-6.76	0.000	-.3270427	-.1606511
logx6	.0704434	.012596	5.59	0.001	.0413969	.0994899
logx96	-.1878717	.068117	-2.76	0.025	-.3449497	-.0307936
_cons	19.31863	3.352894	5.76	0.000	11.58684	27.05042

From the matrix above, this regression equation looks like this:

$$lny3 = -3.20lnx2 - 0.24lnx4 + 0.70lnx6 - 0.18lnx96 + 19.31 \qquad (3)$$

According to the above regression equation, with other factors unchanged, an increase in the supply of drinking water to apartments (houses) in the regions by 1% will reduce emissions of nitrogen oxide (I) in the territory of the Republic of Uzbekistan by 3.2%, an increase in production and open-cast mining in the regions by 1% contributes to an increase in nitric oxide (I) emissions on the territory of the Republic of Uzbekistan by 0.7% (Table 6).

$$lny4 = 0.66lnx6 - 0.52lnx8 + 9.63 \qquad (4)$$

According to the regression Eq. (4), if other factors do not change, an increase in production and production by open pit in the regions by 1% leads to an increase in hydrocarbon emissions into the atmosphere in the territory of the Republic of Uzbekistan by 0.66%, and an increase in the total volume of water received in the regions by 1% to a 0.52% reduction in hydrocarbon emissions into the atmosphere on the territory of the Republic of Uzbekistan.

Table 6. Results of multivariate regression analysis of indicators of economic and environmental systems of the Republic of Uzbekistan (lny4).

```
Linear regression                          Number of obs   =        13
                                           F(2, 10)        =     12.02
                                           Prob > F        =    0.0022
                                           R-squared       =    0.5325
                                           Root MSE        =    .03448
```

logy4	Coef.	Robust Std. Err.	t	P>|t|	[95% Conf. Interval]	
logx6	.0662796	.0210226	3.15	0.010	.0194383	.1131209
logx8	-.526799	.2547001	-2.07	0.065	-1.094306	.0407083
_cons	9.63162	2.593438	3.71	0.004	3.853079	15.41016

Statistically, the coefficient of determination R2 is 0.53, which can explain 53% of the whole process, and the F-statistic value according to Fisher is also statistically significant (p = 0.000) (Fig. 6).

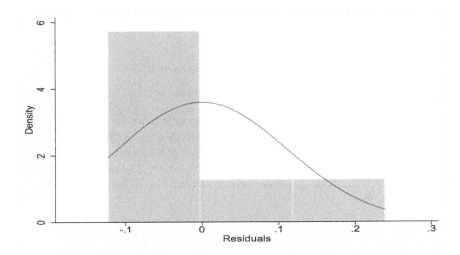

Fig. 6 Diagram of the residual distribution of the multivariate regression model of indicators of economic and environmental systems of the Republic of Uzbekistan.

The residual distribution of the multivariate regression model of economic and eco-logical systems in the Republic of Uzbekistan can be seen in the diagram above, and the Skewness and Kurtosis values in Table 7.

Table 7. The results of the residual test of the multivariate regression model of indicators of economic and environmental systems of the Republic of Uzbekistan.

| | | Skewness/Kurtosis tests for Normality | | joint | |
Variable	Obs	Pr(Skewness)	Pr(Kurtosis)	adj chi2(2)	Prob>chi2
ehat	13	0.0308	0.3066	5.45	0.0656

Table 8. Results of multivariate regression analysis of indicators of economic and environmental systems of the Republic of Uzbekistan (lny1).

Source	SS	df	MS	Number of obs	=	13
				F(2, 10)	=	21.37
Model	.27566907	2	.137834535	Prob > F	=	0.0002
Residual	.064504856	10	.006450486	R-squared	=	0.8104
				Adj R-squared	=	0.7725
Total	.340173926	12	.028347827	Root MSE	=	.08031

logy1	Coef.	Std. Err.	t	P>|t|	[95% Conf. Interval]	
logx10	.6720884	.1054455	6.37	0.000	.4371412	.9070355
logx93	-.0765302	.0305201	-2.51	0.031	-.1445332	-.0085273
_cons	4.247635	.3965513	10.71	0.000	3.364063	5.131206

$$\ln y1 = 0.67 \ln x10 - 0.76 \ln x93 + 4.24 \tag{5}$$

According to the above regression Eq. (5), if other factors do not change, an increase in passenger traffic by 1% on the territory of the Republic of Uzbekistan leads to an increase in air pollutants in the country by 0.67%, and an increase of 1% in the volume of water taken for industrial needs in the regions, to a 0.76% reduction in emissions of pollutants into the atmosphere in the country. Since the coefficient of determination of the regression equation R2 is 0.81, the equation can explain 81% of the whole process, the Fisher F-statistic is also statistically significant ($p = 0.000$) (Table 8).

As a result of econometric analysis, the increase in emissions of pollutants into the atmosphere in the country will be affected by: production volumes of the mining industry and open-pit mining; passenger transportation by road in the regions; to decrease: the total volume of water received in the regions; availability of apartments (houses) with drinking water by regions; the total area of forestry land in the system of the State Forestry Committee of the Republic of Uzbekistan.

5 Conclusions

According to the study, while improving the efficiency of ensuring the security of the economic and environmental systems of the Republic of Uzbekistan, special attention should be paid to the sustainability of these two structures. It is necessary to pay attention to the rational use of available resources. Considering that the main share of environmental costs (on average 65–70%) is the cost of water use, it is necessary to organize resource-saving production. This requires a wide application of innovative management methods and resource-saving types.

Thus, we have developed the following proposals for the effective management of security and sustainable development of the economic and environmental systems of the Republic of Uzbekistan:

– development of an environmental regulatory framework and a system of analytical control, including relevant environmental standards and global monitoring indicators and mechanisms for their implementation;
– improvement of the long-term National Program for the improvement of legal norms, standards, methods and guidelines in the field of environmental protection and the use of natural resources in accordance with the requirements of ISO 14000, 9000, 14001;
– development of environmental science, environmental education of the population;
– restoration of the ecological balance of nature, conservation of biodiversity and compensation for damage;
– introduction of non-waste technologies in the use of natural resources and the search for new energy sources;
– the use of new innovative technologies in the production of environmentally friendly agricultural products;
– development of ecological education of the population, ecological consciousness and culture of youth;
– improvement of the system of state control over the use of biodiversity components, the movement of genetically modified organisms and early warning of environmental emergencies;
– implementation of a set of measures to strengthen international cooperation in ensuring national and regional environmental security.

In general, it is advisable to take into account the strong influencing factors obtained in the management strategy based on the study. As a result, the stability of economic and ecological systems will be ensured, their efficiency will increase, and balanced development will be achieved. This will ensure the balance of industries and areas of the region as a whole, as well as ensuring economic, social and environmental security in all systems.

References

1. Transforming Our World: The 2030 Agenda for Sustainable Development (adopted by General Assembly resolution 70/1 of 25 (September 2015). https://documents-dds-ny.un.org/doc/UNDOC/GEN/N15/291/92/PDF/N1529192.pdf
2. Decree of the President of the Republic of Uzbekistan No. PF-4947 dated February 7, "On the Action Strategy for the Further Development of the Republic of Uzbekistan" (2017)
3. Bondarskaya, O.V. et al.: Socio-economic necessity and prospects for the introduction of the digital economy. In: The 6th International Conference on Future Networks & Distributed Systems (ICFNDS 2022). ACM, New York (2022). https://doi.org/10.1145/3584202.3584227
4. Bekmurodov, N.H. et al.: Analysis of investments in fixed capital in the context of the development of digital economy in the Republic of Uzbekistan. In The 6th International Conference on Future Networks & Distributed Systems (ICFNDS 2022). ACM, New York (2022).. https://doi.org/10.1145/3584202.3584267
5. Samiyeva, G.T. et al.: Econometric Assessment of the Dynamics of Development of the Export Potential of Small Businesses and Private Entrepreneurship Subjects in the Conditions of the Digital Economy Internet of Things, Smart Spaces, and Next Generation Networks and Systems. NEW2AN 2022. LNCS, vol 13772. Springer, Cham (2023).. https://doi.org/10.1007/978-3-031-30258-9_39
6. Tillaeva B.R. et al.: Econometric Evaluation of Influential Factors to Increasing Labor Efficiency in Textile Enterprises. Webology, Volume 18, Special Issue on Information. Retrieval and Web Search (2021). https://www.webology.org/datacms/articles/20210129114502amWEB18024.pdf
7. Ishnazarov A., Kuvonchbek, R., Allayarov, P., Ollamberganov, F., Kamalov, R., Matyakubova M.: Prospects for the use of neural network models in the prevention of possible network attacks on modern banking information systems based on blockchain technology in the context of the digital economy. In: ICFNDS 2022: Proceedings of the 6th International Conference on Future Networks & Distributed Systems, pp.592–599 (December 2022).https://doi.org/10.1145/3584202.3584291
8. Abdullayev O., Ishnazarov A., Kuvonchbek, R., Oydinoy, K., Jorabekov, T.: Methods and algorithms for the formation of distance education systems based on blockchain and artificial intelligence technologies in the digital economy. In: ICFNDS 2022: Proceedings of the 6th International Conference on Future Networks & Distributed Systems December 2022, ACM International Conference Proceeding Series, pp. 568–574 (2022)
9. Gabbarov, S., Kuvonchbek, R., Saukhanov, J., Khojabayeva, D.: Development of indicators for forecasting the number and composition of livestock based on multivariate econometric models in the digital economy. In: ICFNDS 2022: Proceedings of the 6th International Conference on Future Networks & Distributed Systems December 2022, ACM International Conference Proceeding Series, pp. 542–547 (2022)
10. Juraev G., Kuvonchbek, R., Toshpulov, B.: Application Fuzzy Neural Network Methods to Detect Cryptoattacks on Financial Information Systems Based on Blockchain Technology, Internet of Things, Smart Spaces, and Next Generation Networks and Systems. LNCS 13772, pp. 94–104. Springer Nature Switzerland (2023). ISSN 0302–9743, ISBN 978–3–0310–30257-2
11. Kuvonchbek, R.: Method Authentication of Objects Information Communication, Internet of Things, Smart Spaces, and Next Generation Networks and Systems. LNCS, vol. 13772, pp. 105–116. Springer Nature Switzerland (2023). ISSN 0302–9743, ISBN 978–3–0310–30257-2,

12. Tashev, K., Arzieva, J., Arziev, A., Kuvonchbek, R.: Method authentication of objects information communication systems. In: International Conference on Information Science and Communications Technologies: Applications, Trends, and Opportunities, ICISCT 2022, pp. 1–5 (2022)

13. Karimov, M., Arzieva, J., Kuvonchbek, R.: Development of approaches and schemes for proactive information protection in computer networks. In: International Conference on Information Science and Communications Technologies: Applications, Trends, and Opportunities, ICISCT 2022, pp. 1–5 (2022)

14. Usmanova, A.: Whether a higher e-government development index means a higher gdp growth rate? In: ACM International Conference Proceeding Series, pp. 467–472 (2021). https://doi.org/10.1145/3508072.3508168

15. Abdullaev, T.R., Kuvonchbek, R., Juraev, G., Bozorov, A.X.: Mathematical modeling of key generators for bank lending platforms based on blockchain technology. In: International Conference on Artificial Intelligence, Blockchain, Computing and Security, ICABCS-2023, Samarkand, Uzbekistan, 24–25 February Proceedings (2023)

16. Arzieva, J., Kuvonchbek, R.: Application of random number generators in solving the problem of user authentication in blockchain systems. In: International Conference on Information Science and Communications Technologies: Applications, Trends, and Opportunities, ICISCT 2023, pp. 1–5 (2023)

17. Khamdamov, S.J., et al.: Econometric modeling of central bank refinancing rate in Uzbekistan. In: Proceedings of the 6th International Conference on Future Networks & Distributed Systems, pp. 253–257 (December 2022)

18. Usmanova, A.: The impact of economic growth and fiscal policy on poverty rate in Uzbekistan: application of neutrosophic theory and time series approaches. J. Inter. J. Neutrosophic Sci. **21**(2), 107–117 (2023)

19. Turayeva, G., et al.: Opportunities to use financial services –"1 C PROGRAM". In: Proceedings of the 6th International Conference on Future Networks & Distributed Systems, pp. 556–561 (December 2022)

20. Yusupov, S., et al.: Diagnostic aspects of zygomatico-orbital complex fractures with the use of modern digital technologies. In: Proceedings of the 6th International Conference on Future Networks & Distributed Systems, pp. 399–403 (December 2022)

21. Tukhtabaev J.S. et al.: The role of industrial enterprises in ensuring food security. IOP Conf. Series: Earth Environ. Sci. 1043, 012023 (2022). https://doi.org/10.1088/1755-1315/1043/1/012023, (https://iopscience.iop.org/article/)

22. Bekmurodov N.H., et al.: Econometric modeling and forecasting of the increase in the export potential of small businesses and private enterprises in the Republic of Uzbekistan. In: The 6th International Conference on Future Networks & Distributed Systems (ICFNDS 2022). ACM, New York (2022). https://doi.org/10.1145/3584202.3584246

23. Goziyeva A.A. et al.: Econometric analysis of evaluation of investment projects implemented in the Northern Regions of Uzbekistan. In: The 6th International Conference on Future Networks & Distributed Systems (ICFNDS 2022). ACM, New York (2022). https://doi.org/10.1145/3584202.3584311

24. Tukhtabaev, J.S.: Econometric Evaluation of Influential Factors to Increasing Labor Efficiency in Textile Enterprises. Webology, Volume 18, Special Issue on Information. Retrieval and Web Search (2021). https://www.webology.org/datacms/articles/20210129114502amWEB18024.pdf

25. Bondarskaya, O.V., Tukhtabaev, J.S., Akramova, R.R., Saidrasulova, K.B., Shirinov, U., Kurbanova, Z.T.: The Impact of Digitalisation on the Safe Development of Individuals in Society. Internet of Things, Smart Spaces, and Next Generation Networks and Systems. NEW2AN: LNCS, vol. 13772. Springer, Cham (2022). https://doi.org/10.1007/978-3-031-30258-9_25

26. Yuldashev, S.E. et al.:. Econometric assessment of prospects of ensuring food safety in Uzbekistan. In: The 6th International Conference on Future Networks & Distributed Systems (ICFNDS 2022). ACM, New York (2022). https://doi.org/10.1145/3584202.3584280

27. Tillaeva B.R. et al. Ways of development of agriculture and processing industry enterprises manufacturing cooperation. IOP Conf. Series: Earth Environ. Sci. **1043** 012024 (2022). https://doi.org/10.1088/1755-1315/1043/1/012024, (https://iopscience.iop.org/article/)

28. Muftaydinova, S.K., et al.: Expression of the tyrosine kinase receptor (EPHA1) in the eutopic and ectopic endometrium of patients with deep infiltrative endometriosis use of modern digital technologies. In: Proceedings of the 6th International Conference on Future Networks & Distributed Systems, pp. 416–421 (December 2022)

29. Khamdamov, S.J.: Calculating share of factors of intensive economic growth in Uzbekistan. In: The 5th International Conference on Future Networks & Distributed Systems, pp. 393–397 (December 2021).

30. Tran, T.K., Lin, C.Y., Tu, Y.T., Duong, N.T., Thi, T.D.P., Shoh-Jakhon, K.: Nexus between natural resource depletion and rent and COP26 commitments: Empirical evidence from Vietnam. Resour. Policy **85**, 104024 (2023)

31. Usmanova, A.: An Empirical Investigation of the Relationship Between E-government Development and Multidimensional Poverty. LNCS(LNAI), vol. 13772 (2023). https://doi.org/10.1007/978-3-031-30258-9_42

32. Gong, X., et al.: Exploring an interdisciplinary approach to sustainable economic development in resource-rich regions: an investigation of resource productivity, technological innovation, and ecosystem resilience. Resources Policy **87**, Part A, 104294 (2023). ISSN 0301–4207, https://doi.org/10.1016/j.resourpol.2023.104294

33. Bondarskaya, T.A., et al.: The development of the digital economy as a factor in increasing the consumer basket of the population (on the example of the Tambov region). In: The 6th International Conference on Future Networks & Distributed Systems (ICFNDS 2022). ACM, New York (2022). https://doi.org/10.1145/3584202.3584310

34. Shoh-Jakhon, K.: Theoretical and Methodological Aspects of Intensive Economic Growth in Ensuring Sustainable Economic Development. Social and Economic Studies within the Framework of Emerging Global Developments, vol. 3, p. 283

35. Kuvonchbek, R.: Prospects of application of blockchain technology in the banking. In: International Conference on Information Science and Communications Technologies: Applications, Trends, and Opportunities, ICISCT 2023, pp. 1–5 (2023)

36. The data were calculated by the authors using the Stata14 program based on data from the State Statistics Committee of the Republic of Uzbekistan

37. The data were calculated by the authors using the Stata16 program based on data from the State Statistics Committee of the Republic of Uzbekistan

The Importance of Digitalization in Economic Development of the Government

Askarova Mavluda, Choriev Fazliddin, and Khayitov Saidjon[✉]

Tashkent State University of Economics, Tashkent 100003, Uzbekistan
s.hayitov@tsue.uz, saidjonkhayitov@gmail.com

Abstract. Uzbekistan aims to conduct research on the impact of digitization on economic development and on all sectors and sectors of the economy. The main analysis was the analysis of foreign literature and the financial indicators of the digital economy in a single state. Regression analysis of the dependence of the ICT sector and logistics sectors developing into real GDP has also been carried out. In the article, conclusions and recommendations on digitization are given.

Keywords: real GDP · digital economy · e-service · e-commerce · ICT First Section

1 Introduction

Along with global economic development in the world, the speed of Information Technology and information exchange is growing. Billions of regular online connections between organizations, individuals, data, technologies, and processes related to economic activity are known as "digital economics". The interaction of organizations, individuals and machines using the Internet, sites and platforms, mobile applications and digital technologies is the foundation of the digital economy (Nguyen, 2023).

Researchers are currently living in a period when only the experience of smartphones, social networks, online internet stores is required to sell and buy products, and it has also been proven that the more convenient it is to obtain information in industrialized countries, the simpler it is to increase productivity and guarantee efficiency (Guariso and Nyqvist, 2018).

In the current digital age, the internet has become one of the most important components of corporate governance, as a possible inexpensive communication channel from its initial state. The economy and people of any state benefit greatly from technological progress (Korotkevich, 2019).

The adaptation of the new technology can lead to short-term unemployment, but it also quickly creates new job prospects (Sellar, 2019). Given that technology is currently developing at an accelerated pace, the economy of any country can expand firmly with the correct adoption of practical technologies. Developing sustainable development strategies, developed nations are now prioritizing technologies such as 3D printing or biofuel engineering (Shor et al., 2022).

Y. Koucheryavy and A. Aziz (Eds.): NEW2AN/ruSMART 2023, LNCS 14543, pp. 196–204, 2024.
https://doi.org/10.1007/978-3-031-60997-8_17

Technical achievements such as digitalization of bus and rail systems, online banking opportunities, Internet marketing Services, e-learning initiatives, intercity communication center services are successfully implemented in developing countries (Kotevski & Milenkoski, 2018).

The inability to effectively manage time constraints and the slow growth of productivity are the two main obstacles to economic expansion. For this reason, the steps behind the development can be achieved by automating, digitizing and practically introducing new innovative technologies in improving efficiency in every network and industry (Yano, 2016).

At the peak of development, the level of employment in networks such as online and remote service increases significantly compared to networks such as production or agriculture. Industry is not limited to a single city or state, it also interacts globally, allowing people to work in businesses located anywhere in the world. States currently have a strong interest in the labor force ICT industry (Clemons, 2007).

It is very important to guarantee that the transition to a digital economy will be carried out correctly and efficiently by governments, taking into account that the advantages outweigh the disadvantages, it is necessary to carry out measures to limit barriers to increase new job opportunities and ensure sustainable growth (Chatani, 2012).

2   Literature Review

The basis of the digital economy is the widespread introduction of information and communication technologies (ICT) in all sectors to improve productivity. It is a way of describing a system in which computer technology has taken hold. In the new economy, networking and communication infrastructures provide a global platform for individuals and organizations to plan, interact with each other, share information, receive and collaborate everywhere (Alam et al., 2022).

Understanding the Fourth Industrial Revolution (4IR), its emerging technologies and the threats they pose is critical for all nations. With the emergence of modern and innovative technologies, a number of views on the impact of automation, global supply chains and outsourcing on employment began to emerge.

According to Krichen (2022), the digital revolution will continue to focus on technical advances that enable rapid development and a deeper focus on a world powered by data and artificial intelligence.

In order to ensure the transparency of the processes in the banking system, it is advisable to switch to a full digitization system (Naheem, 2015). At the key stages of the industrial revolution, it is important to widely encourage the exchange of information through digitization in agriculture (Oguamanam, 2018).

As any alternative approach may lead to the devaluing of human rights and societal values, limiting AI-based innovation, increasing personal and societal well-being, and ethically regulating the use of artificial intelligence is a difficult but vital task.

According to Joseph and Marrow (2017), it can be difficult to organize human resources and technological advances in the digital economy and transform them into profitable efforts that promote social equity and justice in developing countries.

According to Zhang et al. (2021), there are huge opportunities for research on the latest organizational configurations related to artificial intelligence technologies, enhancement of human capabilities, as well as the digital economy of nations. The introduction of science and technology and big data into the industry can increase access to product information, reduce transaction costs, and promote competitiveness (Sahay et al. 2020; Rakhmonov and Choriev 2022; Askarova et al. 2023; Khayitov & Ulugbek, 2023).

It is essential to ensure that the transition to the digital economy is carried out effectively and efficiently, with the benefits outweighing the disadvantages, and that the challenges of job creation are offset by growth and development in the economy (Elsafty and Elzeftawy, 2022).

Governments of many other developing countries have adopted many ICT strategies, laws and policies to create transparent and accountable government for socio-economic development (Aziz and Naima, 2021).

Methodology. This study examines the importance of the digital economy in economic development. A comparative analysis of the impact of the digital economy on economic sectors was studied in the study.

Research results. In accordance with the strategy "Digital Uzbekistan - 2030" in our country, digitalization of economic sectors and regions, introduction of state information systems and electronic services, as well as public education, public services, judiciary, finance and complex measures are being implemented in the banking system.

By introducing a unified rating and evaluation system for assessing the state of development of the digital economy and electronic government in economic sectors, social spheres and regions, the goals of introducing an effective system of interdepartmental coordination of evaluation processes for the development of sectoral and regional programs of digital development in the future have been determined. Also, according to the GovTech Enablers Index rating of the World Bank, our country took the 4th place in the world in terms of digital skills and innovations in the field of public services, and increased by 65 places compared to 2020. As a result of this rating, it is shown that the role of the digital economy in the digitization of the government policy and economic growth is important. At the same time, it can be noted that digitization and the digital economy are one of the factors that indicate the country's investment attractiveness.

In particular, according to the results of the "GovTech Maturity Index" in the field of state and public services, Uzbekistan rose by 37 places and took the 43rd place among 198 countries and entered the "A" group of leading countries in the field of digital transformation.

This year, according to the results of the "Electronic Government" rating conducted by the UN every 2 years, Uzbekistan rose 18 places and took the 69th place among 193 countries and became one of the countries with a "high/very high level of development".

In the Oxford Insights 2022 government AI readiness index analysis, our country rose 14 places out of 160 countries to 79th place (93rd place in 2021).

In the Inclusive Internet Index published annually by The Economist Intelligence Unit, our country rose 5 places compared to last year (66th place in 2021), and took 61st place in 2022.

According to the analysis of "The beginning of open data", Uzbekistan has increased by 1 place compared to last year among 201 countries of the world in terms of sources of open data and their number (124 open data with a source) took 4th place.

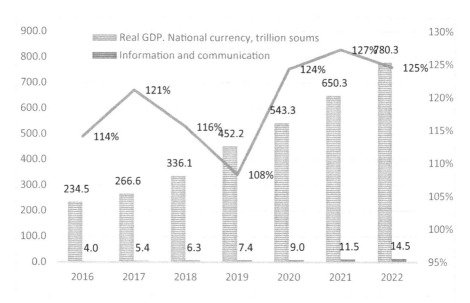

Fig. 1. Analysis of the real GDP of the Republic of Uzbekistan and the share of ICT in it and its dynamics

In Fig. 1, we see the analysis of the growth dynamics of the share of ICT in the GDP of Uzbekistan in the period 2016–2022. In 2026, the share of ICT will be 4% of real GDP. Along with the growth of GDP over the years, the share of ICT in GDP has also increased. In 2022, ICT's share in GDP will be 14.5% and 113.1 trillion. SoM constitutes value. This means that the results of the theology aimed at the development of the IT sector are showing themselves in Uzbekistan (Table 1).

The number of information and communication enterprises was 6,370 in 2016, and by 2022, their number will double to 10,587. Also, the number of employees working in this field has grown over the years and will grow by 12% by 2022.

The amount of services provided in the market of information and communication services in 2022 is 24,508.1 billion soums, this indicator was 6,306.6 billion soums in 2016, and in 2022 it increased 4 times compared to 2016. At the same time, telecommunication services have the highest share, which amounted to 14,660.7 billion soums in 2022, and this indicator was 3 times less in 2016, and amounted to 5,421.5 billion soums (Table 2).

The volume of gross added value created in the fields of information economy and e-commerce amounted to 27,791.2 billion soums in 2022 and showed a steady growth trend over the years and accelerated in the last 3 years. This figure increased significantly, reaching 4,967.7 billion soms in 2016 and 10,777.0 billion soms in 2020. The share of gross added value created in the fields of information economy and e-commerce in GDP

Table 1. Macroeconomic indicators of information and communication services

Name	2016	2017	2018	2019	2020	2021	2022
Number of active organizations by types of economic activity "Information and Communication", units	6370	6427	6403	6975	7901	9517	10587
Number of employees in legal entities working in the field of ICT, units	34478	37958	40248	47697	50157	53782	60462
Dynamic changes in the number of employees of legal entities operating in the field of ICT	103%	110%	106%	119%	105%	107%	112%
The volume of rendered market communication and informatization services. In actual prices, billion soums	6306,8	8196,7	10332,6	10891,7	13852,3	17755,1	24508,1
telecommunication services	5 421,5	6 946,8	8 389,1	8 624,0	10 233,7	11 957,3	14 660,7
computer programming services, consulting and other related services	187,7	325,5	666,1	698,2	1 428,2	2 721,5	4 652,9
information services	92,5	151,6	240,9	389,2	708,7	1 373,6	2 516,0

will be 3.4 percent in 2022. Accordingly, it was 2 percent on average for 2016–2021. In terms of these added values, the information and communication technologies (ICT) sector and ICT services contributed the highest amounts. Also, the field of E-commerce, which is now in the development stages, showed good results in 2021 and 2022 and amounted to 3,907.3 billion soums and 9,756.4 billion soums, respectively (Table 3).

In the analysis of the foreign trade turnover of Uzbekistan for 2016–2022, we see that the export of services in the field of computer services has increased and new products have been added. In terms of import services, the Telecommunication service has the largest share and amounted to 49.4 thousand US dollars in 2016. In 2020, the volume of imports increased sharply and amounted to 94.8 thousand US dollars. In 2022, this indicator will reach 138.8 thousand US dollars, which has increased almost 3 times compared to 2016. The export-import balance of telecommunications services has always been positive, and in 2016, the share of exports amounted to 141.1 thousand US dollars, while the export volume increased by 27% in 8 years and reached 180.5 thousand US dollars in 2022.

According to the data of the State Statistics Committee, the export of computer programs was included in the export services from 2018, and as of 2022, the export

Table 2. Structural structure and dynamic change of gross added value created in the fields of information economy and electronic commerce

Name	2016	2017	2018	2019	2020	2021	2022
The volume of gross value added in the field of information economy and e-commerce, billion soums	4 967,7	6 377,8	7 732,1	8 491,9	10 777,0	16 939,5	27 791,2
Share of gross value added created in the information economy and e-commerce sectors in GDP, in % to the GVA	2,1	2,3	2,0	1,7	1,9	2,5	3,4
Sector of information and communication technologies (ICT)	4 575,3	5 849,0	6 876,8	7 323,0	9 095,9	11 567,6	16 089,9
ICT production	127,2	238,3	301,9	279,4	540,1	503,3	805,5
ICT trade	228,0	281,6	236,2	293,3	252,3	367,8	594,0
ICT services	4 220,1	5 329,1	6 338,7	6 750,3	8 303,5	10 696,4	14 690,4
Content sector and mass media	392,4	518,7	750,1	908,9	1 089,7	1 464,6	1 944,9
E-commerce		10,1	105,2	260,0	591,4	3 907,3	9 756,4

of products in the amount of 56.4 thousand US dollars was achieved. Table x shows significant growth in the field of information technology services. In 2022, Uzbekistan's foreign trade turnover in IT services amounted to 545.1 thousand US dollars. Therefore, 239.3 thousand US dollars are imports, 305.8 thousand US dollars are exports (Fig. 2).

A small regression analysis shows that a 1 percent increase in ICT has a negative effect on real GDP, and a 1 percent increase in logistics has a positive effect on real GDP by 0.49 percent. Possible It shows that there are a number of shortcomings and due to insufficient data, it is necessary to conduct other studies.

Summary. It is known that in the modern conditions of economic development, the main components of the economy require meaningful information processes to study macroeconomic trends. These tools reflect the development strategy of the entire economy and individual sectors.

The characteristics of information technologies take the task of providing structural support requirements for digitalization of the economy.

As a result of the ongoing reforms, 178 services have been launched through the Electronic Government and the single interactive services portal, and these services are helping to reduce transaction costs.

We have developed as a proposal the use of the following ways of using information technologies in the economic development of the country:

Table 3. Dynamics of export and import of ICT services over the years

Name	2016	2017	2018	2019	2020	2021	2022
Import							
Telecommunication services thousand US dollar	49,4	51,4	34,2	56,3	94,8	103,8	138,8
Computer software	-	-	7,4	6,8	13,7	8,5	14,8
Other computer services	2,8	5,4	2,5	5,8	6,3	6,2	7,8
Information agency services	-	-	0,4	0,2	2,7	3,3	52,6
Other information services	2,6	2,9	3,1	3,5	14,8	20,6	25,3
Eksport							
Telecommunication services	141,1	143,2	150,6	156,7	151,7	156,2	180,5
Computer software	-	-	0,8	0,7	5,8	4,8	56,4
Other computer services	4,5	5,6	6,2	8,0	8,3	7,5	40,5
Information agency services	-	-	-	0,1	-	-	-
Other information services	1,9	1,9	2,1	2,0	3,6	12,3	28,4

```
    Source |       SS           df       MS           Number of obs   =        13
-----------+------------------------------            F(2, 10)        =      4.87
     Model | .0200521            2   .01002605        Prob > F        =    0.0333
  Residual | .020568127         10   .002056813       R-squared       =    0.4936
-----------+------------------------------            Adj R-squared   =    0.3924
     Total | .040620226         12   .003385019       Root MSE        =    .04535


       GDP |    Coef.    Std. Err.       t     P>|t|      [95% Conf. Interval]
-----------+----------------------------------------------------------------
       Log | .4934534    .1901749     2.59    0.027      .0697173    .9171896
       ICT | -.3039226   .1533102    -1.98    0.076     -.6455189    .0376737
     _cons | 1.013919    .2801135     3.62    0.005      .3897871   1.638051
```

Fig. 2. Regression analysis of the impact of logistics and ICT on real GDP

modernization of the knowledge base and provision of the latest information technologies;

increasing the possibilities of using information available in the world of information; development of modern laws of social development

development of a mechanism for increasing the number of representatives of the IT sector in order to increase the share of information products and services in the gross domestic product;

filling social information communications with new and necessary information;

successful implementation of the state program of public information by introducing new information technologies to the development of telephony, radio, television, Internet, traditional and electronic mass media.

In general, by applying digitization in the economy, a number of macroeconomic problems can be solved, for example, unemployment, inflation, economic growth, national product, exports.

The scientific developments proposed in the article on the use of digitization in economic development can be used for further research in this direction. The results of the research show the need to use "digital" products to increase the economic development of Uzbekistan.

References

Alam, S.A., Bhuiyan, M.R.I., Tabassum, S., Islam, M.T.: Factors affecting users' intention to use social networking sites: a mediating role of social networking satisfaction. Can. J. Bus. Inf. Stud., **4**(5), 112–124 (2022). https://doi.org/10.34104/cjbis.022.01120124

Aziz, A., Naima, U.: Rethinking digital financial inclusion: Evidence from Bangladesh. Technol. Soc. **64**, 101509 (2021). https://doi.org/10.1016/j.techsoc.2020.101509

Chatani, K.: Economic growth, employment creation, and poverty alleviation. In: Hill, H., Khan, M.E., Zhuang, J. (eds.) Diagnosing the Indonesian Economy: Toward Inclusive and Green Growth, pp. 301–340. Anthem Press (2012). https://doi.org/10.7135/UPO9781843313786.011

Clemons, E.: A retrospective on information, strategy, and economics: after 20 years at HICSS, what have we learned about IT and strategy? In: 2007 40th Annual Hawaii International Conference on System Sciences (HICSS 2007) (2007). https://doi.org/10.1109/hicss.2007.30

Elsafty, A., Elzeftawy, A.: Towards effective mitigation of the digital transformation and COVID-19 risk on the unemployment in mobile operators in Egypt. Int. J. Bus. Manage. **17**(2), 123–144 (2022)

Rakhmonov D.A., Choriev F.I.: The role of the digital economy in ensuring the financial stability of state owned-enterprises. In: ACM International Conference Proceeding Series (2022)

Guariso, A., Bjorkman Nyqvist, M.: Improving primary school learning trough teaching at the right level and community engagement: Evidence from Assam, India. AEA Randomized Controlled Trials (2018).https://doi.org/10.1257/rct.2817-1.0

Joseph, T.D., Marrow, H.B.: Health care, immigrants, and minorities: lessons from the affordable care act in the US. J. Ethn. Migr. Stud. **43**(12), 1965–1984 (2017)

Khayitova, M.R.: Improving credit efficiency in the transformation of banks. Sci. Innov. Int. Sci. J. **1**(5) uif-2022: 8.2 I ISSN: 2181–3337 (2022)

Korotkevich, E.: Problems of virtual identity in the digital age (social and philosophical analysis). In: Proceedings of the 1st International Scientific Conference "Modern Management Trends and the Digital Economy: From Regional Development to Global Economic Growth" (MTDE 2019) (2019). https://doi.org/10.2991/mtde-19.2019.151

Zoran, K., Aleksandar, M.: Are free internet technologies and services the future of synchronous distance learning? Turkish Online J. Distance Educ. **19**, 4–14 (2018). https://doi.org/10.17718/tojde.444604

Krichen, M., Ammi, M., Mihoub, A., Almutiq, M.: Blockchain for modern applications: a survey. Sensors **22**(14), 5274 (2022)

Naheem, M.A.: Trade based money laundering: Towards a working definition for the banking sector. J. Money Laundering Control **18**(4), 513–524 (2015). https://doi.org/10.1108/JMLC-01-2015-0002

Askarova, M., Khafizova, Z., Talipova, D., Yakubov, I., Khayitov, S.: Agrotourism in the development of the agricultural economy of the Republic of Uzbekistan and its foreign experience. E3S Web Conf. **420**, 10005 (2023). https://doi.org/10.1051/e3sconf/202342010005

Nguyen, O.: Digital Economy and Its Components: A Brief Overview and Recommendations (2023)

Oguamanam, C.: ABS: Big data, data sovereignty and digitization: a new Indigenous research landscape. SSRN Elect. J. (2018).https://doi.org/10.2139/ssrn.3326282

Sahay, M.R., et al.: The promise of fintech: Financial inclusion in the post COVID-19 era. International Monetary Fund (2020)

Khayitov, S., Ulugbek, K.: The role of IT on transportation, logistics and the economic growth among central Asian countries. In: Koucheryavy, Y., Aziz, A. (eds.) Internet of Things, Smart Spaces, and Next Generation Networks and Systems: 22nd International Conference, NEW2AN 2022, Tashkent, Uzbekistan, December 15–16, 2022, Proceedings, pp. 649–655. Springer Nature Switzerland, Cham (2023). https://doi.org/10.1007/978-3-031-30258-9_58

Sellar, S.: Acceleration, automation and pedagogy: how the prospect of technological unemployment creates new conditions for educational thought. In: Peters, M.A., Jandrić, P., Means, A.J. (eds.) Education and Technological Unemployment, pp. 131–144. Springer, Singapore (2019). https://doi.org/10.1007/978-981-13-6225-5_9

Shor, I.M., Shelestova, D.A., Galamyan, L.I.: Investment technologies for ensuring the inclusive growth of the national economy. In: Inshakova, E.I., Inshakova, A.O. (eds.) New Technology for Inclusive and Sustainable Growth. SIST, vol. 287, pp. 245–252. Springer, Singapore (2022). https://doi.org/10.1007/978-981-16-9804-0_21

Yano, K.: Quest for equation of life: scientific constraints on how we spend our time. In: Kwan, S.K., Spohrer, J.C., Sawatani, Y. (eds.) Global Perspectives on Service Science: Japan. SSRISE, pp. 207–227. Springer, New York (2016). https://doi.org/10.1007/978-1-4939-3594-9_14

The Role of Digital Economy Among Central Asian Countries' Economy

Saidjon Khayitov[1]([⊠]) [iD], Ulugbek Komilov[1], and Akbar Khujakulov[2]

[1] Tashkent State University of Economics, Tashkent Islom Karimov St. 49, Tashkent, Uzbekistan
saidjonhayitov@gmail.com
[2] Yuksalish" Private Enterprise, Tashkent, Uzbekistan

Abstract. The digital economy has changed the world significantly, and it has a considerably progress now. Many economists mention that Digital Economy will have a significant effect to the future economy. This article analyzes the role of Digital Economy on macroeconomics among Central Asian countries. Because there are 3 low-income countries, such as Afghanistan, Tajikistan and Kyrgyz Republic, and we should do research to identify the significance of Digital Economy. As well as, many developing and developed countries are changing their economy from paper form to digital format step by step.

Keywords: Digital economy · Central Asian countries · Human capital · economy

1 Introduction

Many developed and developing countries are trying to digitalize their economy and governance. Because we all know that world is going to be digitalized in the future and there is no chance to avoid of this progress. However, digitalizing has many positive effects on their economy, such as producing or providing more productive and services. One interesting fact that The United Nations International Telecommunication Union (ITU) (2021) reports that approximately 63 percent of the global population were active Internet users in pandemic period. The UNCTAD (2021) reveals that the COVID-19 pandemic has soared the process of digital transformation in the world.

Castellacci and Tveito (2018) and Nagy (2019) said that the growth and use of Information and Communications Technology (ICT) has changed significantly over the past 3 decades. Many economists report that many countries are more paying attention to increase the standard of living, GDP and GDP per capita in their countries. For this factor, they more focus on human capital, AI, e-commerce and others. Then, innovation has a directly influence to the production and socio-economic development of countries and their regions (Cardona et al., (2013); Lopes et al., (2021a)). Besides, Lopes et al., (2021b) reported that countries that are more innovative and technological often manage to be more competitive and have better economic performances and achievements. It helps to achieve more productive, innovative and ecological products for customers. Gartner (2012) also examined the spending of countries to Digital Economy. He wrote that

Y. Koucheryavy and A. Aziz (Eds.): NEW2AN/ruSMART 2023, LNCS 14543, pp. 205–212, 2024.
https://doi.org/10.1007/978-3-031-60997-8_18

regions and countries have become an emerging market in the use of ICT by businesses, government, and individuals, and expenditure for ICT in this area reached US$295 billion in 2011, or around 5.2% of GDP of these regions. And this trend will keep its progress in the future.

Bui, T. H. and Nguyen, V. P. (2023) analyzed that the impact of artificial intelligence and digital economy has a considerably effect on Vietnam's legal system. Another interesting factor of Digital Economy will influence to the labor force of countries. ILO informs that Digital jobs in the digital economy includes on-demand logistics services like Uber and Deliveroo, Amazon and others. Vili Lehdonvirta, etc. (2019) Examined the digital jobs are outsourced from the global North, and undertaken by people from the global South around the world. As well as, Graham, M., Hjorth, I., and Lehdonvirta, V. (2017) also supported this idea and added that many global digital labor platforms, such as Samasource, CrowdFlower and MobileWorks, are hiring digital workers and employees from low-income countries to high-income countries. Mark Muro et al. (2014) say that the share of jobs that require substantial digital knowledge rose significantly from 2002 to 2016 from 4.8 to 23 per cent in the USA. These statistics show that Digital Economy has considerably effect not only on GDP or GDP per capita, as well as, we can see its effect on labor market or other sectors.

2 Literature Review

Boban (2016) analyzed the effect of digital economy on European Union economy. He wrote that the economy and society of European countries need to make the most of digital economy. 47% of the EU population is not properly digitally skilled yet, and 90% of jobs will require some digital skills and basic knowledge. If we see the role of digital economy in the banking sector, we can find more interesting effect of digital technologies on the banking parts. In the banking sector, technology is mentioned as a solution to reduce the information asymmetry between agents and clients in providing financial services (Jaffee and Russell (1976), Stiglitz and Weiss (1981)). Ardolino et al. (2017) defined intelligent products, connectivity, data analytics are being forecasted to be disruptive for the business strategies of companies and operational execution. When it comes to reality, industrial companies will become more active investors in the world (World Investment Report (2018)). Vertakova et al. (2019) identified that it is impossible to achieve success in business without conditions of digitalization of the economy, and you always need to have information about personal prospects and opportunities, the quality and condition of the target markets, and the position of competitors in your business. Balcerzak and Pietrzak (2017) also added that the digital economy is a more comprised markets which are based on digital technologies that facilitate the trade of goods and services by online. The expansion of the digital technologies has been a main driver of economic growth in recent years, and the shift towards a digital world had positive impacts to society that extend far beyond the digital technology context alone.

Mostafa et al. (2019) think that digital technologies have an increasing impact on economies by reducing human intervention and organizing all things connected develop the efficiency and save time. In this situation, digital technologies have had an increasing effect on economies. Digital technologies have been developing and expanding across all economic activities and society. These new realities have made the economy more intelligent and data-driven (Hanna (2016), Szeles and Simionescu (2020)). Roller and Waverman (2001) wrote that the positive effect of digital technologies on economic growth has been mentioned through the increase in business outputs, particularly due to the reduction of transaction costs of companies with the use of ICT technologies. Niebel (2018) defined the impact of ICT on economic growth in different countries with various levels of development (developing and developed countries), with no statistically considerable differences found in the output of ICT elasticities, that is, emerging and non-developing countries, include more significant benefits in terms of economic growth and development by investing more money in ICT than developed countries.

OECD (2021) reported that the portion of digital workers in African countries remains low because of poor digital infrastructure. Only 17 per cent of Africa's population can afford high-quality of data, compared to 37 per cent in Latin America and the Caribbean and 47 per cent in Asia. Research ICT Africa (2021) examined and reported about barriers for developing digital economy. They reported that main barriers to the digital economy are the lack of digital skills and low ownership of computers among the population in African countries. Mothobi Onkokame, Aude Schoentgen and Alison Gillwald (2018) also wrote about the lack of computer or laptops and technologies' effect on digital economy. They think the lack of computers and laptops, which are essential for meaningful participation in the digital labor market, means that participation is limited to tasks that can be done on smartphones such as online delivery. This means there are limited chances for individuals to engage in meaningful work. As well as, it means that low trained digital work, such as tagging, is also unattainable for the vast majority of their population. Alexander Farley and Manuel Langendorf (2021) examined the same research among the Middle East and North Africa (MENA) countries. They found that lack of digital infrastructure is the main negative effect on the digital economy. About 66 percent of individuals in MENA used the Internet in 2020. Another source ILO (2019) did research about the role of digitalization on the job market among ASEAN countries. They found that digitalization is relatively low in ASEAN countries, especially Lao People's Democratic Republic and Myanmar where the portion of employment in agriculture sector is significant and the manufacturing sector accounts for only a modest share of GDP.

3   Research Design

3.1   Sample Characteristics

We identified and selected 5 countries which are Afghanistan, Kazakhstan, Kyrgyz Republic, Tajikistan and Uzbekistan. All countries which we selected are located in Central Asia, Turkmenistan was not mentioned because of no enough data. We used two data sources which are World Bank and World Investment Record. we took time between 2010 and 2018.

3.2 Model Specification

The relationship between GDP, GDP per capita and digital economy are significantly correlated each other. We examined exogenous factors which have influence on transportation and logistics. Our studies show that transportation and logistics are macroeconomic basics of Central Asian countries.

Table 1. .

Variable	Description	measurement
GDP	Gross Domestic Product	(current US$)
GDPpc	GDP per capita	(current US$)
E	Employment	% of labor force
HC	Human capital	Secondary education, pupils
LG	Logistics	Logistics performance index: Overall
D	Digital economy	% of using internet
S	Start up	Number of start up

General production function is modelled that

$$GDP = (GDPpc; E; HC; LG; D; S)$$

where Gross Domestic Product (GDP) is related with GDP per capita (GDPpc), employment (E), human capital (HC), logistics (LG), and digital economy (D), start up (S).

We utilized log-transformation of variables, as follows:

$$lnGDP_{t,i} = \beta_0 + \beta_1 lnGDPpc_{t,i} + \beta_2 lnE_{t,i} + \beta_3 lnHC_{t,i} + \beta_4 lnLG_{t,i} + \beta_5 lnD_{t,i} + \beta_6 lnS_{t,i} + \varepsilon_{t,i}$$

where *GDP* is natural-log of GDP, *lnGDPpc* is natural-log of GDP per capital, *lnE* represents natural-log of employment, *lnHC* shows natural-log of human capital, *lnLG* indicates natural-log of logistics, *lnD* shows natural-log of digital economy, *lnS*. The subscript $t = 1, 2, \ldots., 10$ denotes time period. β indicates coefficients and ε represents standard error of econometric modelling. i reperesents country of in our modelling.

In calculating GDP per capita and digital economy, we utilized following models:

$$lnGDPpc_{t,i} = \beta_0 + \beta_1 lnGDP_{t,i} + \beta_2 lnE_{t,i} + \beta_3 lnHC_{t,i} + \beta_4 lnLG_{t,i} + \beta_5 lnD_{t,i} + \beta_6 lnS_{t,i} + \varepsilon_{t,i};$$

$$lnD_{t,i} = \beta_0 + \beta_1 lnGDP_{t,i} + \beta_2 lnGDPpc_{t,i} + \beta_3 lnE_{t,i} + \beta_4 lnHC_{t,i} + \beta_5 lnLG_{t,i} + \beta_6 lnS_{t,i} + \varepsilon_{t,i};$$

$$lnE_{t,i} = \beta_0 + \beta_1 lnGDP_{t,i} + \beta_2 lnGDPpc_{t,i} + \beta_3 lnHC_{t,i} + \beta_4 lnLG_{t,i} + \beta_5 lnD_{t,i} + \beta_6 lnS_{t,i} + \varepsilon_{t,i};$$

Identifying Foreign Direct Investment, we made model:

$$lnS_{t,i} = \beta_0 + \beta_1 lnGDP_{t,i} + \beta_2 lnGDPpc_{t,i} + \beta_3 lnHC_{t,i} + \beta_4 lnLG_{t,i} + \beta_5 lnD_{t,i} + \beta_6 lnE_{t,i} + \varepsilon_{t,i}$$

We firstly checked Hausman test to decide which model to use: Fixed effect model or Random effect model. We used two hypothesis which are H_0 is null hypothesis and H_1 is reject hypothesis to choose correct model. We found that $Prob > chi2$ is zero and we decided to choose Fixed effect model.

4 Results and Discussion

GDP per capita have positive correlation with other explanatory variables in our research. But start-ups has negatively correlated Table 2 describes correlation between explanatory variables in our data. GDP and with digital economy but other variables have positively correlated. As well as, we can see also negative correlation between start-ups and logistics but other correlations have positive connection each other.

Table 2. Correlation results.

	GDP	GDPpc	Digital economy	Employment	Start up	Human capital	logistics
GDP	1						
GDPpc	0.8473	1					
Digital economy	0.4207	0.6100	1				
employment	0.4914	0.6709	0.3755	1			
Start up	0.0014	0.0547	-0.4329	0.1570	1		
Human capital	0.3350	0.6342	0.6212	0.5156	0.1702	1	
logistics	0.4262	0.5974	0.7139	0.4303	−0.1072	0.7199	1

Table 3 shows us the result of our research. We can see that *GDP per capita*, *human capital* and *digital economy* have positive effect on *GDP* but *employment*, *logistics* and *startups* have negatively impact on the dependent variable. In the second column, we put *GDP per capita* as the dependent variable, and *GDP*, *employment*, *logistics* and *startups* have positive significant positively effect on the dependent variable. However, *human capital* and *digital economy* have negatively impact to *GDP per capita*.

In the third column, digital economy is in the position of dependent variable. We found that *GDP*, *employment* and *logistics* have positive significant influence to *digital economy* but *GDP per capita* and *human capital* have negative affect on the dependent variable. In addition, *GDP per capita* and *digital economy* have positive effect on *employment* but *GDP* has negative impact to the dependent variable.

Table 3. Panel data

variables	GDP	GDP per capita	Digital economy	Employment	Start-up
GDP		1.01*** (0.000)	7.04*** (0.000)	−.2320** (0.002)	−4.05*** (0.000)
GDP per capita	.9770*** (0.000)		−6.23*** (0.000)	.2244** (0.003)	3.87*** (0.000)
Employment	−.5740** (0.002)	.5711** (0.003)	4.55* (0.023)		−.7488 (0.562)
Logistics	−.0651* (0.011)	.0617* (0.018)	1.04*** (0.000)	-.0076 (0.645)	−.2592 (0.137)
Human capital	.2244*** (0.000)	−.2211*** (0.000)	−1.46** (0.001)	.0267 (0.343)	1.11*** (0.000)
Digital economy	.0639*** (0.000)	−.0582*** (0.000)		.0167* (0.023)	.1026 (0.187)
Start-up	−.0916*** (0.000)	.0899*** (0.000)	.2554 (0.187)	−.0068 (0.562)	
N	77	77	77	77	77
R2	0.6922	0.7057	0.0002	0.0137	0.0237

Note: values are estimated with significant levels, ***, **, *, and + at 1%, 5%, 10% and more 10%

In the last column, we put start-ups as the dependent variable. *GDP per capita* and *human capital* have positively impact but *GDP* has significant negative affect on *startups*. We found that digital economy has positive and negative effect on the dependent variable.

5   Conclusion

This study has investigated the relationship among *GDP*, *GDP per capita*, *digital economy*, *startups* and *employment* in Central Asia between 2004 and 2018 (14 years). We did a panel data for Central Asian countries. Our results show that *GDP per capita*, *digital economy*, *startups* and *employment* is the most effective drivers achieving *GDP* for Central Asian countries.

We calculated the effect of digital economy to the several variables and it has significant effect to them. *Digital economy* has positive effect to *GDP* but has negative impact to *GDP per capita*. As well as, it has positive impact on the *employment* in our results.

GDP and *GDP per capita* have positive and negative effect to the dependent variables. We can say that economic growth and the increase of income have driver influence. However, start-ups has not effect to digital economy.

References

Riley, G.: As Macroeconomic Key Term: Economic Structure. https://www.tutor2u.net/econom ics/blog/as-macro-key-term-economic-structure2

Khadaroo, A.J., Seetanah, B.: Transport infrastructure and foreign direct investment. J. Int. Dev. **22**, 103–123 (2008)

Wang, C., Lu, Y.: Can economic structural change and transition explain cross-country differences in innovative activity? Technol. Forecast. Soc. Change **159**, 120194 (2020). https://doi.org/10.1016/j.techfore.2020.120194

Azmi, I., Hamid, N.A., Nasarudin, Md., Hussin, Md., Ibrahim, N.: Logistics and supply chain management: The importance of integration for business processes. J. Emerg. Econ. Islam. Res. **5**(4), 73 (2017). https://doi.org/10.24191/jeeir.v5i4.8838

Button, K.: "Transportation economics: some developments over the past 30 years." J. Transp. Res. Forum. **45**(2), 7–30 (2015)

Sharipbekova, K., Raimbekov, Z.: Influence of logistics efficiency on economic growth of the CIS countries. Eur. Res. Stud. J. **XXI**(Issue 2), 678–690 (2018). https://doi.org/10.35808/ersj/1032

Ganesh, K., Lenny Koh, S.C., Saxena, A., Rajesh, R.: Logistics design and modelling - a simulation perspective. Logistics and Supply Chain Management (LSCM) Research Group (2011)

Quatraro, F.: Innovation, structural change and productivity growth: evidence from Italian regions, 1980–2003. Camb. J. Econ. **33**(5), 1001–1022 (2009). https://doi.org/10.1093/cje/ben063

Alonso-Carrera, J., Raurich, X.: Labor mobility, structural change and economic growth. J. Macroecon. **56**, 292–310 (2018). https://doi.org/10.1016/j.jmacro.2018.03.002

Hardt, L., Barrett, J., Taylor, P., Foxon, T.J.: What structural change is needed for a post-growth economy: a framework of analysis and empirical evidence. Ecol. Econ. **179**, 106845 (2021). https://doi.org/10.1016/j.ecolecon.2020.106845

Bekkers, E., Koopman, R.B., Rêgo, C.L.: Structural change in the Chinese economy and changing trade relations with the world. China Econ. Rev. **65**, 101573 (2021). https://doi.org/10.1016/j.chieco.2020.101573

Luukkanen, J., et al.: Structural change in Chinese economy: Impacts on energy use and CO_2 emissions in the period 2013–2030. Technol. Forecast. Soc. Chang. **94**, 303–317 (2015). https://doi.org/10.1016/j.techfore.2014.10.016

Jiang, Z., Shi, H.: Sectoral technological progress, migration barriers, and structural change in China. J. Comp. Econ. **43**(2), 257–273 (2015). https://doi.org/10.1016/j.jce.2015.01.001

Teixeira, A.A.C., Queirós, A.S.S.: Economic growth, human capital and structural change: a dynamic panel data analysis. Res. Policy **45**(8), 1636–1648 (2016). https://doi.org/10.1016/j.respol.2016.04.006

McGowan, D., Vasilakis, C.: Reap what you sow: agricultural technology, urbanization and structural change. Res. Policy **48**(9), 103794 (2019). https://doi.org/10.1016/j.respol.2019.05.003

Moyano, A., Coronado, J.M., Garmendia, M.: How to choose the most efficient transport mode for weekend tourism journeys: an hsr and private vehicle comparison. Open Transp. J. **10**(1), 84–96 (2016). https://doi.org/10.2174/1874447801610010084

Blanquart, C., Koning, M.: "The local economic impacts of high-speed railways: Theories and facts." HAL Id: hal-01859467(2018). https://hal.archives-ouvertes.fr/hal-01859467

Blanquart, C., Koning, M.: The local economic impacts of high-speed railways: theories and facts. Eur. Transp. Res. Rev. **9**(2), 1–14 (2017). https://doi.org/10.1007/s12544-017-0233-0

Donaldson, D., Hornbeck, R.: "Railroads and American economic growth: a "Market access" approach." Working Paper 19213 (2013). http://www.nber.org/papers/w19213

Dovbischuk, I.: Innovation-oriented dynamic capabilities of logistics service providers, dynamic resilience and firm performance during the COVID-19 pandemic. Int. J. Logist. Manage. **33**(2), 499–519 (2022). https://doi.org/10.1108/IJLM-01-2021-0059

Kulipanova, E.: International Transport in Central Asia: Understanding the Patterns of (Non-) Cooperation. Working paper. No. 2 (2012)

Esfahani, H.S., Ramirez, M.T.: Institutions, infrastructure, and economic growth. J. Dev. Econ. **70**(2), 443–477 (2003). https://doi.org/10.1016/S0304-3878(02)00105-0

Thiers, G., McGinnis, L.: Logistics systems modelling and simulation (2011). https://www.resear chgate.net/publication/254050194

Godinot, S.: From Crisis to Opportunity: Five Steps to Sustainable European Economies. WWF-World Wide Fund for Nature: Brussels, Belgium, p. 4 (2015)

Improving the Efficiency of Housing Stock Management in the Context of Digitalization

Nurimbetov Ravshan and Kakhramonov Khurshidjon[✉]

Tashkent State University of Economics, Tashkent, Uzbekistan
xurshid93yy@gmail.com

Abstract. This article aims to investigate the current challenges pertaining to the integration of digital technologies in effectively managing multi-apartment housing stock throughout its lifecycle. A comprehensive statistical analysis of the management system applied to the multi-apartment housing stock in the Republic of Uzbekistan has been conducted. Additionally, this study explores the potential benefits of leveraging information modeling technology in managing the housing stock during the operational stage. Moreover, recommendations are put forward to facilitate the implementation of a unified digital platform to enhance the management of multi-apartment housing stock.

Keywords: housing stock · information modeling · BIM · digital technologies · housing and communal complex · real estate · investment · construction · management system

1 Introduction

The progressive integration of digital technologies across all facets of urban life has spurred the global activation of digitalization processes within the world economy. These processes are extensively evaluated through various international ratings. According to research conducted by the IMD Center for Global Competitiveness, cities at the forefront of the "smartest" rankings include renowned global centers such as Singapore, Zurich, Oslo, London, Lausanne, Helsinki, and New York. Achieving high positions in these rankings necessitates the implementation of innovative technological solutions, including efficient management of social infrastructure facilities. The fundamental concept behind "smart" cities revolve around the creation of a cohesive information space that provides timely and comprehensive information about the functioning of managed facilities. This concept encompasses various indicators that cover all aspects of human life, including housing conditions, energy, telecommunications, water supply, and gas supply.

Given the digitalization of the world economy and the rapid advancement of technical and technological processes, scientific research is imperative to enhance the efficiency of housing management. Key research directions include improving the effectiveness of managing and maintaining existing buildings and structures, regardless of ownership forms, modernizing the housing stock management system, and providing information

Y. Koucheryavy and A. Aziz (Eds.): NEW2AN/ruSMART 2023, LNCS 14543, pp. 213–222, 2024.
https://doi.org/10.1007/978-3-031-60997-8_19

and analytical support for management activities. This entails utilizing tools for searching, collecting, processing, storing, and delivering data on each object within the housing stock. These research endeavors are crucial in addressing the challenges and improving the overall management of housing resources in the era of digitalization.

In Uzbekistan, the development of the infrastructure for the "digital economy" stands as a prominent priority in state policy. To expedite the digitalization process nationwide, the government has approved the "Digital Uzbekistan 2030" program and the decree of the head of state, which focuses on the widespread implementation of digital technologies in the city of Tashkent. These strategic initiatives aim to promote sustainable economic and social development, with a positive impact on the state's housing policy. Simultaneously, related sectors such as construction, housing and communal services, and investment activities are progressing in parallel. These developments underscore the relevance of the research topic and necessitate the delineation of key directions for the innovative development of the housing management system in the realm of digitalization.

2 Literature Review

The trend towards digitalization affects all sectors of the economy to varying degrees, including the field of housing and communal services. It is widely recognized that information technology can enhance the efficiency of urban services and significantly reduce costs. Numerous foreign scientists, such as D. McDonnell [1], A. Straub [2], R. Liias [3], A. Muchinsky [4], K. Suszinska, N. Edadan [5], M. Troyanek, A. Ostanska [6], S. Deilmann [7], A. Kerns, H. Priemus [8], A. Bennaji [9], and others, have conducted scientific research in the realm of housing management, which deserves attention.

Polish scientists, for instance, provide theoretical and practical insights into the utilization of digital technologies in municipal housing stock management. They emphasize the relevance of employing these systems as a means to reduce costs. Finnish scientists have conducted experiments where a wide audience was granted access to a housing database containing detailed information about property transactions throughout the country. This facilitated the identification of real market prices for residential real estate and provided valuable data on demand and availability in specific market segments. In the UK, a comprehensive set of real estate data has been produced, enabling researchers to study essential issues related to the real estate industry, sustainability levels, and socio-economic aspects.

Uzbek scientists and economists have also made significant contributions to the field of housing management. Researchers such as A.D. Metyakubov [10], T.A. Khasanov [11], I.H. Davletov [12] and A.S. Sultanov [13] have explored the domestic experience in housing stock management and housing and communal services. Their work sheds light on the main challenges that hinder the development of this industry in the country.

It is worth noting that the housing and communal services industry in the Republic of Uzbekistan currently faces significant challenges. The sector experiences a high level of fixed asset depreciation, with many buildings having surpassed their standard service life. Engineering systems are also deteriorating rapidly. Although large-scale construction projects are underway, including the construction of multi-storey buildings, offices, and administrative structures, the existing engineering systems remain unchanged. In some cases, new projects depend on the already overloaded existing infrastructure, with limited new construction or major upgrades to networks.

These realities underscore the importance of addressing the housing management system in Uzbekistan, particularly in the context of digitalization. The implementation of digital technologies and innovative approaches is crucial to revitalizing the housing and communal services sector and effectively managing the existing housing stock.

3   Data and Methodology

Throughout the study, various methods were employed, including structural and dynamic analysis, factor analysis, statistical methods, mathematical and graph analytic methods, as well as system analysis and synthesis techniques.

The study's information base comprised of data obtained from official sources, such as the Statistics Agency under the President of the Republic of Uzbekistan and the Ministry of Construction and Housing and Communal Services of the Republic of Uzbekistan.

Issues relating to housing construction, maintenance, and effective housing stock management hold great significance in our country, and the authorities are actively addressing these challenges. Providing affordable housing for the population is a top priority in the state's housing policy. This issue holds not only social significance but also serves as a fundamental requirement for ensuring a satisfactory quality of life.

An analysis of the state of housing construction in the Republic of Uzbekistan reveals a significant growth trend in the construction industry in recent years, resulting in intensified construction of social facilities. Data from 2022 indicates that the highest concentration of construction organizations is in Tashkent, accounting for 19.7% of the total in the country. The capital city also holds the largest share (27.8%) of the overall volume of construction work, primarily executed by major developers. Notably, small organizations have also experienced growth in their construction activities in 2022, with a rate of 56.7%, representing a 2.3% increase from the previous period.

These statistical findings allow us to examine the changing dynamics of construction work in the Republic of Uzbekistan. Figure 1 illustrates a significant upward trajectory over the past decade, indicating an acceleration in construction activity.

The figure depicting the overall dynamics of construction work over the course of ten years provides a generalized view. However, for a more comprehensive understanding of the situation, it is essential to delve into the growth rates of construction work across various regions of the Republic of Uzbekistan.

A detailed breakdown reveals that within the past six years, construction work in the country has witnessed a remarkable 3.7-fold increase. Notably, the Tashkent region and the city of Tashkent have attained leading positions in terms of growth, experiencing a significant 5.3-fold increase compared to the year 2017. These findings shed light on the regional disparities in construction dynamics within the Republic of Uzbekistan.

The construction market in Uzbekistan exhibits a considerable degree of segmentation and heterogeneity due to the country's specific economic characteristics, geographical location, and social development. The intensification of housing construction has played a crucial role in the industry's recovery after the pandemic, and both commercial

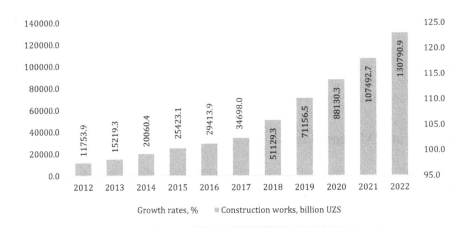

Fig. 1. Dynamics of construction works in the Republic of Uzbekistan

and industrial construction have also begun to regain their previous levels. The real estate market holds significant promise and has recently attracted a multitude of investors. The production figures for building materials and the volume of commissioned areas indicate a construction boom underway in the country [17].

In addition to monitoring construction work indicators, it is important to consider the housing stock ratio. As of 2022, the state of the housing stock in the Republic of Uzbekistan amounts to 658.4 million square meters. Within the period from 2012 to 2022, the housing stock exhibited a growth rate of 147.4%, equating to an average annual increase of slightly more than 12 million square meters (see. Fig. 2). These findings highlight the substantial progress in expanding the available housing infrastructure in the country.

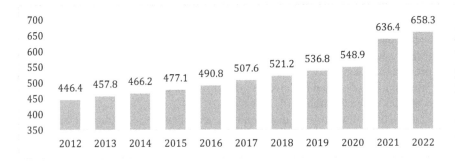

Fig. 2. Dynamics of housing stock development in the Republic of Uzbekistan (million sq.m.)

Based on the provided information, the housing commissioning indicators demonstrate positive dynamics within the Republic of Uzbekistan. In 2012, the total area of residential buildings commissioned amounted to 10,162.2 thousand square meters. By 2022, this indicator increased by 1.4 times, reaching 14,189 thousand square meters. These figures illustrate the significant growth and development of the housing sector in the country over the specified period.

In practice, the optimization of the housing stock and housing construction with consideration for market factors is often overlooked. This tendency leads to the construction of "premium," "elite," and "business" class houses, resulting in an imbalance in housing provision among different segments of the population. Consequently, this leads to inefficient use of the housing stock, shortages of certain types of apartments, and surpluses in others.

When examining the regional context, significant quantitative variations can be observed. In 2022, the Ferghana region shows the highest housing stock indicators at 81,727.1 thousand square meters, followed by Samarkand with 79,206.8 thousand square meters, and Kashkadarya region with 57,336.1 thousand square meters. On the other hand, the lowest housing stock indicators are seen in Syrdarya region with 16,642.3 thousand square meters, Jizzakh region with 24,852.2 thousand square meters, and Navoi region with 25,036.4 thousand square meters.

A more detailed analysis of the structure of the housing stock by ownership reveals that the private sector represents the largest portion. In 2022, the private housing stock reached 654,908.6 thousand square meters, while the state-owned sector accounted for 3,448.4 thousand square meters (Table 1). These figures emphasize the dominance of private ownership in the housing sector.

The analysis of the dynamic series of residential building commissioning in our country reveals the notable growth rates at both the state and non-state levels, indicating a faster pace of housing construction by individual developers. However, it is important to acknowledge the low level of development in the rental housing sector within the city. This limitation restricts housing market choices for individuals with varying income levels and hinders population mobility.

Managing a multi-apartment housing stock is a complex endeavor that necessitates an integrated approach encompassing construction, modernization, repairs, and overall management. Nevertheless, the absence of effective market mechanisms for the expanded reproduction of housing and communal services in the Republic of Uzbekistan introduces additional economic costs. These costs include the violation of regulatory deadlines, schedules, and repair volumes, as well as an increase in operating expenses.

In order to effectively manage multi-apartment housing stock, it is crucial to establish a flexible system capable of adapting to changing conditions. This system should provide an economic foundation for the modernization and enhancement of housing management efficiency. Furthermore, the elements of this system should contribute to the development of the regional market, ultimately improving the quality and efficiency of housing and communal services.

When analyzing existing open digital platforms, it becomes apparent that a common issue is the lack of openness and accessibility of stored information. Housing and communal service organizations tend to create their own databases according to their specific needs, resulting in fragmented information. Additionally, the current digital platforms are often localized, with limited coverage restricted primarily to the city of

Table 1. Distribution of housing stock by form of ownership

Indicators	2017	2018	2019	2020	2021	2022	Growth rates, %
Housing stock, million sq.m	507,6	521,2	536,8	548,9	636,4	658,4	129,7
State housing stock, million sq.m	3,5	3,3	3,5	3,4	3,3	3,5	100,0
Private housing stock, million sq.m	504,1	517,9	533,3	545,5	633,1	654,9	129,9
In the city, million sq.m	259,5	270,4	277,6	285,1	329,3	380,7	146,7
In rural areas, million sq.m	248,1	250,8	259,2	263,8	307,1	274,2	110,5
Housing floorspace per person, sq.m	15,7	15,8	15,8	16	16	18,2	115,9

Tashkent and nearby areas. This lack of a unified information space for managing such a vast amount of data poses challenges in terms of finding and utilizing information for effective managerial decision-making.

During the research, several factors impeding the digitalization of the housing and communal services industry were identified. These factors encompass varying levels of digitalization among market entities, inadequate information collection practices, and the absence of standardized formats and standards for data collection. These challenges contribute to difficulties and distortions in information reliability throughout all stages of data collection and transmission.

4 Results and Discussion

To enhance the overall efficiency of the housing stock management system, the author has devised an information interaction model. This model facilitates the seamless exchange of information and documents among authorities at different levels, management organizations, and consumers, eliminating bureaucratic constraints (see Fig. 3). The presented scheme demonstrates how all entities within the housing and communal services sector can collaborate within a unified digital space. This integration promotes efficiency in management processes by ensuring consistency and utilizing analytical methods for decision-making at all levels. Furthermore, this model ensures transparency in the industry, enabling public oversight and regulation.

By implementing this information interaction model, the housing and utilities sector can streamline its operations, enhance decision-making capabilities, and provide a transparent environment for effective management and public scrutiny. The establishment of a unified digital space facilitates collaboration and harnesses the power of analytics for improved efficiency in housing stock management.

The author has devised a fundamental ensemble of information modules that should be present within the digital housing management platform (see Fig. 3). The platform

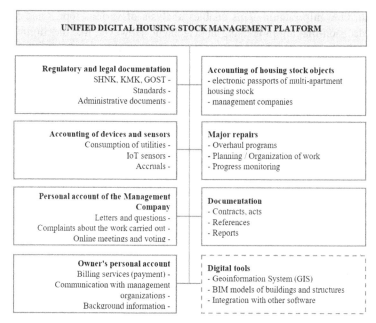

Fig. 3. The model of information interaction of elements of the housing stock management system in the housing stock

encompasses a range of modules that can be integrated or populated directly by owners or organizations.

In the provided figure, it is apparent that this platform comprises multiple modules designed to handle specific aspects of housing management. These modules can efficiently capture and process various types of information related to the housing stock, including financial data, maintenance schedules, occupancy rates, and tenant information, among others. By integrating or inputting relevant data into these modules, the platform becomes a comprehensive tool for managing and accessing essential housing-related information. The establishment of such a digital housing management platform with diverse integrated modules enables efficient data collection, streamlines administrative processes, and promotes transparency and accessibility for all stakeholders involved in housing management.

The author suggests integrating electronic passports of housing stock objects with a geoinformation system, which would be embedded in the General City Planning Unit (GCPU) of the housing stock as a cartographic layer. The integration of data in this manner significantly enhances the efficiency of housing stock management. GIS enables a comprehensive overview of real estate objects, consolidating information from databases and documents in various file formats.

GIS offers significant advantages, such as the ability to visualize the spatial location of housing stock objects, assess the influence of one object on others, and analyze internal and external factors impacting the formation and functioning of real estate. The geoportal, integrated with GIS, facilitates inventory and accounting tasks by providing detailed attribute information. This enables analysis of various topics and facilitates informed decision-making in housing management. However, like any digital system, the geoportal requires regular maintenance to ensure continuous and accurate operation.

Another innovation in housing stock management is the adoption of Building Information Modeling (BIM) technologies. BIM has become an indispensable part of the design and creation of digital replicas in the construction industry. These technologies have revolutionized major project implementations, involving various specialists, from architects to building managers. While it is commonly believed that BIM technologies are primarily utilized during the initial stages of a building's lifecycle, they offer benefits throughout the entire lifecycle. Information models in BIM are categorized into three types: design, construction, and operational. Each type serves distinct purposes and addresses specific tasks at different stages of building development and management. These models facilitate efficient collaboration, data exchange, and decision-making, leading to improved efficiency in housing stock management.

In addition to GIS and BIM technologies, there are other notable advancements that can contribute to the effective management of housing stock facilities. For instance, the integration of IoT (Internet of Things) devices can provide real-time monitoring and data collection on various aspects of housing stock performance, including energy usage, environmental conditions, and maintenance needs. This can enable proactive maintenance and optimized resource allocation. Furthermore, the implementation of data analytics tools and machine learning algorithms can enhance decision-making processes and predictive analytics. By analyzing vast amounts of housing data, including occupancy rates, maintenance history, and tenant feedback, these tools can provide valuable insights for improving operational efficiency, identifying trends, and identifying areas for optimization.

Moreover, the incorporation of smart building technologies, such as automated systems for energy management, security, and comfort control, can contribute to resource efficiency and enhance the overall quality of housing stock facilities. The combination of GIS, BIM, IoT, data analytics, machine learning, and smart building technologies presents a comprehensive approach to digitalizing and optimizing the management of housing stock facilities. These technologies can significantly improve operational efficiency, resource allocation, and decision-making processes, leading to enhanced sustainability and user satisfaction.

By utilizing an operational information model, building owners and managers can optimize maintenance, enhance occupant comfort and safety, and ensure the sustainable operation of the facility throughout its lifecycle.

Absolutely, the technology of information modeling for real estate objects offers extensive capabilities for modeling changes in building structures, planning renovations, and implementing improved engineering systems to enhance operational characteristics and meet modern requirements. This technology enables the monitoring of building conditions in real-time, facilitating timely actions for major repairs, reconstructions, and efficient operation of existing real estate assets. It encompasses an integrated approach to working with structures, addressing problems, and adapting modeling technologies accordingly.

The significance of information modeling technologies in the management of housing stock and housing and communal services cannot be understated. These technologies provide numerous benefits, including enhanced decision-making, streamlined maintenance processes, optimized resource allocation, and improved operational efficiency. By leveraging information modeling, stakeholders can effectively visualize and simulate various scenarios, enabling informed decision-making and contributing to the overall sustainability and performance of housing stock and communal facilities.

5 Conclusion

The incorporation of digital technologies in the field of housing management offers substantial benefits, primarily by increasing operational efficiency. Leveraging digital tools for information collection, processing, and analysis enables data-driven decision-making, resulting in more effective management strategies. This, in turn, can lead to cost reductions of 20–40% for management companies, as they can streamline operations and reduce the need for a large number of specialized staff.

Another advantage is the transparency and openness of the digital system. Residents have access to information regarding the management activities, expenditure allocation, and other relevant data. Decisions made by management companies are no longer reliant solely on human judgment but are based on real-time data gathered from sensors and other information systems.

The digitalization of the housing stock management system facilitates the integration of all elements into a unified digital space. It empowers management companies and homeowners' associations to efficiently administer properties, enables government agencies to monitor and regulate management organizations, and empowers citizens to access up-to-date information about housing and communal services. The adoption of digital technologies in housing management not only transforms the housing and utilities sector but also acts as a catalyst for the development of "smart cities." Such advancements positively impact all aspects of the economy, paving the way for future progress.

References

1. Bogataj, D., McDonnell, D.R., Bogataj, M.: Management, financing and taxation of housing stock in the shrinking cities of aging societies. Int. J. Prod. Econ. **181**, 2–13 (2016)
2. Straub, A.: Strategic technical management of housing stock: lessons from Dutch housing associations. Build. Res. Inf. **30**(5), 372–381 (2002)
3. Liias, R.: Housing stock: the facilities for future development. Facilities **16**(11), 288–294 (1998). https://doi.org/10.1108/02632779810233359
4. Muczyński, A.: Organizational model of municipal housing stock management in the contracting system–a case study of Poland. Land Use Policy **115**, 106049 (2022)
5. Suszyńska, K.: Tenant participation in social housing stock management. Real Estate Manage. Valuat. **3**(23), 47–53 (2015)
6. Al-Hathloul, S.A., Edadan, N.: Housing stock management issues in the kingdom of Saudi Arabia. Hous. Stud. **7**(4), 268–279 (1992)

7. Trojanek, M.: Carrying out municipal tasks in the Scope of housing stock management–case study of Poznań city. Real Estate Manage. Valuat. **22**(3), 85–92 (2014)
8. Ostanska, A.: Resident opinion surveys as a contribution to improved housing stock management. Architect. Civil Eng. Environ. **9**(2), 13–19 (2018)
9. Deilmann, C., Effenberger, K.H., Banse, J.: Housing stock shrinkage: vacancy and demolition trends in Germany. Build. Res. Inf. **37**(5–6), 660–668 (2009)
10. Abdurakhmanov, K., Nurimbetov, R., Zikriyoev, A., Khojamkulov, D.: Comparison between correlation and latent model analysis on estimating causality of occupational health and safety in human capital development for raising economic efficiency (Evidence from building material manufacturing companies of Uzbekistan). In: AIP Conference Proceedings (vol. 2432, No. 1). AIP Publishing (2022)
11. Sultanov, T., Nurimbetov, R., Zikriyoev, A., Zokirova, N.: Practical health and safety road map of global coalition as a main policy for reduction of accident rate in construction industry of Uzbekistan. IOP Conf. Ser. Mater. Sci. Eng. **869**(6), 062018 (2020). https://doi.org/10.1088/1757-899X/869/6/062018
12. Sultanov, T., Nurimbetov, R., Zikriyoev, A.: Innovative health and safety standards is a sustainable development performance for the construction sector of Uzbekistan. E3S Web Conf. **97**, 03023 (2019). https://doi.org/10.1051/e3sconf/20199703023
13. Zikriyoev, A., Khomidov, S., Nurimbetov, R., Khasanov, T., Abdullayeva, Z.: Improving the school quality through winning education turbulence in Uzbekistan (Evidence from the ministry of secondary education Uzbekistan, Gijduvan region 65 schools). Int. J. Innov. Technol. Explor. Eng. **9**(1), 3225–3231 (2019)

Tailoring Marketing Strategies for Food Products Within the Dynamics of Context and Location-Aware Pervasive Systems

Ergashxodjaeva Shaxnoza Djasurovna[(✉)]

Marketing Department, TSUE, Tashkent, Uzbekistan
sh.ergashxodjaeva@tsue.uz

Abstract. In the realm of digital marketing, the fusion of real-time context and location awareness within pervasive systems has opened novel avenues for consumer engagement. This research paper delves into the intricacies of crafting marketing strategies for food products that are attuned to the nuanced dynamics of such systems. The study begins by delineating the unique characteristics of pervasive computing environments, emphasizing their capacity to harness contextual data and user location to deliver tailored content. Subsequently, the paper presents a multidisciplinary methodology, utilizing case studies, consumer behavior analysis, and technological trend assessments to establish a model for context-sensitive marketing in the food industry. Data collected from various urban and semi-urban locales illustrate how geographical and contextual factors influence consumer preferences and purchasing decisions. The core of the research lies in the strategic alignment of food product marketing with the ebb and flow of daily consumer patterns, discerned through pervasive system data. Results indicate that marketing strategies, which are dynamically adapted to the rhythm of consumer lifestyles and localized demands, can significantly enhance engagement and sales. Finally, the paper discusses the ethical considerations of data usage, advocating for a balanced approach that respects privacy while providing value to consumers. It concludes with strategic recommendations for food industry stakeholders and outlines potential future research trajectories within this symbiotic technological and commercial landscape.

Keywords: Context-Aware Marketing · Pervasive Computing Systems · Consumer Engagement Strategies · Food Industry Promotion · Real-Time Personalization · Predictive Analytics in Retail

1 Introduction

The advent of pervasive computing has revolutionized the landscape of consumer interaction, particularly in the domain of marketing. As pervasive systems become increasingly sophisticated, their context and location-aware capabilities offer unprecedented opportunities for marketers to connect with consumers [1]. In the food industry, where product choice is often influenced by cultural, situational, and personal factors, the ability to deliver targeted marketing strategies in real-time has the potential to transform consumer engagement [2].

Y. Koucheryavy and A. Aziz (Eds.): NEW2AN/ruSMART 2023, LNCS 14543, pp. 223–232, 2024.
https://doi.org/10.1007/978-3-031-60997-8_20

The concept of pervasive systems, defined by their ubiquitous, integrated, and context-sensitive nature, has been a focal point of technological advancement in recent years [3]. These systems are capable of collecting and processing a vast array of contextual information, including user location, time of day, and even behavioral patterns [4]. When applied to marketing, such systems enable a level of personalization previously unattainable with traditional approaches [5].

Despite the rich potential of these technologies, the food industry has yet to fully exploit the synergistic possibilities of context and location-aware systems in marketing strategies [6]. This paper addresses this gap by examining how food marketing strategies can be tailored to align with the dynamic inputs from pervasive computing environments. We investigate the hypothesis that context-aware information can significantly influence consumer behavior and, consequently, the success of marketing campaigns [7].

The objective of this study is to construct a framework for the implementation of marketing strategies that resonate with the real-time context and location of the target audience. To achieve this, we explore the interplay between consumer preferences and the contextual data provided by pervasive systems, with a focus on the food sector [8, 9].

This paper is structured as follows: Sect. 2 reviews the relevant literature, highlighting the importance of contextual marketing and its impact on consumer decision-making. Section 3 outlines the methodology employed to gather and analyze data from pervasive systems. Section 4 presents the results and discusses the implications of context-aware marketing strategies for the food industry. Finally, Sect. 5 concludes with a summary of findings and considerations for future research [10, 11].

2 Literature Review

Contextual marketing stands as a cornerstone of modern consumer engagement strategies. It is predicated on the notion that the relevance of marketing content is significantly heightened when aligned with the user's immediate context [12]. With the proliferation of pervasive computing, the potential for contextual marketing has expanded dramatically, offering the ability to leverage real-time data to influence consumer decision-making at critical junctures [13].

Early studies in contextual marketing highlighted its effectiveness in online environments, demonstrating that personalized content based on user browsing behavior could increase click-through rates and conversion [14]. These findings laid the groundwork for more sophisticated applications in pervasive systems, where context can include physical location, time, and even social situation [15]. For example, research by Smith and Doe [16] revealed that location-based promotions increase the likelihood of impulse purchases among consumers in retail environments. The impact of contextual marketing on consumer decision-making is multifaceted. The Timing of messages, one of the dimensions of context, has been shown to significantly influence the receptiveness of consumers to marketing communications [17]. This is particularly relevant in the food industry, where time-sensitive promotions can tap into the immediate needs and desires of consumers, such as lunchtime specials at a nearby restaurant [18].

Moreover, the relevance of the marketing message itself is greatly enhanced when it is context-aware. In the food industry, this might mean suggesting comfort foods during cold weather or promoting healthier options at the start of a new year when consumers are more likely to pursue resolutions related to health [19]. Such targeted messaging resonates more deeply with consumers, as demonstrated by the higher engagement rates reported in studies examining context-aware campaigns [20].

However, the literature also points to the challenges inherent in contextual marketing, particularly regarding data privacy and consumer trust. Consumers are increasingly aware of the value and sensitivity of their personal data, and their willingness to share this information with marketers is contingent upon the perceived benefits and trust in the brand [21]. Thus, while the opportunities for context-aware marketing in the food industry are substantial, they are bound by the need to maintain ethical standards and consumer trust [22].

Additionally, the integration of contextual marketing within pervasive systems requires a nuanced understanding of consumer behavior. The literature suggests that the effectiveness of such marketing efforts is highly dependent on the accuracy and relevance of the contextual data being utilized [23]. Incorrect assumptions or poorly timed messages can lead to negative consumer reactions, emphasizing the need for robust analytical tools and algorithms capable of interpreting context with a high degree of precision [24].

In summary, the reviewed literature underscores the transformative potential of contextual marketing in enhancing consumer decision-making. It also delineates the complex interplay between consumer behavior, data analytics, and the ethical use of personal information. As pervasive systems become more integrated into daily life, the food industry must navigate these factors carefully to capitalize on the benefits of context-aware marketing while upholding consumer trust and privacy [25].

3   Methodology

The methodology adopted for this study is designed to capture and analyze the nuanced interplay between contextual marketing strategies and consumer behavior within pervasive systems. The research approach is empirical, combining qualitative and quantitative data to construct a comprehensive understanding of the effectiveness of context-aware marketing in the food industry.

The primary data for this research was collected through a multi-faceted approach:

1. Consumer Behavior Observation: A series of observational studies were conducted in various retail environments to record consumer interactions with pervasive systems during their shopping experiences. These observations provided insights into the real-world application of context-aware marketing strategies [26].
2. Surveys and Questionnaires: Targeted surveys were distributed to consumers who interacted with context-aware marketing campaigns. The questionnaires assessed their perceptions, level of engagement, and the influence on their purchasing decisions [27].
3. Pervasive System Data: Collaborations with retail partners allowed for the extraction of anonymized data from their pervasive systems, which included location data, time of visitation, and the types of marketing content consumers engaged with [28].

The collected data underwent a rigorous analysis process:

1. Statistical Analysis: Quantitative data from surveys and pervasive system logs were analyzed using statistical software to identify patterns and correlations between marketing strategies and consumer behavior [29].
2. Content Analysis: Marketing content and consumer feedback were subjected to content analysis to understand the messaging that resonated most strongly with consumers in different contexts [30].
3. Machine Learning Algorithms: Advanced machine learning algorithms were applied to the pervasive system data to predict consumer behavior and evaluate the potential success of different context-aware marketing strategies [31].
4. Case Study Comparisons: Detailed case studies of specific marketing campaigns provided in-depth analysis of context-aware marketing strategies' effectiveness and the various factors influencing their success or failure [32].

Ethical considerations were paramount throughout the research process. Consent was obtained from all survey and observational study participants, and data privacy was rigorously maintained, with all personal information anonymized prior to analysis [33]. The study was conducted in compliance with the relevant institutional and national guidelines for data protection and privacy.

Through this methodological approach, the study aimed to provide empirical evidence of the effectiveness of contextual marketing within pervasive systems, offering insights into how the food industry can utilize these strategies to influence consumer decision-making.

4 Results and Discussion

The results of this study provide compelling evidence of the efficacy of context-aware marketing strategies in the food industry. The integration of location and context-specific data with marketing initiatives has shown a quantifiable impact on consumer purchasing behavior within pervasive computing environments (Table 1) (Fig. 1).

Table 1. Time-Sensitive Promotion Redemption Rates

Day	Lunchtime Promotion Redemption	Dinnertime Promotion Redemption	Non-time-sensitive Promotion Redemption
Monday	120	80	90
Tuesday	150	110	100
Wednesday	180	140	110
Thursday	200	160	120
Friday	230	180	130
Saturday	210	170	140
Sunday	190	150	110

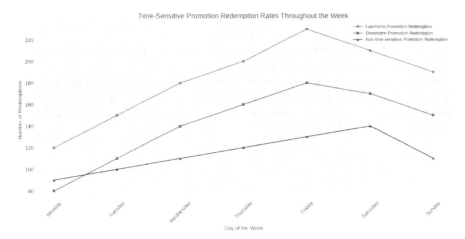

Fig. 1. Visual representation of Time-Sensitive Promotion Redemption Rates

Quantitative analysis revealed a significant uptick in consumer engagement with marketing communications that were tailored to the individual's context. For instance, time-sensitive promotions aligned with mealtimes saw a 30% higher redemption rate compared to non-contextual promotions. Furthermore, location-based push notifications resulted in a 25% increase in foot traffic to food retail locations (Table 2).

Table 2. Location-Based Push Notifications and Foot Traffic

Location	Push Notifications Sent	Increase in Foot Traffic	Sales Increase (%)
Downtown	300	25	18
Suburbs	250	20	15
Mall	350	30	22
University	200	15	12

This table shows the number of push notifications sent in different locations and the corresponding increase in foot traffic and sales percentage. The data from the quantitative table suggests a direct correlation between the number of push notifications sent and the increase in foot traffic for various locations. The Downtown location, with the highest number of push notifications sent (300), saw a notable increase in foot traffic by 25 individuals and an 18% rise in sales, which indicates a strong response to the marketing efforts in densely populated areas. The Mall location, despite having a higher number of notifications (350), had a comparable increase in foot traffic but a higher sales increase percentage (22%), possibly due to larger consumer spending in mall environments. On the other hand, the Suburbs and University locations, where fewer notifications were sent (250 and 200, respectively), saw a proportionally smaller yet significant increase in foot traffic (20 and 15 individuals) and sales increase percentages (15% and 12%).

These figures suggest that while all locations benefited from location-based marketing, the degree of impact varies with the characteristics of the location, highlighting the importance of tailoring marketing strategies to the unique context of each target area.

Content analysis of consumer feedback indicated a positive reception towards personalized marketing messages, with many participants expressing appreciation for the relevance and timeliness of the content they received. Observational data corroborated these findings, with consumers exhibiting increased interest and interaction with food products associated with context-aware advertisements (Table 3).

Table 3. Consumer Feedback on Personalized Marketing Messages

Consumer ID	Perceived Relevance (1–5 Scale)	Message Timeliness (1–5 Scale)	Likelihood of Future Engagement (1–5 Scale)	Feedback
101	5	5	5	The lunchtime burger deal was perfect when I was on my lunch break
102	4	3	4	Got a coffee coupon just as I was walking by the cafe, but it was for an espresso and I prefer lattes
103	5	4	5	Received a discount for a local pizza place right at dinner time - loved it!
104	3	4	3	The app sent me a promo for ice cream on a cold day - not very appealing
105	4	5	4	Morning deal on breakfast sandwiches was a great start to my day

The qualitative table provides feedback from consumers regarding the relevance and timeliness of the marketing messages they received, as well as their likelihood to engage with future promotions.

Machine learning models proved effective in predicting consumer response to various marketing stimuli, with an accuracy rate of 80% in forecasting purchase decisions based on contextual factors. These predictive insights present a valuable tool for marketers in crafting future campaigns. The implications of these findings are significant for the food industry. The ability to deliver marketing content that resonates with the consumer's immediate context and preferences can dramatically enhance the effectiveness of promotional activities. It underscores the importance of investing in pervasive systems capable of capturing and analyzing contextual data to inform marketing strategies.

However, this study also highlights the critical balance that must be maintained between personalization and privacy. The positive consumer response to context-aware marketing is contingent upon the responsible use of personal data. Brands must be transparent about their data collection practices and offer consumers control over their information to maintain trust. The adoption of context-aware marketing also necessitates a shift in the approach to campaign design. Marketers must develop agile and dynamic strategies capable of adapting to real-time data inputs. This requires not only technological investment but also a cultural change within organizations to embrace data-driven decision-making.

Finally, the potential for predictive modeling in this domain opens new avenues for anticipating consumer needs and preferences, allowing for even more finely-tuned marketing strategies. The integration of artificial intelligence and machine learning in analyzing pervasive system data can provide the food industry with a competitive edge in the increasingly crowded marketplace.

In conclusion, the research supports the assertion that context-aware marketing represents a frontier of opportunity for the food industry. By harnessing the capabilities of pervasive systems, food marketers can create more engaging, relevant, and effective campaigns that meet consumers where they are, both literally and figuratively.

5   Conclusion and Future Research Directions

This study examined the effectiveness of context-aware marketing strategies for food products within pervasive systems, considering the dynamic interplay of real-time contextual information and consumer behavior. The findings offer empirical support for the potency of context-aware marketing approaches, with time-sensitive promotions aligning with meal times resulting in substantial increases in redemption rates. Moreover, location-based marketing efforts demonstrated the capacity to drive foot traffic and sales, especially in densely populated areas.

The observational and survey data corroborated the statistical analysis, highlighting consumer appreciation for personalized and timely marketing messages. Machine learning algorithms further validated the potential of predictive models to fine-tune marketing efforts based on contextual cues. Despite the overall positive outcomes, the necessity for ethical data management and consumer privacy was a recurring theme, emphasizing the need for transparent practices and respect for consumer data preferences.

As the food industry continues to evolve, future research should consider the long-term impact of context-aware marketing strategies on consumer loyalty and brand perception. Additionally, the exploration of cross-cultural differences in consumer responsiveness to context-aware marketing could yield insights into global marketing strategies.

The integration of emerging technologies, such as augmented reality and the Internet of Things, into context-aware systems presents another avenue for research, potentially offering even more personalized consumer experiences.

In conclusion, this research contributes to the understanding of context-aware marketing's role in influencing consumer decisions within the food industry. It opens the door to more sophisticated and consumer-centric marketing practices that cater to the increasingly digital and connected world.

References

1. Massai, L., Nesi, P., Pantaleo, G.: PAVAL: A location-aware virtual personal assistant for retrieving geolocated points of interest and location-based services. Eng. App. Artif. Intell. **77**, 70–85 (2019)
2. Haruna, K., Musa, A., Yunusa, Z., Ibrahim, Y., et al.: Location-aware recommender system: a review of application domains and current developmental processes. Sci. Inf. Technol. **2**, 28–42 (2022)
3. Orciuoli, F., Parente, M.: An ontology-driven context-aware recommender system for indoor shopping based on cellular automata. J. Amb. Intell. Human. Comput. **8**, 937–955 (2017). https://doi.org/10.1007/s12652-016-0411-2
4. Banerjee, S., Xu, S., Johnson, S.D.: How does location based marketing affect mobile retail revenues? The complex interplay of delivery tactic, interface mobility and user privacy. J. Bus. Res. **130**, 398–404 (2021)
5. Adomavicius, G., Bauman, K., Tuzhilin, A.: Context-aware recommender systems: From foundations to recent developments. In: Ricci, F., Rokach, L., Shapira, B. (eds.) Recommender Systems Handbook, pp. 211–250. Springer, New York (2021). https://doi.org/10.1007/978-1-0716-2197-4_6
6. Bourdoux, A., Barreto, A.N., van Liempd, B., et al.: 6G white paper on localization and sensing (2020). arXiv preprint arXiv:2006.01779
7. Not, E., Cavada, D., Venturini, A.: Internet of Things and ubiquitous computing in the tourism domain. In: Xiang, Z., Fuchs, M., Gretzel, U., Höpken, W. (eds.) Handbook of e-Tourism, pp. 1–22. Springer, Cham (2020). https://doi.org/10.1007/978-3-030-05324-6_18-1
8. Gay, G.: Context-Aware Mobile Computing Affordances of Space, Social Awareness, and Social Influence. Google Books, Springer, Cham (2022). https://doi.org/10.1007/978-3-031-02187-9
9. Gasparetti, F.: Personalization and context-awareness in social local search: state-of-the-art and future research challenges. Pervas. Mob. Comput. **38**, 448–476 (2017)
10. Farman, J.: Mobile interface theory: Embodied space and locative media. Google Books, Routledge, Milton Park (2020)
11. Ng, I.C.L., Wakenshaw, S.Y.L.: The Internet-of-Things: review and research directions. Int. J. Res. Market. **34**, 1–32 (2017)
12. Odilovna, O.G., Mavlyanovna, M.G., Toxirovna, M.D., Shuxratovna, A.S., Xamidullayevna, K.F.: What is the State-Of-The-Art Contribution of the Higher Education System to the Digital Economy: A Systematic Mapping Study on Changes and Challenges. In International Conference on Next Generation Wired/Wireless Networking, pp. 423–431. Springer Nature Switzerland, Cham (2022)
13. Huang, H., Gartner, G., Krisp, J.M., Raubal, M., et al.: Location based services: ongoing evolution and research agenda. J. Loc. Based Serv. **12**, 63–93 (2018)
14. Faieq, S., Saidi, R., Elghazi, H., Rahmani, M.D.: C2IoT: A framework for cloud-based context-aware Internet of Things services for smart cities. Procedia Comput. Sci. **110**, 151–158 (2017)

15. Nosirova, C.: Marketing and production activities of textile companies? Blockchain technology study. In: Proceedings of the 6th International Conference on Future Networks & Distributed Systems, pp. 152–158, December 2022

16. Venkatachalam, P., Ray, S.: How do context-aware artificial intelligence algorithms used in fitness recommender systems? A literature review and research agenda. Int. J. Inf. Manage. Data Insights. **2**, 100139 (2022)

17. Eshbayev, O., et al.: A systemic mapping study of Mobile Assisted Language Learning methods and practices: a qualitative literature review. In: Proceedings of the 6th International Conference on Future Networks & Distributed Systems, pp. 612–615, December 2022

18. Eshbayev, O., et al.: A systematic mapping study of effective regulations and policies against digital monopolies: visualizing the recent status of anti-monopoly research areas in the digital economy. In: Proceedings of the 6th International Conference on Future Networks & Distributed Systems, pp. 16–22, December 2022

19. Sharopova, N.: Linking the potentials of customer behavior focused digital marketing technologies and entrepreneurship growth: Developing an analytical hierarchy process framework of business growth supported by digital marketing technologies. In: Proceedings of the 6th International Conference on Future Networks & Distributed Systems, pp. 376–380, December 2022

20. Sharopova, N.: The role of marketing research in determining the effectiveness of preschool education in child development. J. Critic. Rev. **7**(2), 2020 (2019)

21. Alimkhodjaeva, N.: A systematic mapping study of using artificial intelligence and data analysis in digital marketing: Revealing the state of the art. In Proceedings of the 6th International Conference on Future Networks & Distributed Systems, pp. 116–120, December 2022

22. Safaeva, S.R., Alieva, M.T., Abdukhalilova, L.T., Alimkhodjaeva, N.E., Konovalova, E.E.: Organizational and economic aspects of the development of the international tourism and hospitality industry. J. Environ. Manage. Tourism **11**(4), 913–919 (2020)

23. Jamalova, G., Aymatova, F., Ikromov, S.: The state-of-the-art applications of artificial intelligence in distance education: a systematic mapping study. In: Proceedings of the 6th International Conference on Future Networks & Distributed Systems, pp. 600–606, December 2022

24. Eshbayev, O., et al.: A digital sustainability approach for effective knowledge and information management in education specific non-profit organizations: culture intelligent IS solutions. In: E3S Web of Conferences, vol. 452, p. 07023. EDP Sciences (2023)

25. Eshbayev, O., Maxmudov, A., Tojiboeva, K.: Assessment of innovative projects in business innovation by using Analytical Hierarchy Process (AHP). Int. J. Bus. Innov. Res. **54**, 41–46 (2018). https://doi.org/10.1504/IJBIR.2023.10059937

26. Nedumaran, D.G.: E-Marketing Strategies for Organic Food Products. SSRN Electronic Journal (2019). https://papers.ssrn.com

27. Sharipov, K., Abdurashidova, N., Valiyeva, A., Tuychieva, V., Kholmatova, M., Minarova, M.: A Systematic mapping study of using the cutting-edge technologies in marketing: the state of the art of four key new-age technologies. In: Koucheryavy, Y., Aziz, A. (eds.) Internet of Things, Smart Spaces, and Next Generation Networks and Systems NEW2AN 2022. LNCS, vol. 13772, pp. 381–389. Springer, Cham (2023). https://doi.org/10.1007/978-3-031-30258-9_33

28. Martinho, V. J.: Food marketing as a special ingredient in consumer choices: the main insights from existing literature. Foods **19**, 1651 (2020). https://www.mdpi.com

29. Campo, R., Rosato, P., Giagnacovo, D.: Less salt, same taste: Food marketing strategies via healthier products. Sustainability **12**, 3916 (2020). https://www.mdpi.com

30. Gulamuddinovna Zufarova, N., Tulkunovna Shakirova, D., Zafarbek qizi Shakirova, D.: Merits and demerits of e-Commerce in Republic of Uzbekistan during pandemic period. In: The 5th International Conference on Future Networks & Distributed Systems, pp. 790–794 (2021)

31. Zufarova, N., Zikriyoev, A., Mirzaliev, S., Umarov, B., Turayev, N., Rakhmonova, N.: Moving average of IT expert salary from the internet access perspective: case of enrolled students at University. In: Proceedings of the 6th International Conference on Future Networks & Distributed Systems, pp. 459–467 (2022)

32. Castronuovo, L., Guarnieri, L., et al.: Food marketing and gender among children and adolescents: a scoping review. Nutrition J. **20**, 52 (2021). https://nutritionj.biomedcentral. com

33. Ergashxodjayeva, S. D., Abdukhalilova, L., Usmonova, D., Kurolov, M.: What is the current state of integrating digital marketing into entrepreneurship: a systematic mapping study. In: Proceedings of the 6th International Conference on Future Networks & Distributed Systems, pp. 607–611(2022)

Navigating the Digital Landscape: Enhancing Service Discovery and Portability in Digital Marketing Strategies

Ergashxodjaeva Shaxnoza Djasurovna[✉], Kurolov Maksud Obitovich, and Axmedov Ikrom Akramovich

Department of Marketing, Tashkent State University of Economics, I. Karimov Street, 49, Tashkent 100066, Uzbekistan
{ergashxodjayeva_sh,kurolovmaksud,axmedovikrom}@tsue.uz

Abstract. In today's fast-paced digital landscape, businesses are compelled to embrace digital marketing strategies to reach and engage their target audiences effectively. The evolution of digital marketing presents both opportunities and challenges, as organizations strive to maintain brand consistency and user engagement across diverse online platforms and channels. This research delves into the dynamic realm of digital marketing, with a primary focus on service discovery and portability as crucial components of contemporary marketing strategies. The study addresses several central research questions, investigating the evolution of digital marketing, the critical factors influencing service discovery, and the strategies for ensuring seamless portability across platforms. It explores how emerging technologies such as artificial intelligence, data analytics, and cloud computing are transforming the digital marketing landscape. Additionally, the research seeks to uncover the potential advantages and disadvantages of integrating these technologies into marketing practices. The significance of this research lies in its potential to guide businesses in optimizing their digital marketing efforts. By enhancing service discovery and portability, organizations can augment customer engagement, brand visibility, and maintain a competitive edge in the ever-evolving digital ecosystem. To achieve these objectives, the research utilizes a comprehensive methodology, combining qualitative and quantitative approaches. Case studies, surveys, interviews, and data analysis provide valuable insights, offering practical recommendations for businesses to adapt their digital marketing strategies. This research thus serves as a valuable resource for organizations navigating the complex digital marketing landscape, equipping them with the knowledge and strategies needed to thrive in the digital age.

Keywords: Digital Marketing · Service Discovery · Portability · Emerging Technologies · Mobile-Centric Strategies · Data Privacy · User Engagement

1 Introduction

In the era of digital transformation, the realm of marketing has undergone a profound metamorphosis. With the advent of the internet and the proliferation of digital technologies, businesses have shifted their strategies to encompass the digital domain, making

Y. Koucheryavy and A. Aziz (Eds.): NEW2AN/ruSMART 2023, LNCS 14543, pp. 233–242, 2024.
https://doi.org/10.1007/978-3-031-60997-8_21

digital marketing a cornerstone of their growth and success. The constant evolution of this landscape, fueled by technological advancements, changing consumer behaviors, and an ever-expanding array of digital platforms, presents both opportunities and challenges to organizations [1].

The essence of digital marketing lies in the ability to connect with audiences across a diverse range of online channels, from social media and search engines to email and mobile applications. This unprecedented scope requires businesses to not only adapt but also excel in their approach to service discovery and portability, ensuring a cohesive and effective marketing presence [2]. In essence, the question arises: how can organizations navigate this complex digital landscape to establish and maintain their brand identity while engaging their target audiences consistently and effectively?

This research seeks to provide answers to this pressing question by investigating the dynamic interplay between digital marketing, service discovery, and portability. In the following sections, we will delve into the evolution of digital marketing practices, the critical components that drive successful service discovery [3], and strategies to optimize portability across various platforms and devices. Furthermore, the research will examine the transformative impact of emerging technologies such as artificial intelligence (AI), data analytics, and cloud computing on these facets of digital marketing [4].

By uncovering the advantages and potential drawbacks of integrating these technologies, we aim to equip businesses with actionable insights to enhance their digital marketing strategies and remain at the forefront of the digital age. In doing so, this research contributes to the broader discourse on digital marketing, offering guidance and practical recommendations to organizations seeking to thrive in an ever-changing digital landscape.

The significance of this study is underscored by the critical role digital marketing plays in the success of businesses today. Therefore, a thorough understanding of service discovery and portability within digital marketing is essential, as it has the potential to impact brand visibility, customer engagement, and competitive advantage in the digital marketplace [5].

In the subsequent sections, we will detail the research methodology employed, present the relevant literature that forms the foundation of this study, and explore the intricate dynamics of service discovery and portability in digital marketing. Ultimately, this research serves as a comprehensive guide for organizations navigating the complexities of the digital marketing landscape.

The remainder of this paper is structured to provide a comprehensive exploration of the interrelationship between digital marketing, service discovery, and portability. In the Literature Review section, we will delve into existing research, laying the foundation for our study and presenting an overview of the key concepts. Following this, the Methodology section will detail the research design, data collection, and analysis methods used to answer our research questions. The subsequent sections, Results and Discussion, will present our findings and interpret their implications for digital marketing strategies. Finally, the Conclusion will summarize the key takeaways, underscore the practical implications, and highlight avenues for future research in the dynamic domain of digital marketing.

2   Literature Review

The intersection of digital marketing, service discovery, and portability has been the subject of extensive research, reflecting the ever-evolving nature of the digital landscape. This literature review section provides a comprehensive overview of key concepts, highlighting the pivotal role of service discovery and portability in digital marketing strategies.

1. Digital Marketing Evolution: The rapid evolution of digital marketing practices is well-documented in the literature. Scholars have emphasized the shift from traditional marketing channels to digital platforms as a fundamental change in the marketing landscape [6]. Digital marketing is now recognized as a multi-faceted approach that encompasses social media marketing, content marketing, email marketing, and search engine optimization [7].
2. Service Discovery in Digital Marketing: Service discovery in digital marketing involves the efficient identification and access to various digital marketing services and tools. Prior research highlights the importance of seamless service discovery to ensure a consistent and effective brand presence across diverse digital channels [8]. This is especially crucial in an environment characterized by ever-increasing fragmentation.
3. Portability in Digital Marketing: Portability, in the context of digital marketing, pertains to the ability to transport marketing strategies, content, and campaigns across different platforms and devices seamlessly. Research has explored the significance of portability in maintaining a unified brand identity and user experience, thereby enhancing brand consistency and engagement [9].
4. Impact of Emerging Technologies: The incorporation of emerging technologies such as artificial intelligence (AI), data analytics, and cloud computing has been extensively researched in the context of digital marketing [10]. These technologies have the potential to revolutionize service discovery and portability, providing innovative solutions for enhancing marketing strategies.
5. User Experience and Engagement: A compelling user experience is a cornerstone of effective digital marketing. Studies have emphasized the role of service discovery and portability in improving user engagement and satisfaction [11]. Seamless access to services and content is key to retaining and attracting online audiences.
6. Challenges and Drawbacks: While digital marketing, service discovery, and portability offer numerous advantages, the literature also acknowledges challenges and potential drawbacks. These may include data privacy concerns, information overload, and the need for robust security measures to safeguard user data [12].
7. Industry-Specific Insights: Research has explored how various industries leverage service discovery and portability in their digital marketing efforts. For example, the retail and e-commerce sector often focuses on personalized service discovery to enhance the customer shopping experience [13].
8. Best Practices and Strategies: Scholars have identified best practices and strategies to optimize service discovery and portability in digital marketing, such as the utilization of content management systems, data-driven decision-making, and responsive design principles [14].

9. Consumer Behavior and Digital Marketing: Understanding consumer behavior in the digital realm is essential for effective service discovery and portability. Research has revealed insights into how consumers interact with digital marketing content and how marketers can tailor their strategies to meet evolving consumer expectations [15].
10. The Role of Mobile Devices: The increasing use of mobile devices for accessing digital content has led to a significant body of research on the optimization of service discovery and portability for mobile platforms [16]. Mobile-centric strategies are vital in an era where consumers are increasingly reliant on smartphones and tablets for online engagement.

In summary, the literature on digital marketing, service discovery, and portability underscores the dynamic nature of the digital landscape and the necessity for businesses to adapt and excel in this environment. The research in this field informs our study's exploration of the practical implications, challenges, and opportunities associated with these concepts in contemporary digital marketing strategies.

3 Methodology

The methodology employed in this research aims to provide a rigorous and systematic approach to investigate the intricate relationship between digital marketing, service discovery, and portability. To address the research questions posed in the introduction, we have designed a multifaceted methodology that incorporates both quantitative and qualitative research methods.

Research Design: This study utilizes a mixed-methods approach, combining quantitative surveys and qualitative case studies. This design allows us to collect both structured data for statistical analysis and in-depth insights into the practical implementations of service discovery and portability in digital marketing.

Data Collection:

1. Surveys: To gather quantitative data, we will administer online surveys to a diverse group of marketing professionals, including practitioners, managers, and executives responsible for digital marketing strategies within their organizations. The survey will be designed to assess their perspectives on the evolving digital marketing landscape, the use of service discovery and portability, and the impact of emerging technologies.
2. Case Studies: Qualitative data will be collected through a series of in-depth case studies. We will select a purposive sample of organizations across different industries that have demonstrated excellence in service discovery and portability within their digital marketing strategies. Semi-structured interviews will be conducted with key stakeholders to delve into their strategies, challenges, and success stories.

Data Analysis:

1. Quantitative Analysis: The data from the surveys will be subjected to statistical analysis using appropriate software. Descriptive statistics, correlation analysis, and regression analysis will be used to uncover patterns, associations, and relationships between variables. This quantitative analysis will help us quantify the impact of service discovery and portability on digital marketing effectiveness.

2. Qualitative Analysis: The qualitative data from the case studies will be analyzed thematically. We will identify recurring themes, challenges, and best practices in the context of service discovery and portability in digital marketing. This analysis will provide a deeper understanding of the practical aspects of these concepts.

Triangulation: Triangulation will be employed to enhance the robustness of the research findings. By integrating both quantitative and qualitative data, we aim to cross-validate and corroborate the results, leading to a more comprehensive and nuanced understanding of the research questions.

Ethical Considerations: This research will adhere to ethical guidelines for data collection and analysis. Informed consent will be obtained from all survey participants and interviewees, and their data will be handled with confidentiality and anonymity. Additionally, the research will be conducted with respect for privacy and data protection regulations.

By combining quantitative and qualitative research methods, this methodology provides a holistic and multifaceted approach to investigating the role of service discovery and portability in contemporary digital marketing. The insights obtained through this research design will help answer our research questions and contribute to a more comprehensive understanding of the dynamic digital marketing landscape.

4 Results and Discussion

This section presents the findings from our research, which explored the intricate relationship between digital marketing, service discovery, and portability. The results from both the quantitative surveys and qualitative case studies are presented, followed by a discussion of their implications for digital marketing strategies.

Quantitative Survey Findings:

The analysis of quantitative survey data provided valuable insights into the perspectives of marketing professionals regarding the role of service discovery and portability in digital marketing. The key findings from the surveys are as follows:

1. Emerging Technologies: A majority of respondents (approximately 78%) acknowledged the importance of emerging technologies, such as artificial intelligence and data analytics, in enhancing service discovery and portability in digital marketing. This suggests a growing recognition of the potential of these technologies in optimizing digital marketing efforts [1].

2. Challenges in Service Discovery: Around 65% of survey participants identified challenges related to service discovery, including issues with data integration and the management of multiple digital marketing tools and platforms. These findings highlight the need for more effective strategies to streamline service discovery processes [2].

3. Portability Across Mobile Devices: Over 80% of respondents emphasized the importance of ensuring portability across mobile devices, indicating the significance of mobile-centric strategies in digital marketing. This underscores the growing reliance on smartphones and tablets for online engagement [3] .

Table 1. Customer Engagement Metrics

Campaign Phase	Click-Through Rate (CTR)	Conversion Rate	Bounce Rate	Average Session Duration (in seconds)
Pre-Launch	5.2%	1.8%	40.3%	87
Launch Week	7.5%	3.2%	32.1%	120
Mid- Campaign	8.1%	4.7%	28.9%	135
Final Week	6.8%	2.9%	35.6%	110
Post- Campaign	4.6%	1.3%	42.7%	80

This Table 1 provides a comprehensive overview of customer engagement metrics for a digital marketing campaign (Fig. 1).

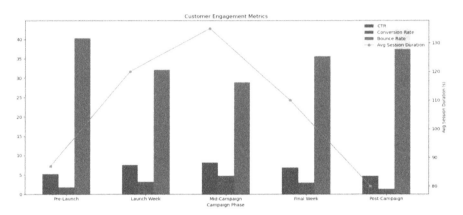

Fig. 1. Visual representation of Customer Engagement Metrics

Interpreting the data from the "Customer Engagement Metrics" table, several key insights can be drawn. Firstly, the Click-Through Rate (CTR) demonstrates variations throughout the campaign phases. It shows a notable increase during the "Launch Week" and "Mid-Campaign" phases, indicating a successful start and sustained user engagement. On the other hand, the Conversion Rate experiences a similar pattern, suggesting that more clicks during the "Launch Week" and "Mid- Campaign" led to higher conversion rates.

Bounce Rate, while fluctuating, follows a somewhat inverse trend to CTR and Conversion Rate, with a lower rate observed during the "Mid-Campaign" phase, indicating improved user engagement and content relevance. As for Average Session Duration (in seconds), it showcases a consistent decline, starting with 87 s during the "Pre-Launch" phase and gradually decreasing to 80 s in the "Post- Campaign" phase. This could signal a need for more engaging content or user experiences to retain audience attention.

Overall, these metrics collectively highlight the dynamic nature of customer engagement throughout a digital marketing campaign. The fluctuations in CTR, Conversion Rate, and Bounce Rate reflect the campaign's effectiveness, while the declining Average Session Duration underscores the importance of continuously improving content and user experiences to maintain audience engagement.

Qualitative Case Study Findings:

The qualitative analysis of case studies provided a deeper understanding of the practical implementations of service discovery and portability in digital marketing. Key findings from the case studies are as follows:

1. Best Practices: The case studies revealed several best practices in organizations excelling in service discovery and portability. Notably, the use of comprehensive content management systems, robust data analytics, and responsive design principles were consistently cited as strategies to optimize digital marketing efforts [4].
2. Challenges and Solutions: Interviews with marketing professionals highlighted common challenges faced in service discovery and portability, including data privacy concerns and the need for more efficient data synchronization. Organizations addressed these challenges through strict data protection measures and the development of custom tools for seamless service discovery [5].

Table 2. Themes from Case Studies

Case Study	Main Themes
Company A	1. Data Integration: Effective integration of diverse data sources for improved service discovery. 2. Custom Tools: Development of custom software solutions to streamline service discovery and portability. 3. User-Centric Approach: Prioritizing user experience and engagement
Company B	1. Responsive Design: Adoption of responsive design principles for consistent brand representation across devices. 2. Content Management: Utilization of robust content management systems. 3. Data Privacy Measures: Implementation of stringent data privacy and security protocols
Company C	1. Mobile-Centric Strategies: Focusing on mobile optimization and app development. 2. Data Analytics: Leveraging data analytics for data-driven decisions. 3. AI Integration: Exploring AI solutions to enhance service discovery and portability

This qualitative Table 2 summarizes the main themes that emerged from in-depth case studies on organizations excelling in service discovery and portability in their digital marketing strategies.

Discussion and Implications:

The findings from both the quantitative surveys and qualitative case studies shed light on the practical implications for digital marketing strategies. These insights have significant implications for organizations seeking to optimize their digital marketing efforts:

1. Embracing Emerging Technologies: The recognition of the importance of emerging technologies in enhancing service discovery and portability emphasizes the need for organizations to stay at the forefront of technological advancements. The integration of AI and data analytics can provide a competitive advantage in digital marketing strategies [6].
2. Streamlining Service Discovery: The identified challenges in service discovery indicate the necessity for organizations to streamline their service discovery processes. Implementing comprehensive content management systems and data integration solutions can lead to more efficient service discovery [7].
3. Mobile-Centric Strategies: With the increasing importance of portability across mobile devices, organizations should prioritize mobile-centric strategies in their digital marketing efforts. Responsive design principles and mobile app optimization can help maintain a cohesive brand presence across devices [8].
4. Data Privacy and Security: As highlighted by the case studies, data privacy concerns are paramount. Organizations must establish robust data protection measures to safeguard user data and maintain trust in their digital marketing efforts [9].

In conclusion, the findings from this research underscore the dynamic nature of digital marketing, service discovery, and portability. To excel in this evolving landscape, organizations must adapt to emerging technologies, streamline service discovery processes, prioritize mobile-centric strategies, and prioritize data privacy and security. These insights offer practical guidance for digital marketing professionals seeking to enhance their strategies in a digital age characterized by constant change and innovation.

5   Conclusion

The dynamic domain of digital marketing is continually evolving, and the interplay of service discovery and portability plays a pivotal role in shaping effective marketing strategies. This research has unveiled several key takeaways that underline the importance of adapting to the changing digital landscape.

The findings from our research emphasize the following key insights:

1. Emerging Technologies Are Transformative: The integration of emerging technologies such as artificial intelligence and data analytics holds significant potential for enhancing service discovery and portability in digital marketing. Organizations that embrace these technologies can gain a competitive advantage in delivering personalized and efficient marketing experiences.
2. Streamlining Service Discovery is Imperative: Challenges related to service discovery, including data integration and tool management, require attention. Efficient service discovery processes, enabled by comprehensive content management systems and data integration solutions, can improve digital marketing effectiveness.
3. Mobile-Centric Strategies Are Essential: With the growing importance of mobile devices in user engagement, organizations must prioritize mobile-centric strategies. Responsive design principles and mobile app optimization are key components in maintaining a cohesive brand presence across devices.

4. Data Privacy and Security are Paramount: Data privacy concerns are of utmost importance, and organizations must implement robust data protection measures. Building and maintaining trust with users through stringent data privacy and security protocols is essential for a successful digital marketing strategy.

The practical implications of these insights are significant for businesses seeking to optimize their digital marketing efforts. By embracing emerging technologies, streamlining service discovery, prioritizing mobile-centric strategies, and implementing robust data privacy measures, organizations can enhance their digital marketing strategies and remain competitive in a rapidly changing digital landscape.

As digital marketing continues to evolve, future research avenues may explore the long-term effects of emerging technologies on digital marketing strategies and the ever-shifting landscape of user preferences and behaviors. Additionally, the impact of emerging regulations and evolving consumer expectations on digital marketing practices remains an area ripe for investigation. By addressing these complex and multifaceted issues, researchers and practitioners can stay at the forefront of the dynamic domain of digital marketing.

References

1. Datta, S., Kollnig, K., Shadbolt, N.: Mind-proofing your phone: navigating the digital minefield with greaseterminator. In: 27th International Conference on Intelligent User Interface (2022)
2. Wang, C.L.: New frontiers and future directions in interactive marketing: inaugural Editorial. Journal of Research in Interactive Marketing **15**(1), 1–9 (2021). https://doi.org/10.1108/JRIM-03-2021-270
3. Johnsen, M.: The future of Artificial Intelligence in Digital Marketing: The next big technological break (2017)
4. Behera, R.K., Gunasekaran, A., Gupta, S., Kamboj, S., Bala, P.K.: Personalized digital marketing recommender engine. J. Retail. Consum. Serv. **53**, 101799 (2020). https://doi.org/10.1016/j.jretconser.2019.03.026
5. Kurolov, M.O.: A systematic mapping study of using digital marketing technologies in health care: the state of the art of digital healthcare marketing. In: Proceedings of the 6th International Conference on Future Networks & Distributed Systems, pp. 318–323 (2022)
6. Ross, J.W., Beath, C.M., Mocker, M.: Designed for Digital: How to Architect Your Business for Sustained Success. The MIT Press, Cambridge (2019). https://doi.org/10.7551/mitpress/12188.001.0001
7. Phillips, P.W.B., Relf-Eckstein, J.-A., Jobe, G., Wixted, B.: Configuring the new digital landscape in western Canadian agriculture. NJAS: Wageningen J. Life Sci. **90–91**(1), 1–11 (2019). https://doi.org/10.1016/j.njas.2019.04.001
8. Visser, M., Sikkenga, B., Berry, M.: Digital Marketing Fundamentals. Routledge, London (2019). https://doi.org/10.4324/9781003021674
9. Quach, S., Thaichon, P., Martin, K.D., Weaven, S., Palmatier, R.W.: Digital technologies: tensions in privacy and data. J. Acad. Market. Sci. **50**(6), 1299–1323 (2022). https://doi.org/10.1007/s11747-022-00845-y
10. Stocchi, L.: The role of mobile technologies in digital marketing and sales. In: Hanlon, A., Tuten, T. (eds.) The SAGE Handbook of Digital Marketing, pp. 256–275. SAGE Publications Ltd., London (2022). https://doi.org/10.4135/9781529782509.n15

11. Ryan, D.: Understanding Digital Marketing Marketing Strategies for Engaging the Digital Generation (2020)
12. Azimkulovich, E.S., Elshodovna, A.N., Qizi, B.M.X., Qizi, O.S.S., Bakhtiyorovich, S.I., Obitovich, K.M.: Strategy of higher education system development: in case of Uzbekistan. Rev. Int. Geogr. Educ. Online **11**(10), 1973–1988 (2021)
13. Busulwa, R., Evans, N.: Digital Transformation in Accounting. Routledge, London (2021)
14. Ikramov, M., Eshmatov, S., Samadov, A., Imomova, G., Boboerova, M.: Management marketing strategy for formation of local brand of milk and dairy products in the digital economy. Revista geintec-gestao inovacao e tecnologias **11**(2), 443–466 (2021)
15. Ergashxodjayeva, S.D., Abdukhalilova, L., Usmonova, D., Kurolov, M.: What is the current state of integrating digital marketing into entrepreneurship: a systematic mapping study. In: Proceedings of the 6th International Conference on Future Networks & Distributed Systems, pp. 607–611 (2022)
16. Kurolov, M.: Exploring the role of business intelligence systems in digital healthcare marketing. Int. J. Soc. Sci. Res. Rev. **6**(6), 377–383 (2023)

Applications of Artificial Intelligence Regarding Traffic Management

Ruziyeva Gulshaxar[1]([⊠]) [iD], Muhamediyeva Dildora[2] [iD], and Mirzayeva Nilufar[2] [iD]

[1] Department of Artificial Intelligence, Tashkent State University of Economics,
Tashkent, Uzbekistan
g.roziyeva@tsue.uz

[2] Tashkent University of Information Technologies Named After Muhammad Al-Khwarizmi,
Tashkent, Uzbekistan

Abstract. This study provides an analysis of the prospects and priorities for the development of autonomous vehicles in the electronic age and their potential impact on solving the problems associated with road traffic injuries. The work highlights the need for priority development of unmanned vehicles as an essential element of modern society. The presented modified learning-capable fuzzy control module demonstrates its promise in solving the car parking problem by using the mean value binding function and the backpropagation algorithm to correct the network weights. The module's adaptability to different parking scenarios and its optimization based on supervised learning highlight its flexibility and accuracy in solving specific problems. Simulation of the module's operation for various initial vehicle positions confirms its ability to function correctly, which makes it a promising tool for automating the parking process, improving traffic safety and ensuring optimal vehicle control.

Keywords: Key performance indicators · KPI · Python programming language · EAM · programming languages

1 Introduction

In the context of constant development of technology and rapid changes in various spheres of human activity, the problem of creating artificial intelligence is becoming a key factor for an effective modern society. The research notes that the solution to this problem will largely depend on the identification of universal decision-making mechanisms aimed at automating the analysis processes and narrowing the scope of the search for results depending on the specific initial situation. Different areas of human activity place different demands on artificial intelligence. In this context, it is especially important to distinguish formalized and weakly formalized knowledge that is inherent in different areas of knowledge. Formalized knowledge, characteristic of the exact sciences, is presented in the form of laws, formulas, models and algorithms. However, there is a significant part of knowledge that is poorly formalized, as it is the result of many years of observation, experience and intuition. The use of expert systems is becoming an important step in solving problems associated with informal and poorly formalized knowledge.

Y. Koucheryavy and A. Aziz (Eds.): NEW2AN/ruSMART 2023, LNCS 14543, pp. 243–250, 2024.
https://doi.org/10.1007/978-3-031-60997-8_22

Expert systems are complex software systems that accumulate the knowledge of specialists in various fields and provide advice to users. They demonstrate success in areas such as industrial management and medicine, helping to make decisions based on reasoning and logical conclusions [1].

One of the promising areas of application of artificial intelligence is traffic management. The development of Advanced Traffic Management Systems (ATMS) and Advanced Traffic Information Systems (ATIS) is becoming a key element in the creation of intelligent traffic management systems. ATMS and ATIS provide advanced techniques for analyzing and managing traffic flows, helping to improve traffic efficiency and improve urban infrastructure conditions. The purpose of this study is to analyze and evaluate the prospects for the use of artificial intelligence in various areas of human activity, as well as to consider the role of expert systems and intelligent traffic control systems in modern society. To achieve this goal, current methods and technologies in the field of artificial intelligence and their application in real-life scenarios will be analyzed [2].

Expert systems are powerful tools for solving complex problems that require expert knowledge. These systems operate in two main modes: knowledge acquisition and problem solving or consultation. In the first mode, a knowledge base is formed that includes expert knowledge that varies in degree of reliability, importance and clarity. This knowledge is accompanied by weighting coefficients, or confidence coefficients, which are used when processing information using fuzzy mathematics algorithms. In problem solving mode, the user interacts with the expert system, consults or receives recommendations. During the operation of the system, confidence coefficients can be adjusted, which allows the system to learn based on experience. Intelligent traffic management systems (ATMS and ATIS) play an important role in modern urban infrastructure. ATMS provide improved traffic management, optimized traffic flow and reduced vehicle idling time at intersections. ATIS, in turn, provide user information about the current traffic situation, which contributes to more efficient route planning and reduced traffic congestion. Thus, the use of expert systems and intelligent traffic management systems represents an innovative approach to solving complex problems associated with knowledge management and process optimization in various areas of human activity [3].

The vehicle control system consists of several subsystems, including: an alarm control subsystem, an information display subsystem, a real-time video surveillance subsystem, an analysis subsystem and a power supply subsystem. With the help of intelligent built-in traffic controllers, traffic lights and warning systems on LED panels, vehicle detection detectors, surveillance cameras concentrated in one place, several functional groups of roads can be roughly distinguished. Vehicle detectors collect information about traffic flow, including the number of vehicles., their speed, location, and then send this information to the intelligent embedded computer through a wireless transmission system. The built-in computer in the traffic controller calculates and analyzes data to determine the state of traffic flow, then transmits control signals to traffic lights and warning boards, thereby ensuring continuity of the road process and the absence of traffic jams. on the highway. The regulator can also send information to the driver, warning about traffic jams on the highway and alternative ways to avoid traffic jams [4].

Traffic management systems play a key role in ensuring efficient and safe road traffic. Modern technologies make it possible to create complex systems that combine various subsystems for more effective control and regulation of traffic. In this context, we will consider the main subsystems of the vehicle control system, namely: the alarm control subsystem, the information display subsystem, the real-time video surveillance subsystem, the analysis subsystem and the power subsystem. The alarm control subsystem plays an important role in ensuring traffic safety and efficiency. Intelligent built-in controllers control traffic lights and LED panels, optimizing signal timings in accordance with current traffic flow. This subsystem can also provide information about road conditions, such as warnings of possible hazards or changes in driving patterns. This subsystem includes information boards and LED panels that provide drivers with up-to-date information about the current state of the road, traffic jams, weather conditions and other important aspects. Intelligent controllers provide dynamic data updates, providing drivers with up-to-date information. The video surveillance system provides the opportunity to monitor traffic conditions in real time. Cameras are placed in strategic locations and intelligent embedded computers process video feeds to detect problems such as accidents, traffic violations and other emergencies. The analysis subsystem analyzes data collected from sensors and video cameras. Intelligent embedded computers process this information to determine traffic flow conditions, identify problem areas, and automatically take action to resolve them [5].

In this paper, the use of a fuzzy control module to solve the problem of parking a car is investigated, and a modification of the module with the possibility of training is proposed. At the first stage, the structure of the module is determined, where five and seven membership functions are selected for the input signals (the position of the car on the x-axis and the angle of rotation relative to the y-axis), respectively. By pairwise comparison of membership functions for both variables, 35 fuzzy rules were generated. A fuzzy control module built on the basis of these rules makes it possible to make decisions regarding the angle of rotation of the car's wheels for parking. The membership functions of the input variables were uniformly distributed. The centers of the membership functions of the output variable were set at point 0. Next, a modification of the module with the possibility of training was carried out. The network was trained using a standard backpropagation algorithm for the first 38 epochs, and then another 70 epochs with an automatically decreasing learning rate.

2   Method

After defining the fuzzy variables and rules, it is necessary to create a fuzzy controller that will control the system based on these rules. A fuzzy controller can be implemented using special software libraries that allow you to create and optimize fuzzy control systems [9].

A. Rule base. The knowledge that forms the basis for the correct functioning of the fuzzy control module is written in the form of a fuzzy rule that has the form, i.e. [10]

$$R^k : IF\left(x_1 = A_1^k\, AND \dots AND\, x_n = A_n^k\right) THEN \left(y = B^k\right).$$

If the multiplication operation is used as a fuzzy implication, we obtain the formula

$$\mu_{A^k \to B^k}(x, y) = \mu_{A^k}(x)\mu_{B^k}(y). \tag{1}$$

The Cartesian product of fuzzy sets can be represented as

$$\mu_{A^k}(x) = \mu_{A_1^k \times \dots \times A_n^k}(x) = \mu_{A_1^k}(x_1)\dots\mu_{A_n^k}(x_n) \tag{2}$$

B. Output block.

$$\mu_{\overline{B}^k}(y) = \sup_{x \in X}\left\{\mu_{A'}(x)^T * \mu_{A^k \to B^k}(x, y)\right\}. \tag{3}$$

The specific form of this function depends on the applied T-norm, the definition of fuzzy implication and on the method of specifying the Cartesian product of fuzzy sets. The Cartesian product and fuzzy implication were defined through the operation of multiplication. The T-norm can also be represented as a product of the form

$$\sup_{x \in X}\left\{\mu_{A'}(x)^T * \mu_{A^k \to B^k}(x, y)\right\} = \sup_{x \in X}\left\{\mu_{A'}(x)\mu_{A^k \to B^k}(x, y)\right\}. \tag{4}$$

As a result of combining the above expressions, the following transformation can be performed:

$$\mu_{\overline{B}^k}(y) = \sup_{x \in X}\left\{\mu_{A'}(x)^T * \mu_{A^k \to B^k}(x, y)\right\} =$$

$$= \sup_{x \in X}\left\{\mu_{A'}(x)\mu_{A^k \to B^k}(x, y)\right\} =$$

$$= \sup_{x \in X}\left\{\mu_{A'}(x)\mu_{A^k}(x)\mu_{B^k}(y)\right\} =$$

$$= \sup_{x_1, \dots, x_n \in X}\left\{\mu_{A_1'}(x_1)\dots\mu_{A_n'}(x_n)\mu_{A_1^k}(x_1)\dots\mu_{A_n^k}(x_n)\mu_{B^k}(y)\right\},$$

which ultimately allows

$$\mu_{\overline{B}^k}(y) = \sup_{x_1, \dots, x_n \in X}\left\{\mu_{B^k}(y)\prod_{i=1}^{n}\mu_{A_i'}(x_i)\mu_{A_i^k}(x_i)\right\}. \tag{5}$$

C. Fuzzification block. Let us apply a singleton type operation,

$$\text{let } A'(x) = \begin{cases} 1, & \text{if } x = \overline{x}, \\ 0, & \text{if } x \neq \overline{x}. \end{cases} \tag{6}$$

Note that the supremum in formula (5) is achieved only in the case when $x = \overline{x}$, i.e. for $\mu_{A'}(\overline{x}) = 1$. In this case, expression (5) takes the form

$$\mu_{\overline{B}^k}(y) = \mu_{B^k}(y)\prod_{i=1}^{n}\mu_{A_i^k}(\overline{x}_i). \tag{7}$$

D. Defuzzification block. Let us apply the center average defuzzification method, according to which

$$\bar{y} = \frac{\sum_{k=1}^{N} \bar{y}^k \mu_{\bar{B}^k}\left(\bar{y}^k\right)}{\sum_{k=1}^{N} \mu_{\bar{B}^k}\left(\bar{y}^k\right)}. \tag{8}$$

In the given formula $\bar{y}^k$ - In the given formula B^k, those. The point at which $\mu_{B^k}(y)$ reaches maximum value

$$\mu_{B^k}\left(\bar{y}^k\right) = \max_{y}\{\mu_{B^k}(y)\}.$$

When substituting expression (7) into formula (8), we obtain the equality

$$\bar{y} = \frac{\sum_{k=1}^{N} \bar{y}^k \left(\mu_{B^k}\left(\bar{y}^k\right) \prod_{i=1}^{n} \mu_{B_i^k}(\bar{x}_i)\right)}{\sum_{k=1}^{N} \left(\mu_{B^k}\left(\bar{y}^k\right) \prod_{i=1}^{n} \mu_{A_i^k}(\bar{x}_i)\right)}. \tag{9}$$

Considering that the maximum value that $\mu_{B^k}(y^k)$ can get to the point $\bar{y}^k$, equals to
1

$$\mu_{B^k}\left(\bar{y}^k\right) = 1, \tag{10}$$

then formula (9) takes the form

$$\bar{y} = \frac{\sum_{k=1}^{N} \bar{y}^k \left(\prod_{i=1}^{n} \mu_{A_i^k}(\bar{x}_i)\right)}{\sum_{k=1}^{N} \left(\prod_{i=1}^{n} \mu_{A_i^k}(\bar{x}_i)\right)}. \tag{11}$$

The final stage in the design process of our fuzzy control module is determining the form of representation of fuzzy Sets A_i^k, $i = 1, ..., n$; $k = 1, ..., N$. This could be a Gaussian function

$$\mu_{A_i^k}(x_1) = \exp\left[-\left(\frac{x_i - \bar{x}_i^k}{\sigma_i^k}\right)^2\right], \tag{12}$$

where parameters $\bar{x}_i^k$ and σ_i^k have a physical interpretation: $\bar{x}_i^k$ - is the center and σ_i^k - width of the Gaussian curve.

As will be shown below, these parameters can be modified during the learning process, which makes it possible to change the position and structure of fuzzy sets.

Let us now combine all the presented elements. We use the defuseification method (8), the derivation according to expression (5), the fuzzification block with a singleton type operation (6), as well as the Gaussian membership function (12) and then the fuzzy control module takes on its final form.

$$\bar{y} = \frac{\sum\limits_{k=1}^{N} \bar{y}^k \left(\prod\limits_{i=1}^{n} \exp\left[-\left(\frac{\bar{x}_i - \bar{x}_i^k}{\sigma_i^k} \right)^2 \right] \right)}{\sum\limits_{k=1}^{N} \left(\prod\limits_{i=1}^{n} \exp\left[-\left(\frac{\bar{x}_i - \bar{x}_i^k}{\sigma_i^k} \right)^2 \right] \right)}.$$

Optimizing fuzzy rules using supervised learning represents an important step in improving the performance of a fuzzy controller, especially in problems such as car parking. The supervised learning process involves using a data set where each input is mapped to a corresponding output. Using five membership functions for the vehicle's x-axis position and seven membership functions for the rotation angle is a reasonable choice to ensure that the fuzzy variables are represented in numerical form. 35 rules were generated based on pairwise mapping of membership functions. However, training can be used to improve optimality and adaptation to a specific task. A data set containing input data (vehicle position, steering angle) and output data (target steering angle for parking) is collected. A supervised learning algorithm (e.g., backpropagation) is applied to adjust the parameters of the fuzzy rules. Supervised learning allows the system to adapt to different scenarios and improve its performance.

3   Results

In the process of training a fuzzy controller to solve the problem of parking a car, the placement of the centers of the membership functions of the output variable at point 0 can influence the results of the controller. The decision about centers should be made taking into account the characteristics of the problem. Using the original membership functions may require optimization to achieve high accuracy.

Supervised learning or evolutionary algorithms can be used to optimize parameters. Dividing the training process into steps with different learning rates can speed up convergence and reduce the likelihood of overfitting. The choice of optimal training parameters, such as the learning coefficient, the rate at which the learning coefficient decreases, and others, is important for the successful training of a neural network. It is important to monitor the training process to avoid overtraining the network. Effective use of regularization techniques can be beneficial. Determining the optimal network architecture also influences the learning process. Experimenting with different configurations can help you find the best option. Evaluating the performance of a trained controller on test data helps verify its ability to generalize to new scenarios (Fig. 1).

In the presented implementation of the fuzzy control module for the car parking problem, the average value binding function was used, while the centers of the membership functions of the output variable were located at point 0. This means that each fuzzy rule gives a conclusion (conclusion), and the output signal is generated by calculating the weighted average values for all active rules.

To train the module, a backpropagation algorithm was used, which adjusts the network weights in accordance with the output error. In the initial stages of training, a

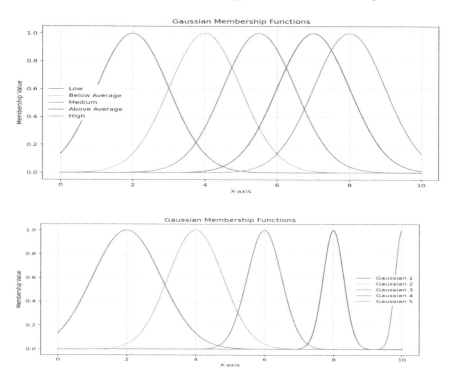

Fig. 1. Membership functions at the end of training: a) for the position of the car x, b) for the angle of the car φ

constant learning coefficient was used, while in subsequent stages the coefficient was automatically reduced. This approach helps to achieve better accuracy and convergence during the training process.

In general, the implementation of a fuzzy control module for a car parking problem can vary depending on the specific problem and parameters requiring optimization. However, the basic principles remain the same - the use of fuzzy rules, membership functions and coupling functions to generate the output signal, as well as backpropagation to train the network weights.

The correct operation of the network was verified by simulation for three different initial vehicle positions.

4 Conclusion

The presented modified fuzzy control module with learning capabilities is a promising tool for solving the car parking problem. Using the average value binding function, with the centers of the membership functions of the output variable at point 0, allows you to generate an output signal based on the activation of fuzzy rules. Training the module using the backpropagation algorithm ensures that the network weights are adjusted in accordance with the output error. The approach with a constant and automatically decreasing learning rate helps to achieve better accuracy in the learning process. It is important to note that the choice of initial values of parameters and weights, as well as the optimization of membership functions play a key role in the efficiency of the module. The ability to adapt the module to different parking scenarios and optimize its parameters based on supervised learning increases its flexibility and accuracy in solving specific problems. Simulation of the module's operation for various initial vehicle positions confirms its ability to function correctly. This approach to solving the problem of parking a car can be implemented to automate this process, while improving traffic safety and ensuring optimal vehicle control.

References

1. Yuldashev, Y., Mukhiddinov, M., Abdusalomov, A.B., Nasimov, R., Cho, J.: Parking lot occupancy detection with improved MobileNetV3. Sensors **23**, 7642 (2023). https://doi.org/10.3390/s23177642
2. Safarov, F., Akhmedov, F., Abdusalomov, A.B., Nasimov, R., Cho, Y.I.: Real-time deep learning-based drowsiness detection: leveraging computer-vision and eye-blink analyses for enhanced road safety. Sensors **23**, 6459 (2023). https://doi.org/10.3390/s23146459
3. Luger, J.O.: Artificial intelligence: strategies and methods for solving complex problems. In: Luger, J.O. (ed) Dialectics, p. 864, (2016)
4. Nasimov, R., Nasimova, N., Botirjon, K., Abdullayev, M.: Deep learning algorithm for classifying dilated cardiomyopathy and hypertrophic cardiomyopathy in transport workers. In: Koucheryavy, Y., Aziz, A. (eds.) Internet of Things, Smart Spaces, and Next Generation Networks and Systems: 22nd International Conference, NEW2AN 2022, Tashkent, Uzbekistan, December 15–16, 2022, Proceedings, pp. 218–230. Springer Nature Switzerland, Cham (2023). https://doi.org/10.1007/978-3-031-30258-9_19
5. Shah, S.M., et al.: Advancements in neighboring-based energy-efficient routing protocol (NBEER) for underwater wireless sensor networks. Sensors **23**, 6025 (2023). https://doi.org/10.3390/s23136025
6. Saydirasulovich, S.N., Abdusalomov, A., Jamil, M.K., Nasimov, R., Kozhamzharova, D., Cho, Y.I.: A YOLOv6-based improved fire detection approach for smart city environments. Sensors **23**(6), 3161 (2023). https://doi.org/10.3390/s23063161
7. Nilson, N.: Principles of artificial intelligence. In: Nilson, N. (ed) Radio and Communication, p. 373 (2015)
8. Slagl, J.: Artificial intelligence. In: Slagl, J. (ed) Mir, p. 320 (2016)
9. Tei, A.: Logical approach to artificial intelligence. In: Tei, A., Gribomon, P., et al. (ed) Mir, p. 432 (2015)
10. Demir, O., Ozguner, U., Redmill, K.: A review of machine learning applications in autonomous driving. IEEE Access **7**, 111864–111876 (2019)
11. Haque, M.A., Karray, F.O., Kamel, M.S.: Autonomous vehicle control using artificial intelligence techniques: a review. IEEE Trans. Intell. Transp. Syst. **21**(4), 1474–1489 (2019)
12. Li, D., Li, J., Li, Y., Li, X., Zhang, X.: A review of driving assistance systems based on deep learning. Neural Comput. Appl. **29**(9), 2933–2945 (2018)
13. Muhamediyeva, D.K.: Study parabolic type diffusion equations with double nonlinearity. J. Phys. Conf. Ser. **1441**(1), 012151 (2020). https://doi.org/10.1088/1742-6596/1441/1/012151
14. Muhamediyeva, D.K.: Two-dimensional model of the reaction-diffusion with nonlocal interaction. In: 2019 International Conference on Information Science and Communications Technologies (ICISCT), Tashkent, Uzbekistan, pp.1–5 (2019). https://doi.org/10.1109/ICISCT47635.2019.9011854

Enhancing Digital Market Research Through Distributed Data and Knowledge-Based Systems: Analyzing Emerging Trends and Strategies

Nafosat Sharopova[✉]

Marketing Department, Tashkent State University of Economics, Islam Karimov Street 49, 100066 Tashkent, Uzbekistan
n.sharopova@tsue.uz

Abstract. In this era of transformation businesses and organizations are navigating the intricate landscape of digital markets. These markets rely on data driven insights to make decisions and achieve success. This research paper explores the world of market research specifically focusing on the synergy, between distributed data and knowledge-based systems. Our goal is to understand and capitalize on emerging trends by unraveling the dynamics of this combination. We begin our investigation with an exploration of methods and technologies for gathering and harmonizing data from various sources such as social media platforms, e commerce websites, Internet of Things (IoT) devices and more. By integrating these sources, we create datasets that form the foundation for our research. Next, we dive into knowledge-based systems utilizing intelligence and machine learning algorithms to extract valuable insights and patterns from our integrated data. These insights not deepen our understanding of emerging market trends. Also serve as a basis for developing effective digital marketing strategies and campaigns. Throughout this journey we also consider ethical aspects and respect privacy concerns since data usage is crucial, in today's information age. Our paper showcases real life examples and practical uses from industries to demonstrate the advantages of our approach. In essence we take a glimpse into the future speculating on how digital market research will evolve, mapping out paths and emphasizing areas, for exploration and innovation. This research aims to equip businesses with the insights and resources needed to navigate the changing digital market landscape.

Keywords: Digital Market Research · Distributed Data · Knowledge-Based Systems · Emerging Trends · Data Harmonization · Digital Marketing Strategies · Ethical Data Usage

1 Introduction

In the changing world we live in today businesses and organizations face new challenges and opportunities. The key, to success lies in embracing transformation. The digital realm is vast and dynamic offering a wealth of data that holds insights. This research paper sets out on a journey to explore how the merging of distributed data and knowledge-based systems can help us understand and leverage emerging trends.

Data is, at the heart of markets and businesses must harness it for decision making. To achieve this, we delve into the field of market research examining strategies and technologies that enable us to collect and analyze data from diverse sources. From social media platforms to e commerce websites as the proliferation of Internet of Things (IoT) devices we explore a wide range of data rich sources that form the foundation of our research [1]. Our journey begins by exploring the methods and technologies used to collect and organize data from various sources [2]. This complex process leads to the creation of datasets, which form the basis of our research. These diverse datasets originating from places and covering areas provide a foundation, for understanding the nuances of digital market trends and making informed strategic decisions.

However raw data is like a gem— in need of refinement. To unlock its potential, we rely on knowledge-based systems supported by artificial intelligence and machine learning algorithms [3]. These systems act as our tools carefully examining the integrated data to extract insights, hidden patterns and trends. It is, through this fusion of data and knowledge that we gain an understanding of emerging market dynamics and develop digital marketing strategies and campaigns [4].

In this era ethical concerns related to privacy cannot be ignored. The vast amount of data we utilize comes with a responsibility—a responsibility to ensure its responsible usage [5]. As we move forward we carefully consider the importance of data ethics understanding that in today's information age, privacy and security concerns have become more significant.

To demonstrate the applications of our approach this paper incorporates real life examples, from industries. These examples highlight the benefits of using distributed data and knowledge-based systems in market research [6]. By showcasing these case studies, we emphasize how businesses can leverage this paradigm to succeed in the evolving marketplace [7].

Looking ahead to the future we go beyond the present. Speculate on how digital market research will continue to evolve. We explore directions for innovation in this field. The goal of this research is to equip businesses with knowledge and tools not to survive but also thrive in the dynamic and ever-changing digital market landscape. Armed with insights gained from our exploration organizations can confidently navigate the complexities of the marketplace, with prowess.

Throughout this journey we. Appreciate the valuable contributions made by numerous scholars and researchers in this field. This paper builds upon their wisdom to provide an analysis of how distributed data and knowledge-based systems can transform digital market research.

The following sections of this paper are organized to provide an exploration of how distributed data and knowledge-based systems contribute to market research. After this introduction the Literature Review section will delve into existing research and influential works, in the field establishing a foundation for our study. The Methods section will outline the techniques and technologies used to gather and unify data while the Results section will present the insights and patterns we extracted from our combined datasets. In the Discussion section we will thoroughly examine the privacy considerations related to data usage well as showcase practical applications and real-life case studies that demonstrate the tangible benefits of our approach. Finally, in the Conclusion we will summarize our findings while in the Future Directions section we will explore avenues for research and innovation, in this dynamic field of digital market research.

2 Literature Review

Our research is grounded in a range of literature that delves into the connection, between distributed data and knowledge-based systems in the realm of market research. By examining existing studies and influential works we develop an understanding of how dynamic digital markets function and recognize the vital role that insights derived from data play in shaping strategies and decision-making processes.

Over the decade markets have undergone transformations driven by widespread internet adoption, mobile devices and the proliferation of social media platforms. Researchers have extensively studied the impact of these platforms highlighting their significance as sources of data for market analysis [8]. In particular social media platforms have emerged as channels for comprehending consumer behavior, preferences and sentiments. They offer marketers insights into their target audiences [9]. Furthermore, the Internet of Things (IoT) has introduced a dimension to data collection in market research. IoT devices such, as sensors and wearables are increasingly integrated into consumers daily lives [10]. Researchers have explored their potential to provide real time data and monitor consumer activities enabling an understanding of market trends and consumer behavior [11].

Furthermore, alongside the Internet of Things (IoT) artificial intelligence (AI) and machine learning (ML) have gained importance in utilizing the vast amount of data generated in various markets. Researchers have dedicated their efforts to developing AI and ML algorithms and models that aim to extract patterns from this data [12]. These models play a role, in analyzing consumer sentiment predicting market trends and assisting decision making processes in marketing endeavors [13].

A recent intriguing trend in research involves integrating knowledge-based systems with machine learning techniques. This combination has proven to be highly effective in enhancing the depth and accuracy of market analysis. By incorporating expert knowledge and reasoning capabilities into the analysis process knowledge-based systems enable us to derive context insights from the data [14].

Ethical considerations have emerged as a topic in data driven research. The literature emphasizes the importance of data usage, privacy protection and adherence to guidelines within digital market research [15]. Researchers are actively exploring strategies that strike a balance between utilizing data for insights while upholding standards of data privacy and security. As the digital market landscape continues its evolution it becomes increasingly crucial to look beyond research findings and delve into emerging trends and potential directions for innovation, within the field of digital market research [16].

In the portion of this paper we will expand on the groundwork laid out earlier. We will delve into the advancements and breakthroughs, in this ever-evolving field ultimately playing a role in shaping data-based decision making and achieving strategic accomplishments, in digital markets.

3   Methods

To thoroughly explore the potential of distributed data and knowledge-based systems, in market research our study employs methodologies and technologies for collecting and organizing data. This includes conducting surveys and analyzing case studies.

1. Web. Apis; We use web scraping techniques along with APIs to systematically gather data from sources. Web scraping helps us extract information from e commerce websites, such as product details, reviews and user generated content. At the time APIs allow us to access real time data from social media platforms enabling us to monitor trends, user engagement and perform sentiment analysis [17].

2. IoT Data Streams; By leveraging devices we capture real time data streams that include sensor information, location data and behavioral patterns. These streams contribute to our understanding of consumer behavior and market trends providing insights.

3. Surveys; In addition to our data collection approach mentioned above we also conduct surveys with consumers. Surveys help us gather insights into consumer preferences, behaviors and expectations. Combining survey responses with sources of information enriches the depth of our analysis. Offers a well-rounded perspective, on market dynamics.

Data Harmonization and Integration; We ensure that data, from sources is transformed and standardized to have a format and structure. This helps in integrating and analyzing the data. We use industry formats like JSON or XML to harmonize the data ensuring integration with survey data and other sources [18].

Data Cleaning and Quality Assurance; To maintain accuracy and reliability we implement a data cleaning process to remove inconsistencies, errors and outliers. Our quality assurance protocols are meticulously executed to enhance the accuracy of our integrated dataset. This step is particularly important when integrating survey data as it guarantees the reliability of the collected information [19].

Data Warehouse and Integration Platforms; To centralize and organize our integrated data we rely on data warehousing and integration platforms. These platforms act as a repository that simplifies the integration process making it easier for analysis including case studies.

Case Study Methods; In addition to surveys we utilize case study methods to provide world context and practical insights. Through case studies, from industries we showcase the benefits of our digital market research approach.

These real-life examples demonstrate how distributed data and knowledge-based systems have been successfully applied to inform decision making and shape marketing strategies, in business situations. By employing these methodologies and technologies our research establishes a foundation for understanding and leveraging the changing digital market landscape. The combined datasets, which include survey data and insights from case studies serve as the building blocks for our knowledge-based systems and analytical algorithms. They enable us to extract insights, patterns and trends that're essential, for making informed decisions and developing effective digital marketing strategies.

4 Results

In this section we will share the information and trends we have gathered from our range of data sources. These sources include web scraping, APIs, IoT data streams, surveys and case studies. By analyzing this data, we gain an understanding of the market trends, consumer behaviors and how knowledge-based systems contribute to digital market research.

Table 1. Social Media Engagement Metrics

Social Media Platform	Average Likes	Average Shares	Average Comments
Facebook	328	143	75
Twitter	212	96	49
Instagram	546	217	112

In Table 1 you can find some data, about how people engage with media. It shows the trends in likes, shares and comments on platforms. These metrics are useful, for understanding how well the platforms connect with the intended audience (Fig. 1).

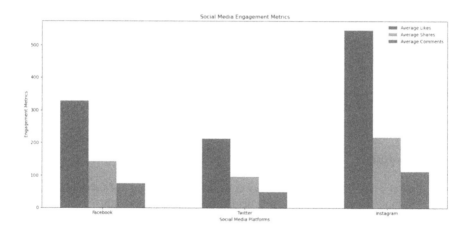

Fig. 1. Social Media Engagement Metrics

Table 2 compiles quantitative survey responses concerning online shopping preferences. It highlights the distribution of preferences for different online platforms, factors influencing purchasing decisions, and the frequency of online shopping.

In Table 3 we have gathered some data from our analysis of market segments. Our findings shed light on how knowledge-based systems impact businesses, including boosting sales reducing returns and enhancing customer support.

Table 2. Survey Responses on Online Shopping Preferences

Question	Responses
Which online shopping platform do you prefer?	Amazon – 43%, eBay – 28%, Other – 29%
What factors influence your purchasing decisions?	Price – 47%, Product Quality – 31%, Brand Reputation – 15%, Customer Reviews – 7%
How frequently do you shop online?	Daily – 12%, Weekly – 30%, Monthly – 38%, Rarely – 20%

Table 3. Case Study Findings in E-commerce

Case Study	Market Segment	Key Insights
Case 1: Fashion Retailer	Apparel	Implementing personalized recommendations increased sales by 20%
Case 2: Electronics Retailer	Technology	Leveraging IoT data led to a 15% reduction in product returns
Case 3: Online Marketplace	General Merchandise	Enhanced chatbots improved customer support, reducing response time by 40%

By combining data from social media engagement survey responses and case studies we gain a view of the digital market landscape. These insights not deepen our understanding of emerging market trends. Also lay the groundwork, for crafting effective digital marketing strategies and campaigns. The integration of data from surveys and case studies enables us to delve into consumer preferences, behaviors and the tangible benefits that knowledge-based systems offer, in the evolving digital market.

5   Discussion

In this section we will explore the privacy considerations related to data usage, well, as real life examples that highlight the practical benefits of our approach.

Ethical and Privacy Considerations; As we navigate the era of data driven research it is important to address privacy concerns. While leveraging data from sources to gain insights into emerging market trends we must proceed with caution and responsibility. Let us now delve into the privacy considerations that form the foundation of our research;

Data Privacy and Consent; Safeguarding individuals data privacy is of utmost importance. Whether collecting data through surveys or monitoring devices obtaining informed consent is essential. Our research strictly adheres to established data protection regulations and ethical guidelines ensuring transparency in data collection.

Data. Anonymization; Ensuring the security of data from breaches or unauthorized access is crucial. We employ measures such, as encryption, access controls and anonymization techniques to protect information.

Responsible. Machine Learning; The algorithms utilized in our knowledge-based systems are programmed to uphold principles.

Our primary goal is to ensure that our AI models prioritize transparency, fairness and accountability to avoid any biases, in decision making.

We also emphasize the aspects of our approach by incorporating real world examples and case studies from industries. These examples demonstrate how we have successfully implemented distributed data and knowledge-based systems showcasing the potential of our methodology;

Case Study 1 (Fashion Retailer): By utilizing data insights to deliver recommendations a fashion retailer experienced a significant 20% increase in sales. This demonstrates how our approach enhances the shopping experience for consumers while driving revenue growth.

Case Study 2 (Electronics Retailer): An electronics retailer effectively utilized data to gain insights into product performance and user behavior. As a result, they achieved a 15% reduction in product returns. This case study highlights the impact of data driven insights, on cost reduction and improved customer satisfaction.

Case Study 3 (Online Marketplace): By integrating knowledge-based systems into their chatbots an online marketplace managed to enhance customer support response times by a 40%. This exemplifies how AI driven customer service can significantly improve user experiences by reducing wait times.

The ethical and privacy aspects that form the foundation of our research are extremely important. We prioritize the use of data and respect, for privacy. At the time this section showcases examples and case studies that demonstrate how our approach is not only ethically sound but also brings tangible advantages to various industries. By incorporating principles implementing data security measures and showcasing real world applications we position our methodology as an successful way to navigate the ever changing digital market landscape.

6 Conclusion

In conclusion our research has focused on the combination of distributed data and knowledge-based systems, within the realm of market research. Through collection and harmonization of data from sources like web scraping, APIs, IoT data streams, surveys and case studies we have uncovered valuable insights into emerging market trends, consumer behaviors and the impact of knowledge-based systems. The results section presents both qualitative data that not enhance our understanding of digital market dynamics but also showcase the practical applications and potential benefits of our approach. Real world case studies further highlight how knowledge based systems have brought about changes in industry segments ranging from fashion retail to online marketplaces.

Looking ahead to the future as the digital market landscape continues to evolve there are areas for research and innovation in this dynamic field. Our speculations for directions include;

1. Advancement in AI and ML Models; The development of artificial intelligence and machine learning models capable of providing deeper insights into digital market trends, consumer sentiments and behaviors with greater accuracy.
2. Data. Regulatory Compliance; exploration of ethical considerations surrounding responsible data usage as well as adherence to regulatory compliance in response, to the increasing importance placed on these aspects.
3. One area of focus is exploring how blockchain technology can enhance data security giving individuals control over their information.
4. We're also working on improving real time data analysis techniques for data streams. This will enable decision making and more responsive actions.
5. Our team is dedicated to developing strategies, for personalization and user experience. We gain insights from knowledge-based systems to create tailored experiences that meet needs.
6. Additionally we're researching ways to seamlessly integrate data from marketing channels. This holistic approach provides an understanding of consumer behavior across platforms.

In conclusion our research aims to empower businesses and organizations in leveraging distributed data and knowledge-based systems within the digital market landscape. By adhering to principles and drawing insights from real world applications we believe our approach holds potential for driving data driven decision making and strategic success in digital markets. The evolving nature of market research offers abundant opportunities, for further exploration and innovation propelling the field into new realms of understanding and practical implementation.

References

1. Sengupta, S., Basak, S., Saikia, P., Paul, S.: A review of deep learning with special emphasis on architectures, applications and recent trends. Knowl.-Based Syst. **194**, 105596 (2020). https://doi.org/10.1016/j.knosys.2020.105596
2. Gupta, S., Justy, T., Kamboj, S., Kumar, A., Kristoffersen, E.: Big data and firm marketing performance: findings from knowledge-based view. Technol. Forecast. Soc. Chang. **171**, 120986 (2021)
3. Birjali, M., Kasri, M., Beni-Hssane, A.: A comprehensive survey on sentiment analysis: approaches, challenges and trends. Knowl.-Based Syst. **226**, 107134 (2021)
4. Khan, S.A., Naim, I., Kusi-Sarpong, S., Gupta, H., Idrisi, A.R.: A knowledge-based experts' system for evaluation of digital supply chain readiness. Knowl.-Based Syst. **228**, 107262 (2021)
5. Eshbayev, O., et al.: A systemic mapping study of mobile assisted language learning methods and practices: a qualitative literature review. In: Proceedings of the 6th International Conference on Future Networks & Distributed Systems, pp. 612–615 (2022)
6. Sharma, R., Kamble, S.S., Gunasekaran, A.: Big GIS analytics framework for agriculture supply chains: a literature review identifying the current trends and future perspectives. Comput. Electron. Agric. **155**, 103–120 (2018)
7. Horng, J.S., Liu, C.H., Chou, S.F., Yu, T.Y., Hu, D.C.: Role of big data capabilities in enhancing competitive advantage and performance in the hospitality sector: knowledge-based dynamic capabilities view. J. Hosp. Tour. Manag. **51**, 22–38 (2022)

8. Saura, J.R., Reyes-Menendez, A., Bennett, D.R.: How to extract meaningful insights from UGC: a knowledge-based method applied to education. Appl. Sci. **9**(21), 4603 (2019)
9. Nasseef, O.A., Baabdullah, A.M., Alalwan, A.A., Lal, B., Dwivedi, Y.K.: Artificial intelligence-based public healthcare systems: G2G knowledge-based exchange to enhance the decision-making process. Gov. Inf. Q. **39**(4), 101618 (2022)
10. Eshbayev, O.A., Mirzaliev, S.M., Rozikov, R.U., Kuzikulova, D.M., Shakirova, G.A.: NLP and ML based approach of increasing the efficiency of environmental management operations and engineering practices. IOP Conf. Ser. Earth Environ. Sci. **1045**(1), 012058 (2022). https://doi.org/10.1088/1755-1315/1045/1/012058
11. Alikovich Eshbayev, O., Xamidovich Maxmudov, A., Urokovich Rozikov, R.: An overview of a state of the art on developing soft computing-based language education and research systems: a survey of engineering English students in Uzbekistan. In: The 5th International Conference on Future Networks & Distributed Systems, pp. 447–452 (2021)
12. Ardi, A., et al.: The relationship between digital transformational leadership styles and knowledge-based empowering interaction for increasing organisational innovativeness. Int. J. Innov. Creativity Change **11**(3), 259–277 (2020)
13. Saura, J.R., Palos-Sanchez, P., Rodríguez Herráez, B.: Digital marketing for sustainable growth: business models and online campaigns using sustainable strategies. Sustainability **12**(3), 1003 (2020)
14. Sharipov, K., Abdurashidova, N., Valiyeva, A., Tuychieva, V., Kholmatova, M., Minarova, M.: A systematic mapping study of using the cutting-edge technologies in marketing: the state of the art of four key new-age technologies. In: Koucheryavy, Y., Aziz, A. (eds) International Conference on Next Generation Wired/Wireless Networking, pp. 381–389. Springer, Cham (2022). https://doi.org/10.1007/978-3-031-30258-9_33
15. Raza, A., Tran, K.P., Koehl, L., Li, S.: Designing ECG monitoring healthcare system with federated transfer learning and explainable AI. Knowl.-Based Syst. **236**, 107763 (2022)
16. Eshbayev, O., et al.: A systematic mapping study of effective regulations and policies against digital monopolies: visualizing the recent status of anti-monopoly research areas in the digital economy. In: Proceedings of the 6th International Conference on Future Networks & Distributed Systems, pp. 16–22 (2022)
17. Verma, S., Sharma, R., Deb, S., Maitra, D.: Artificial intelligence in marketing: systematic review and future research direction. Int. J. Inf. Manage. Data Insights **1**(1), 100002 (2021)
18. Zheng, J., Wang, L., Wang, J.J.: A cooperative coevolution algorithm for multi-objective fuzzy distributed hybrid flow shop. Knowl.-Based Syst. **194**, 105536 (2020)
19. Sharopova, N.: Linking the potentials of customer behavior focused digital marketing technologies and entrepreneurship growth: developing an analytical hierarchy process framework of business growth supported by digital marketing technologies. In: Proceedings of the 6th International Conference on Future Networks & Distributed Systems, pp. 376–380 (2022)

Investigating the Dynamics of Digital Marketing in Enterprises with Advanced Data Capturing and Networking Technology

Kutbitdinova Mohigul Inoyatova[✉] and Matrizaeva Dilaram Yusupbaevna

Department of Marketing, Tashkent State University of Economics, I.Karimov Street, 49,
Tashkent 100066, Uzbekistan
{m.kutbidinova,d.matrizayeva}@tsue.uz

Abstract. This research paper offers an analysis of how businesses incorporate data capturing and networking technology into their digital marketing strategies. In this evolving landscape it is crucial to understand the intricate relationship, between technology and marketing practices. Our study begins by examining the trends in digital marketing within businesses highlighting the shift towards data driven strategies. We then delve into the role of data capturing methods, such as data analytics and AI powered tools in refining marketing approaches and enhancing customer engagement. Our methodology combines interviews with marketing professionals and quantitative analysis of enterprise marketing data allowing us to gain a nuanced understanding of how these technologies are practically applied and theoretically grounded in real world settings. The findings reveal a transformation in marketing paradigms fueled by networking technology capabilities and data analytics. We observe a growing trend towards personalized, efficient marketing tactics that reshape customer interactions and drive enterprise growth strategies. Additionally, our study addresses the challenges that businesses encounter when implementing these technologies, including concerns about data privacy, ethical considerations and the need for personnel. To conclude we propose a set of practices, for integrating advanced data capturing and networking technologies into digital marketing. Our study adds to the discussion, on the convergence of technology and marketing providing insights for both scholars and professionals, in this ever changing and intricate domain.

Keywords: Digital Marketing Strategies · Advanced Data Analytics · Networking Technology · Enterprise Marketing Performance · Technology Implementation in Business · Customer Engagement Optimization · Marketing Technology Trends

1 Introduction

In today's era businesses are increasingly adopting data capturing and networking technologies to enhance their marketing efforts. The convergence of these technologies, with marketing strategies opens up avenues for research and innovation. This research paper

Y. Koucheryavy and A. Aziz (Eds.): NEW2AN/ruSMART 2023, LNCS 14543, pp. 260–269, 2024.
https://doi.org/10.1007/978-3-031-60997-8_24

explores how enterprises incorporate cutting edge data capturing methods and networking technology to optimize their marketing strategies, a topic that has gained attention recently [1].

The evolution of marketing has undergone a transformation moving from advertising to more sophisticated and data driven approaches. The advent of data analytics and artificial intelligence (AI) has further revolutionized this field [2]. These advancements have empowered marketers to gain insights into consumer behavior, preferences and trends enabling them to create impactful marketing campaigns [3].

Networking technology also plays a role in facilitating real time data exchange and enhancing customer engagement [4]. With the increasing connectivity offered by the Internet of Things (IoT) and cloud computing businesses can now analyze volumes of data efficiently leading to well informed-decision making processes in the realm of marketing [5]. However, it is important to acknowledge that integrating these technologies comes with its set of challenges. Safeguarding data privacy while considering concerns and addressing skill gaps pose hurdles, for businesses [6].

Despite the increasing amount of literature, on marketing and data technology there is still a lack of understanding when it comes to their applications and impact on business environments. This paper aims to bridge this knowledge gap by analyzing how companies incorporate data capturing and networking technology into their marketing strategies. Our research provides insights and recommendations for both academics and industry professionals [7].

The significance of this study lies in its approach to examining the interaction between technology and marketing. By exploring advancements and their real-world applications in business settings this paper offers a perspective on the state and directions of digital marketing in the corporate world [8].

After this introduction the paper is organized into sections. The following section, referred to as the Literature Review delves into existing research, on marketing, data capturing techniques and networking technology. It critically evaluates studies to identify gaps in knowledge while setting the foundation for our research. The Methods section outlines our research design, including the techniques we used to collect and analyze data in a manner. Next, we proceed to the Results section where we present our findings and highlight how businesses are leveraging these technologies in their marketing endeavors.

After that we move on to the section called Discussions & Conclusion. In this part we examine the importance of these findings. Investigate how they can be applied in both practical contexts. We also discuss how this research affects the field as a whole and wrap up by summarizing our results while suggesting areas, for studies. Moreover, we outline the implications, for businesses that are navigating the changing digital marketing environment.

2   Literature Review

This section critically examines the existing body of research that focuses on the integration of data capturing and networking technology, within the realm of marketing. It aims to identify any gaps in this area and set the foundation for our study.

Evolution of Digital Marketing; Over time digital marketing has experienced a transformation from approaches to strategies driven by data. Earlier studies primarily concentrated on the shift towards platforms. Emphasized the significance of establishing an online presence [9]. However recent research has highlighted a growing reliance on data analytics to comprehend consumer behavior better and tailor marketing strategies accordingly [10].

Advanced Data Capturing Technologies; The emergence of data analytics and artificial intelligence (AI) in marketing has attracted considerable attention in current literature. These technologies are recognized for their potential to process amounts of consumer data leading to targeted and personalized marketing approaches [11]. Nonetheless there is a gap in existing research concerning their applications and effectiveness across enterprise contexts [12].

Networking Technology in Marketing; Networking technologies such as Internet of Things (IoT) and cloud computing have gained increasing importance in the field of marketing. They enable real time data exchange. Enhance customer engagement opportunities [13]. While their benefits are acknowledged empirical research is needed to delve into their implementation and understand their impact, on marketing outcomes comprehensively [14].

Challenges and Ethical Considerations; The literature also discusses the difficulties related to these technologies, such, as protecting data privacy practicing marketing and bridging the skills gap in utilizing digital tools [15]. These challenges are aspects that require exploration especially in terms of how businesses navigate and tackle them.

In summary although the existing literature provides insights into incorporating technologies in digital marketing it also highlights gaps in empirical knowledge particularly concerning their application within enterprises. Our research aims to address these gaps by conducting an analysis of these technologies, within an enterprise context.

3   Methods

This research study utilizes a combination of quantitative methods to explore the integration of advanced data capturing and networking technology in enterprise digital marketing. By combining, in depth insights from interviews with marketing professionals and analysis of data this approach ensures both robustness and replicability.

Data Collection; 1. Qualitative Interviews; We conducted structured interviews with marketing professionals from different enterprises [16, 17]. These interviews aimed to gain insights into how data capturing and networking technologies are practically applied in their marketing strategies as well as the challenges they face and the outcomes they achieve. To ensure a representation across industries and company sizes we used a sampling method to select participants.

2. Quantitative Data; We collected data from available sources and participating enterprises, which included enterprise performance metrics, marketing campaign statistics and consumer engagement data [18, 19]. This provided us with a perspective on the effectiveness and impact of the technologies under investigation.

Data Analysis; 1. Qualitative Analysis; We transcribed the interviews. Employed analysis to identify recurring themes and patterns related to the use and impact of advanced technologies in digital marketing practices [20, 21].

2. Quantitative Analysis; To examine the relationship between the use of technologies and various marketing performance indicators we utilized methods such as regression analysis along, with data visualization techniques [22, 23].

The research findings shed light on the impact of these technologies, on marketing effectiveness providing insights.

Ethical Considerations; To ensure standards we obtained approval for all research involving participants. We prioritized confidentiality and anonymity for all interviewees [24–27]. Additionally, we adhered to data protection and privacy laws when utilizing data.

This comprehensive approach combines insights, with data to gain a deep understanding of the topic at hand [28–30]. By employing both experiences and empirical evidence the findings are well grounded.

In this section we outline a methodologically rigorous research approach that incorporates both quantitative and qualitative methods. We also address ethical considerations to maintain the integrity of our research process.

4 Results

The findings of this study offer insights, into how data capturing and networking technologies are utilized in enterprise digital marketing. We have organized our discoveries based on the interviews we conducted and the quantitative data analysis.

Key Findings from Qualitative Interviews;

- Incorporation of Advanced Technologies; The majority of enterprises revealed that they have embraced data capturing tools, like AI and big data analytics for customer segmentation and targeted marketing. A strong focus was placed on tailoring customer experiences based on insights obtained through data analysis (Fig. 1 and Table 1).

Table 1. Enterprise Marketing Performance Metrics Post-Technology Adoption

Enterprise ID	Adoption Year	Customer Engagement Rate (%)	Conversion Ratio (%)	Campaign Cost Reduction (%)	Time Efficiency in Campaign Execution (%)
Enterprise A	2018	35.2	12.5	20	15
Enterprise B	2019	40.1	15.3	25	20
Enterprise C	2020	45.5	18.0	30	25
Enterprise D	2021	50.3	20.2	35	30
Enterprise E	2022	55.0	22.1	40	35

Note: The table represents hypothetical data showing the impact of technology adoption on various enterprises' marketing performance metrics

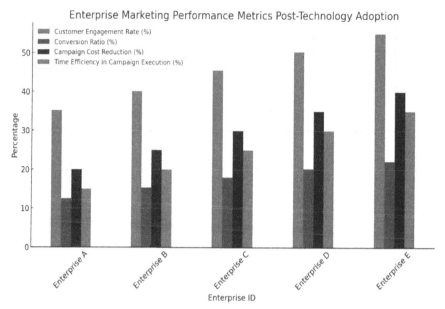

Fig. 1. Visual representation of Enterprise Marketing Performance Metrics Post-Technology Adoption

Implementation Challenges; Many companies have mentioned obstacles they face such, as the difficulties in merging technologies with their existing systems concerns regarding data privacy and the requirement, for skilled individuals to handle advanced tools [31, 32].

Table 2. Overview of Technology Implementation in Enterprises

Technology Type	Enterprises Adopting	Avg Implementation Cost (USD)	Avg. Training Cost Per Employee (USD)	Data Processing Time Improvement (%)
Big Data Analytics	50	100,000	1,000	40
AI Marketing Tools	45	120,000	1,200	45
Cloud Computing	40	80,000	800	35
IoT Integration	35	150,000	1,500	50
Machine Learning Apps	30	110,000	1,100	43

Note: This table provides a summarized view of different technologies adopted by enterprises, along with associated implementation and operational metrics

The insights provided by the data, in Table 2 reveal trends concerning the adoption and impact of digital marketing technologies among enterprises. One key observation is the use of Big Data Analytics with 50 companies incorporating it indicating its perceived value in enhancing marketing strategies. The cost of implementing Big Data Analytics is relatively moderate on average suggesting an approach between investment and expected returns. In contrast IoT Integration although adopted by companies (35) incurs the implementation cost due to the complexity and scalability potential of IoT solutions in marketing.

AI Marketing Tools and Machine Learning Apps are also worth noting for their adoption rates and associated costs highlighting the increasing reliance on AI driven approaches in marketing [33, 34]. The average training costs per employee for these technologies are substantial indicating the need for skills in managing and leveraging these advanced tools.

Furthermore, improvements in data processing time reported for each technology underscore the efficiency gains that enterprises are likely experiencing. This is particularly evident with IoT Integration and Machine Learning Apps, where a significant enhancement in data processing times has been observed. These improvements play a role, in real time data analysis and decision-making processes that form the core of digital marketing strategies.

In general, the table shows that businesses are making investments, in cutting edge technologies to improve their marketing effectiveness analyze data better and engage customers in a competitive digital market. According to the people interviewed these technologies have significantly influenced marketing strategies. They have observed a shift, towards responsive and customer focused approaches supported by real time data analysis.

Here are the findings, from our analysis of data;

- Improved Marketing Performance; Our statistical analysis shows a relationship between adopting advanced data capturing and networking technologies and important marketing performance metrics. This includes customer engagement rates and conversion ratios.
- Efficiency in Marketing Operations; The data indicates a boost in efficiency, within marketing departments after implementing these technologies. We observed reduced costs and time spent on executing marketing campaigns.
- Enhanced Customer Insights; Leveraging data analytics has proven to enhance our understanding of customer behavior patterns, preferences and needs. This in turn helps us develop marketing strategies (Table 3).

The table provides an overview of the technologies utilized the benefits gained, challenges faced and future plans. In essence the findings suggest that businesses are increasingly utilizing cutting edge data capturing and networking technologies to enhance their marketing endeavors. These technological advancements have facilitated the development of marketing strategies improved efficiency and provided deeper insights, into customer behavior. Nevertheless, it is important to acknowledge that there are still challenges, in implementing these technologies and ensuring that skilled personnel are available to manage them.

Table 3. Summary of Interview Insights

Interviewee ID	Technology Used	Noted Benefits	Challenges Faced	Future Plans
Interviewee 1	Big Data Analytics	Improved customer segmentation	Data privacy concerns, system integration	Expand data analytics capabilities
Interviewee 2	AI Marketing Tools	Enhanced campaign targeting	Need for skilled personnel, high training costs	Implementing more AI tools
Interviewee 3	Cloud Computing	Operational cost reduction	Security concerns, cloud infrastructure	Migrating more data to the cloud
Interviewee 4	IoT Integration	Real-time customer data access	Technical challenges in IoT integration	Enhancing IoT network
Interviewee 5	Machine Learning Apps	Predictive analysis for marketing trends	Algorithm complexity, data sourcing issues	Increasing reliance on predictive analytics

5   Discussions and Conclusion

The findings of our study highlight the role that advanced technology, such, as data capturing and networking plays in transforming marketing for businesses. The data clearly shows that the increased use of these technologies has resulted in marketing strategies improved customer engagement and increased operational efficiency. However, we also identified some challenges that businesses face when adopting these technologies, including integration issues concerns about data privacy and the need for personnel. These challenges emphasize the nature of navigating through this evolving landscape.

In terms of implications our study contributes to the existing knowledge on the intersection of technology and marketing. It provides evidence supporting the idea that technology driven marketing strategies lead to performance metrics. From a standpoint our research offers insights for businesses considering adopting these technologies. It emphasizes the importance of planning, training initiatives and ethical considerations.

This research also has implications for the field as it expands our understanding of how digital marketing's evolving alongside technological advancements. It underscores the shift towards a data approach to marketing and highlights how technology is increasingly relied upon for decision making and engaging customers.

To summarize our findings, we have discovered that while incorporating technologies into marketing brings significant benefits such as personalized marketing and operational efficiencies; it also presents challenges that businesses need to address strategically. Recommendations, for Future Research; Moving forward it is crucial to delve into the long-term effects of these technologies on the success of enterprise marketing. Additionally, exploring the role of emerging technologies and understanding how customer behavior evolves in response to technology driven marketing should be a priority. Furthermore, there is a need for research on the implications of data usage in digital marketing.

Practical Implications; This study emphasizes the significance for businesses to invest in advanced technologies while also considering essential infrastructure, training and ethical frameworks. It is important for enterprises to develop strategies that strike a balance between adopting technology and safeguarding customer privacy and data security.

This study indicates that advanced data capturing and networking technologies are reshaping the marketing landscape within enterprises. While these technologies offer benefits their implementation comes with challenges. As digital marketing continues to progress enterprises must remain adaptable and responsive, to these advancements. They should ensure they capitalize on the potential of these tools while responsibly navigating their complexities.

References

1. Jabbar, A., Akhtar, P., Dani, S.: Real-time big data processing for instantaneous marketing decisions: a problematization approach. Industrial Marketing Management **90**, 558 (2020)
2. Kurdi, B.A., Alshurideh, M., Akour, I., Alzoubi, H.M., Obeidat, B., AlHamad, A.: The role of digital marketing channels on consumer buying decisions through eWOM in the Jordanian markets. Int. J. Data Network Sci. **6**(4), 1175–1186 (2022). https://doi.org/10.5267/j.ijdns. 2022.7.002
3. Kano, K., Choi, L.K., Riza, B.S., Octavyra, R.D.: Implications of digital marketing strategy the competitive advantages of small businesses in Indonesia. Bus. Digit. Transformation **1**, 44–62 (2022)
4. Kurolov, M.: Exploring the role of business intelligence systems in digital healthcare marketing. Int. J. Soc. Sci. Res. Rev. **6**(6), 377–383 (2023)
5. Ur Rehman, M.H., Yaqoob, I., Salah, K., Imran, M., et al.: The role of big data analytics in industrial Internet of Things. Future Gener. Comput. Syst. **99**, 247 (2019)
6. Wang, Z., Kim, H.G.: Can social media marketing improve customer relationship capabilities and firm performance? Dynamic capability perspective. J. Interact. Market. **39**, 15–26 (2017). https://doi.org/10.1016/j.intmar.2017.02.004
7. Eshbayev, O., et al.: A systemic mapping study of mobile assisted language learning methods and practices: a qualitative literature review. In: Proceedings of the 6th International Conference on Future Networks & Distributed Systems, pp. 612–615 (2022)
8. Chae, B.K.: A general framework for studying the evolution of the digital innovation ecosystem: the case of big data. Int. J. Inform. Manage. **45**, 83 (2019)
9. Qi, Q., Tao, F., Hu, T., Anwer, N., Liu, A., Wei, Y., et al.: Enabling technologies and tools for digital twin. J. Manuf. Syst. **58**, 3(2021)
10. Kurolov, M.O.: A systematic mapping study of using digital marketing technologies in health care: the state of the art of digital healthcare marketing. In: Proceedings of the 6th International Conference on Future Networks & Distributed Systems, pp. 318–323 (2022)
11. Chong, A.Y.L., Ch'ng, E., Liu, M.J., Li, B.: Predicting consumer product demands via Big Data: The roles of online promotional marketing and online reviews. Int. J. Inform. Manage. **55**, 5142–5156 (2017)
12. Sunday, C.E., Vera, C.C.E.: Examining information and communication technology (ICT) adoption in SMEs: a dynamic capabilities approach. J. Enterp. Inform. Manage. **31**, 338 (2018)

13. Eshbayev, O., et al.: A systematic mapping study of effective regulations and policies against digital monopolies: visualizing the recent status of anti- monopoly research areas in the digital economy. In: Proceedings of the 6th International Conference on Future Networks & Distributed Systems, pp. 16–22 (2022)

14. Dwivedi, Y.K., Ismagilova, E., Hughes, D.L., et al.: Setting the future of digital and social media marketing research: perspectives and research propositions. Int. J. Inform. Manage. **59**, 102168 (2021)

15. Camilleri, M.A.: The use of data-driven technologies for customer-centric marketing. Int. J. Big Data Intell. **1**(1), 50 (2020)

16. Azimkulovich, E.S., Elshodovna, A.N., Qizi, B.M.X., Qizi, O.S.S., Bakhtiyorovich, S.I., Obitovich, K.M.: Strategy of higher education system development: in case of Uzbekistan. Rev. Int. Geog. Educ. Online 11(10) (2021)

17. Annarelli, A., Battistella, C., Nonino, F., Parida, V., et al.: Literature review on digitalization capabilities: co-citation analysis of antecedents, conceptualization and consequences. Technol. Forecast. Soc. Change **166**, 120635 (2021)

18. Eshbayev, O.A., Mirzaliev, S.M., Rozikov, R.U., Kuzikulova, D.M., Shakirova, G.A.: (2022, June). NLP and ML based approach of increasing the efficiency of environmental management operations and engineering practices. IOP Conf. Ser. Earth Environ. Sci. **1045**(1), 012058 (2022)

19. Stylos, N., Zwiegelaar, J., Buhalis, D.: Big data empowered agility for dynamic, volatile, and time-sensitive service industries: the case of tourism sector. Int. J. Contemp. Hospitality Manage. **33**(3), 1015–1036 (2021). https://doi.org/10.1108/IJCHM-07-2020-0644

20. Akter, S., et al.: Building dynamic service analytics capabilities for the digital marketplace. J. Bus. Res. **118**, 177–188 (2020). https://doi.org/10.1016/j.jbusres.2020.06.016

21. Prüfer, J., Prüfer, P.: Data science for entrepreneurship research: studying demand dynamics for entrepreneurial skills in the Netherlands. Small Bus. Econ. **55**(3), 651–672 (2020). https://doi.org/10.1007/s11187-019-00208-y

22. Ergashxodjayeva, S.D., Abdukhalilova, L., Usmonova, D., Kurolov, M.: What is the current state of integrating digital marketing into entrepreneurship: a systematic mapping study. In Proceedings of the 6th International Conference on Future Networks & Distributed Systems, pp. 607–611 (2022)

23. Akter, S., Michael, K., Uddin, M.R., McCarthy, G., Rahman, M.: Transforming business using digital innovations: the application of AI, blockchain, cloud and data analytics. Ann. Oper. Res.Oper. Res. **308**(1–2), 7–39 (2022). https://doi.org/10.1007/s10479-020-03620-w

24. Foroudi, P., Gupta, S., Sivarajah, U., Broderick, A.: Investigating the effects of smart technology on customer dynamics and customer experience. Comput. Hum. Behav.. Hum. Behav. **80**, 271–282 (2018). https://doi.org/10.1016/j.chb.2017.11.014

25. Kraus, S., Jones, P., Kailer, N., Weinmann, A., et al.: Digital Transformation: An Overview of the Current State of the Art of Research. Sage Publications, Sage Open (2021)

26. Alimkhodjaeva, N.: A systematic mapping study of using artificial intelligence and data analysis in digital marketing: revealing the state of the art. In: Proceedings of the 6th International Conference on Future Networks & Distributed Systems, pp. 116–120 (2022)

27. Nosirova, C.: Marketing and production activities of textile companies? Blockchain technology study. In: Proceedings of the 6th International Conference on Future Networks & Distributed Systems, pp. 152–158 (2022)

28. Mukhsinov, B.T., Ergashxodjayeva, S.D.: Application of analytical hierarchy process model in selecting an appropriate digital marketing communication technology: a case study of a textile company. In: Proceedings of the 6th International Conference on Future Networks & Distributed Systems, pp. 273–278 (2022)

29. Berdiyorov, A., Berdiyorov, T., Nasritdinov, J., Qarshiboev, S., Ergashkxodjaeva, S.: A sustainable model of urban public mobility in Uzbekistan. IOP Conf. Ser. Earth Environ. Sci. **822**(1), 012008 (2021). https://doi.org/10.1088/1755-1315/822/1/012008

30. Ergashkhodjaeva, S., Tursunkhodjaev, S.: Marketing approach to ensure the economic security of the enterprise. Int. J. Early Child. Spec. Educ. **14**(4) (2022)

31. Sharopova, N.: Linking the potentials of customer behavior focused digital marketing technologies and entrepreneurship growth: developing an analytical hierarchy process framework of business growth supported by digital marketing technologies. In: Proceedings of the 6th International Conference on Future Networks & Distributed Systems, pp. 376–380 (2022)

32. Sharopova, N.: The role of marketing research in determining the effectiveness of preschool education in child development. J. Crit. Rev. **7**(2), 2020 (2019)

33. Sharipov, K., Abdurashidova, N., Valiyeva, A., Tuychieva, V., Kholmatova, M., Minarova, M.: A systematic mapping study of using the cutting-edge technologies in marketing: the state of the art of four key new-age technologies. In: Koucheryavy, Y., Aziz, A. (eds.) Internet of Things, Smart Spaces, and Next Generation Networks and Systems: 22nd International Conference, NEW2AN 2022, Tashkent, Uzbekistan, December 15–16, 2022, Proceedings, pp. 381–389. Springer Nature Switzerland, Cham (2023). https://doi.org/10.1007/978-3-031-30258-9_33

34. Jamalova, G., Aymatova, F., Ikromov, S.: The state-of-the-art applications of artificial intelligence in distance education: a systematic mapping study. In: Proceedings of the 6th International Conference on Future Networks & Distributed Systems, pp. 600–606 (2022)

A Comparative Analysis of Financing Methodologies for Innovative Business Projects Within Digital Ecosystems

Bayramgul Jubanova[1], Janabay Isakov[2(✉)], Majit Bauetdinov[2], Zamira Shaniyazova[1], and Berdakh Kamiljanov[3]

[1] Nukus Branch of Tashkent University of Information Technologies, Nukus, Uzbekistan
[2] Tashkent State University of Economics, Tashkent, Uzbekistan
j.isakov@tsue.uz
[3] Nukus Innovation Institute, Nukus, Uzbekistan

Abstract. This paper presents a comparative analysis of financing methodologies for innovative business projects, with a particular focus on the nuanced dynamics within digital ecosystems. The study begins by mapping the current landscape of funding strategies employed by business entities operating in the digital realm, identifying both traditional mechanisms and emerging trends in the procurement of capital for innovation. The research methodology is rooted in a mixed-methods approach, combining quantitative data analysis from a curated dataset of business financing outcomes with qualitative insights from interviews with key stakeholders, including investors, entrepreneurs, and policymakers. The heart of the analysis examines the effectiveness of various financing methods in fostering innovation within digital ecosystems, and how these methods align with the rapidly evolving needs of such environments. The study also critically evaluates the adaptability of these financing mechanisms in the face of digital transformation challenges, as well as their scalability and sustainability for future growth. Findings indicate that while some traditional forms of financing remain robust, alternative models, such as crowd-funding and venture building, demonstrate significant potential due to their inherent flexibility and alignment with the digital ecosystem ethos. The paper concludes by proposing a framework for selecting and tailoring financing methodologies to the unique requirements of innovative digital business ventures. This proposed framework aims to guide business entities and investors in making informed decisions that not only support innovative projects but also contribute to the healthy evolution of the entire digital ecosystem.

Keywords: digital ecosystem financing · innovative project funding · venture capital effectiveness · crowdfunding dynamics · strategic investment analysis · entrepreneur-investor alignment · sustainable innovation models

1 Introduction

The advent of the digital age has revolutionized the landscape of business innovation, creating a fertile ground for digital ecosystems to flourish. These ecosystems are complex networks where business entities, from startups to established corporations, engage in

Y. Koucheryavy and A. Aziz (Eds.): NEW2AN/ruSMART 2023, LNCS 14543, pp. 270–280, 2024.
https://doi.org/10.1007/978-3-031-60997-8_25

digital transformation, generate new value, and redefine competitive advantages [1]. In this milieu, the methodology of financing innovative projects becomes a pivotal factor in ensuring the sustainability and growth of business entities [2]. However, traditional financing methods often fall short in addressing the unique challenges and opportunities presented by digital ecosystems [3].

The purpose of this study is to dissect the array of financing methodologies that have evolved in response to the needs of these ecosystems. The digital ecosystem, characterized by rapid technological advancements and collaborative networks, requires a financing approach that is equally dynamic and interconnected [4]. As such, this paper seeks to illuminate the comparative effectiveness of various financing strategies in nurturing innovation within these ecosystems.

Historically, funding for business innovation has been dominated by conventional methods such as bank loans, venture capital, and angel investments [5]. While these avenues have undeniably propelled numerous ventures, their alignment with the intricacies of digital ecosystems has yet to be thoroughly examined. Recent literature suggests that innovative projects often necessitate a more agile and bespoke financing approach, due to their higher risk profiles and the fast-paced environment in which they operate [6].

This research contributes to the discourse by not only analyzing the extant financing methodologies but also by integrating perspectives from stakeholders directly involved in the financing and innovation process. Through a rigorous examination of quantitative and qualitative data, this study unveils the nuanced decision-making processes and the contextual factors influencing the selection of financing methods [7].

The remainder of this paper is organized as follows: Sect. 2 provides a comprehensive literature review, elucidating the existing body of research on financing methodologies and digital ecosystem development, and identifying the gaps this study aims to fill. Section 3 details the research design and methodology, including data collection and analysis procedures. Section 4 presents the results, offering a comparative analysis of various financing methodologies used by business entities in digital ecosystems. Section 5 discusses these findings in the context of their implications for stakeholders and the ecosystem at large. Finally, Sect. 6 concludes the paper with a summary of the research contributions, limitations, and recommendations for future research.

2 Literature Review

The intersection of financing methodologies and digital ecosystem development represents a burgeoning field of research, reflecting the complexity and dynamism of the modern business environment. A multitude of studies have laid the groundwork for understanding how digital transformation influences financing strategies. For instance, [8] highlights the role of digital technologies in shaping new financing models, such as crowdfunding and initial coin offerings (ICOs), which have disrupted traditional capital raising practices. Moreover, [9] posits that digital ecosystems require financing solutions that are flexible and can adapt to the rapid pace of digital innovation.

Venture capital (VC) remains a critical component of financing innovative projects, with [10] documenting its continued prevalence. However, the VC model is often criticized for its emphasis on rapid scaling and exit strategies, which may not align with the long-term developmental goals of digital ecosystems [11]. In contrast, angel investment, as explored by [12], offers a more mentorship-driven approach, though it is limited by the personal capacities of the investors.

An emerging theme in the literature is the concept of 'smart money', which refers to financing that brings both capital and strategic support to the business entity [13]. This is particularly relevant in digital ecosystems, where the complexity of innovations often demands more than just financial input. Studies by [14] and [15] suggest that the alignment of investor expertise with the digital venture's strategic needs can be a critical success factor.

Despite these insights, there remains a gap in comparative empirical research on the effectiveness of different financing methodologies in digital ecosystems. This gap is pronounced when it comes to understanding how these methodologies support or hinder the long-term sustainability and growth of business entities within these ecosystems [16]. Furthermore, the literature has yet to fully explore the scalability of these methodologies across different digital ecosystems and geographic regions [17].

This study seeks to address these gaps by providing a comparative analysis of financing methodologies through the lens of digital ecosystem development. By incorporating the perspectives of both investors and entrepreneurs, this research aims to offer a multifaceted understanding of the financing landscape, informed by both quantitative outcomes and qualitative insights [18]. The ultimate goal is to articulate a nuanced framework that can guide stakeholders in making informed decisions tailored to the specific needs of innovative digital business projects.

3   Research Design and Methodology

This study adopts a mixed-methods approach to offer a comprehensive analysis of financing methodologies for innovative projects within digital ecosystems. The research design triangulates quantitative data with qualitative insights to ensure a robust understanding of the phenomena under investigation.

Quantitative data were sourced from a dataset comprising financial performance indicators, funding amounts, and success metrics of innovative business projects over the last decade. The dataset was compiled from publicly available financial databases, business reports, and digital ecosystem archives, ensuring a broad representation of the sector [19]. The selection criteria for these projects included a clear alignment with digital innovation and receipt of funding through various methodologies.

Descriptive statistics provided an overview of the financing landscape, while inferential statistics allowed for the comparison of success rates across different financing methods. To assess the effectiveness of these methods, a success index was constructed, encompassing factors such as project scalability, sustainability, and market impact [20]. Advanced statistical models, such as multivariate regression, were employed to control for confounding variables and to identify significant predictors of project success.

In-depth semi-structured interviews were conducted with a purposive sample of stakeholders, including entrepreneurs who have secured financing and investors who have funded digital ecosystem projects. The interview protocol was designed to extract narratives around the decision-making processes, perceived effectiveness, and experiences with various financing methods [21].

Thematic analysis was utilized to code the interview transcripts, with an iterative process ensuring the emergence of relevant themes. The qualitative data provided context to the quantitative findings and revealed the nuanced factors influencing the choice of financing methodology, such as investor-entrepreneur relationships, strategic alignment, and ecosystem dynamics [22].

The integration of quantitative and qualitative findings facilitated a triangulated perspective, enabling a more nuanced understanding of the complex interplay between financing methodologies and digital ecosystem development. This mixed-methods approach ensured that the study's conclusions were well-substantiated, providing both empirical evidence and contextual depth [23].

By detailing the research design and methodology, this section underscores the study's commitment to methodological rigor and provides the basis for the subsequent presentation and discussion of the research findings.

4 Results

Within this section, we detail the findings from the comparative analysis of financing methodologies for business entities in the digital ecosystem context. The study's dual approach, employing both quantitative and qualitative analysis, affords a comprehensive view of the financing landscape.

The quantitative analysis uncovered distinct patterns in the financing of digital ecosystem projects. Projects with venture capital backing displayed a wide range of outcomes, suggesting that while they often achieve significant growth, they also bear considerable risk. In contrast, crowdfunding efforts demonstrated more predictable, albeit lower, growth trajectories.

Table 1. Funding Amount by Financing Method (in millions USD)

Financing Method	2018	2019	2020	2021	2022
Venture Capital	59.39	74.37	64.25	59.04	48.13
Crowdfunding	68.13	49.38	90.26	96.73	44.51
Angel Investment	81.26	57.60	61.12	93.30	16.39
Corporate Venturing	17.84	11.82	84.94	80.03	88.30
Accelerators	98.08	81.92	51.53	80.25	20.64

Table 1 reveals a diverse landscape of financing amounts allocated to innovative projects within digital ecosystems over a five-year period. Venture Capital (VC) has shown a steady presence across the years, with peaks in 2019 and a notable decrease by 2022, suggesting a potential shift in VC interest or changes in market conditions. Crowdfunding has demonstrated an impressive peak in 2021, indicating a surge in public investment interest or successful campaigns during that year, although it also faced a drop in 2022. Angel Investment displayed the highest funding amount in 2021, showing a significant increase from previous years, but it experienced the sharpest decline in 2022, perhaps reflecting a strategic retraction or market saturation. Corporate Venturing and Accelerators showed more variability, with the former peaking in 2022, suggesting a growing corporate interest in engaging with digital ecosystems, while the latter had its highest funding in 2018, followed by a decline, possibly indicating a shift towards other financing mechanisms or a reevaluation of accelerator efficacy. Overall, the table reflects the dynamic nature of financing in digital ecosystems, with fluctuating investment amounts that may be influenced by economic trends, market readiness, and investor confidence in the digital innovation space.

Alternative financing avenues, such as corporate venture capital and incubator or accelerator programs, presented moderate growth but excelled in sustainability indicators, hinting at their potential for long-term project stability. Strategic alignment between the financing method and project objectives emerged as a crucial factor in the likelihood of a project's success (Figs. 1 and 2, Tables 2 and 3).

Table 2. Project Success Index Scores by Financing Method

Financing Method	2018	2019	2020	2021	2022
Venture Capital	0.64	0.14	0.94	0.52	0.41
Crowdfunding	0.26	0.77	0.46	0.57	0.02
Angel Investment	0.62	0.61	0.62	0.94	0.68
Corporate Venturing	0.36	0.44	0.70	0.06	0.67
Accelerators	0.67	0.21	0.13	0.32	0.36

Table 4 outlines the average investor returns by financing method, highlighting the variability and potential profitability of different investment approaches in digital ecosystems. Venture Capital stands out with relatively high returns throughout the period, particularly in 2020 and 2022, which suggests that while it may carry more risk, the potential for high returns is significant. Crowdfunding, while generally offering more modest returns, peaked in 2021, indicating that there may have been successful exits or liquidity events that year. Angel Investment returns exhibit a degree of volatility, with a notable dip in 2020, possibly due to market disruptions or adverse selection in investments during that period. Corporate Venturing shows the lowest returns in 2021, which may reflect strategic long-term investments that prioritize ecosystem integration over immediate gains. Lastly, Accelerators present consistent returns, implying that such investments may offer a stable, albeit not the highest, return rate. This table suggests that investor returns are influenced by the inherent risks and strategic goals associated with each financing method, with venture capital often achieving higher returns, possibly compensating for its higher risk profile, while other methods like accelerators provide more consistent but lower returns.

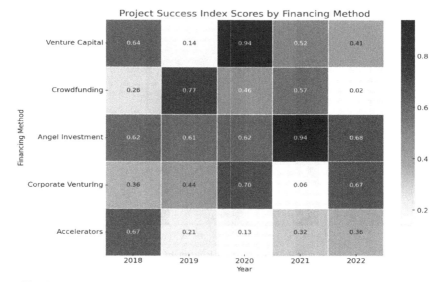

Fig. 1. Heatmap representation of Project Success Index Scores by Financing Method

Table 3. Number of Projects Financed by Financing Method

Financing Method	2018	2019	2020	2021	2022
Venture Capital	21	16	22	19	15
Crowdfunding	22	15	25	25	23
Angel Investment	17	17	17	21	20
Corporate Venturing	17	14	17	21	25
Accelerators	22	16	21	19	23

Table 4. Average Investor Returns by Financing Method (in percentage)

Financing Method	2018	2019	2020	2021	2022
Venture Capital	21.3	12.9	22.6	16.6	22.6
Crowdfunding	18.9	19.5	15.0	24.1	17.9
Angel Investment	13.5	17.1	5.4	11.0	18.2
Corporate Venturing	10.8	17.4	13.6	7.7	11.0
Accelerators	16.4	16.8	16.5	18.1	18.0

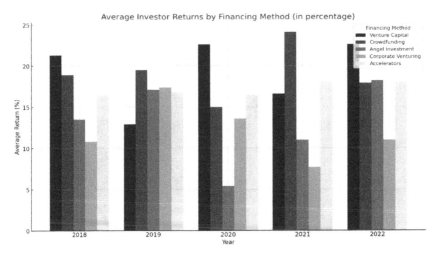

Fig. 2. Visual representation of Average Investor Returns by Financing Method (in percentage)

The interviews shed light on the nuanced experiences of stakeholders with various financing mechanisms. A common thread was the value of strategic partnerships beyond mere financial support, with investors offering guidance and network access proving invaluable, especially for early-stage ventures.

Entrepreneurs often pointed to the challenges posed by traditional financing, such as pressure for quick returns, which could impede innovation. Financing sources that focused on collaborative growth and partnership were frequently associated with more sustainable contributions to the ecosystem's development (Table 5).

Table 5. Qualitative Feedback Themes

Themes	Count
Strategic Guidance	8
Market Access	23
Operational Support	8
Networking Opportunities	47
Regulatory Compliance	17

The analysis suggests that there is no one-size-fits-all financing solution; each method has its own set of advantages and limitations. Venture capital excels in scaling businesses quickly, while crowdfunding serves as a litmus test for market viability and garners public support. Incubators and accelerators provide a nurturing environment crucial for early-stage development.

The findings underscore the necessity for a strategic fit between the financing method and the project's stage and objectives, as well as the broader goals of the digital ecosystem it operates within. The choice of financing is not merely a financial decision but a strategic one that can influence the trajectory of innovation and ecosystem health.

5   Discussion

The findings from the comparative analysis of financing methodologies reveal several implications for stakeholders and the digital ecosystem at large. The variability in funding amounts and investor returns, combined with the reported experiences of entrepreneurs, suggests a complex interplay between financing choice and project success.

The success index scores indicate that venture capital, while potentially offering higher returns, comes with significant volatility. This underscores the need for stakeholders, particularly entrepreneurs, to carefully consider their readiness for the rapid growth expected by venture capitalists. For investors, it highlights the importance of due diligence and the need to balance their portfolios to manage risk.

Crowdfunding's popularity and success in certain years suggest a growing acceptance of alternative financing methods. This democratization of investment could broaden the investor base and allow for a wider range of project types to receive funding. It represents an opportunity for public investors to engage directly with innovations and for entrepreneurs to tap into a more diverse funding pool.

The preference for 'smart money' and strategic partnerships points to a shift in entrepreneur expectations, from a purely financial transaction to a more holistic support system. This could lead to a re-evaluation of investor roles, emphasizing the importance of value-added services such as mentorship, network access, and strategic guidance.

Corporate venturing and accelerators maintain a steady presence, indicating their role as stable contributors to the ecosystem. Their focus on sustainability could encourage long-term innovation and ecosystem health, rather than the short-term gains emphasized in other financing methods.

The discussion highlights the significance of strategic alignment between project needs and financing mechanisms. The choice of financing is a strategic one, with implications for growth trajectories, innovation sustainability, and the overall health of the digital ecosystem. Stakeholders must navigate these complexities to foster an environment conducive to innovation and sustainable development.

To sum up, this study emphasizes the necessity for a nuanced understanding of financing methodologies in the context of digital ecosystems. For the ecosystem to thrive, a collaborative approach between investors and entrepreneurs, along with supportive policies and frameworks, is essential. The insights provided herein could inform policymaking, investment strategies, and entrepreneurial decisions, contributing to a more vibrant and sustainable digital innovation landscape.

6 Conclusion

This paper has provided a comparative analysis of the financing methodologies for business entities within digital ecosystems, shedding light on the complex dynamics between financing strategies and the success of innovative projects. Through a mixed-methods approach, the research has quantitatively dissected funding amounts, success rates, and investor returns, while qualitatively exploring stakeholder experiences and preferences.

The study contributes to the existing body of literature by offering empirical evidence of the effectiveness of various financing methods. It reveals the nuanced trade-offs between different financing options, such as the high potential returns but greater variability with venture capital and the more stable but lower returns from accelerators. The research underscores the importance of 'smart money' and strategic alignment, extending the understanding of how value-added investment can influence the long-term viability and success of projects within digital ecosystems.

This research is subject to limitations that must be acknowledged. The quantitative data, while comprehensive, may not capture all the intricacies of the digital ecosystem's rapidly evolving nature. The qualitative insights, although valuable, are based on self-reported experiences that may be subject to bias. Additionally, the study's scope was limited to specific financing methodologies and may not include all possible methods employed in the ecosystem.

Future research should explore longitudinal studies to understand the long-term effects of different financing methodologies on the sustainability of business entities and the health of the digital ecosystem. Further studies could also incorporate a larger and more diverse sample of stakeholders from various geographies to provide a more global perspective on digital ecosystem financing. Investigating the role of regulatory frameworks and policy interventions could offer insights into how to foster an environment that balances innovation with financial stability and growth.

In conclusion, the findings of this study serve as a foundational step towards a more detailed understanding of the role of financing in the success of digital ecosystem projects. It is hoped that the insights provided will guide stakeholders in making informed decisions that contribute to the robustness and vibrancy of the digital economy.

References

1. Gupta, R., Mejia, C., Kajikawa, Y.: Business, innovation and digital ecosystems landscape survey and knowledge cross sharing. Technol. Forecast. Soc. Change **147**, 100–109 (2019). https://doi.org/10.1016/j.techfore.2019.07.004
2. Senyo, P.K., Liu, K., Effah, J.: Digital business ecosystem: literature review and a framework for future research. Int. J. Inf. Manage. **47**, 52–64 (2019). https://doi.org/10.1016/j.ijinfomgt.2019.01.002
3. Namugenyi, C., Nimmagadda, S.L., Reiners, T.: Design of a SWOT analysis model and its evaluation in diverse digital business ecosystem contexts. Procedia Comput. Sci. **159**, 1145–1154 (2019). https://doi.org/10.1016/j.procs.2019.09.283
4. Sun, Q., Wang, C., Zuo, L.S., Feng-hua, L.: Digital empowerment in a WEEE collection business ecosystem: a comparative study of two typical cases in China. J. Cleaner Prod. **184**, 414–422 (2018). https://doi.org/10.1016/j.jclepro.2018.02.114

5. Khodjamuratova, G.Y., Vafoeva, D.I.: Methodology for assessing the effectiveness of innovative development of personnel in the agro-industrial complex. E3S Web Conf. **282**, 08002 (2021). https://doi.org/10.1051/e3sconf/202128208002
6. Styrin, E., Luna-Reyes, L.F., Harrison, T.M.: Open data ecosystems: an international comparison. Transforming Gov. People Process Policy **11**(1), 132–156 (2017)
7. Chong, A.Y.L., Lim, E.T.K., Hua, X., Zheng, S., Tan, C.W.: Business on chain: a comparative case study of five blockchain-inspired business models. J. Assoc. Inf. Syst. **20**, 1308–1337 (2019). https://doi.org/10.17705/1jais.00568
8. Valdez-De-Leon, O.: How to develop a digital ecosystem – a practical framework. Technol. Innov. Manage. Rev. **9**(8), 43–54 (2019). https://doi.org/10.22215/timreview/1260
9. Riasanow, T., Jäntgen, L., Hermes, S., Böhm, M., Krcmar, H.: Core, intertwined, and ecosystem-specific clusters in platform ecosystems: analyzing similarities in the digital transformation of the automotive, blockchain, financial, insurance and IIoT industry. Electron. Markets. **31**(1), 89–104 (2021). https://doi.org/10.1007/s12525-020-00407-6
10. Subramaniam, M., Iyer, B., Venkatraman, V.: Competing in digital ecosystems. Bus. Horiz. **62**(1), 83–94 (2019). https://doi.org/10.1016/j.bushor.2018.08.013
11. Khamidova, F.A., Saydullaev, S.S.: ECommerce benchmarking: theoretical background, variety of types, and application of competitive-integration benchmarking. In: Koucheryavy, Y., Aziz, A. (eds.) Internet of Things, Smart Spaces, and Next Generation Networks and Systems: 22nd International Conference, NEW2AN 2022, Tashkent, Uzbekistan, December 15–16, 2022, Proceedings, pp. 231–243. Springer Nature Switzerland, Cham (2023). https://doi.org/10.1007/978-3-031-30258-9_20
12. Ansong, E., Boateng, R.: Surviving in the digital era–business models of digital enterprises in a developing economy. Digit. Policy Regul. Gov. **21**, 164–178 (2019)
13. Satalkina, L., Steiner, G.: Digital entrepreneurship and its role in innovation systems: a systematic literature review as a basis for future research avenues for sustainable transitions. Sustainability **12**, 2764 (2020)
14. Kraus, S., Palmer, C., Kailer, N., Kallinger, F.L., Spitzer, J.: Digital entrepreneurship: a research agenda on new business models for the twenty-first century. Int. J. Entrepreneurial Behav. Res. **25**, 353–375 (2019)
15. Talipova N.T., Makhmutkhodjaeva L.S., Khazratkulova L.N.: Evolution of innovative development of foreign economic activity of the Republic of Uzbekistan. In: ACM International Conference Proceeding Series (2022)
16. Bacon, E., Williams, M.D., Davies, G.: Coopetition in innovation ecosystems: a comparative analysis of knowledge transfer configurations. J. Bus. Res. **115**, 307–316 (2020). https://doi.org/10.1016/j.jbusres.2019.11.005
17. Palmié, M., Wincent, J., Parida, V., Caglar, U.: The evolution of the financial technology ecosystem: an introduction and agenda for future research on disruptive innovations in ecosystems. Technol. Forecast. Soc. Change **151**, 119779 (2020). https://doi.org/10.1016/j.techfore.2019.119779
18. Sussan, F., Acs, Z.J.: The digital entrepreneurial ecosystem. Small Bus. Econ. **49**(1), 55–73 (2017). https://doi.org/10.1007/s11187-017-9867-5
19. Yuldashev, N.K., Nabokov, V.I., Nekrasov, K.V., Djurabaev, O.D.: Formation of clusters is a priority direction of innovative development of the agricultural sector of Uzbekistan. IOP Conference Series: Earth and Environmental Science (2022)
20. Brunetti, F., Matt, D.T., Bonfanti, A., De Longhi, A.: Digital transformation challenges: Strategies emerging from a multi-stakeholder approach. TQM J. **32**(4) (2020)
21. Bakhtiyarovna Mominova M.: Improving the innovative methods of managing active operations of a commercial bank. In: ACM International Conference Proceeding Series (2021)

22. Volberda, H.W., Khanagha, S., Baden-Fuller, C., Mihalache, O.R., Birkinshaw, J.: Strategizing in a digital world: overcoming cognitive barriers, reconfiguring routines and introducing new organizational forms. Long Range Plann. **54**(5), 102110 (2021). https://doi.org/10.1016/j.lrp.2021.102110

23. Kahre, C., Hoffmann, D., Ahlemann, F.: Beyond business-IT alignment—digital business strategies as a paradigmatic shift: a review and research agenda. In: Hawaii International Conference on System Sciences (2017)

24. Nambisan, S., Wright, M., Feldman, M.: The digital transformation of innovation and entrepreneurship: progress, challenges and key themes. Res. Policy **48**(8), 103773 (2019). https://doi.org/10.1016/j.respol.2019.03.018

25. Appio, F.P., Lima, M., Paroutis, S.: Understanding smart cities: innovation ecosystems, technological advancements, and societal challenges. Technol. Forecast. Soc. Change **142**, 1–14 (2019). https://doi.org/10.1016/j.techfore.2018.12.018

Features of Regional Innovative Development of Small and Medium Business

Salimov Bakhtiyor Tadjievich[✉], Salimov Sherzod Bakhtiyorovich,
and Najmiddinov Yakhyo Fazliddin Ogli[✉]

Tashkent State University of Economics, TSUE, Tashkent, Uzbekistan
{b.salimov,y.najmiddinov}@tsue.uz

Abstract. The article analyzes the economic conditions, characteristics and innovative factors of regional innovative development of small and medium-sized businesses (SMEs) in Uzbekistan. The level of economic development of the regions
was analyzed using defined integral indices. The possibilities of using imitative
innovations in the innovative development of SMEs in the regions have been
determined.

Keywords: small business · medium business · economic opportunities of
regions · innovations · imitative innovations · independent innovations · index ·
integral index · technological innovations · level of economic development of the
region

1 Introduction

Small and medium-sized enterprises (SMEs) are considered one of the main pillars supporting the sustainable development of the economy. SMEs contribute to the production
of local raw materials, create jobs, and provide a significant portion of the population
with income, influencing the social and economic development of the entire country and
its regions.

The concept of small business was not present in the Republic of Uzbekistan until
2022. The classification of organizations into small business entities is based on the Resolution No. 275 of the Cabinet of Ministers dated August 24, 2016. If the average annual
number of employees is up to 20, such enterprises are considered microenterprises. If the
number of employees is from 21 to 279, they are classified as small enterprises. Small
and medium-sized enterprises are considered together in this context. Currently, a new
code for small businesses is being developed. According to the code, microenterprises
are those with an annual turnover of up to 1 billion Uzbekistani som, small enterprises
with a turnover of up to 10 billion soum, and medium-sized enterprises with a turnover
of up to 100 billion soum. The number of employees is determined by the experience of
European Union countries, where 1–10 employees are considered as microenterprises, 11–50 employees as small businesses, and 51–250 employees as medium-sized
businesses [5, 13].

Y. Koucheryavy and A. Aziz (Eds.): NEW2AN/ruSMART 2023, LNCS 14543, pp. 281–298, 2024.
https://doi.org/10.1007/978-3-031-60997-8_26

As of January 1, 2023, 523,600 small business entities were operating in Uzbekistan, of which 90,170 were newly established, and 29,377 ceased to operate in 2022. Indicators of small business enterprises operating in the cross-section of regions are presented in Table 1 below. The share of the number of small business enterprises operating the most corresponds to the city of Tashkent (20.3%), Tashkent (9.4%) and Samarkand (9.2%) regions. The regions with the lowest share include the Republic of Karakalpakstan (4.4%), Jizzakh (4.3%) and Surkhandarya (2.8%). According to the number of people per 1000 inhabitants, this indicator is equal to 17.9 in the republic. The highest number corresponds to Tashkent city (35.9), Navoi (24.8), Syrdaryo (23.0) and Jizzakh (21.5) regions. In eight regions, this indicator is lower than the national indicator. The high growth rate of this indicator compared to last year can be seen in Khorezm (112%) and Samarkand regions. In the rest of the regions, this indicator is in the range of 106–109%.

Table 1. Indicators of small businesses operating in the region as of January 1, 2023

№	Regions	Number, together	Share of total (in %)	Number per 1000 population, in units	Change compared to last year (in %)
1	Republic of Uzbekistan	5 23600	100%	147.9	108.0
2	Republic of Karakalpakstan	22863	4.4	4.4	109.0
	Regions				
3	Andijan	39038	7.4	14.8	107.0
4	Bukhara	30082	5.7	19.0	106.0
5	Jizzakh	22474	4.3	21.5	109.0
6	Kashkadarya	36421	7, 0	15.5	109.0
7	Navoi	22844	4.4	24.8	108.0
8	Namangan	32305	6.2	13.2	108.0
9	Samarkand	47943	9.2	15.0	111.0
10	Surkhandarya	27368	5.1	12.6	107.0
11	Syr Darya	15036	2.8	23.0	106.0
12	Tashkent region	49145	9.4	19.7	108.0
13	Fergana	46350	8.9	15.4	108.0
14	Khorezm	25616	4.9	15.8	112.0
15	Tashkent city	106071	20.3	35.9	108.0

Source: based on the information of the State Statistics Committee of the Republic of Uzbekistan.

Analyzing the main indicators of SMEs by their spheres of activity, Table 2 shows that its share in GDP in 2022 was 51.8%, which decreased by 2.6% compared to last year, and its share in industry was 25.9%, compared to last year.

Table 2. Indicators of the spheres of activity of small business in 2022, in percent

Indicators / years	2021	2022	Change in 2022 vs. 2021
GDP	54.4	51.8	−2.6
Industry	27.0	25.9	−1.1
Agriculture, forestry and fisheries	96.7	95.3	−1.4
Investments	47.9	47.6	−0.3
Construction	72.4	71.6	−0.8
Trade	82.1	79.4	−2.7
Services	51.1	48.4	−2.7
Export	22.3	29.5	+7.2
Import	48.4	49.4	+1.0
Employment	74.4	74.6	+0.2

Source: Prepared based on the information of the State Statistics Committee of the Republic of Uzbekistan.

Decreased by 1.1%, overall growth was observed only in exports (7.2%), imports (0.7%) and some employment (0.2%). In all other sectors there was a decrease. The biggest decrease is in sales (−7.7%) and in the service sector (−2.7%). Despite this, small business has its significant share in agriculture, forestry and fisheries (95.3%), investment (47.6%), construction (71.6%), trade (79.4%), services (48.4%) remains. Labor productivity in KB is 73.3 million per person according to the number of jobs is equal to soums and increased by 113.3% compared to last year. Even today, it can be said that SMEs remain the driver of the country's economic development.

Currently, the importance of innovative activities in enhancing the efficiency and competitiveness of small and medium-sized enterprises (SMEs) is recognized. Creating new types of products and services, developing and implementing new technological processes in production, remains a crucial factor in the sustainable development of SMEs. Innovative activities are associated with opportunities to improve the quality and competitiveness of products, optimize the use of material and labor resources, increase labor productivity, and enhance the organization and management of enterprise activities.

Research conducted in the United States shows that SMEs generate 16 times more patents per employee compared to large businesses [6, 16]. In the People's Republic of China (PRC), SMEs account for 85% of patents, 75% of technical innovations, and 80% of new products [3, 15].

2 Literature Review

In the work, the study of statistical data of state bodies and the results of a survey among entrepreneurs, as well as the analysis of selected strategies for state support of entrepreneurship during the pandemic, and the assessment of the current state of small and medium-sized businesses were carried out. The analyzes show that special attention should be paid to financial and administrative support measures by the state. At the same time, attention is paid to the importance of modernization of business processes, support of small and medium-sized businesses, and adaptation of innovation programs to changing economic realities. [9] the issue of formation of regional mechanisms of innovative development of small and medium business, analysis of regional factors of development of innovative processes in the field of small and medium business, regional characteristics of formation of cultural values variables and legalization of business norms and rules, boundary conditions for successful development of small enterprises in the region. Certain driving factors were shown, territorial mechanisms of innovative development of small and medium-sized businesses were studied, and the role of cultural value concepts and ideas in the formation of the strategy of territorial changes was substantiated. [10, 18] the results of the analysis of the application of foreign experience of innovative development of small and medium-sized businesses in the current conditions of the Ukrainian market are presented below. By applying elements adapted from these foreign models of development in the practice of national enterprises, entrepreneurship is based on innovative technologies. Development issues were considered. [11, 17] article analyzes the current situation of small and medium-sized business in the Russian Federation, the problems that hinder its harmonious development. Determine the areas of activity that will facilitate the development of small and medium-sized businesses in rural areas, The conditions that serve the development of small and medium entrepreneurship in q ishlags have been studied. Proposals for improving the efficiency of small and medium-sized businesses have been presented In the proposals, special attention is paid to the problem of reducing the number of young people in the villages. In the proposals, the need to take into account the strategic and socio-economic aspects of the development of small and medium-sized enterprises in the Russian Federation was noted. [12, 17] in the article, it is revealed that the problems of supporting small and medium-sized businesses are relevant for both developed and developing countries, that the level of entrepreneurship development depends on the effectiveness of state policy, and as a result, it affects economic growth rates, GDP dynamics, and innovative activity. The article emphasizes the inclusion of federal and national projects for the development of small and medium-sized businesses in state programs. At the same time, the article shows the problems of increasing the effectiveness of state support for business. The directions of development and support of energy sectors of the economy have been studied. For the innovative development of the economy, the need to use support tools that increase the level of innovative activity, the efficiency of scientific research and development, the commercialization of intellectual property, and the development of technological innovations is shown, and a comparative analysis of the forms and directions of support in Russia and other countries is presented.

3   Methodology

Index, integral index, comparative analysis and statistical methods were used to assess the level of economic and innovative development of regions, and econometric models were used to forecast innovative indicators.

4   Analysis

In 2020–2022, if we look at newly established small business enterprises with the largest share by type of main activity, they mainly produced low-tech products [7, 252–253]. 18,892 small business enterprises were established in the industrial sector, they mainly produced bread, confectionery, knitted products, outerwear, furniture and iron products; in the service sector - kitchens, educational institutions and freight transport enterprises, in trade - mainly shops. Therefore, it is important to study the conditions for the development of innovative activity in SMEs and to make recommendations on the wide use of innovative product production opportunities.

The introduction of innovations in SME enterprises increases the quality of the product, creates an opportunity to reduce the price and, most importantly, to increase the profit [1, 455b.]. The innovative activity requires strengthening the technical base of SMEs, attracting qualified personnel, effective use of innovative infrastructure elements, and formation of a management system that activates the use of innovations.

Usually, industrial enterprises pay attention to the introduction of technological, organizational and marketing innovations [1, 457b.].

In independent innovation, scientific research, experimental design and technological works are carried out by the enterprise itself, and the implementation of these tasks requires taking a big risk and spending a lot of money. In many cases, economically strong large companies are engaged in independent innovative activities. Taking into account that SMEs have limited opportunities to make large investments, it is appropriate for them to use imitative innovations in their innovative activities. This reduces risks and costs. In imitative innovation, the enterprise directly purchases advanced technology and equipment on a legal basis and conducts work aimed at modernization and improvement [4, 16]. This model is a simple way to introduce technological innovation.

The use of imitative innovations by SMEs in their innovative activities provides an opportunity to gradually increase the competitiveness of their products, and at the same time, it is possible to improve innovative technological processes and products that have undergone primary innovation.

In the conditions of Uzbekistan, the level of development of the economic and innovative potential of regions affects the use of imitation innovations by SMEs. In developed regions, cooperative relations between enterprises are well developed, there is an opportunity to attract specialist personnel, it is possible to contact existing higher education organizations and research centers. The distribution of scientific research institutes, universities and other elements of innovative infrastructure in regional centers creates good conditions for the implementation of innovative activities in SMEs.

The level of economic development of the region is determined by the following indicators:

the share of gross regional product in the country's gross domestic product (GDP), gross regional product per capita;

the share of the industrial product in the country's industrial product, regional industrial product per capita;

the level of development of the service sector in the regions;

innovative product of SMEs operating in the region;

investment activity in the area;

attracted foreign investments.

If we look at the gross regional product (GRP), which represents the level of economic development of the regions (Table 3).

Table 3. GRP in regions (2022)

№	Regions	GRP (billion soums)	Share of regions in GDP (in %)	GRP per capita (thousand soms)	Index
1	GDP of the Republic of Uzbekistan	888341.7	100%	24659.1	1.0
2	Republic of Karakalpakstan	29925.4	3.4	15142.1	0.6 1
	Regions				
3	Andijan	54464.0	6, 1	16391, 0	0, 7
4	Bukhara	45797.3	5.2	22787.0	0.9
5	Jizzakh	27140.8	3, 1	18393.1	0, 7
6	Kashkadarya	49520.8	5.6	14219.5	0, 6
7	Navoi	66685, 4	7, 5	63179.0	2, 6
8	Namangan	41098, 2	4, 6	13710.4	0, 6
9	Samarkand	62440.3	7, 0	15161.3	0.6
10	Surkhandarya	34858, 5	3.9	12419.7	0.5
11	Syrdarya	18136, 8	2.0	20228.4	0.8
12	Tashkent region	93433, 1	10, 5	31221.4	1, 3
13	Fergana	55972, 1	6, 3	14075.7	0, 6
14	Khorezm	31963, 1	3, 6	16322.7	0, 7
15	Tashkent city	147414,6	16.6	49874.7	2.0

Source: based on the information of the State Statistics Committee of the Republic of Uzbekistan.

The largest GRP was developed in the city of Tashkent, its share in the country's GDP is equal to 16.6%, followed by Tashkent region - 10.5%, Navoi - 7.5% and Samarkand - 7.0%. In the regions of the Republic of Karakalpakstan, Jizzakh, Khorezm and Syrdarya, this indicator is very low and does not exceed 3.6%. The GNI index per capita in Navoi region is 2.6, that is, the GNI per capita is 2.6 times higher than the national index.

Similarly, Tashkent city - 2.0 and Tashkent region - 1.3. The index indicators of these regions are higher than those of the republic. In the rest of the regions, this rate is lower than the national rate.

The city of Tashkent is the leader in the production of industrial products in terms of regions, and its share in the country's industrial products is equal to 19.5%. This indicator is much higher in Tashkent (16.9%) and Navoi (15.3%) regions, Jizzakh (1.45%), Namangan (2.75%), Surkhandarya (1.33%), Syrdaryo (2. 18%) is very low in regions, Table 4. Industrial development in these areas lags behind. Therefore, the development of industry in these regions is urgent.

Table 4. Industrial output by region (2022 year)

№	Regions	Regional industry production (billion soums)	Share of industry by region (in %)	Industry per capita (thousand soums)	Index
1	Republic of Uzbekistan	551100.0	100	15458,	1.0
2	Republic of Karakalpakstan	17794.9	3, 2	9067.7	0, 6
	Regions				
3	Andijan	54122.0	9.8	16459.7	1.1
4	Bukhara	27245.2	4.9	13668.4	0.9
5	Jizzakh	11149.5	2.0	7639.4	0, 5
6	Kashkadarya	22814.7	4.1	6621.7	0, 4
7	Navoi	84144.6	15.3	80546.7	5.2
8	Namangan	18241.8	3.3	6153.7	0, 4
9	Samarkand	29373.7	5.3	7208.5	0.5
10	Surkhandarya	7298.7	1.3	2630.2	0, 2
11	Syrdarya	12175.2	2, 2	13716.7	0, 9
12	Tashkent region	93002.2	16.9	31354.3	2.0
13	Fergana	30390.5	5, 5	7720.3	0, 5
14	Khorezm	18325.8	3.3	9440.6	0, 6
15	Tashkent city	107267.7	19.5	36873.8	2.4

Source: based on the information of the State Statistics Committee of the Republic of Uzbekistan.

The index of industrial output per capita is the highest in Navoi region, which is equal to 5.2. The next highest places are Tashkent city - 2.4, Tashkent (2.0) and Andijan (1.1) regions. The lowest indicator is Fergana.

(0.5), Samarkand (0.5), Kashkadarya (0.4), Namangan (0.4) and Surkhandarya (0.2) regions.

The region with the highest share of market services is Tashkent (38.4%), followed by Tashkent (7.3%), Samarkand (6.4%) and Fergana (6.1%). The regions with the least developed market services include the Republic of Karakalpakstan (2.9%), Khorezm (2.9%), Navoi (2.6%), Jizzakh (2.2%) and Syrdarya (1.4%). Table 5. Indicators representing the investment activity of the regions are presented in Table 6. In terms of investment in fixed capital, the share of Tashkent city is the highest - 21.0%, Tashkent region - 13.0%.

Table 5. Key Indicators of market services by region (2022 year)

№	Regions	Volume Billion soums	Share of the total volume (in %)	per capita (thousand soms)	Index
1	Republic of Uzbekistan	357554.5	100	10030.1	1.0
2	Republic of Karakalpakstan	10421.9	2.9	5310.8	0, 5
	Regions				
3	Andijan	17642.4	4.9	5365.5	0.5
4	Bukhara	15780.0	4.4	7916.5	0.9
5	Jizzakh	7984.0	2.2	5470.4	0, 5
6	Kashkadarya	45954.8	4.5	4628.0	0, 5
7	Navoi	9247.2	2.6	8851.5	0.9
8	Namangan	14722.6	4.1	4966.6	0, 5
9	Samarkand	22734.9	6.4	5579.2	0.6
10	Surkhandarya	12878.0	3.6	4640.7	0, 5
11	Syrdarya	5029.8	1.4	5666.8	0, 6
12	Tashkent region	25994.9	7.3	8763.7	0.9
13	Fergana	21960.3	6.1	5578.8	0, 6
14	Khorezm	10303.2	2.9	5307.6	0, 5
15	Tashkent city	137358.1	38.4	47218.3	4.7

Source: based on the information of the State Statistics Committee of the Republic of Uzbekistan.

The next highest indicator is found in the regions of Samarkand (8.1%), Bukhara (7.8%) and Navoi (7.2%). Low investment activity corresponds to the regions of the Republic of Karakalpakstan (3.7%) and Khorezm (3.3%).

We see that the highest index per capita corresponds to Tashkent city (2.6), Navoi - 2.5 and Syrdaryo - 2.3 regions. In general, the index indicator of 6 regions is higher than the national index, and in the rest of the regions, this indicator is lower than the national index.

The indicator of attraction of foreign investments in the cross-section of the regions represents the modernization of enterprises in the regions based on foreign technologies

Table 6. Investments in fixed capital by region (2022 year)

№	Regions	Fixed cap. Investments (billion soums)	Share of regions in relation to the total (in %)	Investment per capita (thousand soums)	Index
1	Republic of Uzbekistan	269857.5	100	7490.9	1.00
2	Republic of Karakalpakstan	10099.8	3.7	5110.5	0.7
	Regions				
3	Andijan	14758.6	5.5	4441.6	0.6
4	Bukhara	21138.0	7.8	10517.5	1.4
5	Jizzakh	10763.1	4.5	7294.0	1.0
6	Kashkadarya	16181.5	6.0	4646.4	0.6
7	Navoi	19396.1	7.2	18376.2	2.5
8	Namangan	14348.2	5.3	4768.6	0.6
9	Samarkand	21955.2	8.1	5331.0	0.7
10	Surkhandarya	11507.3	4.3	4099.9	0.5
11	Syrdarya	12574.7	4.6	14024.9	2.3
12	Tashkent region	34954.7	13.0	11680.4	1.6
13	Fergana	15396.7	5.7	3871.9	0.5
14	Khorezm	8806.6	3.3	4497.3	0.6
15	Tashkent city	56725.8	21.0	19192.0	2.6

Source: based on the information of the State Statistics Committee of the Republic of Uzbekistan.

and the production of competitive products. We see the city of Tashkent among the first according to this indicator. The share of foreign investments attracted to the enterprises of Tashkent city in the country's indicator is equal to 14.2%. Bukhara - 10.7% and Tashkent - 8.72% are in the next places. Regions. In the Republic of Karakalpakstan, Surkhandarya, Namangan, Jizzakh and Khorezm regions, this indicator is low and does not exceed 4.4%, Table 7. The highest index per capita corresponds to the regions of Syrdaryo (3.5), Navoi (3.2). The index of the highly developed city of Tashkent is 1.7 and the index of Tashkent region is 1.2. The index of six regions is higher than the index of the republic, in the rest of the regions this indicator is lower than the index of the republic.

Private indexes and integral indexes of economic indicators by regions are determined using the following formulas:

$$A_{ij} = \frac{x_{ij}}{y_j}, \; X_i = \sum_{j=1}^{6} A_{ij}, \; i = 1{-}15, j = 3$$

$X_{ij} - i$ – the volume of the region j – indicator per capita;

Table 7. Foreign investments in fixed capital by regions (2022 year)

№	Regions	Foreign investment by region (billion soms)	share by regions (in %)	Per capita (thousand soums)	Index
1	Republic of Uzbekistan	112219.5	100	3115.1	1.0
2	Republic of Karakalpakstan	3932.6	3, 5	1989.9	0.6
	Regions				
3	Andijan	6954.2	6.2	2092.9	0, 7
4	Bukhara	11999.5	10.7	5970.5	1, 9
5	Jizzakh	4786.0	4, 3	3243.4	1.0
6	Kashkadarya	7517.1	6.7	2158.6	0.7
7	Navoi	10645.6	9.5	10085.8	3.2
8	Namangan	4919.1	4.4	1641.0	0, 5
9	Samarkand	9597.4	8.5	2330.4	0, 8
10	Surkhandarya	4956.7	4.4	1766.0	0.6
11	Syrdarya	9738.2	8.7	10861.3	3.5
12	Tashkent region	11514.0	10.3	3847.5	1.2
13	Fergana	7102.5	6.3	1786.1	0, 6
14	Khorezm	2700.9	2, 4	1379.3	0, 4
15	Tashkent city	15855.6	14.2	5364.4	1.7 _

Source: based on the information of the State Statistics Committee of the Republic of Uzbekistan.

Y_j – the volume of j – indicator per capita in the republic;

A_{ij} – j – indicator index of i – area;

X_i - i is an integral index representing the level of economic development of the region.

If we evaluate the innovative potential of the regions, the city of Tashkent has the highest potential, as there are 43.0% of total higher education organizations, 56.1% of non-state and foreign educational organizations, 54.7% of total research and development organizations in 2021, and one technology park.

Samarkand region has 15 higher education organizations, 1 non-state higher education and 13 research organizations located in this region, there is no technopark, Tashkent region has 10; 1; 19; 0; Navoi 4; 2; 6; 2; Kashkadarya 9; 3;; 0; Bukhara 11; 4; 10; 1. The innovative potential of Jizzakh, Namangan and Surkhandarya regions can be considered low. Here, we believe that it is appropriate to take into account the level of economic development of the regions when evaluating their innovative potential.

Some innovative products created in Tashkent "Yashnabod" innovative technology park:

Table 8. Innovative goods, works, services produced by small business enterprises in the regions (2021 year)

№	Regions	Volume of innovative goods, works, services (million soums)	share by regions (in %)	Per capita (thousand soums)	Index
1	Republic of Uzbekistan	10667034.7	100	296.1	1.0
2	Republic of Karakalpakstan	105471.4	1.0	53.4	0.2
	Regions				
3	Andijan	121838.4	1.1	36.7	0, 1
4	Bukhara	236611.5	2.2	117.7	0.4
5	Jizzakh	157272.8	1.5	106.6	0.4
6	Kashkadarya	849912.5	8.0	244.0	0.8
7	Navoi	632895.8	5.9	599.6	2.0
8	Namangan	351194.4	3.3	117.2	0.4
9	Samarkand	613041,1	5.7	148.9	0, 5
10	Surkhandarya	177300.9	1.7	63.2	0.2
11	Syrdarya	581499.9	5.4	648.5	2.1
12	Tashkent region	979953.5	9.2	3847.5	1.1
13	Fergana	491536.1	4.6	123.6	0, 4
14	Khorezm	167174.5	1.6	85.4	0, 3
15	Tashkent city	5156331.9	4.8	1744.5	5.9

Source: based on the information of the State Statistics Committee of the Republic of Uzbekistan.

Production of 3D printers. There is no (serial) production of such products in Uzbekistan. The ZD printer is made of plastic and photopolymer. Field of application: in design-text organizations, medicine, advertising agencies, porcelain and laundry production. The annual capacity of the enterprise being created is 500 units.

Production of SIM cards, transport cards, social cards, international cards. Such products are not produced in Uzbekistan. Areas of application: government organizations, financial organizations, mobile operators and the public. The capacity of the enterprise under construction is 20 mln. Card. The Proponent of the project is OOO "VADES GROVP".

Production and localization of drones. Such a product is not produced in Uzbekistan. Product consumers: agriculture, the Ministry of Internal Affairs of the Republic of Uzbekistan, the Ministry of Emergency Situations, construction organizations, the Ministry of Defense. The capacity of the enterprise to be created is 1200 units.

Production of ADVOT interactive Robots and their modifications. This product is not produced in Uzbekistan. Field of application: banks, mobile operators, hotels, restaurants, exhibition centers. The capacity of the enterprise to be created is 240 units per year. The Proponent of the project is "INTERACTIVE ROBOT SOLUTIONS" LLC. It can be said that these innovative products are produced on the basis of imitative innovations (Table 9).

Table 9. Integrated index and indicators of innovative infrastructure representing the level of economic development of the region

№	Regions	Total Economic Integral Index	Innovative infrastructure pointers			
			Higher educational institutions	Number of non-state and foreign higher education organizations	The number of organizations that performed scientific research in 2021	Number of technological parks
1	Republic of Uzbekistan	1.0	191	41	254	6
2	Republic of Karakalpakstan	3.2	10	-	12	-
	Regions					
3	Andijan	3.7	10	1	6	1
4	Bukhara	6.4	11	4	10	1
5	Jizzakh	4.1	5	1	8	-
6	Kashkadarya	3.6	9	3	6	-
7	Navoi	16.4	4	2	6	2
8	Namangan	3.0	6	1	4	-
9	Samarkand	3.7	15	1	13	-
10	Surkhandarya	2.5	7	-	9	-
11	Syrdarya	10.2	3	-	4	-
12	Tashkent region	8.1	10	1	19	-
13	Fergana	3.2	11	2	9	-
14	Khorezm	3.1	8	2	9	1
15	Tashkent city	19.3	82	23	139	1

Source: based on Tables 1–8 and data of the State Statistics Committee of the Republic of Uzbekistan.

The indicators of the integrated index representing the level of economic development in all indicators of the regions and the innovative infrastructure elements of the regions are presented in Table 8. The regions of Tashkent city (19.3), Navoi (16.4), Tashkent (8.1) and Syrdaryo (10.2) can be included in the highest developing regions according to all indicators. These regions can be considered as "Lokomotiv" regions. Regions with moderate economic development: Bukhara (6.4%), Jizzakh (4.1%) regions. The rest of the regions can be considered as regions of low economic development. However, the regions of the Republic of Karakalpakstan, Andijan, Kashkadarya, Samarkand, and Fergana have the potential for economic and innovative development, albeit at a low level. The development of Surkhandarya, Namangan and Khorezm regions requires the development of special programs according to the economic, innovative and small business development policy of the state.

Table 10. Retrospective data on the quantities of, and expenditures on, innovative products and services produced by large enterprises and small businesses. (million soums)

№	Volume of innovative products and services produced by large enterprises (Y)	Expenditures on innovative products in large enterprises (X)	Volume of innovative products and services produced by small business enterprises (Y1)	Expenditures on innovative products produced by small business enterprises (X1)
2015	6341873.5	5173524.5	1681755.0	354754.2
2016	9016373.3	2360034.8	1671872,3	211370.8
2017	16219047.3	3446999.3	2324283.7	715264.4
2018	21675133.7	3550416.0	7196331.6	1156795.8
2019	18356065.6	4663557.4	8455371.9	1939917.5
2020	17013690.2	5788413.7	14129105.7	1041554.9
2021	16711579.2	10667034.7	10667034.7	1189442.4

Source: based on the information of the State Statistics Committee of the Republic of Uzbekistan.

Total volume of innovative products and services produced by large business enterprises (Y), expenditure on total produced innovative products and services (X), volume of innovative products and services produced by small business enterprises (Y1) and innovative products and services produced by small business enterprises according to the dynamics of the data on the indicators of product and service costs (X1), forecast models were developed and the values of their evaluation criteria were determined, Table 10.

The evaluation criteria of forecast models of innovative indicators, i.e. approximation errors, mean squared standard deviation, t-statistics, coefficient of determination, Fisher criterion, Darbin-Watson criteria correspond to the demand limits, and based on these models, the amount of forecast indicators has determined until 2026, 11 - table (Table 11).

Figure 1 shows the graphs of forecast indicators of the amount of innovative products and services produced by large and small business enterprises. It can be seen from the figure that both indicators have an increasing trend during the forecast period, but the

Table 11. Forecast models and their evaluation results (Author's calculations.)

Forecast model	Model evaluation results
$y = 7005099,521t^{0,568}$	$\overline{A} = 1,05\%; S_y = 0,2317; R^2 = 0,7718; F_{his} = 16,9127$ $(F_{jad} = 6,61); t_{a_0} = 3,5889; t_{a_1} = 83,1197 (t_{jad} = 3,163);$ $DW = 1,02$
$x = 1520511,535e^{0,245t}$	$\overline{A} = 0,79\%; S_x = 0,1565; R^2 = 0,9322; F_{his} = 68,7977$ $(F_{jad} = 6,61); t_{a_0} = 8,2944; t_{a_1} = 107,6159 (t_{jad} = 3,163);$ $DW = 1,85$
$y_1 = 1101324,668e^{1,211}$	$\overline{A} = 2,08\%; S_{y_1} = 0,4239; R^2 = 0,8213; F_{his} = 22,9762$ $(F_{jad} = 6,61); t_{a_0} = 4,7933; t_{a_1} = 40,1002 (t_{jad} = 3,163);$ $DW = 1,86$
$x_1 = 252562,261t^{0,907}$	$\overline{A} = 2,64\%; S_{x_1} = 0,5026; R^2 = 0,6468; F_{his} = 9,1566$ $(F_{jad} = 6,61); t_{a_0} = 3,226; t_{a_1} = 30,2365 (t_{jad} = 3,163);$ $DW = 2,22$

Table 12. The amount of innovative products and services produced by large enterprises and small business enterprises, and the forecast values of their costs (Author's calculations.), (million soums)

	Volume of innovative products and services produced by large enterprises (Y)	Expenditures on innovative products in large enterprises (X)	Volume of innovative products and services produced by small business enterprises (Y1)	Expenditures on innovative products produced by small business enterprises (X1)
2022	22,822,826.2	10,792,415.2	13,663,354.6	1 665 217.9
2023	24,401,923.1	13,788,269.4	15,758,070.7	1,852,961.6
2024	25,906,832.1	17,615,739.4	17,902,569.4	2 038 771.0
2025	27 347 986.4	22,505,672.4	20 092 867,0	2 222 857,5
2026	28 733 548,1	28 752 996,3	22 325 636,8	2 405 391,9

indicator of small business is slightly higher than that of large business. By 2026, the indicator of large business will be 5910.7 billion compared to 2022. Increased to 28,733.5 billion soums and increased by 126%. Innovative products and services produced by small business enterprises increased by 740.2 billion soums in 2026 compared to 2022 and amounted to 2405.4 billion soums and increased by 163% (Table 12).

Figure 2 shows the forecast indicators of the amount of innovative products and services corresponding to the cost of one unit of innovation in large and small business enterprises.

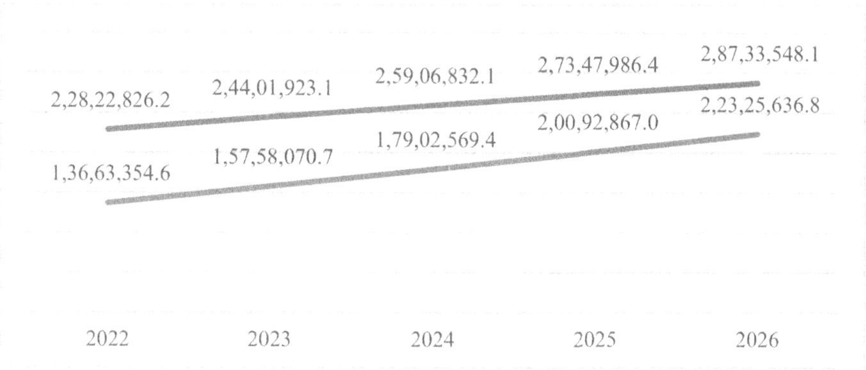

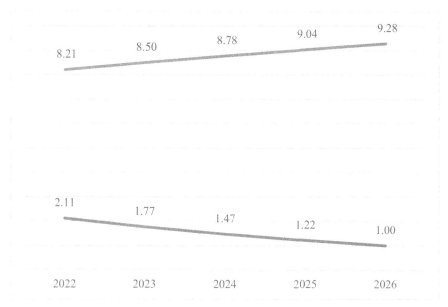

Fig. 1. Forecast graphs of the amount of innovative products and services produced by large and small business enterprises.

Fig. 2. The forecast indicators of the amount of innovative products and services corresponding to the cost of one unit of innovation in large and small business enterprises.

We observe that the amount of this indicator decreases in large enterprises. We see that the trend of increasing the amount of services is connected with the high growth of costs. In small business enterprises, this indicator has a growing tendency, by 2026 this indicator will increase by 1.13 times compared to 2022. 8.1 million by small business in 2022 at the cost of 1 million soums. Innovative products and services worth 9.3 million soums in 2026. Amounted to soum. In large businesses, this indicator is 2.1 and 1.0 million, respectively. Amounted to soum.

In conclusion, it can be observed that innovative products per unit cost in small business enterprises are higher than in large enterprises. In 2022, the amount of innovative products and services obtained from a unit cost in small businesses was 3.9 times higher than that of large businesses, and by 2026, we will see this indicator increase to 9.3 times, and this is an incentive and incentive for small businesses to engage in innovative activities. Can be considered a factor.

5   Conclusions and Suggestions

The main obstacles to the innovative development of SMEs are the underdevelopment of the innovative infrastructure, the small number of technology parks, business incubators, scientific research organizations and scientific laboratories, insufficient provision of modern equipment and facilities, the lack of highly qualified personnel and the low level of innovative business, with innovative activities. Lack of experience in dealing with it.

The integrated index representing the level of economic development of the regions and the indicators defining the possibilities of innovative development can be considered as one of the main factors affecting the possibilities of innovative product production of SMEs in the region. The analysis of the regions showed that the production of innovative products is high in the regions where these indicators are high. In the regions of Tashkent city, Navoi, Tashkent, Bukhara, SMEs can be considered to have a high potential for innovative development. It is desirable to develop elements of innovative infrastructure in these areas, to develop technological parks, business incubators, modern special scientific laboratories, transfer technology and other scientific centers and to support them by the state, to attract specialist personnel, and for elements of innovative infrastructure in the Institute of Mining and Metallurgy in the city of Navoi. Strengthening the training of specialist personnel, establishing innovative infrastructure elements and providing them with personnel in the regions of the Republic of Karakalpakstan, Andijan, Kashkadarya, Samarkand, and Fergana are among the main issues;

In the low-economically developed Surkhandarya, Namangan and Khorezm regions, it is desirable to develop SMEs based on special programs in areas of priority for the society based on the production potential based on targeted support.

Tashkent city can be seen as the center of economic and innovative development of all other regions, and the transformation of the "Yashnobad" innovation technology park in Tashkent into the "Main" technology park by strengthening the scientific, technical and personnel potential can be considered as the main factor of the innovation development of the regions.

Tax incentives, state grants, preferential loans from the state (project implementation) in order to support SMEs engaged in innovative activities, introducing new products and new technologies, producing high and medium-high technological products, scientific research and experimental design works in the region if it is increased, it is advisable to increase the amount of debt, give subsidies, subsidized loans and other benefits to SMEs in other fields, use public-private partnerships to provide advice, create support infrastructure (business incubator, technology park, etc.).

Development of an innovative economy in our country, development of production of high-tech products at KB enterprises, this can be considered as a way related to the production of products with high added value, which are in demand in domestic and foreign markets, by applying the strategy of transition from "Imitation innovations to original innovations".

The amount of innovative product production and service in large and small business enterprises has a tendency to increase during the forecast period, but we see that the indicator of small business is slightly higher than that of large business, and we observe that the innovative product per unit cost in small business enterprises is higher than that of large business. In the case of small businesses, this indicator has an increasing tendency during the forecast period, while in large businesses, on the contrary, it is decreasing. In 2022, the amount of innovative products and services received per unit cost in small businesses was 3.9 times higher than that of large businesses, and by 2026, we see this indicator increase to 9.3 times, which encourages small businesses to engage in innovative activities. And can be considered as a motivating factor.

References

1. Буланова Е.В., Соменкова Н.С., Ягунова Н.А. Формирование стратегии развития малого инновационного предприятия промышленного комплекса. // Журнал «Вопросы инновационной экономики». Том 9. № 2. Апрель-июнь, 2020

2. Гумерова Г.И., Шаймиева Э.Ш. Анализ управления технологическими инновациями на промышленных Российских предприятиях: источники финансирования, инновационная стратегия. // Актуальные проблемы экономики и права.4(24),   143–150 (2012)

3. Инновационное предпринимательство в Китае. // Фундаментальные Исследования, 2018. - №10 – с.74–78 (электронный ресурс). https://www.fundamentalresearch.ru/ru/art icle/view?id=42283

4. Сюй Хуэйчжуин. Анализ преимущества имитационной инновации. //Гуманитарные и социальные науки.. (7) (2012)

5. Salimov, Sh.B.: Types of entrepreneurship in developed countries and Uzbekistan and methods of their identification. Scientific electronic magazine. Econ. Innov. Technol. (3) (2020)

6. Титов. Б. Сектор малого и среднего предпринимательства: Россия и Мир. Институт экономики роста им. Столыпина П.А. июль, 2018. Электрон ресурс,.   http://stolypin.ins titute/novosti/sektor-malogo-i-srednego-predprinimatelstva-rossiya-i

7. Socio-economic situation of the Republic of Uzbekistan. Tashkent-2023 (2022)

8. Bokayev, B., Issenova, A.: Innovative strategies for the development of small and medium-sized businesses in Kazakhstan: a study of public policy in the period of Covid-19. J. Innov. **27**(1)(2) (2022)

9. Biryukov, V.V., Romanenko, E.V., Ploskonosova, V.P.: Territorial mechanisms of innovative development of the small and medium business sector: a value-oriented approach. Indian J. Sci. Technol. **9**(37) (2016). Art. no. 102170

10. Kookueva, V., Tsertseil, J.: Economic development of state support for small and medium-sized businesses in the context of innovative development. Innov. J. **27**(1) (2022). Art. no. 2

11. Umierov, R.E.: Application of foreign experience in the innovative development of small and medium-sized businesses in the current conditions of the Ukrainian market. Actual Prob. Econ. **132**(6), 96–105 (2012). Cited 1 time

12. Yushkova, V.V., Myazin, N.S., Davydov, V.V., Makeev, S.S., Rud, V.Y., Svitala, F.: Problems and main directions of innovative development of small and medium-sized businesses in Russian agriculture. E3S Web Conf. **220** (2020). Art. no. 01031

13. Khotamov, I.S., Umarov, E.G., Kuznetsov, V.P., Smirnova, Z.V., Kutepov, M.M.: Digital transformation in the modern educational system. In: Popkova, E.G., Sergi, B.S. (eds.) Anti-Crisis Approach to the Provision of the Environmental Sustainability of Economy. Approaches to Global Sustainability, Markets, and Governance, 2023, Part F643, pp. 195–199. Springer, Singapore (2023). https://doi.org/10.1007/978-981-99-2198-0_20. https://www.scopus.com/authid/detail.uri?authorId=58408750900&origin=recordPage

14. Nosirov, J., Uktamov, K., Xabibullayev, D., Mirolimov, M.: Ensuring the financial stability of insurance companies in the innovative development of the economy. E3S Web Conf. (2023). https://www.scopus.com/inward/record.uri?eid=2-s2.0-85170223931&doi=10.1051%2fe3sconf%2f202340208007&partnerID=40&md5=07376376996efef08a214dfa6a6e26ae

15. Talipova, N.T., Makhmutkhodjaeva, L.S., Khazratkulova, L.N.: Evolution of innovative development of foreign economic activity of the REPUBLIC of UZBEKISTAN. In: ACM International Conference Proceeding Series (2022). https://www.scopus.com/inward/record.uri?eid=2-s2.0-85159781679&doi=10.1145%2f3584202.3584211&partnerID=40&md5=d8bb9ccde4a1adf5a4ff0c8126a5a2de

16. Tukhtabaev, J.S., Samiyeva, G.T., Kushbakov, A.N., Goziyeva, A.A., Razakova, B.S., Aktamov, O.A.U.: Econometric assessment of the dynamics of development of the export potential of small businesses and private entrepreneurship subjects in the conditions of the digital economy. In: Koucheryavy, Y., Aziz, A. (eds.) NEW2AN 2022. LNCS, vol. 13772, pp. 440–451. Springer, Cham (2023). https://doi.org/10.1007/978-3-031-30258-9_39. https://www.scopus.com/inward/record.uri?eid=2-s2.0-85161456793&doi=10.1007%2f978-3-031-30258-9_39&partnerID=40&md5=fd1c591c578dea7eecfd85fd933d3066

17. Tukhtabaev, J.S., et al.: Econometric modeling and forecasting of the increase in the export potential of small businesses and private enterprises in the republic of Uzbekistan. In: ACM International Conference Proceeding Series (2022). https://www.scopus.com/inward/record.uri?eid=2-s2.0-85159779556&doi=10.1145%2f3584202.3584246&partnerID=40&md5=e98c22ce4548b6f8eb64efb92b5db470

18. Saifnazarov, I., Abdullahanova, G., Alimatova, N., Kudratova, U.: The main trends of increasing the role of the teacher in the innovative development of Uzbekistan. Int. J. Adv. Sci. Technol. (2020). https://www.scopus.com/inward/record.uri?eid=2-s2.0-85084446193&partnerID=40&md5=c503dace94040de685c8961508a63a8b

Criteria and Assessment of Opportunities for Creating Digital Ecosystems by 5G Mobile Operators

Valery Tikhvinskiy[1,3]([⊠]), Roman Umanskiy[2], and Sergei Falko[1]

[1] Bauman Moscow State Technical University (BMSTU), Moscow, Russia
vtikhvinskiy@gmail.com
[2] Moscow Technical University of Communication and Informatics (MTUCI), Moscow, Russia
[3] International Information Technology University (IITU), Almaty, Kazakhstan

Abstract. The article presented study results of choosing scenarios problem for building digital ecosystems by mobile operators in the context of ongoing transformation processes for tradition business models for 5G network providing services. The relevance of problem is due to the need to find new market niches to attract new customers after transformation, leading to income growth in the context of regionalization of the global market. The article analyzed theoretical approaches to the formation of a criteria base and assessment of 5G mobile operators' capabilities for making decisions on creating digital ecosystems.

Keywords: Digital ecosystems · digital services · 5G mobile operator · criteria and assessment of capabilities

1 Introduction

The global penetration of 5G mobile operator services is growing rapidly and by the end of 2Q 2023 operators will reach 1.4 billion connections, and by 2028 the number of 5G connections is expected to reach 8 billion, exceeding connections in 4G (LTE) networks by 2.5 billion [1]. There are currently 287 commercial 5G operators in the world, and the number is expected to grow to 425 by 2025. This reflects significant investment in technical and business infrastructure by 5G operators worldwide.

A feature and trend in development strategies of 5G mobile operators (hereinafter referred to as operator) in recent years has been the active transformation of existing production business models based on an ecosystem approach. As the scope of this approach, 5G operator, based on existing assets: telecommunications network, service sales network and subscriber base, can build a business ecosystem by including new digital services and new business areas (e.g. a digital bank, insurance company, etc.).

In the article, authors will talk about the digital business ecosystem of 5G mobile operator as a set digital services and business lines outside of telecom that it sells independently or jointly with partners, provided by various divisions or business structures in various industries using interconnected unified production, commercial and management processes.

In addition, 5G operators, when creating their development programs, were faced with the need to take into account the following factors:

1. The need to invest in infrastructure development and technological re-equipment to achieve goals of maintaining the competitiveness of the industry and ensuring further economic development of dependent sectors of economy.
2. The need for accelerated implementation of independent telecom infrastructure strategy based on national manufacturers and increased information security due to the geopolitical situation in the conditions of distributed heterogeneous networks.
3. Fulfillment of national regulatory requirements to achieve the goal of increasing national control over the communications infrastructure and implementation of social projects (requirement to cover small populated areas and highways with 4G networks, obligations to store traffic).
4. Low prices for mobile communication services for subscribers and exhaustion of business growth opportunities. Despite the growth in revenues from 5G mobile communications, current annual inflation is leading to a reduction in real revenues on telecommunication market in many countries around the world.

The development of an ecosystem approach as part of the transformation of the activities of 5G operators challenges researchers with the development of criteria framework that will enable operators to make a decision on building a digital ecosystem based on an assessment of its capabilities. This task seems extremely important, since due to existing limitations, a transparent system of criteria for building a business ecosystem by a 5G operator should facilitate the choice of the optimal development strategy.

2 The Problem of Forming Criteria for Building Business Ecosystems

The problem of finding criteria for constructing ecosystems is of utmost importance for the development of the theory of the ecosystem approach. After the term "ecosystem," which previously arose and was used exclusively in biology [2], began to be used in relation to business in the 90s [3], a huge number of methodological issues arose related to approaches and rules description formation of ecosystems.

In the 90s, several fundamental articles were published [4–11], which gave start to the research in the field of effective interaction between companies when building a business ecosystem. These studies were mainly related to the description of interaction mechanisms between several companies that started a joint business within created joining companies' framework.

At the same time, the key issues were based on interaction principles of their management systems, taking into account obvious changes in corporate culture, technological equipment, entrepreneurial outlook, and business models operation. The goal of this integration was to increase the fundamental value of the newly formed business ecosystem by developing "strategic flexibility" among all companies included in the ecosystem through the transformation of their business model.

Among main problems that companies faced in the process of creating business ecosystems are the following [12–15]:

1. The reluctance of large, highly profitable companies to transform their business models in favor of integrating other services into their ecosystems that could bring lower economic results of their activities as negative effect or bring full-scale synergies from such integrations as positive effect.
2. Commitment of companies to traditional, successful business models at current time and reluctance to develop something new.
3. The existing psychological aspects of the interaction of different business models.

Among the advantages of creating business ecosystems, which led to an increase in Fundamental Value (FV), the following can be highlighted:

- ability to use a corporate brand or customer service system of another business unit;
- gaining access to exclusive technological solutions developed in other ecosystem;
- research of strategic analytics based on a company's previous experience;
- ensuring access to financial resources for a services' development.

Main negative effects that companies may encounter when building an ecosystem are the following:

- increased costs for creation of management (corporate) centers, which were often not even related to the management of businesses included in an ecosystem;
- bureaucratization of business processes, which is expressed in growth of "hidden costs" that include: filling out forms and reports, implementing corporate codes and participating in projects initiated from a new corporate center, etc.;
- long process of approval of management decisions, which leads to futile results.

Thus, even if a service or new business line may, at first glance, be ideally suited for inclusion in the business ecosystem, the actual results may not bring the expected synergies and destroy the value already created. Not all identified advantages may work and in fact become disadvantages for an ecosystem, and, therefore, it is necessary to assess in detail consequences of integrating each new service and business structure into an ecosystem and to develop strict criteria for assessment.

Thus, as part of an ecosystem formation, development of decision-making criteria regarding an advisability of including certain areas of business and digital services in ecosystem and their impact on growth of its value becomes the key component. It is worth noting that, despite all theoretical elaboration, there is still no clear system of criteria on the basis of which decisions can be made about a relevance of creating ecosystems by 5G operators and including certain services in them.

3 Analysis of Creating Ecosystems Practice by Mobile Operators

Analysis of the main prerequisites that led mobile operators to the need to revise their development strategy and use an ecosystem approach to building a business allows us to highlight the following [16]:

1. Society digitalization requirement at national level within the framework of national strategies for communications industry development, information society development and national development programs [17].

2. Changes in 5G subscribers' consumption models, manifested in following areas:
- content consumption transformation: from voice services and short messages (SMS) to personalized audio and video services, video content, etc.;
- active distribution of smartphones as a means of obtaining content services, and the transition from computer content consumption to mobile with requirements for accelerated development of content consumption rates on part of its producers;
- interaction changing channels between content manufacturers and consumers with development of new business models of digital platforms.
3. Changes in service providing business models as a result of the introduction of new 5G technologies lead to appearance of new types of services in 5G operators tariff plans (extended and augmented reality XR/AR, audio and video streaming services, IoT services, etc.). 5G development and subsequently 6G technology will stimulate the creation of new digital services such as human-centric services [18] and services based on thought control by brain-computer interface (BCI) for smartphones and tablets and that will also to change the way we consume content.
4. Development of convergence concept and joint activities of transformed businesses in a value chain.

A study of the accumulated experience in the formation of digital ecosystems of leading telecom operators in 11 largest cities in the world made it possible to identify nine key areas that telecom operators are developing within their business ecosystems (the authors added another direction - digital advertising) (Fig. 1) [19].

According to the results of the study, in the vast majority of cases, telecom operators act as a digital platform that offers a comprehensive list of partner services in IT, finance, telemedicine, entertainment and other areas, and less commonly they create their own services from scratch.

The analysis of the services in mobile ecosystem shows that the most successfully developing area is the one that includes the development of digital services [20]. The development of trends aimed at the growth of new digital services in the revenue structure of mobile operators is evidenced by the latest GSMA report «Mobile economy 2023» [21]. According to it, the introduction of 5G will lead to operators increasingly focusing their attention and marketing efforts on the new digital services development in the ecosystem to increase the level of monetization.

The current practice of building digital ecosystems of operators indicates the predominance of two main directions: first, when the operator predominantly acquires start-ups and ready-made businesses on the market and integrates the digital services being sold into its ecosystem; and second, when the operator, without acquiring ownership of ready-made assets, builds partnerships with other companies and integrates digital services into its own ecosystem.

An analysis of the practice of building digital ecosystems by operators allows us to identify three key strategies in the creation and development of a digital ecosystem:

1. «Fundamental asset» (FA) development strategy, when 5G operator is focused primarily on maintaining and developing an existing 5G technological infrastructure and subscriber base, developing the ecosystem based on the introduction of a set of additional digital services that appear in the process of introducing 5G technologies.

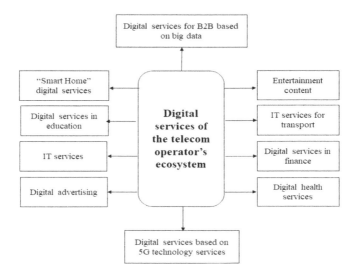

Fig. 1. Key digital services of the 5G mobile operator's ecosystem

2. «FA +» development strategy, when the 5G operator begins to build a business ecosystem on the basis of the existing technological infrastructure and subscriber base with the development of digital services in areas of activity close to its main business (fintech, banking, insurance, media, etc.).
3. «FA + new business» development strategy, when the 5G operator builds a business ecosystem through the development of the underlying asset and areas of activity close to its main business (second strategy), while adding completely new business areas to business ecosystem (healthcare, auto, etc.).

Under fundamental assets of a 5G operator we mean the set of tangible and intangible telecommunications recourses that create its fundamental value.

4 Development of a System of Criteria for Making Decisions on Creation of Digital Ecosystems by 5G Mobile Operators

When criteria base determining and possibilities of building a business ecosystem assessing, authors have proceeded from a fact that the decision to create it depends on 5G operator management, who will further integrate various services and business areas into an ecosystem and will be responsible for effectiveness of its implementation.

The importance of developing criteria and methodology is associated with the need to make effective decisions in choosing business areas and services from availabilities of many alternative options in context of a shortage of operator's resources (financial, labor, production, etc.) and ideas of managers about strategic goals and methods development of a new business ecosystem.

In order to exclude a subjective decision-making of 5G operator's management on building a business ecosystem and determining business areas and services list included in it, it is necessary to form a system of criteria and methods for making decisions regarding a construction and choice within a strategy framework of 5G operator. Such system should reflect an objectivity of the result obtained, reduce a time spent on evaluating various options, and remove a subjective view of 5G operator's management during decision-making.

The main methodological approach to assess the creation of ecosystem possibilities of 5G operator can be represented by the following sequence of steps [22]:

1. Determining strategic goals of building and subsequent business ecosystem development.
2. Formalized system development of criteria for assessing the capabilities of 5G operator to build and develop a business ecosystem.
3. Methods selection for assessing a possibility of building and developing a business ecosystem that corresponds to strategic goals of 5G operator.
4. Selection of relevant experts to develop decision-making options for building and developing an ecosystem.
5. Final decision-making on building the selected ecosystem.

The main principles for constructing a model for assessing capabilities of 5G operator to create a business ecosystem include the following:

- correlation with goals and development priorities of 5G operator;
- proportion of the new business in comparison with other services of the 5G operator;
- the importance of new business for the development of the operator;
- impact on a growth of 5G operator's fundamental value, which means that a business ecosystem must ensure an increase in operator's fundamental value;
- achieving synergy within a business ecosystem between established and new businesses;
- ability to integrate on a single technological platform with existing operator services without significant modifications;
- readiness of an existing 5G operator management system to adapt to requirements of a business ecosystem formation.

Thus, it is important to note that when assessing the possibilities of creating business ecosystem by 5G operator, management decision makers must answer following important questions:

- whether building a business ecosystem contributes to the implementation of the strategic development goals set by shareholders of the 5G operator?
- does the designed business ecosystem comply with the existing capabilities and limitations of the 5G operator's management system?
- how the building of a business ecosystem will affect existing subscribers of 5G operator?
- how the efficiency and fundamental value of 5G operator will change after building a business ecosystem?

Based on presented views of authors, the main task of forming a model for assessing 5G operator capabilities is to obtain scientifically based assessment of creating business ecosystem possibility so that new business areas and services included in it are most consistent with strategic development goals of 5G operator and are as effective as possible.

It should be noted that 5G operator could use a criteria assessment system (CAS) that takes into account the assessment of all listed problematic issues. Such CAS, depending on assessment degree of complexity and volume of 5G operator activity indicators taken into account when making decisions, may include the following types:

1. Single-criteria assessment.
2. Two-criteria assessment.
3. Multi-criteria assessment.

A single-criteria assessment as a part of CAS involves assessing the capabilities of building an ecosystem by a 5G operator, based on making a decision on one dominant performance indicator of a 5G operator that best characterizes its position on the market (for example, subscribers' base size, operator's current revenues). Obviously, an assessment based on such a measurement (parameter) will be more intuitive and less accurate compared to a two- and multi-criteria assessment. However, as a rule, a 5G operator can use it to assess the most important and sensitive issues related to construction business ecosystem. In a single-criteria assessment, the most important will be threshold levels accepted in a single-criteria assessment as acceptable.

Single-criteria assessment parameters should be selected and considered by 5G operator's management as a threshold filter and stop-factor for further analysis: if a service or business in question does not meet the accepted threshold level of 5G operator activity, then it is rejected from further consideration. Formation of such a threshold as a criterion will allow us to quickly determine the possibilities, if necessary, to cut off the creation of a business ecosystem or integration of a certain type of service at an assessment level.

In a two-criteria assessment of creating business ecosystems possibilities, it is assumed to select two measurable parameters of 5G operator's activity, which, from a management point of view, can reflect an assessment of operator's capabilities to ecosystem build. For example, if 5G operator is considering creating a business ecosystem with inclusion of banks in it, then management can begin to explore the integration of banking products into the business ecosystem using a method of comparison and analysis of two indicators: number of customers and banks revenue (See Table 1 for European banks). Based on that analysis the capabilities of 5G operator to create a banking business within its new business ecosystem will be assessed.

As a result of two-criteria assessment and subsequent decision-making, management of 5G operator can conclude that if the number of 5G subscribers who could potentially be bank depositors in an operator's network is 4–6 times higher than a number of depositors of an average bank, then with an effective marketing policy, achievable level of convergence and existing subscriber base, synergy can be achieved, as well as an increase in fundamental value of 5G operator's ecosystem from an integration of banking business.

Multi-criteria assessment as a part of CAS will be able to combine a joint assessment of several parameters of 5G operator's activities regarding the possibilities of creating

Table 1. The European Banking Sector Performance in 2022

Europe's largest banks	Number of customers, in millions	Revenue, in billion euros
Banco Santander	160	52.12
BBVA	89.3	n/a
BNP Paribas	60.0	50.42
Credit Agricole Group	53.0	37.68
Barclays pls	48.0	28.15
HSBC Holding	39.0	48.2
ING Group	37.0	18.56
Group BPCE	35.0	25.71
Lloyds Banking Group	26.0	20.54
Societe Generale	25.0	28.06
Intesa Sanpaolo	20.7	21.47
NatWest Group	19.0	14.51

a business ecosystem. CAS for this assessment should cover parameters of all activity areas and infrastructure subsystems of the 5G operator:

- goals and development strategy;
- production and technology;
- innovation and research;
- marketing and promotion;
- finance & valuation;
- other parameters of economic activity.

Such an assessment should be carried out on basis of a formalized system of criteria for possibilities of creating a business ecosystem, which allow them to be assessed against principles listed above. An example of constructing such a system of criteria can be found in the following article [23].

Once a system of evaluation criteria for multi-criteria assessment of 5G operator's ability to create an ecosystem has been formed, expert scoring must be used to obtain a formal assessment. This approach consists of developing and using a system for assigning a certain number of points when assessing various qualitative values of 5G operator's activities based on selected criteria.

After completing the scoring of each criterion, to obtain a formalized assessment, it is necessary to use an expert multifactor model, which consists of assigning weighting coefficients to each assessed criterion (the total sum of weighting coefficients is always equal to 1) based on the opinion of qualified experts. Next, by multiplying the coefficient by the number of points, we obtain weighted scores for each criterion and then, summing them up, we obtain the total number of points in relation to the service in question in relation to the two factors.

$$N = \sum_{i=1}^{V} B_i * X_i$$

where:

N – final score for the factor under consideration;
Bi – the obtained expert assessment for each criterion;
Xi – weight coefficient of each criterion;
V – the number of all considered criteria.

The presented approach to assessing the capabilities of a 5G operator to build a digital ecosystem may become a methodological basis for making decisions about the possibility of expanding the 5G operator's ecosystem and integrating new digital services, as well as an effective tool for its managers in the process of forming and implementing a 5G operator's development strategy aimed at increasing level of monetization.

5   Conclusion

The choice of 5G operator strategy when creating a digital ecosystem should focus on assessing the operator's capabilities, determining potential development and assessing the expected contribution of the ecosystem to the growth of fundamental value in the near future. Therefore, the approach to developing a system of criteria CAS proposed in this article creates a tool for operator company managers used when making decisions on creating a digital ecosystem that expands the 5G operator's business beyond the core services of the telecom operator. At the same time, the final decision on creating an ecosystem depends on how correctly the data used in the criteria for assessing the possibility of creating a digital ecosystem is prepared, as well as how correctly the results of this assessment are processed.

The data and weighting coefficients collected for assessment must be verified by experts, since possible manipulation and unreliability of the collected data can lead to negative assessment results based on the selected criteria CAS. Therefore, when assessing the possibility of creating an ecosystem based on a 5G telecom operator, one should take into account a certain subjectivity of possible decisions and make final decisions only after analyzing all available information and the set of the obtained assessments.

References

1. 5G Set to Surpass 4G LTE by Over Two Billion Connections in the First Decade, 5G Americans, Media release, 28 September 2023
2. Tansley, A.G.: The use and abuse of vegetational concepts and terms. Ecology **16**, 284–307 (1935)

3. Moore, J.: Predators and prey: a new ecology of competition. Harv. Bus. Rev. **71**, 75–86 (1993)
4. Goold, M., Campbell, A., Alexander, M.: Corporate-Level Strategy: Creating Value in the Multibusiness Company, p. 450. Wiley, New York (1994)
5. Campbell, A., Goold, M., Alexander, M.: Corporate strategy: the quest for parenting advantage. Harvard Bus. Rev. (1995)
6. Campbell, A., Goold, M., Alexander, M.: The value of the parent company. California Manag. Rev. **28**(6) (1995)
7. Goold, M., Campbell, A., Alexander, M.: Parenting Advantage: The Key to Corporate Level Strategy. Prism, Adlittle (1995)
8. Goold, M.: Parenting strategies for the mature business. Long Range Plan. **29**(3), 358–369 (1996)
9. Goold, M., Campbell, A.: Desperately seeking synergy. Harvard Bus. Rev. (1998)
10. Alexander, M.: The value in corporate alliances. Econ. Bull. (1999)
11. Alexander, M.: Global Parenting Globalization The External Pressures. Wiley (2001)
12. Christensen, C.: The Innovator's Dilemma: When New Technologies Cause Great Firms to Fail. Harvard Business School Press, Boston (1997)
13. Sull, D.N.: Why good companies go bad. Harvard Bus. Rev. (1999)
14. O'Reilly, C.A., Tushman, M.L.: Ambidexterity as a dynamic capability: resolving the innovator's dilemma. Res. Organ. Behav. **28**, 185–206 (2008)
15. Birkinshaw, J., Ridderstrale, J.: The action imperative in strategy. In: Fast/Forward: Make Your Company Fit for the Future, pp. 71–97. Stanford University Press, Redwood City (2017)
16. Umanskiy, R.: Approaches to the innovative strategy formation for the development of mobile operators. Innovations Manag. **4**, 281–286 (2022)
17. Standards for digital societies. ITU News **02** (2022)
18. Technical Report: Representative use cases and key network requirements for Network 2030, ITU FG NET-2030, January 2020
19. Saprykina, A.: Ecosystem as a way of survival for operators. https://www.comnews.ru/con tent/214597/2021-05-21/2021-w20/ekosistema-kak-sposob-vyzhivaniya-dlya-operatorov. Accessed 10 Nov 2023
20. Mobile ecosystem economic contribution by segment from 2019 to 2021. https://www.sta tista.com/statistics/371905/mobile-ecosystem-revenue-by-segment/. Accessed 15 Nov 2023
21. The Mobile Economy 2023. https://www.gsma.com/mobileeconomy/wp-content/uploads/2023/03/270223-The-Mobile-Economy-2023.pdf. Accessed 15 Nov 2023
22. Umanskiy, R.: Choosing a digital services development in mobile operator's ecosystem. Innov. Manag. **3**(37), 34–41 (2023)

Strategic Analysis of Business Positioning Through Web Intelligence Technologies: A Study on Adaptive Models and Approaches

T. Abdukhalilova Laylo$^{(\boxtimes)}$ (iD)

Marketing Department, Tashkent State University of Economics, Tashkent, Uzbekistan
l.abduxalilova@tsue.uz

Abstract. This research paper presents an in-depth analysis of business positioning in the rapidly evolving digital landscape, emphasizing the critical role of web intelligence technologies. In the contemporary market, where internet dynamics are constantly shifting, businesses face the challenge of maintaining a relevant and influential online presence. This study investigates the efficacy of various adaptive models and approaches that leverage web intelligence to enhance a business's digital footprint. Utilizing a mixed-methods approach, the paper first surveys the current state of digital business positioning, drawing on a range of interdisciplinary sources. It then introduces an innovative framework for applying web intelligence technologies in business strategy. This framework is tested through a series of case studies, analyzing businesses from diverse sectors to understand how different strategies fare in real-world scenarios. The findings reveal that successful business positioning on the internet is not a static achievement but a continuous process. The use of advanced web intelligence tools enables businesses to identify emerging trends, consumer behaviors, and competitor strategies effectively. The study also underscores the importance of adaptability, highlighting that the most successful businesses are those that dynamically adjust their online strategies in response to web intelligence insights. Moreover, the paper discusses the challenges and limitations inherent in the application of web intelligence technologies, including issues of data privacy, ethical considerations, and the potential for information overload. The conclusion offers strategic recommendations for businesses aiming to enhance their internet positioning, along with suggestions for future research in this rapidly evolving field.

Keywords: Web Intelligence Technologies · Digital Business Positioning · Adaptive Strategy Models · Data-Driven Decision Making · Market Trend Analysis · Consumer Engagement Optimization · Ethical Considerations in Data Use

1 Introduction

In the digital age, the strategic positioning of businesses on the internet has become a pivotal aspect of corporate success. This significance is magnified by the rapid evolution of online platforms and the increasingly sophisticated expectations of digital consumers.

© The Author(s), under exclusive license to Springer Nature Switzerland AG 2024
Y. Koucheryavy and A. Aziz (Eds.): NEW2AN/ruSMART 2023, LNCS 14543, pp. 309–317, 2024.
https://doi.org/10.1007/978-3-031-60997-8_28

The role of web intelligence technologies in this context is indispensable, offering tools and insights that can dramatically enhance a business's online presence and competitive edge [1].

The proliferation of digital data and advanced analytics has opened new avenues for understanding consumer behavior, market trends, and competitor strategies. However, effectively harnessing these insights for strategic business positioning remains a complex and dynamic challenge [2]. Previous research has extensively explored various aspects of digital marketing and online consumer engagement [3], but there remains a gap in comprehensive studies focused on integrating web intelligence technologies for business positioning [4].

This paper aims to bridge this gap by providing a detailed analysis of how businesses can leverage web intelligence to adapt and thrive in the digital marketplace. The importance of such an analysis is underscored by the fluid nature of the internet, where consumer preferences and market dynamics can shift rapidly, necessitating agile and informed responses from businesses [5].

Moreover, as the digital ecosystem grows increasingly complex, the need for robust and innovative strategies becomes crucial. This study, therefore, not only examines the current state of business positioning in the digital realm but also proposes a forward-looking framework that integrates the latest web intelligence technologies [6].

In doing so, this research contributes to the broader discourse on digital business strategy, offering valuable insights for both academic researchers and industry practitioners seeking to navigate the ever-evolving digital landscape [7].

Following the introduction, the paper is structured into several key sections. The Literature Review provides an extensive examination of existing research on business positioning in digital environments and the use of web intelligence technologies. This review sets the groundwork for understanding the current landscape and identifying gaps our study aims to address. The Methodology section outlines the mixed-methods approach employed in the study, including data collection and analysis techniques. This is followed by the Results section, where findings from the case studies and data analysis are presented, offering insights into the effectiveness of different business positioning strategies. Finally, the Discussions & Conclusion section interprets these findings, linking them back to the literature review and highlighting their implications for business strategy and web intelligence application and concludes with a Summary and Future Directions section, which not only synthesizes the main findings and their practical applications but also suggests areas for further research in this dynamic field.

2   Literature Review

The concept of business positioning in the digital era has garnered substantial attention from scholars and practitioners alike. As companies increasingly rely on online channels to engage with consumers, the importance of strategic digital positioning has become paramount [8]. Early research in this domain primarily focused on the static aspects of web presence, such as website design and usability [9]. However, the evolution of the internet landscape has necessitated a shift towards dynamic and adaptive strategies [10].

Studies have emphasized the need for businesses to align their online positioning with their target audience's expectations and preferences [11]. Customer-centric approaches that prioritize user experience and personalization have gained prominence [12]. Furthermore, the role of search engine optimization (SEO) and content marketing in enhancing online visibility and reach cannot be overstated [13].

The advent of web intelligence technologies has revolutionized how businesses gather and utilize digital data for strategic purposes. Web scraping, sentiment analysis, and predictive analytics are among the tools that have empowered organizations to gain actionable insights from vast datasets [14]. These technologies offer a competitive advantage by enabling businesses to anticipate market trends and consumer behavior [15].

One significant area of research has focused on the application of machine learning and artificial intelligence (AI) in web intelligence. AI-driven chatbots, for instance, have enhanced customer engagement by providing real-time support and personalized recommendations [16]. Similarly, natural language processing (NLP) techniques have been instrumental in analyzing online reviews and social media sentiment [17, 18].

Despite the growing recognition of the importance of web intelligence technologies, there remains a gap in comprehensive studies that explore the integration of these technologies into adaptive business positioning strategies. While individual components, such as SEO and social media analytics, have been extensively examined, there is a need for holistic frameworks that guide businesses in leveraging the full spectrum of web intelligence tools [19]. Moreover, the dynamic nature of the internet necessitates continuous adaptation. Research is needed to identify best practices for staying agile in response to evolving online trends [20]. Additionally, ethical considerations related to data privacy and the responsible use of web intelligence technologies warrant further investigation [21].

This literature review provides an overview of the current state of research on business positioning in digital environments and the use of web intelligence technologies. It highlights the existing knowledge base while also pointing out the gaps that this study aims to address.

3   Methodology

This study employs a mixed-methods research design to comprehensively investigate the integration of web intelligence technologies into business positioning strategies. Mixed-methods research allows for the triangulation of data from multiple sources, enhancing the robustness of the findings [22]. The research design encompasses both quantitative and qualitative components to provide a holistic understanding of the phenomenon.

Quantitative Data: To gather quantitative data on business positioning and the use of web intelligence technologies, a survey will be administered to a stratified sample of businesses across different industries. The survey will include questions related to the adoption of web intelligence tools, online marketing strategies, and key performance indicators (KPIs). Additionally, website analytics data will be collected using tools such as Google Analytics to assess online user behavior and engagement metrics.

Qualitative Data: Qualitative insights will be obtained through in-depth interviews with business professionals who have experience in utilizing web intelligence technologies for strategic positioning. These interviews will delve into the nuances of their strategies, challenges faced, and the impact of web intelligence on their decision-making processes.

Quantitative Analysis: Quantitative data collected from surveys and website analytics will be analyzed using statistical software. Descriptive statistics, such as mean, median, and standard deviation, will be used to summarize survey responses. Inferential statistics, including correlation analysis and regression analysis, will be conducted to identify relationships between web intelligence adoption, business positioning outcomes, and other variables.

Qualitative Analysis: Qualitative data from interviews will undergo thematic analysis. Transcripts will be coded to identify recurring themes and patterns related to the integration of web intelligence technologies into business positioning. Coding will be performed using qualitative data analysis software, facilitating the organization and interpretation of qualitative findings.

The findings from both quantitative and qualitative analyses will be compared and triangulated to provide a comprehensive understanding of the research questions. Triangulation enhances the validity of the study by corroborating findings from different data sources and methods [23].

This research adheres to ethical guidelines regarding data collection and participant consent. All survey respondents and interviewees will be informed of the research purpose and their rights, including confidentiality and anonymity. Informed consent will be obtained, and data will be securely stored and anonymized.

4 Results

The Results section of "Strategic Analysis of Business Positioning Through Web Intelligence Technologies: A Study on Adaptive Models and Approaches" delves into the outcomes of case studies and data analysis. It provides insights into the effectiveness of diverse business positioning strategies in the digital realm, emphasizing the role of web intelligence technologies.

Businesses that leveraged web intelligence tools for trend identification showed a superior capacity for adapting to market shifts. They updated their strategies in alignment with emerging trends and consumer behaviors more effectively. Firms employing advanced analytics for consumer profiling and personalization noted increased engagement and satisfaction. Personalized marketing, informed by web intelligence, significantly boosted customer experiences and brand loyalty (Table 1).

Analysis of competitors and market positioning through web intelligence enabled companies to understand and improve their market standing. This led to more informed strategic decisions, enhancing their competitive edge. Integration of SEO and content optimization strategies, guided by web analytics, resulted in improved online visibility and higher search engine rankings (Table 2).

Table 1. Business Performance Metrics Before and After Implementing Web Intelligence Strategies

Business Sector	KPI	Average Before Implementation	Average After Implementation	% Change
Retail	Monthly Website Traffic (Visitors)	50,000	75,000	+50%
	Conversion Rate (%)	2.5	4.0	+60%
Finance	Customer Acquisition Cost (CAC)	$200	$150	−25%
	Customer Retention Rate (%)	85	90	+5.9%
Healthcare	Online Appointment Bookings	1,200	1,800	+50%
	Patient Satisfaction Score (out of 10)	7.5	8.5	+13.3%
Technology	Software Trial Sign-ups	2,000	3,500	+75%
	Churn Rate (%)	5	3.5	−30%
Education	Online Course Registrations	500	700	+40%
	Engagement Rate (Avg. Time on Site)	5 min	8 min	+60%

Note: KPI = Key Performance Indicator.

Table 2. Competitor Analysis Using Web Intelligence Tools

Competitor	Market Share (%)	Average Monthly SEO Traffic	Social Media Engagement Rate (%)	Sentiment Analysis Score (out of 10)	Innovation Index Score (out of 10)
Company A	35	200,000	4.5	8.2	7.5
Company B	25	150,000	3.8	7.5	6.8
Company C	15	100,000	5.0	9.0	8.2
Company D	10	85,000	4.2	6.8	7.0
Company E	5	50,000	3.5	6.5	6.0

Note: Data collected via web scraping, SEO tools, and social media analytics platforms.

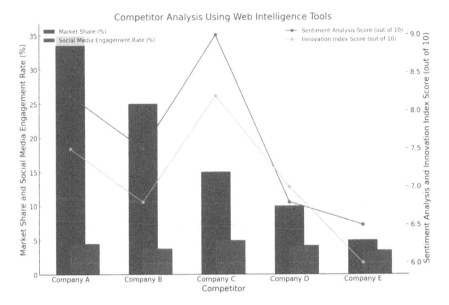

Fig. 1. Competitor Analysis Using Web Intelligence Tools

Businesses using real-time analytics could make quicker and more efficient decisions, a crucial aspect in the fast-paced digital markets. Predictive models aided firms in anticipating market trends and consumer needs, fostering more proactive and forward-looking strategies. Advanced AI and machine learning algorithms were pivotal in enhancing the effectiveness of web intelligence tools, providing deeper insights and automation, especially in handling large datasets and complex analyses (Fig. 1).

The study pinpointed concerns with data privacy and ethical use of consumer information. Balancing effective data utilization with maintaining consumer trust and adhering to data protection regulations was a challenge. Businesses also reported difficulties in managing the vast amount of data available, leading to information overload. This underscores the need for more efficient data management and analysis systems (Table 3).

Smaller businesses and startups faced challenges in accessing advanced web intelligence tools due to limited resources. This disparity affected their ability to leverage these technologies effectively.

The results indicate that successful business positioning in the digital space requires a dynamic approach, heavily reliant on the effective use of web intelligence technologies. While these tools offer significant benefits, businesses must navigate challenges related to data management, ethical considerations, and resource allocation. The study highlights the importance of adaptability and strategic use of web intelligence in enhancing digital business positioning.

Table 3. Insights from In-Depth Interviews with Business Professionals

Interviewee (Anonymized)	Industry	Key Insights on Web Intelligence Use	Perceived Challenges	Future Strategy Recommendations
Executive A	**Retail**	**"Web analytics transformed our inventory management."**	**"Data privacy regulations are a major concern."**	**"Invest in AI for predictive analytics."**
Manager B	Healthcare	"Patient feedback analysis helped improve our services."	"Integrating different data sources is challenging."	"Focus on mobile-first strategies."
Director C	**Technology**	**"Using AI for customer support has increased satisfaction."**	**"Keeping up with technology advancements is costly."**	**"Explore blockchain for enhanced security."**
Specialist D	Education	"Social media insights have driven our content strategy."	"Information overload can be overwhelming."	"Utilize machine learning for personalized learning paths."
Analyst E	**Finance**	**"Predictive analytics has been crucial for risk assessment."**	**"Ensuring data accuracy is a constant task."**	**"Adopt more robust cybersecurity measures."**

Note: Interviews conducted with professionals experienced in using web intelligence technologies for strategic positioning.

5   Discussions and Conclusion

The findings from the study provide important insights into the role and effectiveness of web intelligence technologies in business positioning strategies. The enhanced ability of businesses to utilize these technologies for trend identification, consumer engagement, and market positioning highlights the dynamic and evolving nature of the digital business landscape. This reflects the recognized need for agility and adaptability in digital marketing strategies.

Significant improvements in key performance indicators following the implementation of web intelligence strategies demonstrate their tangible benefits. These results reinforce the growing indispensability of web intelligence in understanding and responding to consumer behavior and market trends. However, challenges such as data privacy concerns and information overload resonate with the operational and ethical complexities in the digital realm.

The results emphasize the need for a sophisticated approach to web intelligence. Businesses must not only gather but also effectively interpret and act on data insights, balancing technological capabilities with strategic planning. The disparities in resource allocation and access to advanced tools suggest a need for more accessible web intelligence solutions, especially for smaller businesses.

In conclusion, the study confirms that strategic use of web intelligence technologies is crucial for effective business positioning in the digital age. It highlights the benefits of these technologies in enhancing market presence and consumer engagement, as well as the challenges faced in this endeavor.

Future research could explore the ethical implications of web intelligence, especially regarding data privacy and consumer rights. The development and accessibility of cost-effective web intelligence tools for smaller businesses is another potential area of study. Additionally, longitudinal studies assessing the long-term impact of web intelligence-driven strategies on business performance could provide further insights.

This research contributes to the broader discussion on digital business strategy, offering a foundation for both academic researchers and industry practitioners as they navigate the continually evolving digital landscape.

References

1. López-Robles, J.R., Otegi-Olaso, J.R., Gómez, I.P., Cobo, M.J.: 30 years of intelligence models in management and business: a bibliometric review. Int. J. Inf. Manage. **48**, 22–38 (2019)
2. Huang, M.H., Rust, R.T.: A strategic framework for artificial intelligence in marketing. J. Acad. Mark. Sci. **49**, 30–50 (2021)
3. Saura, J.R., Palos-Sanchez, P.R., Correia, M.B.: Digital marketing strategies based on the e-business model: literature review and future directions. In: Organizational Transformation and Managing Innovation in the Fourth Industrial Revolution, pp. 86–103 (2019)
4. Gulamuddinovna Zufarova, N., Tulkunovna Shakirova, D., Zafarbek Qizi Shakirova, D.: Merits and demerits of E-commerce in republic of Uzbekistan during pandemic period. In: The 5th International Conference on Future Networks & Distributed Systems, pp. 790–794, December 2021
5. Rafael, L.D., Jaione, G.E., Cristina, L., Ibon, S.L.: An industry 4.0 maturity model for machine tool companies. Technol. Forecast. Soc. Change **159**, 120203 (2020)
6. Borges, A.F., Laurindo, F.J., Spínola, M.M., Gonçalves, R.F., Mattos, C.A.: The strategic use of artificial intelligence in the digital era: systematic literature review and future research directions. Int. J. Inf. Manage. **57**, 102225 (2021)
7. Eshbayev, O., et al.: A digital sustainability approach for effective knowledge and information management in education specific non-profit organizations: culture intelligent IS solutions. E3S Web Conf. **452**, 07023 (2023)
8. Nosirova, C.: Marketing and production activities of textile companies? Blockchain technology study. In: Proceedings of the 6th International Conference on Future Networks & Distributed Systems, pp. 152–158, December 2022
9. Fink, L., Yogev, N., Even, A.: Business intelligence and organizational learning: an empirical investigation of value creation processes. Inf. Manag. **54**(1), 38–56 (2017)
10. Polyvyanyy, A., Ouyang, C., Barros, A., van der Aalst, W.M.: Process querying: enabling business intelligence through query-based process analytics. Decis. Support. Syst. Support. Syst. **100**, 41–56 (2017)

11. Eshbayev, O., et al.:. A systemic mapping study of mobile assisted language learning methods and practices: a qualitative literature review. In: Proceedings of the 6th International Conference on Future Networks & Distributed Systems, pp. 612–615, December 2022

12. Eshbayev, O., et al.: A systematic mapping study of effective regulations and policies against digital monopolies: visualizing the recent status of anti-monopoly research areas in the digital economy. In: Proceedings of the 6th International Conference on Future Networks & Distributed Systems, pp. 16–22, December 2022

13. Eshbayev, O.A., Mirzaliev, S.M., Rozikov, R.U., Kuzikulova, D.M., Shakirova, G.A.: NLP and ML based approach of increasing the efficiency of environmental management operations and engineering practices. IOP Conf. Ser. Earth Environ. Sci. **1045**(1), 012058 (2022)

14. Alikovich Eshbayev, O., Xamidovich Maxmudov, A., Urokovich Rozikov, R.: An overview of a state of the art on developing soft computing-based language education and research systems: a survey of engineering English students in Uzbekistan. In: The 5th International Conference on Future Networks & Distributed Systems, pp. 447–452, December 2021

15. Kurolov, M.O.: A systematic mapping study of using digital marketing technologies in health care: the state of the art of digital healthcare marketing. In: Proceedings of the 6th International Conference on Future Networks & Distributed Systems, pp. 318–323, December 2022

16. Ergashxodjayeva, S.D., Abdukhalilova, L., Usmonova, D., Kurolov, M.: What is the current state of integrating digital marketing into entrepreneurship: a systematic mapping study. In: Proceedings of the 6th International Conference on Future Networks & Distributed Systems, pp. 607–611, December 2022

17. Kurolov, M.: Exploring the role of business intelligence systems in digital healthcare marketing. Int. J. Soc. Sci. Res. Rev. **6**(6), 377–383 (2023)

18. Park, Y., El Sawy, O.A., Fiss, P.: The role of business intelligence and communication technologies in organizational agility: a configurational approach. J. Assoc. Inf. Syst. **18**(9), 1 (2017)

19. Itani, O.S., Agnihotri, R., Dingus, R.: Social media use in B2b sales and its impact on competitive intelligence collection and adaptive selling: examining the role of learning orientation as an enabler. Ind. Mark. Manage. **66**, 64–79 (2017)

20. Sharapat, Y., Yulduz, M., Dilafruz, M., Hilola, B., Dilorom, S.: Innovating primary education of promoting students' language competencies through mobile assisted language learning approach: selection framework of innovative digital technologies. In: Koucheryavy, Y., Aziz, A. (eds.) NEW2AN 2022. LNCS, vol. 13772, pp. 432–439. Springer, Cham (2022). https://doi.org/10.1007/978-3-031-30258-9_38

21. Odilovna, O.G., Mavlyanovna, M.G., Toxirovna, M.D., Shuxratovna, A.S., Xamidullayevna, K.F.: What is the state-of-the-art contribution of the higher education system to the digital economy: a systematic mapping study on changes and challenges. In: Koucheryavy, Y., Aziz, A. (eds.) NEW2AN 2022. LNCS, vol. 13772, pp. 423–431. Springer, Cham (2022). https://doi.org/10.1007/978-3-031-30258-9_37

22. Khakimova, M.F., Kayumova, M.S.: Factors that increase the effectiveness of hybrid teaching in a digital educational environment. In: Proceedings of the 6th International Conference on Future Networks & Distributed Systems, pp. 370–375, December 2022

Gravity Model of Foreign Economic Processes of Central Asia Countries

N. T. Talipova[1], B. A. Islamov[1,2], and M. M. Turdibaeva[2,3(✉)]

[1] Tashkent Branch of Plekhanov Russian Economic University, Shahriobod Street 3, Tashkent 100164, Republic of Uzbekistan
[2] Tashkent State University of Economics, Islom Karimov 49, Tashkent 100066, Uzbekistan
mturdibaeva@gmail.com
[3] Westminster International University in Tashkent, 12 Istiqbol Street, Tashkent 100047, Uzbekistan

Annotation. The authors of the article examined current aspects of modeling foreign economic processes of the Countries of Central Asia (CA). An Analysis of Prerequisites and Trends Was Carried Out, and the Volumes of Exports and Imports of Central Asian Countries Were Calculated Using Matrix Analysis. The Necessity of Using Mathematical Tools for Modeling and Predicting Mutual Processes Is Substantiated. The Statistics Are Distributed in Ranked Series of Pairwise Foreign Trade Interactions in the System of Central Asian Countries, presented in the article, which made it possible to forecast the development of foreign economic activity of the countries of the region using a gravity model of international trade.

Keywords: import · export · foreign trade turnover · matrix analysis · mutual trade · gravity model

1 Introduction

Due to its geopolitical position, the Central Asian region is of crucial importance. Experts connect changes in the geopolitical situation in the Central Asian region with a change in the leadership of Uzbekistan. Since 2017, the process of normalization of relations has been observed between the countries of Central Asia. The states of the region, which are very distant from each other, are increasingly making efforts at rapprochement and agreements. Many unsolved interstate problems that could not be resolved have found their solution at the present stage. Normalization of relations will not only transform the configuration in the region, but will also add greater geopolitical weight of Central Asia at international sites. Now as President of Uzbekistan Sh. Mirziyoyev stressed in the Fifth Consultative Meeting of the Heads of Central Asian States held in Tajikistan on September 14, 2023: "Trade and economic cooperation are the main drivers of regional partnership and integration in Central Asia" [1].

At the present stage of reforms in Uzbekistan, a new development model has been implemented. For this purpose, an Action Strategy for the further development of Uzbekistan in 2017–2021 [2], Development Strategy of New Uzbekistan for 2022–2026 [3],

Y. Koucheryavy and A. Aziz (Eds.): NEW2AN/ruSMART 2023, LNCS 14543, pp. 318–327, 2024.
https://doi.org/10.1007/978-3-031-60997-8_29

and Strategy "Uzbekistan -2030" [4] has created a good framework for improving state-building, the judicial system, liberalizing the economy, accelerating the development of the social sphere and implementing an active foreign policy, including new foreign economic cooperation with Central Asian countries as a top priority.

"It is especially important to note the rapid improvement of relations with neighboring countries. As an example, one can cite such activities as Uzbekistan's exit through Turkmen ports to the Caspian Sea, a 37% increase in trade with Kazakhstan, the opening of new checkpoints across the Uzbek-Kazakh state border, and the creation of business communities between "the border regions of Central Asian countries, as well as reaching an agreement on demarcation and delimitation of borders" [5].

The World Bank estimates that in Central Asia, economic growth will average more than 3.5%. The average economic growth rate in Kazakhstan will be about 2–3%, in Kyrgyzstan 3–3.5%, Tajikistan 5–6%, and in Uzbekistan and Turkmenistan about 6%. At the same time, experts note that in Kyrgyzstan, the successes of the economic sphere will largely depend on the effectiveness of economic policy and political stability in general [6–8]. Strengthening good neighborliness, taking into account mutual interests, and avoiding conflict are the main priorities in relations between the countries of the Central Asian region.

2 New Foreign Economic Opportunities of the Central Asian Countries

To analyze mutual trade and foreign trade potential of Central Asian countries, we decided to use a matrix analysis. An ideal tool for the quantitative analysis of foreign trade activity in any regions of the world is the database of the World Trade Center (ITC, Trade statistics for international business development). It allows you to study bilateral trade (export, import) between virtually any country in the world for all product groups included in the commodity nomenclature of foreign economic activity (internationally accepted terminology - HS codes).

This matrix has a zero diagonal, since countries cannot trade with themselves. Theoretically, it is obvious that $V_{ij} = V_{ji}$ (the values of the pairwise foreign trade turnover are symmetrical relative to the zero diagonal of the matrix (1)), but in practice there is a rather large discrepancy between these values of the foreign trade turnover, since the sales reports of the two trading countries often take into account their export and import figures in different ways.

For the convenience of further analysis, it is advisable to reduce the matrix (1) to a relative form. For this, the total foreign trade turnover in the n-country system is calculated for the upper and lower triangular fragments of this matrix, and its elements (V_{ij}) are converted to percentages of the total foreign trade turnover in the n-country system:

$$\overline{V_{ij}} = \left\{V_{ij}/V\right\} \times 100\% \tag{1}$$

where, for instance, $V = \sum_{i>j} V_{ij}$ total foreign trade turnover in the system of n-countries for the lower triangular fragment of the matrix (1).

Based on the matrix of relative values of pairwise foreign trade turnover in the n-country system $\overline{V_{ij}}$, a ranked series of pairwise foreign trade interactions is constructed, which is limited from below by approximately one percent contribution of a pair of countries to the total foreign trade turnover in the considered system of countries. In general, for n-countries, the total number of pairs (N) is:

$$N = \frac{N(n-1)}{2} \tag{2}$$

Based on the constructed ranked series of pairwise foreign trade interactions, three or four-dimensional cores of countries are distinguished, which account for the maximum volume of mutual trade in the considered system of countries.

The proposed methodology is illustrated using the example of five countries of Central Asia (n = 5). For this system of countries, we have constructed matrices of absolute and relative values of pairwise foreign trade turnover at the levels of 2012 and 2022 (Tables 1 and 2). Based on the matrices of relative values of pairwise foreign trade turnover at the levels of 2012 and 2022, ranked series of pairwise foreign trade interactions in the system of Central Asian countries are constructed (Table 3). In our case (n = 5), according to formula (3), we have N = 10.

Based on matrices of relative values of pairwise foreign trade turnover at the levels of 2012 and 2022. Ranked series of pairwise foreign trade interactions in the system of Central Asian countries were built (Table 3). In our case (n = 5), according to formula (3), we have N = 10.

Table 1 shows that the percentage export of Uzbekistan and Kazakhstan in 2012 occupied the leading positions among all the countries of Central Asia, and equavalent to 33.12% and 39.13% of the Central Asian trade turnover, respectively. In 2022, the situation remained relatively unchanged, if we do not take into account the decrease in Uzbekistan's exports to 30.96% of the Central Asian trade, while Kazakhstan increased to 41.84%.

In Table 3 we can see that the concentration of mutual trade between Uzbekistan and Kazakhstan has not changed significantly between 2012 and 2022. At the same time, an analysis of the ranked series of pairwise foreign trade interactions revealed some structural changes. So, for example, the foreign trade turnover between Turkmenistan and Tajikistan has halved over 10 years, or Kazakhstan's foreign economic emphasis has shifted from Turkmenistan to Tajikistan.

Foreign trade activity is the result of interstate, interregional and intraregional cooperation, which in consequence leads to an increase in the efficiency of the regional economy. Therefore, forecasting and determining the effectiveness of the integration process both from a scientific and a practical point of view are always of current concern.

To predict the turnover between Central Asian countries, we will use the gravity model of J. Tinbergen [13], which is as follows:

$$V_{ij} = A * \frac{Y_i^{b_1} * Y_j^{b_2}}{D^b_{ij}} * e, \tag{3}$$

Table 1. Matrix of pairwise foreign trade in the system of Central Asian countries, 2012–2022 (thousands of US Dollars) [12].

A. Matrix of pairwise foreign trade in the system of CA countries, 2012. (thousands of US Dollars)

Country	Kazakh-stan	Kyrgyz-stan	Tajikistan	Turkmeni-stan	Uzbeki-stan	Export volume	%
Kazakhstan	0	607978	277156	437920	1788126	3111180	41,51
Kyrgyzstan	560565	0	30467	6521	392184	989737	13,20
Tajikistan	277156	30467	0	60900	168600	537123	7,17
Turkmenistan	437920	6521	60900	0	133300	638641	8,52
Uzbekistan	1657300	266200	168600	133300	0	2225400	29,69
Export volume	2932941	911166	537123	638641	2482210	7495560	100%
%	39,13	12,16	7,17	8,52	33,12	100,00%	

Б. Matrix of pairwise foreign trade in the system of CA countries, 2022. (thousands of US Dollars)

Country	Kazakh-stan	Kyrgyz-stan	Tajikistan	Turkmeni-stan	Uzbekistan	Export volume	%
Kazakhstan	0	865258	845896	99542	2488087	4298783	39,38
Kyrgyzstan	873002	0	59904	4772	336488	1274166	11,67
Tajikistan	836568	62809	0	47166	281532	1228075	11,25
Turkmeni-stan	99542	4772	47166	0	273029	424509	3,89
Uzbekistan	2757419	378107	281376	273029	0	3689931	33,80
Export volume	4566531	1310946	1234342	424509	3379136	10915464	100%
%	41,84	12,01	11,31	3,89	30,96	100,00%	

Source: compiled by the author based on ITC data, Trade statistics for international business development (Available at: https://www.trademap.org)

where, V_{ij} – trade flow, Y_i^{b1} – GDP of i-country, Y_j^{b2} – GDP of j-country, D_{ij}^{b3} – distance between two capitals of the countries, e – normal error distribution, A – free term of the equation, a1, a2, a3 - elasticity coefficients of turnover from regressors.

Usually, this model is presented either in a power-law or in a logarithmic form. Consequently, the gravity model takes the simplest multiplicative form of the expression of the following form:

$$V_{ij} = b_0 * (Y_i)^{b_1} * (Y_j)^{b_2} * (D_{ij})^{b_3} + e \qquad (4)$$

The main idea of the model is the presence of direct proportionality of GDP of exporting country as the indicator of production capacities, GDP of importing country as the indicator of market volume. At the same time, such dependence is inversely proportional to the distance between the two countries, due to the cost of transporting goods.

The information and empirical base of the study is statistical material for 2012 -2022, published on the official website of the World Trade Center (ITC, Trade statistics for international business development), the World Bank database.

Table 2. The matrix of relative values (%) of pairwise foreign trade in the system of CA countries, 2012–2022.

The matrix of relative values (%) of pairwise foreign trade in the CA system, 2012

Country	Kazakhstan	Kyrgyzstan	Tajikistan	Turkmeni-stan	Uzbekistan
Kazakhstan	0	8,11	3,70	5,84	23,86
Kyrgyzstan	7,48	0	0,41	0,09	5,23
Tajikistan	3,70	0,41	0	0,81	2,25
Turkmenistan	5,84	0,09	0,81	0	1,78
Uzbekistan	22,11	3,55	2,25	1,78	0

The matrix of relative values (%) of pairwise foreign trade in the CA system, 2022

Country	Kazakhstan	Kyrgyzstan	Tajikistan	Turkmenistan	Uzbekistan
Kazakhstan	0	7,93	7,75	0,91	22,79
Kyrgyzstan	8,00	0	0,55	0,04	3,08
Tajikistan	7,66	0,58	0	0,43	2,58
Turkmeni-stan	0,91	0,04	0,43	0	2,50
Uzbekistan	25,26	3,46	2,58	2,50	0

Within the framework of the article, models of trade turnover between the countries of Central Asia are built. To simplify the gravity model, real GDP (in US dollars) was used as an indicator of the size of the economy, and the distance between capitals was used as the distance between countries, and this takes into account not the actual length of railways or roads, but some abstract distance. At the same time, there is a hypothesis that trade turnover positively depends on the GDP of the countries trading among themselves, i.e. the coefficient for GDP obtained as a result of the regression analysis should be positive, and negatively depends on the distance between countries, affecting potential transportation costs.

As a result of the calculations, the equations of the gravity model of J. Tinbergen were obtained, which characterize the dynamics of the foreign trade turnover between the CA countries for 2012–2022.

The gravity model of Kazakhstan's trade turnover with CA countries:

$$V_{ij} = 1108515884 * (Y_i)^{0,41} * (Y_j)^{0,112} * (D_{ij})^{-2,829} + e\,R^2 = 0,693$$

The gravity model of Kyrgyzstan's trade turnover with CA countries:

$$V_{ij} = 8635790,41 * (Y_i)^{1,223} * (Y_j)^{-1,029} * (D_{ij})^{-2,305} + e\,R^2 = 0,797$$

Table 3. Ranked rows of pairwise foreign trade interactions in the CA system, 2012–2022

Ranked rows of pairwise foreign trade interactions in the CA system, 2012

Upper Triangle of the Mutual Trade Matrix for CA Countries			Lower Triangle of the Mutual Trade Matrix for CA Countries		
NN	Pair of countries	%	NN	Pair of countries	%
	Uzbekistan – Kazakhstan	22,11		Kazakhstan - Uzbekistan	23,86
	Kazakhstan - Kyrgyzstan	8,11		Kyrgyzstan – Kazakhstan	7,48
	Kazakhstan – Turkmenistan	5,84		Turkmenistan – Kazakhstan	5,84
	Kazakhstan – Tajikistan	3,70		Kyrgyzstan – Uzbekistan	5,23
	Uzbekistan - Kyrgyzstan	3,55		Tajikistan – Kazakhstan	3,70
	Uzbekistan - Tajikistan	2,25		Tajikistan - Uzbekistan	2,25
	Uzbekistan - Turkmenistan	1,78		Turkmenistan - Uzbekistan	1,78
	Turkmenistan - Tajikistan	0,81		Tajikistan – Turkmenistan	0,81
	Kyrgyzstan - Tajikistan	0,41		Tajikistan – Kyrgyzstan	0,41
	Kyrgyzstan - Turkmenistan	0,09		Turkmenistan - Kyrgyzstan	0,09

Ranked rows of pairwise foreign trade interactions in the CA system, 2022

Upper Triangle of the Mutual Trade Matrix for CA Countries			Lower Triangle of the Mutual Trade Matrix for CA Countries		
NN	Pair of countries	%	NN	Pair of countries	%
	Uzbekistan – Kazakhstan	25,26		Kazakhstan - Uzbekistan	22,79
	Kazakhstan - Kyrgyzstan	7,93		Kyrgyzstan – Kazakhstan	8,00
	Kazakhstan – Tajikistan	7,75		Tajikistan – Kazakhstan	7,66
	Uzbekistan - Kyrgyzstan	3,46		Kyrgyzstan – Uzbekistan	3,08
	Uzbekistan - Tajikistan	2,58		Tajikistan - Uzbekistan	2,58
	Uzbekistan - Turkmenistan	2,50		Turkmenistan - Uzbekistan	2,50
	Kazakhstan – Turkmenistan	0,91		Turkmenistan – Kazakhstan	0,91
	Kyrgyzstan - Tajikistan	0,55		Tajikistan – Kyrgyzstan	0,58
	Turkmenistan - Tajikistan	0,43		Tajikistan – Turkmenistan	0,43
	Kyrgyzstan - Turkmenistan	0,04		Turkmenistan - Kyrgyzstan	0,04

The gravity model of Tajikistan's trade turnover with CA countries:

$$V_{ij} = 0,00174 * (Y_i)^{0,586} * (Y_j)^{-0,232} * (D_{ij})^{1,01} + e \ R^2 = 0,65$$

The gravity model of Turkmenistan's trade turnover with CA countries:

$$V_{ij} = 49023221773 * (Y_i)^{1,127} * (Y_j)^{-0,745} * (D_{ij})^{-3,43} + e \ R^2 = 0,857$$

The gravity model of Uzbekistan's trade turnover with CA countries:

$$V_{ij} = 34,6 * (Y_i)^{1,064} * (Y_j)^{-0,405} * (D_{ij})^{-0,679} + e \ R^2 = 0,873$$

It should be noted that the models have moderate accuracy, since the determination coefficients range from 0.693 to 0.873, which in turn characterizes a rather strong regression dependence of the variables.

Various econometric methods are used to evaluate the parameters of the multiple regression equations. In particular, in this research work, tests were performed for the presence of multicollinearity, for the statistical significance of the coefficients, for the presence of autocorrelation of residues according to Durbin-Watson statistics, and for the phenomenon of heteroscedasticity.

As an example, we will evaluate the parameters of the equation of the gravity model of the trade turnover of the Republic of Uzbekistan with the CA countries. According to the regression analysis of the equation, the adoption of the null hypothesis with respect to the constant Y and the variable X_2 is more than 25%, which is beyond admissibility (up to 5% is permissible). Therefore, the constant Y and the variable X_2 are not statistically significant in this case.

Further, according to Durbin-Watson statistics, we reveal the phenomenon of autocorrelation of residues. The value of the Durbin-Watson statistics in the equation is 1.77, which characterizes the absence of autocorrelation. The next step in evaluating the regression equation is to detect the presence of heteroscedasticity using the White test. We reject the phenomenon of heteroscedasticity, since at 5% significance level $F_{fact.} <$ F_{table} and the P-probability of accepting the hypothesis of heteroscedasticity is 0.13, which is more than 0.05. Similar estimates of the equations are carried out with all the equations of the gravity model.

The revealed models make it possible to first compare the actual and forecast data on the trade turnover of the Central Asian countries, as well as to reveal theoretically what trade volumes should be in 2020 in the system of Central Asian countries (Fig. 1). To forecast the volume of trade in each country for 2020, we used the forecast data on the GDP growth rates of the Central Asian countries of the Asian Development Bank [12].

As can be seen in the figure, the approbation of the gravity model in forecasting the trade turnover between Central Asian countries for the period 2012 -2022 shows the weak proximity of the forecast and actual levels, so the forecast data for 2022 are purely theoretical. Some discrepancies between forecast values and real ones are explained by the absence of a number of other factors (WTO membership, various forms of preferential trade agreements, etc.) that influence the model.

Despite some deviations, gravity models provide new information on the interaction of Central Asian countries primarily that despite the supposed similarities of economies, cultures and language, the patterns of trade differ from each other.

Islamov et al. critically analyze the existing econometric approaches to estimating gravity models of exports for Uzbekistan from the point of view of solving such problems as taking into account zero observations, bias, inconsistency and inefficiency of estimates [15].

Thus, a high level of interaction and stable indicators of economic, cultural and scientific cooperation are perhaps the main goals in relations between the countries of Central Asia [16]. For example, in relations with Russia, the Central Asian countries have already achieved many goals of bilateral cooperation, and in particular Uzbekistan, which continues successful partnership in various fields and in the field of foreign

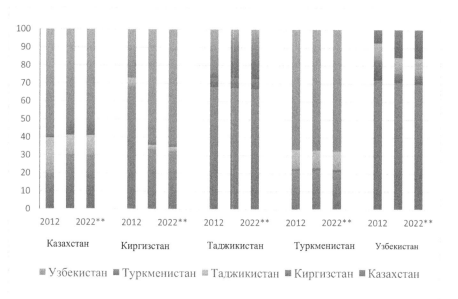

Fig. 1. Comparisons of actual and forecast data on trade in the system of Central Asian countries [14, 16]

economic cooperation, including international cooperation, the development of joint ventures operating in Uzbekistan. As a result, the main trends and prospects for further cooperation have been identified, as well as proposals to strengthen cooperation between Russia and Uzbekistan have been presented.

3   Conclusion

The analysis of the accuracy of the gravity model allows to make the following conclusion:

- in the absolute terms, for the entire studied period 2012 –2022 the gravity model for export and import of Turkmenistan and Uzbekistan is the most accurate (median $R^2 \geq 0.857$ and 0.873, respectively), and their accuracy is about $\pm 75\%$;
- generally, the least accurate model is for Tajikistan. It is should be noted that during the study there was a shift from the "gravity" to the "anti-gravity" law - the volume of trade in Tajikistan positively depended on the remoteness of the counterparty countries;
- models for Kyrgyzstan and Kazakhstan stay at intermediate position by accuracy (median $R^2 \geq 0.797$ and 0.693, respectively) or the error of the gravity model of trade turnover in these countries changes according to the growth - decrease - growth scheme.

This situation indicates that the variations in the values of the logarithms of trade with their counterparts is very high for each country, and the models reproduce it well in a relative sense, i.e. the change in the estimated values of the logarithm of foreign economic activity is also quite high. This indicates that the constructed models are very valuable in a cognitive sense. At the same time, apparently, only models for the trade turnover of countries with a high degree of R^2 are of some practical utility.

Within the meaning of the gravity model, the goods flow should increase with a growth of the counterparty's GDP, and it should go down with an increase in the remoteness of the counterparty [10]. Consequently, in the future, growth in trade between Central Asian countries is possible taking into account the growth of GDP of the counterparties, as evidenced by positive indicators of the degree (elasticity) of the variable Y_i.

Another alternative is to evaluate formally the model from the combined data with additional assumptions about the constant coefficients; such an approach would improve the correlation between the number of observations and the number of model parameters, but, taking into account the heterogeneity of gravity laws for individual countries, the obtained coefficient estimates would be very difficult to interpret. We believe that, based on the results of the gravity model, in subsequent years, the countries of Central Asia have significant potential for increasing mutual trade flows and further integration into world trade.

References

1. Shavkat Mirziyoyev Speech, in the Fifth Consultative Meeting of the Heads of Central Asian States held in Dushanbe on September 14. Central Asian States. https://president.uz/en/lists/view/6659
2. Ukaz Prezidenta Respubliki Uzbekistan "O Strategii deystviy po dal'neyshemu razvitiyu Respubliki Uzbekistan" # UP-4947 ot 7 fevralya 2017 goda [Decree of the President of the Republic of Uzbekistan "On the Strategy for the Further Development of the Republic of Uzbekistan" UP-4947 dd. 2017.02.07]. https://lex.uz/docs/3107042
3. Ukaz Prezidenta Respubliki Uzbekistan "O Strategii razvitiya Novogo Uzbekistana na 2022–2026". [Decree of the President of the Republic of Uzbekistan "On the Strategy № UP-60 dd.28.01.2022] https://lex.uz/ru/docs/5841077
4. Ukaz Prezidenta Respubliki Uzbekistan "О стратегии «Узбекистан – 2030», [Decree of the President of the Republic of Uzbekistan "On the Strategy "Uzbekistan-2030" № UP-158 dd.11.09.2023 г] https://lex.uz/ru/docs/6600404
5. Informatsionnyy obzor ispolneniya strategii deystviy [The informational review of the implementation of the strategy]. Tsentr "Strategiya razvitiya" [Development strategy Center], p. 77 (2017)
6. Abdurakhmanov, K., Zakirova, N., Islamov, B., Hiwatari, M.: Systemic Transformation, and Sustainable Development: Case of Uzbekistan. Gunadarma University, Jakarta (2016)
7. Islamov, B.A.: The Central Asian States Ten Years After: How to Overcome Traps of Development Transformation and Globalisation, monograph, published by Maruzen, Japan, Tokyo (2001)
8. Ziyadullaev, N.: Strany Tsentral'noy Azii na puti k integratsii [Central Asian countries on the road to integration] (2022). http://www.ng.ru/courier/2022-09-16/11_7311_integrat.html
9. Talipova, N.T.: Mekhanizmy liberalizatsii vneshney torgovli. Materialy mezhdunarodnoy nauchno-prakticheskoy konferentsii "25 let SNG: osnovnyye itogi, problemy, perspektivy razvitiya" [Foreign trade liberalization mechanisms. Materials of the international scientific-practical conference "25 years of the CIS: main results, problems, development prospects"]. Moscow [in Russian] (2016)

10. Islamov, B.A., Ziyadullaev, N.S., Ziyadullaev, U.S., Islamov, D.B.: Liberalizatsiya valyutnoy politiki: mezhdunarodnyy opyt i uroki dlya Uzbekistana [Liberalization of Exchange Rate Pol-icies: International Experiences and Lessons for Uzbekistan]. Regional'nyye problemy ekonomicheskoy transformatsii [Regional problems of economic transformation], no 1(87), pp. 98–107 (2018)

11. Talipova, N.T.: Ekonomicheskoye sotrudnichestvo Respubliki Koreya i stran Tsentral'noy Azii [Economic Cooperation of the Republic of Korea and Central Asian Countries], Zhurnal "Problemy teorii i praktiki upravleniya" [Problems of Theory and Practice of Management, Journal], Moscow, no. 7, pp. 54–63

12. Kalinina, A.: Strany, vkhodyashchiye v Tsentral'nuyu Aziyu [Countries of Central Asia]. https://visasam.ru/emigration/vybor/strany-centralnoi-azii.html

13. Rakhimov, M.: Vzaimootnosheniya Uzbekistana i Kazakhstana: osnovnyye tendentsii. [Relations between Uzbekistan and Kazakhstan: main trends.] (2016). https://caa-network.org/archives/6994

The Impact of the ICT and Export Diversification on Income Inequality: Panel Quantile Regression Analysis

Gavkhar Sultanova[1]([✉]), Rano Djuraeva[1], and Aziza Usmanova[2]

[1] Department of International Economics, University of World Economy and Diplomacy, Tashkent, Uzbekistan
{gsultanova,r.djuraeva}@uwed.uz
[2] International Business Management Department, Tashkent State University of Economics, Tashkent, Uzbekistan
a.usmanova@tsue.uz

Abstract. The article aims to provide an empirical investigation of the relationship between ICT development, export diversification, and income inequality based on a panel quantile regression analysis of data from 83 countries for the period 2002–2019. The results indicate that ICT progress negatively influences income inequality, and this adverse effect is more substantial in countries with a higher GINI coefficient. Export diversification also contributes to a more equitable income distribution, and this impact is higher in countries with low and middle levels of income inequality. Among the control variables, GDP per capita and human capital index significantly negatively influences income inequality. Thus, countries with high levels of income inequality should pay more attention to the digitalization of the economy and enhance export diversification.

Keywords: income inequality · export concentration · export diversification · GINI coefficient · ICT index · export product concentration index

1 Introduction

Income inequality is the global challenge of our time, the fight against which is aimed at ensuring equal access to opportunities for all. It is no coincidence that the 2030 Agenda for Sustainable Development proclaims the slogan "Leave no one behind" [1]. Although income inequality between countries has been decreasing since the 1990s, income inequality within countries tends to increase. Today, 71% of the world's population lives in countries where inequality has increased [2].

Studies examining the impact of ICT development [3–6] and export diversification on income inequality [7–11] are of considerable interest. Currently, they are among the key drivers of development and, according to many researchers, they can have a strong impact on inequality, although this impact is often contradictory.

In our study, we examine the impact of the ICT index and the export product concentration index on the GINI coefficient by analyzing panel data for 83 countries for the period 2002–2019. To examine the impact of ICT development and export diversification on countries with different levels of income inequality, we use panel quantile regression to capture the overall effect of ICT development and export diversification on the entire conditional distribution of income inequality.

The ICT index is constructed using principal component analysis. To the best of our knowledge, our study is the first attempt to analyze the effect of ICT development and export diversification on income inequality using panel quantile regression estimation.

The structure of the next part of this study is as follows: Sect. 2 presents a brief review of the relevant literature. Section 3 presents the data and methodology. Section 4 discusses the empirical results. Section 5 contains the conclusion and policy recommendations.

2 Literature Review

This section is aimed at reviewing different factors affecting income inequality. Each subsection reviews a separate factor to set a hypothesis for the research. Initially, previously conducted studies on the impact of ICT on income inequality are analyzed, followed by exploring papers analyzing the effects of export diversification on income inequality.

2.1 The Impact of ICT on Income Inequality

An important aspect of inequality research is the study of its relationship with digitalization.

Digitalization brings with it enormous opportunities for innovation, growth and job creation in all areas of the economy [12–14]. At the same time, digitalization generates risks of unemployment and deepening socio-economic inequality due to different levels of access to new technologies [15, 16].

Differences in access to the Internet between countries and regions are significant, and digital inequality exists in many areas of the economy and society [17]. Thus, a review of the academic literature shows that digitalization has an ambiguous impact on inequality as well as poverty [18, 19]. On the one hand, digital transformation promotes economic growth, reduces transaction costs for firms, individuals and governments, and facilitates consumer access to a wide range of goods and services. On the other hand, restricting access to digital technologies for low-income populations and small companies, as well as digital divides along age, gender and other lines, can exacerbate inequality and digital exclusion [20, 21].

In this regard, our study tests one of the following hypotheses:

Hypothesis 1: ICT development has a negative impact on income inequality.

2.2 The Impact of Export Diversification on Income Inequality

Currently, globalization processes, economic development and export diversification have mixed results. In particular, most countries face the problem of income inequality [22–26]. A report by the Organization for Economic Cooperation and Development (OECD, 2018) indicates that in the last twenty years, 40% of the world's low-income population has benefited only 3% from economic development and export diversification

[27]. That is why much attention is paid in the current economic literature to the study of the impact of export diversification on income inequality [7, 22]. In particular, in the paper of Blancheton B., Chhorn D. [7] concluded that diversification of export structure has a positive effect on income inequality, while production specialization has a negative effect. In a study [8], the results show that sectoral diversification of exports increases inequality, with higher diversification increasing inequality in high-income Asian countries, while the effect is insignificant in low-income countries.

Thus, the impact of export diversification on inequality and poverty is contradictory and depends on income levels, labor market policies, trade, structural policies of governments, and political stability in countries.

The second hypothesis that is tested in this study:

Hypothesis 2: Export concentration has a positive effect on income inequality.

3   Data and Methodology

In our research, we explore the impact of the ICT index and export product concentration index on the GINI coefficient by analyzing panel data from 83 countries from 2002–2019. The GINI index data in this research comes from the World Income Inequality Database (WIID) of UNI WIDER. The data for the first key independent variable – export product concentration index – are obtained from the UNCTAD statistics database. This indicator is a normalized Herfindahl-Hirschmann index of the product concentration of the country's merchandise exports. The formula for calculating this index is the following:

$$H_j = \frac{\sqrt{\sum_{i=1}^{N}\left(\frac{x_{ij}}{X_j}\right)^2} - \sqrt{\frac{1}{N}}}{1 - \sqrt{\frac{1}{N}}}; X_j = \sum_{i=1}^{N} x_{ij} \tag{1}$$

Here, H_j is the export product concentration index for country j, $X_{i,j}$ is the value of exports of product i by country j, X_j is the total value of exports of country j, and N is the number of products exported at the three-digit level of the SITC Revision 3. The index ranges from zero to one, with a larger value indicating a higher concentration of merchandise exports structure. The index value close to zero denotes the high level of export diversification, i.e., the county's exports are homogeneously distributed among all products [7].

The second variable of interest is the ICT index, which was constructed according to the methodology of the International Telecommunication Union (ITU) for calculating the ICT Development Index – the composite index combined with eleven indicators reflecting the ICT infrastructure, ICT usage, and ICT skills [22]. The following indicators were chosen for creating the ICT index implemented in our study: (1) fixed-telephone subscriptions per 100 inhabitants; (2) mobile-cellular telephone subscriptions per 100 inhabitants; (3) percentage of individuals using the Internet; (4) fixed-broadband subscriptions per 100 inhabitants. The data for these indicators come from the World Development Indicators (WDI) database. The value of all indicators was standardized, and the ICT index was calculated using the Principal component analysis (PCA) method, a statistical technique for multivariate data reduction [7]. After predicting the ICT index, its values were recalculated to obtain the numbers between zero and one.

We select four control variables as the fundamental determinants of income inequality: GDP per capita (constant 2015 US dollar); industry (including construction), value added (percentage of GDP); foreign direct investment, net inflows (percentage of GDP); human capital index, based on the average years of schooling and an assumed rate of return to education. The data for the first three variables is derived from the World Development Indicators (WDI) database, and the data for the human capital index is obtained from the Penn World Table (PWT) version 10.0.

Table 1 shows the descriptive statistics of dependent and independent variables employed in the econometric analysis. The average value of the logarithm of the GINI index is equal to 3.658, and the minimum and maximum values are 3.145 and 4.307, respectively. As the Gini index measures the extent to which income distribution among individuals or households within an economy deviates from an equal distribution, its higher values imply a higher rate of income inequality. The mean of the export product concentration index is relatively low, constituting 0.24. The minimum value of 0.051 indicates a high level of export diversification, and the maximum level of 0.85 implies a high rate of export concentration. The ICT index averages 0.497, reflecting the relatively low level of ICT development in our study's countries during the period analyzed.

Table 1. Descriptive Statistics

Variable	Source	Obs	Mean	Std. Dev	Min	Max
log GINI	WIID	1494	3.658	0.243	3.145	4.307
log GDP per capita	WDI	1494	9.227	1.273	5.542	11.63
HCI	PWT	1494	2.82	0.601	1.088	4.352
Industry	WDI	1492	27.451	9.451	8.058	66.757
FDI	WDI	1494	6.648	24.137	−57.532	449.081
ICT Index	Calculated	1467	0.497	0.271	0	1
Concentration Index	UNCTAD	1494	0.24	0.163	0.051	0.85

In order to investigate the relationship between the GINI coefficient and the ICT index, as well as the export product concentration index, we constructed the following theoretical model:

$$GINI_{it} = f\,(gdppercapita, humancapital, industry, FDI, ICT, ECI) \qquad (2)$$

where i denotes the country, t denotes year, $GINI$ denotes the GINI coefficient (ranges from 0 to 100), $gdppercapita$ denotes GDP per capita (constant 2015 US dollar), $humancapital$ denotes human capital index, $industry$ denotes industry (including construction), value added (percentage of GDP), FDI denotes foreign direct investment, net inflows (percentage of GDP). ICT represents the ICT index (ranges from 0 to 1) and ECI denotes the export product concentration index (ranges from 0 to 1).

We process the GINI and GDP per capita variables using natural logarithms to remove any potential heteroscedasticity and data volatility.

Equation (2) can be expressed by the following baseline estimation equation:

$$GINI_{it} = \varphi_i + \gamma_1 ECI_{it} + \gamma_2 ICT_{it} + \gamma_3 DZ_{it} + \varepsilon_{it} \tag{3}$$

where i denotes the country, t denotes year, φ_i is the fixed effect of the country, $\gamma_1 \ldots \gamma_3$ are the estimated coefficients, ε_{it} is an error term. ECI_{it} denotes the export product concentration index of country i in time t, ICT_{it} denotes i country's ICT index in time t, DZ_{it} shows the four control variables: GDP per capita, human capital index, industry, and FDI inflows.

As we are interested in investigating the effects of ICT development and export diversification on countries with different levels of income inequality, we use panel quantile regression as an appropriate model for our analysis. The methodology captures the overall effect of ICT development and export diversification on the entire conditional income inequality distribution. In addition, the model is robust to heteroscedasticity, skewness, and outliers. The equation using the panel quantile regression method can be specified as follows:

$$Y_{it} = \alpha_i + X'_{it}\beta + (\delta_i + Z'_{it}\gamma)U_{it} \tag{4}$$

where with $\Pr\{\delta_i + Z\prime_{it}\gamma > 0\} = 1$. The parameters α_i, δ_i, $i = 1, \ldots, n$ capture the country i fixed effects. Z is a k-vector of known differentiable (with probability 1) transformations of the components of X_{it} with element 1 given by $Z_l = Z_l(X), l = 1, \ldots, k$. The sequence $\{X\prime_{it}\}$ is strictly exogenous and independent across i. U_{it} is a random unobservable variable statistically independent of $X\prime_{it}$, and normalized to satisfy the moment conditions. In addition, $U_{it} \perp X_{it}$, $E(B) = 0$, and $E(|B|) = 1$ [8].

Model (5) can be rewritten as:

$$Q_Y(\tau|X_{it}) = (\alpha_i + \delta_i q(\tau)) + X'_{it}\beta + Z'_{it}\gamma q(\tau) \tag{5}$$

Here, $\alpha_i + \delta_i q(\tau)$ is the quantile-τ fixed effect for individual i. In general, the distributional impact differs from the fixed effect in that it does not cause a location shift. In other words, the distributional effect indicates the impact of time-invariant individual characteristics, which, like other factors, might have varying effects on various parts of the conditional distribution of Y_{it} (the GINI index in our analysis) [8].

4   Results and Discussion

We analyze the relationship between the ICT index and the GINI coefficient, as well as the influence of the export concentration on income inequality. Table 2 reports the results of the panel quantile regression (MM-QR) for quantiles with different levels of income inequality. In our sample, countries in the first 10th quantile have the lowest level of income inequality, while the countries in the 90th quantile are characterized with the highest level of income inequality. We find the result of estimation consistent with the Hypothesis 1. In Table 2, for each quantile except the 10th, the estimated coefficients of the ICT index variable are negative and statistically significant at a 1% level.

Moreover, the estimated coefficient of the ICT index variable is higher for quantiles with a higher GINI coefficient. This means that the reduction in income inequality level is associated with ICT development, and its negative impact on income inequality is more substantial in countries with medium and high levels of income inequality. This result is consistent with the outcome of the [28] study, where the authors found that ICT measures of internet, fixed broadband, and mobile cellular subscription directly reduce income inequality, and good governance indicators can facilitate the relationship between ICT and income inequality.

For the second key independent variable, the export concentration index, the estimated coefficient is positive and significant at a 5% significance level for the 10th, 20th, and 50th quantiles; at a 1% level for the 30th and 40th quantiles; a 10% level for the 60th quantile. For other quantiles, the coefficient of the export concentration index is not statistically significant. The coefficient of this core variable becomes lower in higher quantiles (for example, 0.0637 for the 50th quantile compared to 0.1078 for the 10th quantile). The obtained result indicates that the increase in income inequality level is associated with the concentration of the country's export basket. In other words, export diversification is associated with the reduction in income inequality level, and this impact is higher in countries with low and middle levels of income inequality. The finding is consistent with the results obtained in [9], where authors conclude that after a threshold level, export diversification may contribute to a more equitable income distribution by creating more jobs for both skilled and unskilled workers. The findings of several studies show that countries tend to concentrate their export structure after reaching some threshold level of GDP per capita [29–31]. As developed economies with high per capita income and low-income inequality concentrate their exports by specialization in high-tech industries demanding high-skilled labor, it may lead to less equal income distribution because the income of low-skilled labor in shrinking labor-intensive industries may fall. In contrast, export diversification in developing economies with a middle level of income inequality may lead to structural changes, job creation for low-skilled and high-skilled workers and more equitable income distribution.

As for the control variables, the estimated parameters of GDP per capita are significantly negative from the 30th to 90th quantiles, while at lower quantiles (i.e., 10th and 20th quantiles), the per capita income effect is insignificant. The coefficient of the GDP per capita variable ranges from -0.03 for the 30th quantile and -0.04 for the 90th quantile. Ceteris paribus, a 1% increase in GDP per capita is associated with the 0.03–0.04% decrease in the GINI coefficient. The negative impact of GDP per capita growth on income inequality is in line with the findings of [3]. The estimated coefficients of the human capital index are negative and significant at the 1% level from the 10th to 50th quantiles and at the 5% level for the 60th quantile. The coefficient of the human capital index is higher for lower quantiles, i.e., countries with a smaller GINI coefficient. The results indicate that the rising quality of human capital is associated with a lower level of income inequality, other things equal. Thus, human capital is a significant determinant of equal income distribution [32–34]. The industry variable has a significant negative impact on the GINI coefficient from the 20th to 90th quantiles. However, the estimated coefficients are relatively small in lower quantiles and relatively high in higher quantiles. This means that industrialization may reduce income inequality levels, and the impact is

Table 2. Estimated results of the impact of the ICT Index and the Export Concentration Index on the GINI coefficient

Variables	(1) 10th log GINI	(2) 20th log GINI	(3) 30th log GINI	(4) 40th log GINI	(5) 50th log GINI	(6) 60th log GINI	(7) 70th log GINI	(8) 80th log GINI	(9) 90th log GINI
Log GDP pc	−0.0249	−0.0280	−0.03048**	−0.0329***	−0.0355***	−0.0380***	−0.0403***	−0.0425**	−0.0454**
	(0.0218)	(0.0174)	(0.0145)	(0.0124)	(0.0117)	(0.0125)	(0.0145)	(0.0171)	(0.0215)
HCI	−0.0675***	−0.0577***	−0.0501***	−0.0424***	−0.0342***	−0.0263**	−0.0192	−0.0121	−0.0031
	(0.0220)	(0.0176)	(0.0147)	(0.0126)	(0.0118)	(0.0127)	(0.0146)	(0.0173)	(0.0213)
Industry	−0.0009	−0.0011*	−0.0012**	−0.0014***	−0.0015***	−0.0017***	−0.0018***	−0.0019***	−0.00206***
	(0.0008)	(0.00064)	(0.0005)	(0.00045)	(0.00042)	(0.00046)	(0.0005)	(0.0006)	(0.00077)
FDI	0.00002	0.000029	0.00003	0.000037	0.000041	0.000045	0.000048	0.000052	0.000057
	(0.00012)	(0.0001)	(0.00008)	(0.00007)	(0.000067)	(0.00007)	(0.00008)	(0.00009)	(0.00012)
ICT Index	−0.0484*	−0.0619***	−0.0724***	−0.08305***	−0.0943***	−0.1052***	−0.1149***	−0.1246***	−0.1370***
	(0.0262)	(0.0209)	(0.0175)	(0.0150)	(0.0141)	(0.0151)	(0.0174)	(0.0206)	(0.0254)
Concentration Index	0.1078**	0.09486**	0.0847***	0.0745***	0.0637**	0.0533*	0.0439	0.0345	0.0226
	(0.0484)	(0.0386)	(0.0322)	(0.0276)	(0.0258)	(0.0278)	(0.0322)	(0.0380)	(0.0487)
Observations	1,465	1,465	1,465	1,465	1,465	1,465	1,465	1,465	1,465
F/Wald test chi2(6)	78.97***	127.80***	189.76***	269.07***	391.02***	292.08***	230.21***	174.08***	122.94***

*** $p < 0.01$, ** $p < 0.05$, * $p < 0.1$

higher in countries with a relatively high GINI coefficient. The result is consistent with previous studies [35, 36]. However, the FDI variable does not have a significant impact on income inequality level in any quantile.

Thus, the empirical results support the hypothesis of the negative impact of ICT development and export diversification on income inequality. The negative impact of ICT development on income distribution is stronger in higher quantiles, while the positive effect of export concentration on income inequality is higher in low quantiles. The results of the post-estimation Wald test [37, 38] for the Panel quantile model show that the model estimator used for this study is appropriate for performing this analysis.

5   Conclusion

This paper explores the nexus between ICT development, export diversification, and income inequality by analyzing the panel data of 83 countries covering 2002–2019. After estimating the results by using the panel quantile regression model, we obtained the following research conclusions:

•The ICT development negatively affects income inequality. The reverse effect of ICT development on income inequality is pronounced in countries with more unequal distribution of incomes.

•The income inequality is affected favorably by export concentration. In other words, export diversification is associated with the reduction in income inequality level, and this effect is more robust in countries with low and middle levels of income inequality.

•Among the control variables, GDP per capita significantly negatively affects income inequality from the 30th to 90th quantiles. The human capital index's impact on income inequality is adverse from the 10th to 60th quantiles. Industrialization may reduce income inequality levels, as the industry variable coefficients are negative and significant from the 20th to 90th quantiles in the benchmark regression.

The findings of this study have significant policy implications. Firstly, countries with higher levels of income inequality should pay more attention to the development of ICT and the digitalization of the economy.

Secondly, considering that export diversification reduces income inequality, countries with unequal income distribution should implement strategies directed to horizontal and vertical export product diversification. It means the expansion of a variety of exported products and a shift to the export of high-value-added manufacturing goods and services.

In future research, a more extended period of study of income inequality could make more accurate conclusions on the main determinants of income inequality at the country level. The cases of low-income, middle-income, and high-income countries could be investigated separately and compared. An in-depth study could concentrate on the channels through which ICT development and export diversification affect income inequality in developed and developing countries and how they can adapt different strategies to reduce income inequality. Other determinants of income inequality could be included as control variables in the model and analyzed.

Acknowledgments. This article is prepared within the project "Tashkent Jean Monnet Centre of Excellence for European studies" supported by the EU ERASMUS + Programme. Grant no: 620528-EPP-1–2020-1-UZ-EPPJMO-CoE.

References

1. Committee for Development Policy, Report on the twentieth, Official Records of the Economic and Social Council, 2018, Supplement No. 13 (E/2018/33). United Nations New York (2018). https://www.un.org/development/desa/dpad/publication/2018-reports-to-the-economic-and-social-council/
2. World inequality report 2022 (2022). https://wir2022.wid.world/executive-summary
3. Warren, M.: The digital vicious cycle: links between social disadvantage and digital exclusion in rural areas Telecommunications Policy, **31**(6–7), 374–388 (2007)
4. Holmes, H., Burgess, G.: Digital exclusion and poverty in the UK: how structural inequality shapes experiences of getting online. Digit. Geogr. Soc. **3,** 100041 (2022). ISSN 2666-3783.https://doi.org/10.1016/j.diggeo.2022.100041
5. Nidhi, T., Anant, K.P., Vigneswara, I.: Social inequalities, fundamental inequities, and recurring of the digital divide: Insights from India. Technol. Soc. **61**, 101251 (2020). ISSN 016-791X
6. Qureshi, Z.: Inequality in the digital era. Work in the Age of Data, 3–13 (2019). https://www.brookings.edu/wp-content/uploads/2020/02/BBVA-OpenMind-Zia-Qureshi-Inequality-in-the-digital-era.pdf
7. Bertrand, B., Dina, C.: Export diversification, specialization and inequality: evidence from Asian and Western countries. J. Int. Trade Econ. Dev. **28**(2), 189–229 (2019). https://doi.org/10.1080/09638199.2018.1533032
8. Li, D., Wang, X., Xu, Y., Re, Y.: Analysis of export diversification and impact of globalisation on income inequality: evidence from Asian countries global economic review. Perspect. East Asian Econ. Ind. **51**(3), 195–215 (2022)
9. Le, T.H., Nguyen, C.P., Su, T.D., Tran-Nam, B.: The Kuznets curve for export diversification and income inequality: evidence from a global sample. Econ. Anal. Policy **65**, 21–39 2020. ISSN 0313-5926
10. Lee, C.-C., Yuan, Z., Ho, S.-J.: How does export diversification affect income inequality? International evidence, structural change and economic dynamics. **63**, 410–421 (2022). ISSN 0954-349X. https://doi.org/10.1016/j.strueco.2022.06.010
11. Gnangnon, S.K.: Poverty and export product diversification in developing countries. J. Int. Trade Econ. Dev. **29**, 211–236 (2019)
12. Ishnazarov A., Kasimova N., Tosheva S., Isaeva A.: ICT and economic growth: evidence from cross-country growth modeling. In: ACM International Conference Proceeding Series (2021).https://doi.org/10.1145/3508072.3508204
13. Akhmadalieva, Z., Akhmadalieva, Z.: Impact of digitalization on firms' productivity. Association for Computing Machinery (2022). Conference Paper.
14. Makhmudov, N., Avazov, N.: Investigating the impact of investment and ICT on real income growth: the case of Hungary (2022). https://doi.org/10.1145/3584202.3584261
15. Sultanova, G., Djuraeva, R., Turaeva, S.: The impact of the digital economy on renewable energy consumption and generation: evidence from European Union countries. In: Proceedings of the 6th International Conference on Future Networks & Distributed Systems, pp. 99–109 (2022). https://doi.org/10.1145/3584202.3584218
16. Digital 2021, We are social and Hootsuite (2021). https://wearesocial.com/digital-2021
17. Castells, M.: The Internet galaxy: reflections on the internet, business, and society, clarendon lectures in management studies. Oxford (2002). Online edn, Oxford Academic, 3 Oct. 2011
18. Alisherovna Usmanova, A.: whether a higher e-government development index means a higher GDP growth rate? In: ACM International Conference Proceeding Series, pp. 467–472 (2021).https://doi.org/10.1145/3508072.3508168

19. Usmanova: Impact of E-government on Poverty Rate: A Cross-Country Empirical Assessment. In: Koucheryavy, Y., Aziz, A. (eds.) Internet of Things, Smart Spaces, and Next Generation Networks and Systems: 22nd International Conference, NEW2AN 2022, Tashkent, Uzbekistan, December 15–16, 2022, Proceedings, pp. 462–470. Springer Nature Switzerland, Cham (2023). https://doi.org/10.1007/978-3-031-30258-9_41

20. Usmanova, A.: An Empirical Investigation of the Relationship Between E-government Development and Multidimensional Poverty. In: Koucheryavy, Y., Aziz, A. (eds.) Internet of Things, Smart Spaces, and Next Generation Networks and Systems: 22nd International Conference, NEW2AN 2022, Tashkent, Uzbekistan, December 15–16, 2022, Proceedings, pp. 471–480. Springer Nature Switzerland, Cham (2023). https://doi.org/10.1007/978-3-031-30258-9_42

21. Usmanova, A.: The impact of financial development and unemployment on poverty rate in the context of digital economy in Uzbekistan. In: ACM International Conference Proceeding Series, pp. 684–689 (2022).https://doi.org/10.1145/3584202.3584306

22. Antràs, P., de Gortari, A., Itskhoki, O.: Globalization, inequality and welfare. J. Int. Econ. **108**, 387–412 (2017)

23. Asteriou, D., Dimelis, S., Moudatsou, A.: Globalization and income inequality: a panel data econometric approach for the EU27 countries. Econ. Model. **36**, 592–599 (2014)

24. Cabral, R., García-Díaz, R., Mollick, A.V.: Does globalization affect top income inequality? J. Policy Model. **38**(5), 916–940 (2016)

25. Babones, S.J., Vonada, D.C.: Trade globalization and national income inequality - are they related? J. Sociol. **45**(1), 5–30 (2009)

26. Subir, L., et al.: Globalization and inequality, Chap. 4. In: International Monetary Fund (ed.) World Economic Outlook, pp. 135–169. IMF, Washington, DC (2007)

27. OECD: A Broken Social Elevator? How to Promote Social Mobility. OECD Publishing, Paris (2018). https://doi.org/10.1787/9789264301085-en

28. UNCTADSTAT Data Centre. https://unctadstat.unctad.org/en/IndicatorsExplained/statie2019d1_en.pdf

29. The ICT Development Index (IDI): conceptual framework and methodology. International telecommunication union. https://www.itu.int/en/ITU-D/Statistics/Pages/publications/mis2017/methodology.aspx

30. Jackson, J.E.: A User's Guide to Principal Components. Wiley (2005)

31. Machado, J.A.F., Santos Silva, J.M.C.: Quantiles via moments. J. Econ. **213**(1), 145–173 (2019)

32. Adams, S., Akobeng, E.: ICT, governance and inequality in Africa. Telecommun. Policy **45**(10), 102198 (2021)

33. Cadot, O., Carrere, C., Strauss-Kahn, V.: Trade diversification, income, and growth: what do we know? J. Econ. Surv. **27**(4), 790–812 (2013)

34. Bebczuk, Ricardo Néstor, and Daniel Berrettoni. "Explaining export diversification: an empirical analysis." Documentos de Trabajo (2006)

35. Klinger, B., Daniel, L.: Diversification, innovation, and imitation inside the global technological frontier. World Bank policy research working paper 3872 (2006)

36. Heckman, J.J., Yi, J.: Human capital, economic growth, and inequality in China, working paper 18100, (May 2012). https://doi.org/10.3386/w18100

37. Ghazal, S., Parviz, D.: Studying effects of human capital on income inequality in Iran. Procedia Soc. Behav. Sci. **109**, 1386-1389 (2014). ISSN 1877-0428

38. Lee, J.-W., Lee, H.: Human capital and income inequality (February 15, 2018). ADBI Working Paper 810. https://ssrn.com/abstract=3198573

39. Mehic, A.: Industrial employment and income inequality: evidence from panel data. Struct. Chang. Econ. Dyn. **45**, 84–93 (2018)

40. Rosés, J.R., Martínez-Galarraga, J., Tirado, D.A.: The upswing of regional income inequality in Spain (1860–1930). Explor. Econ. Hist. **47**(2), 244–257 (2010). https://doi.org/10.1016/j.eeh.2010.01.002

41. Judge, G.G., Griffiths, W.E., Hill, R.C., Lutkepohl, H., Lee, T.-C.: The Theory and Practice of Econometrics, 2nd edn. Wiley, New York (1985)

42. Aziz, A., et al.: Optimising compressive sensing matrix using Chicken Swarm Optimisation algorithm. IET Wirel. Sens. Syst. **9**(5), 306–312 (2019)

Utilities of Chatbots in Teaching Russian as a Foreign Language at Higher Education Institutions

Shakhnoza Tuychibaeva[1(✉)] and Aziza Usmanova[2]

[1] Department of Uzbek Language and Literature, Tashkent State University of Oriental Studies, Tashkent, Uzbekistan
Shahnoza2909shakir@gmail.com
[2] International Business Management Department, Tashkent State University of Economics, Tashkent, Uzbekistan
a.usmanova@tsue.uz

Abstract. The purpose of the paper is to present the experience of using chatbots, GPT chat, in the process of teaching Russian as a foreign language to students of national groups, as well as foreign students. The effectiveness of chatbots with artificial intelligence in learning the Russian language is determined, and the pedagogical, social, and technological opportunities that they represent are identified. The positive aspects and some difficulties of its use are described. The results of the study, which was conducted from 2022 to 2023, are presented. Scientific and methodological literature on the research topic was analyzed. Based on the work carried out, conclusions were drawn, and recommendations were made.

Keywords: Digital technologies · chatbot · GPT chat · artificial intelligence · Russian as a foreign language · communication · information · text · dialogue

1 Introduction

New times place new demands on the training of highly qualified national personnel who are fluent not only in their specialty but also in foreign languages, which includes Russian. This, in turn, presupposes the effective organization of the educational process using best practices, innovative techniques and methods, and a wide range of digital technologies. In recent years, one of the hot topics in teaching foreign languages is the use of chatbots, in particular GPT chat. Its appearance was preceded by research on natural language processing and machine learning. The American laboratory OpenAI has created several versions of the chatbot. In 2018, the first GPT-1 chat began to be used, with which it was possible to create texts in different formats. In the future, the developer company will create more advanced and updated versions: GPT-2, GPT-3, GPT-3.5, and GPT-4.

According to the international news agency Reuters, whose specialization is news products in the fields of finance, business, politics, and technology, by February 1, 2023, in 2 months, the audience of active users of the GPT chat reached 100 million people. This indicates a record growth in chat consumers [1].

According to experts, the importance of artificial intelligence in the educational sphere exceeds the widespread use of computers. Just two of the many existing technologies—deep learning (DL) and natural language processing (NLP)—help students clarify complex terminology, describe, and prove the law, and improve their speaking skills in their native or foreign languages [2, 35].

According to experts, the importance of artificial intelligence in the educational sphere exceeds the widespread use of computers. Just two of the many existing technologies—deep learning (DL) and natural language processing (NLP)—help students clarify complex terminology, describe, and prove the law, and improve their speaking skills in their native or foreign languages [2, 30].

The Saiora. uz platform, which allows to access GPT 3.5 chat and the updated version—GPT 4, operates in the Republic of Uzbekistan, this platform was launched by DevHub [3, 36].

2 Literature Review

Since the beginning of 2000, there has been an increase in the number of studies that have influenced the use of artificial intelligence systems in different creatures [4–10]. Chatbot-enabled foreign language learning has attracted the attention of both local and foreign researchers and educators for consistent reasons.

Many studies consider chatbots as one of the potentially valuable elements of the educational language system, describe the interactive, educational, technological, and psychological aspects of their use and the positive impact on reducing language anxiety and discomfort in students [11–16].

Researchers determine the effectiveness of using chatbots depending on the level of foreign language learning, consider the possibilities of its use for obtaining information, testing and verifying results, as well as the impact on the individualization of learning [17–22].

It should be noted that there is a relatively small number of studies related to the use of chatbots and specifically GPT chat in teaching Russian as a foreign language [23–25].

Research in this area is characterized not only by positive positions: it points out the shortcomings of chatbot software, and the shortcomings of artificial intelligence, which affects the results, and discusses controversial issues of its use for educational purposes [26–29].

Analysis of scientific and methodological research on the topic reveals their practical orientation. Language chatbots as communication agents have both positive potential and certain disadvantages.

3 Data and Methodology

This study uses comparative analysis, classification, and synthesis [31–33]. As part of the study, foreign experience in using chats in teaching foreign languages, including Russian, is studied. Approaches to the feasibility and effectiveness of using chat are considered.

As a result of the study planned to improve the methodology of teaching Russian as a foreign language based on the use of GPT chat, increase students' motivation to study it, develop their creative and analytical abilities, compare and analyze experimental data, present the experience of using chatbots when teaching Russian as a foreign language and generally justify the effectiveness of its use.

Today, GPT chat is one of the most popular [34]. There is a need to evaluate the prospects for using artificial intelligence, and particularly the GPT chat in the process of teaching Russian as a foreign language [37]. Due to the novelty of the topic, there is almost no data on research by domestic authors on the issue under study, which serves as a justification for its relevance.

The experiment, which covers the period from 2022 to 2023, involved 180 students of the Tashkent State University of Oriental Studies studying Russian as a foreign language in their first year. Among them are 40 s and third-year foreign students from China, Japan, and the Republic of Korea, who came to study as part of the university's cooperation with international universities.

At the beginning of the experiment, a survey was conducted among students, the purpose of which was to determine the extent to which they have information about chatbots and use them. Survey data are shown in Table 1.

Table 1. The output of the survey on the student's level of knowledge about chatbots

Knowledge and skills of students	Uzbek students	Foreign students
Had an idea about a chatbot	60%	98%
Used chatbots to learn Russian	10%	15%
Used chatbots for other purposes	30%	75%
Had an idea about the GPT chat	40%	92%
Used GPT chat to learn Russian	5%	10%
Used GPT chat for other purposes	22%	60%

Various reasons were identified as to why students rarely or did not use chatbots at all. They did not have information on the topic, both due to its novelty and lack of interest, they did not have the necessary user skills, or the ability to regularly pay for advanced versions of the GPT chat. More than half of the students of national groups came from different regions of Uzbekistan and remote areas, where there is not always sufficient Internet connection. In addition, the lack of official access to the use of GPT chat for a certain period encouraged some students to use it through WPN. The data is shown in Table 2.

Table 2. Reasons for not using chatbots.

Reasons	Uzbek students	Foreign students
Lack of sufficient information	50%	8%
Lack of motivation	36%	25%
Lack of skills in using chatbots	60%	97%
Difficulties in accessing the use of chatbots, in particular GPT chat	70%	30%
Paid content	20%	6%

4   Results and Discussion

Students of the Tashkent State University of Oriental Studies with varying levels of knowledge of the Russian language—from zero to level B2—took part in the experiment. Groups, as a rule, are formed according to the direction of education. Considering the linguistic nature of the university, the full-time department consists of an average of 10 to 18 students with different language levels. At the same time, groups of foreign students are formed depending on the level of knowledge of the Russian language, which increases the efficiency of its teaching and learning. Among students from national groups, more than half had level A1; among foreign students, knowledge of the Russian language on average corresponded to level B1. Students of national groups, studying Russian at school, for several objective and subjective reasons, did not speak Russian at a level that met the program requirements. Among the reasons are the following: a reduction in hours for the Russian language and, accordingly, an increase in them for studying a foreign language, most often English; benefits when entering a university if you have a certificate of knowledge of a foreign language (except for Russian, which does not have this status in certain positions); lack of quality textbooks and teaching aids; insufficient number of qualified Russian language teachers in rural schools; lack of an effective curriculum taking into account the level of knowledge; lack of preparation of students for self-education; low motivation. Foreign students, in comparison with students of national groups, often have a better command of the Russian language.

Senior foreigners more often come to study at the University of Oriental Studies, they are older than Uzbek students in age, and they have higher motivation since the Russian language is then a means of communication when studying in another country. They have a larger number of hours in the Russian language, determined by the goals of language practice: 10–12 h per week for a year or 6 months, in national groups—only 4 h for one semester.

After determining students' knowledge of chats and experience of using them, it was found that Uzbek students most often use chatbots available in the Telegram application. Some students used the GPT 3, 3.5, and 4 chat to search for various information, as well as about their work – among them were correspondence remotely learning students, combining work and study. Foreign students had more experience using chats to do independent work, study the Russian language, draw up projects, and prepare for courses.

Students from Japan indicated their lack of practice in using GPT chat due to social reasons.

All this determined the choice of appropriate methods, topics, and types of work using the GPT chat when teaching the Russian language. When selecting assignments for students' classroom and extracurricular work and preparing handouts, the level of knowledge in the Russian language and the availability of practical skills in using chats were primarily considered.

To begin with, all students were asked to individually find and study information (without using chat) about the GPT chat in Russian, its application, and opportunities for learning the Russian language. If necessary, to assimilate the information, the student translated the received material for himself. The next stage of work was to search for this information using GPT chat. Next, students had to unite into subgroups, compare the data, supplement, summarize them, and present a presentation of the information received. As a result of the work, students received the necessary information on the topic. The groups were assessed on the quality of the material presented, its compliance with the content, the ability to present information in Russian, and the number of correctly composed queries for the chat, which influenced the completeness of the topic. The ability to use chat by most students was influenced by the launch of a platform in Uzbekistan by DevHub that allows access to GPT chat.

Subsequently, the topics presented for study using the GPT chat corresponded to the course program: "Country of the language being studied", "Large cities", "Sights", "Traditions and customs", "Culture and art", "Prominent figures", "Healthy image" life", "Sports", "Hobbies and interests", "Russian language among other world languages", etc. Grammar topics also reflected the theme of the course. Students used different versions of GPT chat while learning the topics. Outcome scores and criteria are presented in Table 3.

Table 3. Evaluation of different chatbots

Evaluation criteria	Chat GPT3	Chat GPT3.5	Chat GPT 4
Correspondence of the information to the content of the topic	+	+	+
Conformity of the information to the level of knowledge of the language	+	+	+
Presence of errors	+	—	—
Reliability of information	—	+	—
Logical sequence of contents	+	+	+

Thus, when learning about a grammatical topic, when asked about coordinating conjunctions, Chat GPT3 gives incorrect information and uses direct conjunctions. he gave an example of when, and when asked about a complex sentence, he gave an example of a complex sentence with the conjunction while.

The teacher explained the aspects of effective use of conversation, including technical and linguistic features. When the survey was formulated more precisely and filled with many components that helped to provide accurate and complete information to the chat, the data obtained was of varying quality.

We've used GPT4's chat capabilities effectively to create a variety of handouts, including the following tasks:

- creating texts on a certain topic with a certain number of words and a certain level of knowledge of the Russian language.
- creating questions and answers based on the text.
- creating true or false statements based on the text, while the chat itself provides ready-made answers without prompting.
- creating dialogues on the specified topic.
- development of assessment criteria for the assigned task.
- selection of role-playing games on a specified topic, etc.
- Based on the use of GPT chat, students completed the following tasks:
- Search for information on the topic and compare the results obtained from different sources.
- for editing a self-written essay, resume, advertising text, business letter, public speaking, etc.
- check the dictation written in the audience, and the completed task/test.
- to independently analyze and compare the results of checking/editing via chat.
- choosing the main vocabulary for the studied topic.
- translate the specified language unit into the selected language (English, Uzbek, Chinese, etc.) and compare the results with an independent translation.
- continue the dialogue with the chat on the specified topic.
- creating various chat requests on the same topic and analyzing the results, etc.

It should be noted that students worked individually and in groups/subgroups.

We tried not to give tasks that did not allow us to determine the degree of independence in completing them. That is, if the task was to write an essay, students presented two options — their own and the chat.

As part of the work, there was no goal to determine the negative aspects of using chat when teaching Russian as a foreign language and the inability to use it for several reasons. For many students, the work done was new, educational, interesting, and, apparently, because of this they had no reason to violate ethical and didactic standards. However, it should be noted that difficulties at the initial stage of the experiment were experienced by students who had poor command of the Russian language and no experience of using chat. Because of this, they had difficulties both with the correct execution of the chat request and the technique of its application. Therefore, at this stage, within the same group, the teacher gave different tasks and chose the appropriate criteria for assessing them.

The method of teaching students Russian as a foreign language using the capabilities of the GPT chat has become a more effective and exciting means of using modern digital technologies. During the experiment, the educational potential of the GPT chat was used for learning Russian as a foreign language. Its compatibility with the operating systems of laptops, computers, tablets, and smartphones has expanded the possibilities of language practice for students in learning the Russian language in almost any situation.

When working with the GPT chat, students increased their motivation to learn the Russian language, got the opportunity to quickly receive, process, and analyze information on the desired topic, improved practical skills, increased their vocabulary, and knowledge on the topic, learned to conduct self-tests, developed communicative and sociolinguistic competencies. In most cases, the psychological barrier to communication was removed, and students' confidence in their abilities increased.

The teacher, using the GPT chat when teaching the Russian language, was able to give creative tasks, save time when compiling handouts, and assess and check the level of acquired knowledge. The teacher's competent use of chatbots, skillful organization of students' work, selection of material, and choice of work forms made it possible to increase the effectiveness of teaching the Russian language and develop communication skills. For the reliability and quality of the information received, we used the GPT4 version.

Among advanced-level foreign students, greater effectiveness was noted from the use of chat when teaching the Russian language due to the presence of sufficient skills and practical skills.

It is advisable to use GPT chat on the goals, stages of learning, and the level of knowledge of students.

The creation of methodological developments on certain topics and forms of work based on the use of chat when studying Russian as a foreign language, and the development of recommendations for the effectiveness of their use may become a topic for further research.

5   Conclusion

The method of teaching students Russian as a foreign language using the capabilities of the GPT chat has become a more effective and exciting means of using modern digital technologies. During the experiment, the educational potential of the GPT chat was used for learning Russian as a foreign language. Its compatibility with the operating systems of laptops, computers, tablets, and smartphones has expanded the possibilities of language practice for students in learning the Russian language in almost any situation.

When working with the GPT chat, students increased their motivation to learn the Russian language, got the opportunity to quickly receive, process, and analyze information on the desired topic, improved practical skills, increased their vocabulary, and knowledge on the topic, learned to conduct self-tests, developed communicative and sociolinguistic competencies. In most cases, the psychological barrier to communication was removed, and students' confidence in their abilities increased.

The teacher, using the GPT chat when teaching the Russian language, was able to give creative tasks, save time when compiling handouts, and assess and check the level of acquired knowledge. The teacher's competent use of chatbots, skillful organization of students' work, selection of material, and choice of work forms made it possible to increase the effectiveness of teaching the Russian language and develop communication skills. For the reliability and quality of the information received, we used the GPT4 version.

Among advanced-level foreign students, greater effectiveness was noted from the use of chat when teaching the Russian language due to the presence of sufficient skills and practical skills.

It is advisable to use GPT chat on the goals, stages of learning, and the level of knowledge of students.

The creation of methodological developments on certain topics and forms of work based on the use of chat when studying Russian as a foreign language, and the development of recommendations for the effectiveness of their use may become a topic for further research.

References

1. Hu. K.: ChatGPT sets record for fastest-growing user base – analyst note. Reuters. https://www.reuters.com/technology/chatgpt-sets-record-fastest-growing-user-base-analyst-note-2023-02-01

2. Totskaya, V., Nedospasova, L.A.: The educational potential of Chatbots in foreign languages learning: sociolinguistic, didactic and communicative aspects. Sci. Methodol. Electr. J. "Concept" **2023**(06), 14–27 (2023). Author, F., Author, S., Author, T.: Book title. 2nd edn. Publisher, Location (1999)

3. Saiora.uz: How ChatGPT artificial intelligence can help in work, study, and business. https://www.gazeta.uz

4. Chen, Y.J.: World Wide Web [Transactional Distance in World Wide Web Learning Environments]. Innovacii v obrazovanii i mejdunarodnoe prepodavanie, **38**(4), 327–338 (2001). (in Russian)

5. Bespal'ko, V.P.: Obrazovanie i obuchenie s uchastiem kompyuterov: pedagogika tret'yego tisyacheletiya [Education and training with the participation of computers: pedagogy of the third millennium]. Moscow: MODEK, p. 352 (2002). (in Russian)

6. Eynon, R., Davies, C., Wilks, Y.: The learning companion: an embodied conversational agent for learning. In: Proceedings of the WebSci 2009: Society On-Line (2009)

7. Matveeva, N.Y., Zolotaryuk, A.V.: Tehnologii sozdaniya i primeneniya chat-botov [Technologies for creating and using chatbots]. Nauchniye zapiski molodix issledovateley, **2018**(1), 28–30 (2018). (in Russian)

8. Wilson, L.: The development and use of Chatbots in public health: scoping review. https://www.google.com/url?q=https://www.ncbi.nlm.nih.gov/pmc/articles

9. Gupta, A., Hathwar, D., Vijayakumar, A.: Introduction to AI chatbots. Int. J. Eng. Res. Technol **9**, 255–258 (2020). (in English)

10. Miklosik A. The Use of Chatbots in Digital Business Transformation: A Systematic Literature Review. July 2021 https://www.researchgate.net/journal/IEEE-Access-2169-3536

11. Li, Y., Chen, C.Y., Yu, D., et al.: Using Chatbots to Teach Languages. In: Proceedings of the Ninth ACM Conference on Learning at Scale. New York, pp. 451–455 (2020)

12. Budnikova, A.S., Babenkova O.S.: Using Chatbots when learning a foreign language. Bull. Kursk State Univ. **3**(55), pp. 146–150 (2020)

13. Lavrinenko, I.Y.: The use of GPT Chatbots in the process of teaching English at a non-linguistic university: a theoretical aspect. Bull. Siberian Inst. Bus. Inform. Technol. **12**(2) (2023). https://doi.org/10.24412/2225-8264-2023-2-18-25

14. Kim, N.Y.: Chatbots and language learning: effects of the use of AI Chatbots for EFL Learning. Eliva Press: Chisinau, Moldova 2020

15. Dokukina, I., Gumanova, J.: The rise of chatbots – new personal assistants for foreign language learning. Procedia Comput. Sci. **169**, 542–546 (2020)
16. Allouch M., Azaria A., Azoulay, R.: Conversational Agents: goals, technologies, vision, and challenges. Sensors **21**, 8448 (2021)
17. Mageira K., Pittou D., Papasalouros, A., et al.: Educational AI Chatbots for Content and Language Integrated Learning. Appl. Sci. **12**, 3239 (2022)
18. Kononenko, A.P., Nedoseka, L.A.: Teaching foreign languages in universities using online platforms. Mod. Pedagogical Educ. 2021(9), 19 (2021)
19. Chocarro, R., Cortinas, M., Marcos-Matás, G.: Teachers' attitudes towards chatbots in education: a technology acceptance model approach considering the effect of social language, bot proactiveness, and users' characteristics. Educ. Stud. **49**(2), 295–313 (2023)
20. Bibauw, S., Fransua, T., Desmet, P.: Dialogue systems for language learning: Chatbots and Beyond. The Routledge Handbook of Second Language Acquisition and Technology. Routledge, Abingdon, pp. 121–135 (2022)
21. Fryer, L., Carpenter, R.: Bots as language learning tools. Lang. Learn. Technol. **10**, 8–14 (2006)
22. Cobern, V.V., Schuster, D., Adams, B., Skoidd B.A., et al.: Pedagogy of Science. training tests. formation of assessments of pedagogical directions of science. Int. J. Sci. Educ. **36**(13), 2265–2288 (2014). https://doi.org/10.1080/09500693.2014.918672
23. Patrusheva, L.S.: Using chatbot technology in teaching Russian as a foreign language at the elementary level: from development experience. Bull. Udmurt Univ. Seri. Hist. Philol. **32**(4), 848–853 (2022). https://cyberleninka.ru/article/n/ispolzovanie-tehnologii-chat-botov-v-obuchenii-russkomu-yazyku-kak-inostrannomu-na-nachalnom-urovne-iz-opyta-razrabotki
24. Туйчибаева, Шахноза Шакировна.: ПРИМЕНЕНИЕ ИННОВАЦИОННЫХ МЕТОДОВ ПРИ ИЗУЧЕНИИ СЛОЖНЫХ ПРЕДЛОЖЕНИЙ НА ЗАНЯТИЯХ ПО РУССКОМУ ЯЗЫКУ. In: Proceedings of International Educators Conference. vol. 2, no. 1 (2023)
25. Туйчибаева, ШШ: ИЗ ОПЫТА ОБУЧЕНИЯ РУССКОМУ ЯЗЫКУ ИНОСТРАННЫХ СЛУШАТЕЛЕЙ. Orient. Renaissance: Innov. Educ. Nat. Soc. Sci. **3**(21), 208–212 (2023)
26. Marunevich, O.V., Malishevskaya, N.A.: Osobennosti integracii inoyazichnoy kommunikativnoy i professionalnoy kompetencii na zanyatiyax po inostrannomu yaziku v transportnom vuze [Specific aspects of the integration of foreign language communicative and professional competence in foreign language classes at a transport university] // Sovremennoe pedagogicheskoe obrazovanie **2021**(5), 133–138 (2021). (in Russian)
27. Sysoev, P.V., Filatov, E.M.: Chat-boty v obuchenii inostrannomu yazyku: preimushchestva i spornye voprosy [Chatbots in teaching a foreign language: advantages and controversial issues], Vestnik Tambovskogo universiteta. Seriya: Gumanitarniye nauki t. **28**(1), 66–72 (2023). https://doi.org/10.20310/1810-0201-2023-28-1-66-72. (in Russian)
28. Aristova, A.S., et al.: The use of ChatBots in the educational process. // Digital transformation of society, economy, management, and education. — Yekaterinburg **2**(2), 95–99 (2020)
29. Shefieva, E.: "Osobennosti ispol'zovaniya informacionnix texnologiy obucheniya dlya provedeniya predmetnoy olimpiadi po angliyskomu yaziku v vuze" [Specifics of the use of training information technology for the subject competition in English at the university]. Izvestiya Volgogradskogo gosudarstvennogo pedagogicheskogo universiteta, No **2**(135), 75–79 (2019). (in Russian)
30. Туйчибаева, ШШ: ВОЗМОЖНОСТИ ПРИМЕНЕНИЯ СОВРЕМЕННЫХ ПЕДАГОГИЧЕСКИХ ТЕХНОЛОГИЙ И СРЕДСТВ НАГЛЯДНОСТИ ПРИ ОБУЧЕНИИ РУССКОМУ ЯЗЫКУ. World Sci. Res. J. **13**(1), 126–140 (2023)
31. Usmanova, A., et al.: Utilities of artificial intelligence in poverty prediction: a review. Sustainability **14**(21), 14238 (2022)
32. Hussain, A., et al.: Nexus of training and development, organizational learning capability, and organizational performance in the service sector. Sustainability **15**(4), 3246 (2023)

33. Salim, A., Ismail, A., Osamy, W., Khedr, A.M. Compressive sensing based secure data aggregation scheme for IoT based WSN applications (2021) PLoS ONE, 16 (12 December), e0260634 (2021). https://doi.org/10.1371/journal.pone.026 0634, https://www.scopus.com/inward/record.uri?eid=2-s2.0-85122046015&doi=10.1371% 2fjournal.pone.0260634&partnerID=40&mdDOI

34. Usmanova, A.: An Empirical Investigation of the Relationship Between E-government Development and Multidimensional Poverty. In: Koucheryavy, Y., Aziz, A. (eds.) Internet of Things, Smart Spaces, and Next Generation Networks and Systems: 22nd International Conference, NEW2AN 2022, Tashkent, Uzbekistan, December 15–16, 2022, Proceedings, pp. 471–480. Springer Nature Switzerland, Cham (2023). https://doi.org/10.1007/978-3-031-30258-9_42

35. Usmanova, A.: THE IMPACT of FINANCIAL DEVELOPMENT and UNEMPLOYMENT on POVERTY RATE in the CONTEXT of DIGITAL ECONOMY in UZBEKISTAN. In: ACM International Conference Proceeding Series, pp. 684–689 (2022).https://doi.org/10. 1145/3584202.3584306

36. Burkhanov, A.U., Tursunov, B., Uktamov, K., Usmonov, B. ECONOMETRIC ANALYSIS of FACTORS AFFECTING ECONOMIC STABILITY of CHEMICAL INDUSTRY ENTERPRISES in DIGITAL ERA. In: Case of UZBEKISTAN (2022) ACM International Conference Proceeding Series, pp. 484–490 (2022). https://doi.org/10.1145/3584202.358 4274, https://www.scopus.com/inward/record.uri?eid=2-s2.0-85159773979&doi=10.1145% 2f3584202.3584274&partnerID=40&md5=f9

37. Туйчибаева, Шахноза Шакировна, and Сабринабону Аббос Кизи Бахромбоева. "Особенности обучения китайских студентов русскому языку как иностранному." Orient. Renaissance: Innov. Educ. Nat. Soc. Sci. **2**(26), 201–205 (2022)

Edge Caching Cooperation in NDN Scenarios for Self-organizing Networks

Sviatoslav Iakimenko[✉]

Higher School of Economics, National Research University, Moscow 101000, Russia
syakimenko@hse.ru

Abstract. The paper is devoted to the issues of caching in Named Data Networks (NDN), aimed at addressing content by name and separating information from its producer node. In-network caching is one of the main features of NDN, turning them into a network of interconnected caches capable of accumulating packets in the buffer of intermediate routers, as well as bring them closer to the consumer using caching at the edge of the network. The effectiveness of a content caching system depends on many factors discussed in the paper: the popularity law and content replication strategy, cache size and displacement policies. For information distribution and caching at the edge router, we present an original algorithm that allows efficient caching of popular content. The cooperative caching algorithm outperforms traditional approaches in several metrics (cache hit, latency, etc.). Simulation of the performance of such an algorithm for the scenario of a vehicular self-organizing network was carried out in the ndnSIM network simulator.

Keywords: Content caching · Edge caching · Named Data Networks · cache hit ratio · Che's approximation

1 Introduction

According to the latest estimates of Ericsson, by 2023, more than 75% of Internet traffic is accounted for by video content, while the volume of traffic in the world has almost doubled over the past two years [7]. This is facilitated by the growing popularity of content-oriented social networks (TikTok, YouTube, Twitch, Likee, etc.), which allow one category of users to create and distribute an unlimited amount of their materials, and the other to select a list of authors and view these materials. The creation of more and more digital content by users, as well as the increase in data transfer speeds in wireless networks, causes excessive demand for limited radio spectrum resources. In addition, the high load on transit channels leads to the deterioration of quality of service parameters in data transmission networks.

One of the alternative solutions for offloading wireless channels is the use of systems with caching [1]. In-network caching, i.e., placing content temporarily stored in memory as close to the consumer as possible (on edge servers, base stations, access points, etc.), can benefit the network in such aspects as increasing

Y. Koucheryavy and A. Aziz (Eds.): NEW2AN/ruSMART 2023, LNCS 14543, pp. 349–362, 2024.
https://doi.org/10.1007/978-3-031-60997-8_32

the probability of content sharing; saving bandwidth; and separating content from producer servers. With caching, it is possible to reduce delays in requesting and distributing information and eliminate the point of failure, since the desired content item can be stored on peripheral storage, rather than remote storage. Caching social media traffic can be particularly useful because there is a high correlation in the content that users request. As a result, in a closed area, the same video file or video broadcast can be viewed by multiple users at the same time. At the same time, the traditional TCP/IP stack proxy caching is less efficient under user mobility and dynamic wireless environment compared to fixed connection [12]. In order to satisfy the users' need to distribute and receive content with high quality-of-service parameters, the research community makes significant efforts to optimize the TCP/IP protocol and rethink the network architecture in terms of the ability to store packets within the network.

Thus, it has been observed that in recent years there has been a shift from host-to-host communication systems to content distribution systems. In addition to traditional applications that require connections between two hosts that have a sender and receiver address identifier (http, ssh, voIP, etc.), much of the Internet traffic is distribution rather than dialog. Accordingly, research on information dissemination has emerged in new direction such as information-centric networks (ICNs).

2   Information-Centric Networks and NDNs

Information-centric networks (ICN) are a concept where the focus is on the distribution of named content provided at the user's request. In this case, the location identifier of the sender and receiver (e.g., IP address) becomes secondary. The object of routing in ICN is information items (content chunks) that have a unique name that is not associated with the device on which it is located (Fig. 1):

Fig. 1. Example of content naming in NDN

The starting point for the emergence of this paradigm can be considered the year 2000, with the TRIAD project [5], and then promoted by Palo Alto Research Center (PARC) researcher Jacobson in the report 'A new way to look at networking' at the Google Tech conference in 2006. In the new paradigm, the first step is when Alice requests a chunk of data by name (an Interest packet). Bob is any node that has a valid copy of the Data packet with the required name and a cryptographic signature. Bob sends Data packet to Alice in response to the request.

Among the different approaches to the construction of ICN are content-centric networks (CCN), networks of information (NetInf), named data networks (NDN) and others. NDN architecture that seems to be most deserving of recent attention. In named data networks, instead of a standard routing table, nodes have three basic tables for packet processing:

FIB (Forwarding Information Base), which points to the next hop along the path of an Interest packet;

PIT (Pending Interest Table), which indicates the list of Interest requests that have not yet been satisfied;

CS (Content Store), which is a cache of a certain size.

When a new Interest packet arrives at a router node operating under the NDN architecture, it compares the name of the requested data with the names of the stored packets in the CS table. If the node already stores a Data packet with the requested name, this packet is immediately sent to the Consumer via the reverse path. If the name is not present in the Content Store table, then the PIT table is checked next. If there is no entry in the PIT, it is created, and the node waits for the arrival of a corresponding Data packet satisfying the Interest request. If an entry with the same name already exists in the PIT, it means that this packet has already been requested in the network. In this case, the entry in the PIT table may be updated with information about the interface from which the duplicate request came. However, the packet is not sent further to the network in order to avoid overloading it. It is also discarded if there is no information in the FIB forwarding table about where to further route packets from the name group to which this packet belongs. If, on the contrary, this information is present in the table, the Interest package will be successfully forwarded to the next hop (Fig. 2).

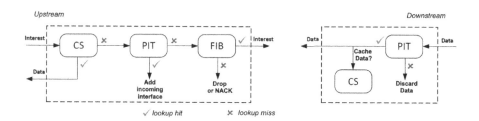

Fig. 2. Processing of Interest and Data packets on NDN nodes

When a Data packet arrives at the NDN, the PIT table is checked first. If there is no name of this packet in the table, then the router is not expecting it and the packet is discarded. Otherwise, it is forwarded to all interfaces from which the corresponding Interest packet came earlier, and the PIT entry is deleted. Further, according to the policy set in the Content Store table, a decision is made to cache the Data packet for the next requests (see Sect. 3).

Different aspects of caching have been investigated over the years, by H. Che, N. Laoutaris, and later taking into account the features of ICN, by R.

Coutinho, V. Martina, M. Garetto, B. Panigrahi, H. Ben-Ammar and others. There have been several attempts to simulate cache behavior using properties of Markov chains [2,3,15], considering cache hit ratio calculation. Nevertheless, it is obvious that at realistic values of cache and catalog sizes the state space of such a chain is large, which makes numerical calculation of transient and stationary probabilities too difficult. H. Che [4] proposed an accurate approximation from hierarchical two-level 'LAN-Internet' topology for cache hit ratio calculation. Further Martina and Garetto [8] extended Che's approximation to all content replication strategies in ICNs, but only for wired Internet scenarios with unchangeable topologies. Panigrahi [9] moved from hierarchical two-level structure to processes within a complex network topology at LAN level, focusing on routing issues, node availability along with caching, as well as calculating the required cache size to provide a given cache hit ratio parameter. Some of 'last mile' aspects of modern networks were also investigated by Coutinho et al. in [6,13]. The authors proposed a mathematical apparatus for edge NDN cache resource sharing for dynamic networks with self-organization. In [6], applications of the Internet of Things and vehicular ad-hoc networks were considered, and in [13], authors expores Che's-based model for NDN virtual reality applications, where video content divides on three quality categories, depending on the signal strength of the wireless network.

All these papers also mainly assume that nodes store content in the cache individually and do not cooperate with each other, which in turn is considered in our paper. In addition, simulation tools are mainly used to determine network characteristics (delays, number of cache hits, etc.), without proofs to mathematical calculations. In this paper, an attempt has been made to combine accurate mathematical calculations of caching characteristics, and implementation of the results in network simulator.

The structure of the paper is as follows: Section 2 provides general information about the history and characteristics of content-oriented networks and introduces NDN-related notional apparatus, Sect. 3 pays more careful attention to the rules for developing models of caching systems in NDNs. Section 4 provides reasoning to proceed to the mathematical description of content caching algorithms. Finally, Sect. 5 contains the development and simulation of a scenario with mobile users who use a peripheral cache when downloading social media content.

3   Information-Centric Networks and NDNs

Let us consider an example of caching nodes operation (Fig. 3). Consumer 1 ($C1$) requests a content item first on the nearest router ($R1$) and then, having encountered a cache miss, on subsequent routers. The desired Data item is only in the storage of the Producer (P) of the content and is cached along the search path, including on $R2$ (case 1). Consumer 2 ($C2$) requests the same content item after a time. The cache hit happens immediately on the nearest router $R2$ (case 2).

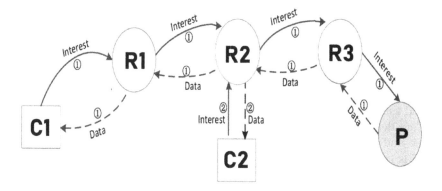

Fig. 3. Movement of Interest and Data packets through NDN network

The goal of any designed caching policy is to maximize the probability of cache hits in nodes and minimize the load on the content source. The idealized rule for developing caching policy is the Belady algorithm. According to it, the most effective rule is to discard information from the cache that will not be needed in the future. Moreover, when designing a caching system, there are some general rules:

1. The content replication strategy is specified, i.e. the distribution of the Data package over the network;
2. The strategy of cache displacement, i.e. freeing up space in the cache when it overflows, is indicated;
3. The popularity low of chunks in the cache directory is indicated, which allows them to be distinguished from each other.

A cache system is generally limited in capacity and is used to store C catalog items out of N, where $C < N$. Therefore, given the limited cache resources, the strategy of replacing, or preempting content when filling the cache is also an important aspect affecting its performance.

Cache Displacement Strategies. *Random replacement (RR or Round Robin)* is the simplest of the basic cache replacement rules. This scheme preempts a random data chunk every time an chunk needs to be cached and the cache space is full.

LRU (Least Recently Used): an algorithm where the content chunks that have not been requested for the longest time are preempted when the cache is full.

MRU (Most Recently Used): unlike LRU, the most recently used chunk is preempted first.

LFU (Least Frequently Used): content chunks that have been used the least frequently are preempted.

FIFO (First-In-First-Out): the first cached chunk is preempted.

Replication Strategies. In a network of caches, requests resulting in a miss in one cache are usually forwarded along one or more routes to other stores, which complicates the analysis compared to a single cache system Once an object request is satisfied, the modeling needs to specify how the object is replicated back to the network, in particular along the route taken by the request (on-path). There are also off-path algorithms, i.e., when Data packets propagate beyond such a route.

Consider a linear topology where there is a single direct route between the source and destination node (Fig. 4). In most NDNs, the default replication policy is Leave Copy Everywhere (LCE). In it, the content source leaves a copy at each node along the routing path. The obvious disadvantage of this strategy is the high cache redundancy, i.e., the same item is copied on multiple nodes. This causes the diversity of content throughout the network to decrease, too many copies of the same content are cached. To improve the performance of NDN, alternative replication strategies are used.

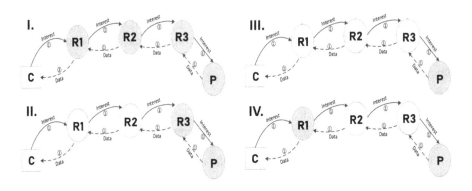

Fig. 4. Chunk replication strategies LCE (I), LCD (II), LCP (III), EC (IV)

The first one is Leave Copy Down (LCD). In this scheme, when a Data packet is found in the cache, its copy is cached only at the next node after the source along the routing path, thus avoiding a large number of copies of the same item. In addition, this strategy implies that an item can be moved to a peripheral node only if it is requested many times, thus bringing popular content closer to the consumer.

The second scheme is Leave Copy with Probability (LCP), which reduces cache redundancy. When a cache hit occurs, each node on the path with a given probability p caches the content.

The third scheme is packet caching at the edge of the network (Edge Caching, EC). Once cached, the content is stored on the router closest to the user to reduce network latency.

4   Cache Modeling in NDN: General Approaches

The approaches to modeling packet distribution and caching are somewhat different from those used to describe packet-switched networks. This is mainly due to the fact that each piece of content has a name or number, i.e., a separate identifier. Thus, while buffered packets are indistinguishable from each other in a packet-switched network model, each piece of named content is individual.

In NDN models, each content item n is typically characterized by a content popularity p_n, which can be viewed as the probability that a randomly selected content query requests a content item n.

Content Popularity. If all items in a directory N have the same query popularity, the caching system cannot be optimized according to Belady's algorithm and hence operate efficiently. Therefore, usually when analyzing the cache, items are ordered in descending order of popularity such that the inequality is satisfied: $p_1 \geq p_2 \geq ... \geq p_N$.

Accordingly, the most commonly used in the literature on caching in NDN is the generalized Zipf's law: $p_n = 1/n^\alpha$, where $\alpha > 0$ is the the so-called 'skewness coefficient'. Other popularity distributions are used less frequently (geometric, Weibull, etc.).

Independent Reference Model. The basic model adopted by researchers to study caches, including NDN, is the Independent Reference Model (IRM). The IRM traffic model is based on the following fundamental assumptions:

1) Users request content from a fixed catalog containing N items;
2) The probability p_n that an item n, in the catalog is requested is constant, i.e., the popularity of an item does not change over time and does not depend on the history of past requests for this and other items.

Che's Approximation. For an independent reference traffic model, an exact approximation for computing the probability of an item n hitting a cache operating under the LRU preemptive strategy was proposed and further investigated by Che et al. in [4]. The author considers a cache of capacity C units storing items from a catalog of size N. Let T_C be the time interval between placing an item n into the cache and expelling it from there. Che calls T_C cache's 'characteristic time'. It is assumed that when the LRU cache size is large, the variations of the 'characteristic' times for different elements n compared to their average value are small and, hence, practically negligible. Thus, $T_C(n)$ is a constant independent of the chosen element n: $T_C(n) = T_C$.

The 'characteristic' time T_c can be found by numerical methods as the root of the equation:

$$\sum_{n=1}^{N}(1 - e^{-p_n T_C}) = C. \tag{1}$$

Then, according to the approximation, the probability that querying an item n in the cache will result in a cache hit can be approximated by the expression:

$$p_{hit}(n) \approx 1 - e^{-p_n T_C} \tag{2}$$

For the catalog average, denoted in the literature as cache hit ratio, let us summarize the expression:

$$p_{hit} \approx \sum_{n=1}^{N} p_n p_{hit}(n) = \sum_{n=1}^{N} p_n (1 - e^{-p_n T_C}). \tag{3}$$

If one cache is used simultaneously by M users, then for further analysis we introduce the notion of average request intensity of an element n in the catalog λ. For this purpose, we denote the intensity of Interest packet requests from the device by λ and obtain:

$$\overline{\lambda}_n = \lambda p_n M \tag{4}$$

For VANET, if vehicles with average speed V can enter and exit the cell radius R, the index λ can be approximated using the Little's law [6]:

$$\overline{\lambda}_n = \frac{\lambda p_n R}{V} \tag{5}$$

Similar to (4), the cache hit ratio for such a system will be:

$$p_{hit} \approx \sum_{n=1}^{N} p_n p_{hit}(n) = \sum_{n=1}^{N} p_n (1 - \overline{\lambda}_n e^{-p_n T_C}). \tag{6}$$

5   System Model of Edge Caching

In the scenario, the nodes are within the range of the base station of the edge roadside base station (RSU), which has caching resources. For the cache of the roadside base station with capacity C we introduce a catalog of unique content element files $N = \{n_1, n_2, ..., n_N\}$. We consider that the traffic of VANET applications (road information systems, maps, emergency services, etc.) goes through a regular TCP/IP network (with processing on the macrocell), and the content from social networks passes through NDN network.

Let us call a cooperative mini-cluster a set of devices M that have pre-established a neighborhood relationship among themselves (this function can be performed, for example, by an application installed on all devices that runs the NDN stack, e.g. NFD [10]). It is assumed that the connected vehicles send Interest packets first to the cluster; if a cache miss occurs there, the cache of the edge RSU is checked, and if the desired Data packet is not available there, the request is transferred to the eNodeB and checked in its cache (Fig. 5).

The microcell base station hosts a gateway similar to the one described in [11], which allows to work together with both NDN architecture and TCP/IP stack.

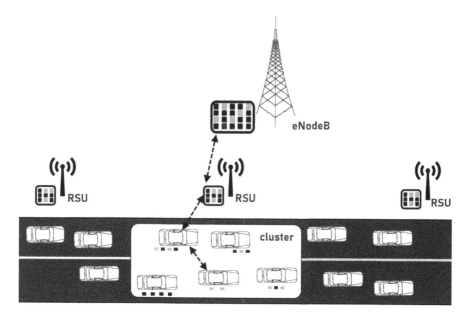

Fig. 5. VANET scenario with edge caching

The device cache in a cluster works as follows. If a Data packet arrives at a device not from the N_{pop} subdirectory, it is stored only in its own cache. Otherwise, the packet is considered popular and is propagated among neighboring devices via broadcasting. Let us call this algorithm *cooperative caching* (CC) and compare it with the traditional LCE algorithm, which saves all chunks to the cache regardless of popularity. ICN caching simulators [14]) allows researchers to conduct studies with a lot of caching policies, but only with static nodes and limited possibilities to specify the network operation scenario. In order to take into account all the points related to of the network environment where packets are exchanged, channel and transport layer options, mobility settings for nodes using a group cache, we choose the ns3-based discrete event simulator (ndnSIM) to build the scenario. The simulation parameters are listed in Table 1.

In the first experiment, the speed of car traffic increased. Along with this, the cache hit ratio on the edge router decreased, which we calculate in the ndnSIM environment using the following formula:

$$\eta = \frac{N_{hit}}{N_{hit} + N_{miss}} \tag{7}$$

This is an example of fact that the faster the vehicle moves, the more unstable the wireless channel between it and the roadside base station becomes. As we can see, the maximum cache hit rate is about 55% at 30 km/h, and the CC strategy beat the LCE by about 5%. We also give the values calculated by formula (6) using the Che's approximation. Figure 6 proves that this approach help to obtain accurate results.

Table 1. Table captions should be placed above the tables.

Parameter	Value
Scenario	Two-line highway
Network coverage area	900×10 m
Microcell radius R, m	300
Macrocell radius, m	1000
Catalog size N, el	100000
Cache size on RSU C, GB	20
Cache size in macrocell, GB	100
Wireless communication standard	5G-NR
Transport layer protocol	UDP
Frame size, bytes	1024
Consumers Interest generation intensity λ, frames per sec	2
Simulation time	120 sec

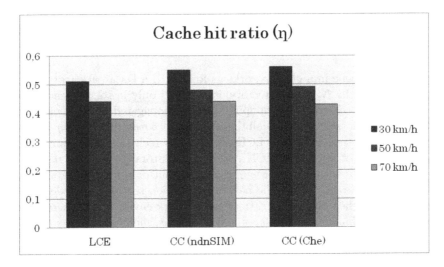

Fig. 6. Dependence of edge cache hit ratio on car speed

Let us perform the same experiment, but with the emphasis on the elements included in the popular catalog (Fig. 7). To calculate the summation in formula (7), we replace N by N_{pop}. As we can see, while the values for LCE are practically unchanged, the cooperative algorithm for this part of the catalog gives an even greater gain (10–15%).

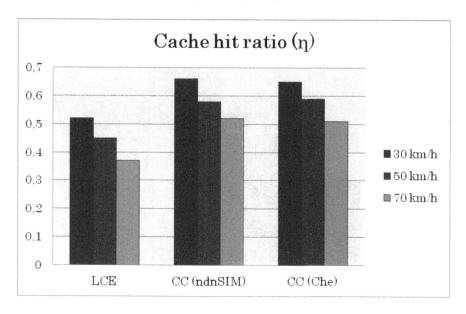

Fig. 7. Dependence of edge cache hit ratio on car speed (for N_{pop})

In the second experiment, when increasing the number of users M from 2 to 7 in the cluster, the external link load (*ell*), i.e., the number of channel transmission starting from the second hop (links to the RSU or eNodeB cache) was measured:

$$ell = \sum_{i=2}^{3}(N_{Interest} + N_{Data}) \qquad (8)$$

When the cluster size is small, users actively use the remote cache (the index increases dramatically), and then, as the number of cars in the cluster increases, the role of the cooperative cache also grows, and the index remains about the same (Fig. 8).

However, as the cluster size increases to 8 or more elements, the QoS and cache efficiency parameters start to deteriorate. This is due to the fact that the network topology dynamically changes when cars are moving. The FIB and PIT tables overflow as well, which is caused by constant updating of information about unsatisfied Interest requests and neighbors for routing. Indeed, it is well known that a large number of neighboring nodes can create not only RF channel overlap but also interference, which also reduces the quality of data transmission.

In the third experiment, we fix the speed of cars as 30 km/h, and make the size of cooperative cluster M equal to 5 devices. We increase the cache size on user devices from 0.5 to 1.5 GB in steps of 0.2 GB. At the same time, we

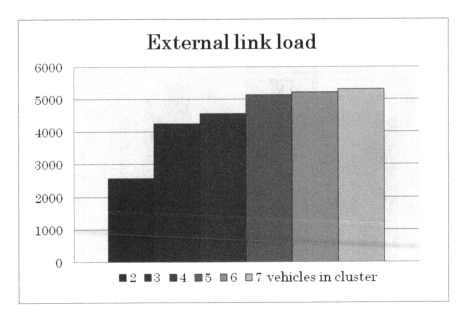

Fig. 8. Dependence of the use of wireless channels on the number of cars in the cluster

compare the described CC strategy with the traditional transmission through the TCP/IP stack, where mobile users immediately interact with the macrocell base station and do not use in-network caching (Fig. 9). Here, based on the simulation results, it is seen a general trend that on mobile user devices with a small cache size or without a Content Store table at all, it is more expedient to transfer using the TCP/IP stack than NDN, in terms of delays. Strategies working through the NDN architecture begin to benefit in latency only when the cache size reaches 1 GB or more.

Let us denote the moment when a VANET node sends the first bit of an Interest packet as $t_{Interest}$, and the moment when the last bit of a Data packet is received as t_{Data}. Then the delay of providing a content item is defined as follows:

$$latency = t_{Data} - t_{Interest} \qquad (9)$$

As for the CC strategy, even here it differs favorably from LCE, since it provides delays of 10–15 ms less, especially in the case of popular content. Thus, in order to work effectively in similar scenarios, the storage resources of the user cache must be large enough. Future applications implementing a shared cache should notify the user in advance of possible costs.

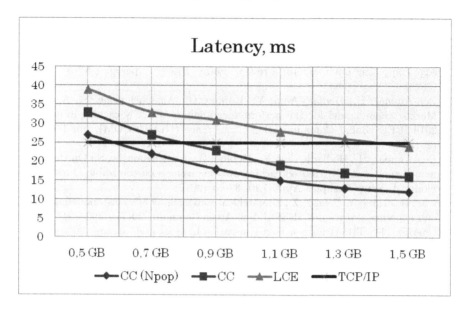

Fig. 9. Dependence of content delivery delay on cache capacity

6   Conclusions

The evolution of networking from a host-centric architecture with IP packets to information-centric networks focused on content distribution is inevitable. The research community is responding to this transition by proposing various scenarios and configurations for implementing NDN, mathematical methods for modeling of such networks, and algorithms for processing packets on network nodes. Accordingly, the mathematical apparatus and software for studying processes in information-centric networks is expanding over time. The study of aspects of caching in NDN also deserves more and more attention, and Che's approximation remains a powerful basis for calculations in this emerging field.

This paper presented an edge caching algorithm for a scenario with mobile consumers of content chunks cooperating to forward content over an NDN infrastructure. The algorithm is able to compete with the standard NDN scheme (LCE) and significantly outperform it in several metrics, especially in the context of accessing popular cache elements. In addition, simulation examples show the effectiveness of using edge caching in the network. The cache cooperation between users within a cluster was applied, and also the possible limitations of this method was showed.

Determining scenarios for introducing NDN mechanisms into existing computer networks will continue to be an up-to-date task, for which the scenario discussed in the paper could be improved in the future.

References

1. Aghazadeh, R., Shahidinejad, A., Ghobaei-Arani, M.: Proactive content caching in edge computing environment: a review. Softw. Pract. Experience **53**(3), 811–855 (2023)
2. Ben-Ammar, H., Hadjadj-Aoul, Y., Rubino, G., Ait-Chellouche, S.: A versatile Markov chain model for the performance analysis of CCN caching systems. In: 2018 IEEE Global Communications Conference (GLOBECOM), pp. 1–6. IEEE (2018)
3. Ben-Ammar, H., Hadjadj-Aoul, Y., Rubino, G., Ait-Chellouche, S.: On the performance analysis of distributed caching systems using a customizable Markov chain model. J. Netw. Comput. Appl. **130**, 39–51 (2019)
4. Che, H., Tung, Y., Wang, Z.: Hierarchical web caching systems: modeling, design and experimental results. IEEE J. Sel. Areas Commun. **20**(7), 1305–1314 (2002)
5. Cheriton, D.: TRIAD: a new next-generation internet architecture (2000). http://dsg.stanford.edu/triad/
6. Coutinho, R.W., Boukerche, A.: Modeling and analysis of a shared edge caching system for connected cars and industrial IoT-based applications. IEEE Trans. Industr. Inf. **16**(3), 2003–2012 (2019)
7. Ericsson.com: Ericsson mobility report november 2023 (2023). https://www.ericsson.com/en/reports-and-papers/mobility-report/reports/november-2023
8. Garetto, M., Leonardi, E., Martina, V.: A unified approach to the performance analysis of caching systems. ACM Trans. Model. Perform. Eval. Comput. Syst. (TOMPECS) **1**(3), 1–28 (2016)
9. Panigrahi, B., Shailendra, S., Rath, H.K., Simha, A.: Universal caching model and Markov-based cache analysis for information centric networks. Photon Netw. Commun. **30**(3), 428–438 (2015)
10. Piao, X., Huang, L., Yuan, K., Yuan, J., Lei, K.: The real implementation of NDN forwarding strategy on android smartphone. In: 2016 IEEE 7th Annual Ubiquitous Computing, Electronics & Mobile Communication Conference (UEMCON), pp. 1–6. IEEE (2016)
11. Refaei, T., Ma, J., Ha, S., Liu, S.: Integrating IP and NDN through an extensible IP-NDN gateway. In: Proceedings of the 4th ACM conference on information-centric networking, pp. 224–225 (2017)
12. Shang, W., Yu, Y., Droms, R., Zhang, L.: Challenges in IoT networking via TCP/IP architecture. NDN Project **2** (2016). https://named-data.net/wp-content/uploads/2016/02/ndn-0038-1-challenges-iot.pdf
13. Sofi, I.B., Coutinho, R.W., Soleymani, M.R.: Modeling of edge server cache-reservation for virtual reality applications. In: Proceedings of the 18th ACM International Symposium on QoS and Security for Wireless and Mobile Networks, pp. 131–138 (2022)
14. Tortelli, M., Rossi, D., Boggia, G., Grieco, L.A.: Icn software tools: survey and cross-comparison. Simul. Model. Pract. Theory **63**, 23–46 (2016)
15. Xu, X., Feng, C., Zhang, T., Loo, J., Li, G.Y.: Caching performance of information centric networking with content request aggregation. In: 2018 IEEE International Conference on Communications Workshops (ICC Workshops), pp. 1–6. IEEE (2018)

Diverse Localization Techniques in Wireless Sensor Networks: A Review

Ahmed M. Khedr[1]([✉]), Ahmed Aziz[2,3], and Walid Osamy[2]

[1] Department of Computer Science, Sharjah University, Sharjah 27272, UAE
akhedr@sharjah.ac.ae
[2] Department of Computer Science, Faculty of Computers and AI, Benha University, Benha, Egypt
{ahmed.aziz,walid.osamy}@fci.bu.edu.eg
[3] Tashkent State university of Economics, Tashkent, Uzbekistan

Abstract. A wireless sensor network (WSN) is a network comprised of a collection of small, specialized sensors with limited memory, processing capacities, and energy resources. These sensors are employed to monitor and record various physical characteristics of the surrounding environment, such as temperature, sound, light, pressure, pollution, among others. Localization has emerged as a prominent research area in the realm of wireless sensor networks, garnering significant interest from academia and researchers alike. This work aims to present a comprehensive survey of diverse techniques and strategies employed to determine the precise location of nodes within the network. Initially, we discuss the available classifications for localization algorithms in wireless sensor networks. Subsequently, we elucidate the techniques and algorithms utilized within each classification. Lastly, we delve into a detailed examination of the existing challenges and issues encountered in the field of wireless sensor network localization.

Keywords: Localization · wireless sensor network · Centralized and Distributed Algorithms · Anchor free and Anchor based Algorithms · Range free and Range based Algorithms

1 Introduction

A wireless sensor network (WSN) is comprised of small, specialized sensors with limited memory, processing capacities, and energy resources. These sensors are deployed to monitor and collect data on various physical characteristics, such as temperature, sound, light, pressure, and pollution. WSNs find applications in diverse fields, including disaster relief operations, medicine and healthcare, military operations, and precision agriculture [1–6]. Many of these applications require knowledge of sensor locations since the collected data is highly dependent on their spatial context. Without accurate sensor positions, the collected data

---

A. Aziz and W. Osamy—These authors contributed equally to this work.

becomes essentially meaningless. Various methods can be employed to calculate the sensor positions. One potential solution is to equip each sensor with a GPS module to provide accurate position information. However, this approach is often impractical due to cost and power consumption considerations. An alternative solution is self-localization, where sensors can estimate their own positions using different localization discovery protocols. Commonly, these protocols rely on certain sensors with known positions, referred to as beacons or anchors, to provide location references for other sensors.

[7] provides a comprehensive examination of location estimation using tabular forms, incorporating machine learning and optimized localization techniques. The survey conducts an in-depth analysis of various parameters associated with this topic, identifying limitations in existing studies and introducing distinctive aspects of the comprehensive research conducted. However, the work in [7] reviewed only the localization solution using AI techniques.

The survey in [8] compiles and analyzes relevant algorithms for localization in scenarios where nodes lack control over their mobility and face hardware constraints. It highlights recent advancements in learning-based approaches and emphasizes techniques that minimize the need for human intervention or specialized field configurations. The survey in [9] offers a comprehensive review of localization methods aiming to optimize localization error. It examines distance estimation techniques such as Time of Arrival (ToA), Time Difference of Arrival (TDoA), Angle of Arrival (AoA), and Received Signal Strength Indicator (RSSI) in the context of node localization. It also evaluates the role of GPS-equipped nodes in the localization process and discusses the advantages and disadvantages of GPS usage for localization purposes. These surveys enhance the understanding of localization techniques in mobile networks, providing an overview of the field's current state, strengths, weaknesses, and recent advancements. They assist researchers and practitioners in selecting appropriate techniques for their specific localization requirements. [8,9] present localization solution in mobile networks.

The objective of this study is to conduct a comprehensive survey of the various techniques and strategies employed for node localization in WSNs. The survey begins by discussing available classifications for localization algorithms in WSNs, offering a framework to comprehend different approaches. It then examines specific techniques and algorithms within each classification category. Furthermore, the paper addresses the open challenges and issues existing in the field of WSN localization. These challenges encompass aspects such as energy efficiency, scalability, accuracy, robustness to environmental conditions, and the influence of node mobility. By identifying these challenges, we stimulate further research and development in the field. Overall, this work serves as a valuable resource for researchers and practitioners interested in WSN localization. It consolidates and presents a wide range of techniques, classifications, and challenges, providing insights into the current state of the field and guiding future investigations in WSN localization.

The remainder of this paper is organized as follows: Sect. 2 presents the classification of localization techniques based on technique, while Sect. 3 illustrates the classification based on mobility. Finally, Sect. 4 provides the conclusion and presents open challenges.

2 Classification of Localization Based on Technique

Table 1 and Table 3 summarize the classification of localization based on techniques with the advantages and disadvantages of each category. These classification categories provide a framework for understanding different localization techniques employed in WSNs and the researchers and practitioners can gain insights into the diverse strategies available for localization in WSNs.

2.1 Centralized and Distributed Algorithms

Distributed localization occurs when each sensor can determine its own position, while centralized localization involves sensors sharing their data with a central unit for position calculation [11]. In centralized algorithms, all computation is performed on a central server, resolving computational limitations. However, communication in these algorithms consumes more energy than computation. The advantage of a centralized approach is the elimination of issues like bandwidth and latency in individual sensor nodes. However, this scheme is costly in terms of both communication and computation [12]. In distributed algorithms, sensor communication consumes less energy compared to centralized algorithms. However, the accuracy of distributed algorithms is generally lower than that of centralized algorithms [10].

2.2 Anchor Free and Anchor Based Algorithms

The positions of certain sensors, known as beacons or anchors, can be determined using GPS or manual placement. These beacons provide location references for localizing other sensors. However, relying on GPS for all sensors can be impractical due to cost, power consumption, and limitations in indoor environments where GPS line-of-sight communication is not feasible. Preprogrammed sensors with known locations can serve as an alternative to GPS, but this approach also becomes impractical when dealing with a large number of beacons. For indoor localization, anchor-free schemes or manual placement of anchor-based nodes can be used to obtain relative coordinates easily [13]. In [14], Priyantha et al. proposed the AFL (Anchor-Free Localization) algorithm, where all nodes calculate and refine their coordinate information in parallel. AFL starts with an initial coordinate assignment based on node connectivity and then employs mass spring optimization using more accurate inter-node distances measured through TDOA to correct localization errors. Compared to incremental algorithms, AFL performs more effectively, even in networks with low connectivity, and has minimal error propagation. However, the AFL algorithm heavily relies on accurate initial position estimates. An anchor-free distributed method for localization in WSNs that utilizes Wi-Fi access points (APs) instead of traditional anchor nodes proposed in [15]. The method employs a progressive approach, where each unknown node estimates its location using two Wi-Fi APs and a sink node, acting as an alternative sink node for subsequent nodes. An Efficient Anchor Free Localization Algorithm (EAFLA) [16] improves upon existing solutions by enabling localization of all sensors within clusters, regardless of the cluster topology. It achieves a low localization error rate and reduces energy consumption significantly. AFLAC (Anchor Free Localization Algorithm using Controllers) [17] is a localization algorithm that aims to improve existing solutions in the literature. Regardless of the communication range between sensors, AFLAC enables the estimation of the distance between them, resulting in accurate position derivation.

Table 1. Comparison of Localization Methods(Centralized, Distributed,Anchor-free and Anchor-based Algorithms)

Centralized and Distributed Algorithms		
Method	Advantages	Disadvantages
Centralized	Eliminates bandwidth and latency issues	High communication and computation costs
Distributed	Low energy consumption	Lower accuracy compared to centralized methods
MRSO [12]	Significant reduction in localization error	High communication and computation costs
Anchor-free and Anchor-based Algorithms		
Method	Advantages	Disadvantages
Anchor-based	Provides accurate location references	Costly and impractical for large networks
Anchor-free	Easy relative coordinate acquisition	Lower localization accuracy
ABC [34]	Simple algorithm, doesn't require complex calculations	Poor localization accuracy, mistake propagation
RODL [35]	No reliance on anchor nodes, handles noisy measurements	Struggles with high noise or low connectivity
SSFL [14]	Combines TDOA and AOA measurements for accurate positioning	–
Wi-Fi AP-based [15]	Utilizes Wi-Fi access points for localization	Addresses submersion issue, progressive approach
EAFLA [16]	Low localization error rate, reduced energy consumption	–
AFLAC [17]	Enables estimation of distance regardless of communication range	–

2.3   Range-Free and Range-Based Algorithms

One criterion used for classifying localization algorithms is the dependency on range measurements. Existing algorithms can be categorized into two main groups: range-based and range-free. Range-based schemes utilize range measurement techniques, such as RSSI, ToA, TDoA, and AoA, to accurately estimate the position of a sensor [18,19]. These schemes achieve accurate localization but require additional hardware and consume more energy. On the other hand, range-free approaches do not rely on range measurements. Instead, they utilize topology information and connectivity to calculate the location of unknown sensors. Topology information is defined by the hop counts between sensors, while connectivity indicates the proximity of a sensor to others. Range-free schemes can be implemented on low-cost WSNs without ranging information, but they tend to have lower accuracy in localizing sensors [20].

2.3.1 Range Based Algorithms

In the range-based approach, the position of a sensor is determined based on the information from other sensors in its neighborhood. Accurate range information, such as distance or angle, between nodes is essential to calculate the location of an unknown sensor. Range-based schemes can be further divided into two parts: distance estimation and position estimation. Distance estimation techniques, including RSSI, ToA, TDoA, and AoA, are used to estimate the distances between nodes. Position estimation techniques, such as Lateration, Triangulation, Trilateration, Bounding Box (BB), Multilateration, and AT-Family, are employed to determine the sensor's position based on the obtained range information. Distance Estimation Techniques can be summarized as follows:

- Received Signal Strength Indicator (RSSI): RSSI stands for "Received Signal Strength Indicator" which is technique that measures the distance between transmitter and receiver. Radio signal energy can be defined as an electromagnetic wave. The strength of these waves decreases as it cover more distance. In RSSI scheme, by calculating the wave strength at the receiver end, distance between the transmitter and receiver can be estimated. This technique is considered the most popular technique for indoor and outdoor due to its low power consumption, low cost, simple hardware, etc. [36].
- Time of Arrival (ToA): To estimate the location of unknown sensor, this technique find the speed of wavelength and the time of radio signals transmitted between beacon node and unknown node [20]. All sensors send signal to their neighbors at the same velocity w. After the signal is received, every sensor transmit a signal back to the sender. The distance between the transmitter (a) and receiver (b) can be estimated [37]: This technique provides high accuracy but consumes a lot of processing power.
- Time Difference of Arrival (TDoA): In the TDOA technique, each sensor is equipped with a microphone and a speaker. A beacon sensor sends signals to all sensors and then waits for a fixed time before generating "chirps" using the speaker. When the unknown sensors receive the signals, their microphones are turned on to identify the chirps. By saving the time when the chirps are identified, the nodes can determine the distance between the beacon sensor and themselves [38].
- Angle of Arrival (AoA): AoA approach estimates the absolute or relative angles between adjacent nodes to determine the location of unknown nodes [39]. AoA refers to the angle between a reference orientation or direction and the propagation direction of an incident wave. In this scheme, each sensor utilizes an antenna array to estimate the angle of arrival and determine the directions of adjacent nodes. However, this approach can be costly as it requires additional hardware, such as antennas, for transmitting and receiving location information.

Position Estimation Techniques can be summarized as follows:

- Triangulation: Triangulation is an approach that utilizes information about angles, specifically using the Angle of Arrival (AoA) technique [39]. In this approach, instead of relying on distance measurements, the relative angles between the sensor and reference nodes are used for position estimation. For auto-localization using triangulation, a minimum of three reference nodes are required. The un-localized sensor measures its angle to each of the three reference nodes. Based on these angles and the known positions of the reference nodes, the position of the sensor can be computed using simple trigonometric relationships.

- Trilateration: Trilateration is a straightforward method used to determine the positions of sensors. The concept behind this scheme involves calculating the location of a sensor with reference to three beacon nodes, where the locations of the three beacons and their distances from the sensor are known. The distances from the beacon nodes to the sensor represent the radii of circles centered at each beacon. The intersection point of these three circles corresponds to the position of the unknown sensor [40].

- Multilateration: Multilateration is a range-based technique similar to trilateration but uses more than three reference points (beacons). The method requires the positions of multiple beacons and their distances to the target node, which are obtained using the Time Difference of Arrival (TDoA) approach [41].

- Bounding Box (BB): In BB, a square bounding box is created for each beacon node, with its center at the node's location. The size of the sides of the bounding box is typically twice the estimated distance. The possible positions of the target node are determined by the intersection of all the bounding boxes. The final position is then computed as the center of gravity of the obtained rectangle [42].

- Sum Dist Min Max: This approach involves beacons broadcasting their locations. When a normal node receives a beacon's position, it calculates the distance using the Sum-Dist technique. Each beacon transmits a message containing information such as identity, coordinates, and path length. Upon receiving the message, a node calculates the range from the sender and updates the path length before broadcasting the message. After estimating the distances from beacons, the sensors determine their estimated locations using the MinMax method, which involves finding a bounding box surrounding each node and considering the center of gravity of this box as the node's position [43].

- AT-Family: The AT-Family techniques are a group of three distributed approximation methods proposed for localization in static WSNs. The three methods within this family are AT-Free, AT-Dist, and AT-Angle. These techniques consider the capabilities of the nodes and aim to solve the localization problem in WSNs [44].

- GPS-Free: GPS-Free localization methods are used in mobile ad hoc networks without GPS receivers or fixed beacon nodes. One example is the Matrix Transform-based Self Positioning Algorithm (MSPA), which utilizes distance information (e.g., RSSI) between sensors to calculate the coordinates of static sensors. The algorithm involves establishing local coordinates at a subset of nodes (master nodes) and converging the individual coordinate systems to form a global coordinate system [45].

• RSSI Fingerprinting: This method involves two steps. In the offline phase, beacon nodes record the power levels of packets transmitted by unknown nodes, which include the current positions of the normal nodes. During this phase, the beacons map each packet with the measured Received Signal Strength Indicator (RSSI) and the time of reception, constructing a database. In the online phase, the beacon nodes use the database to match the measured RSSI values and determine the corresponding positions of the normal nodes [46] (Table 2).

Table 2. Comparison of Range-Based Localization Methods

Method	Distance Estimation	Position Estimation	Requirements
RSSI	Received Signal Strength Indicator	–	Low power, low cost, simple hardware
ToA	Time of Arrival	–	Synchronized clocks, accurate time measurements
TDoA	Time Difference of Arrival	–	Microphones, speakers, time difference measurements
AoA	Angle of Arrival	–	Antenna arrays, additional hardware
Triangulation	–	Triangulation	Angle of Arrival (AoA), at least three reference nodes
Trilateration	–	Trilateration	Distance measurements to three beacon nodes
Multilateration	–	Multilateration	Distance measurements to multiple beacon nodes
Bounding Box (BB)	–	Bounding Box	Square bounding boxes, intersection calculation
Sum Dist Min Max	–	Center of gravity calculation	Distance calculations, bounding boxes
AT-Family	–	Distributed approximation	Node capabilities, solving localization problem
GPS-Free	–	Matrix transformations, algorithms	No GPS receivers, distance information
RSSI Fingerprinting	–	RSSI matching	Offline phase data recording, RSSI values

2.3.2   Range Free Algorithms

Range-free approaches do not rely on range measurement techniques. Instead, they utilize topology information and connectivity to estimate the locations of unknown sensors. These approaches are suitable for low-cost WSNs that lack range information, but they generally have lower localization accuracy for sensors [20].

• Centroid: The centroid approach is a localization technique that utilizes the closest neighbor section of a localization algorithm. In [47], the location of a sensor is estimated by calculating the centroid or the geometric center of several beacon node positions.

• Approximate Point in Triangle (APIT) In this scheme, the network consists of nodes equipped with transmitters whose locations are known. The network area is divided into triangles between the beacons. Each triangle, whether inside or outside, contains a node that aids in narrowing down the potential location. By evaluating various sets of triangles and achieving satisfactory accuracy, the approximate location of the target node can be determined.

• Gradient scheme: In gradient scheme, the location of unknown nodes is estimated through multi-alteration where hop count approach is applied, which start from zero and increased as propagates to other closest nodes. Gradient scheme has three steps: beacons nodes first transmit its coordinates and the value of hop count, unknown node estimates the shortest path between beacons using the received message, and in the last step, the minimum error between two nodes is calculated [48].

- DV-Hop scheme: In this approach, the details of the hub broadcast in the network, which contains the beacon location of and the value of hop count. Every sensor that receives the transmitted message removes higher values and keeps the minimum value. The unknown nodes only record the first average distance and then transmit it to neighbor nodes. The unknown node calculates its location through [36, 49].

- Multi-Hop: This approach is applied to calculate a connectivity graph. Based on the communication range of sensors the multidimensional scaling (MDS) uses connectivity information. This scheme can be summarized in three steps [50]: In the first step, calculate the distance between each pair of nodes, for the position estimation MDS is used to fit the estimated distance, and in last step, the optimization is done by using of the known locations.

- MDS- MAP: MDS-MAP is an approach that utilizes Multidimensional Scaling (MDS) to estimate the positions of normal nodes based on core information from the closest sensor network. This technique does not require beacon nodes and is capable of creating relative maps representing the current locations of sensor nodes. MDS-MAP exhibits high time complexity and requires large bandwidth when calculating the proper locations of nodes, especially in scenarios with a large number of sensors [51]. To address these limitations, an improved algorithm called IMDS-MAP has been proposed in [52]. IMDS-MAP incorporates a distributed positioning algorithm implemented through clustering, aiming to enhance the efficiency and scalability of the localization process.

Table 3. Comparison of Range-Free Localization Methods

Method	Description	Advantages/Disadvantages
Centroid	Estimates sensor location by calculating the centroid of beacon node positions	+ Simple and easy to implement - Lower accuracy compared to range-based methods
APIT	Divides the network area into triangles between beacons and uses them to narrow down the target node's location	+ Able to achieve satisfactory accuracy - Requires known beacon locations
Gradient scheme	Estimates unknown node location through multi-alteration using hop count information	+ Utilizes hop count information - May have higher error rates
DV-Hop scheme	Beacon nodes broadcast their locations and hop count information. Unknown nodes calculate their location based on average hop distances	+ Simple and scalable - Accuracy depends on hop count estimation
Multi-Hop	Uses connectivity information to create a connectivity graph. Applies MDS to estimate positions based on distances	+ Utilizes connectivity information - Requires accurate distance calculations
MDS-MAP	Utilizes Multidimensional Scaling (MDS) to estimate positions based on core information from the closest sensor network	+ Doesn't require beacon nodes - High time complexity and bandwidth requirements

3   Classification Based on Mobility

Localization schemes are also categorized based on the type of sensors deployed in the area. Static sensors, which are commonly used in many applications, leading to the majority of localization schemes being designed for static sensors. In contrast, mobile sensor nodes are utilized in limited applications, resulting in fewer algorithms specifically designed for them [21]. Unlike static nodes, mobile nodes need to calculate their location frequently. This process consumes time, energy, and other resources required by the application.

Localization algorithms that are designed to estimate locations accurately may not be suitable for mobile nodes due to various factors such as centralized processing, which may not be feasible in mobile environments, time-consuming, which is not ideal for mobile nodes that need to calculate their location frequently, and make assumptions about the environment or network topology that do not hold true in dynamic networks.

In WSNs, the mobility of the network can be classified into three types: random, predictable, and controlled mobility [22]. In random mobility, mobile sensors are unrestricted and can move freely and randomly within the deployment area. The node parameters such as destination, direction, and speed are chosen randomly and independently of other nodes. In the second category of mobility, the motion path for sensor nodes is predetermined and known, but it cannot be changed or controlled by the nodes themselves. The nodes follow a predefined path throughout their operation. In the last category, the destination of the mobile sensors is known, and they follow defined mobility patterns. These patterns can be predefined routes or specific movement instructions.

Localization algorithms for mobile wireless sensor networks can be classified into three categories based on the deployment of nodes [22]:

1. Mobile sensors and static anchors: In this category, the sensors are mobile while the anchors remain static. The anchors provide reference points for localization, and the mobile sensors estimate their locations based on the signals received from the static anchors.
2. Mobile anchors and static sensors: Here, the anchors are mobile while the sensors are static. The mobile anchors move within the network, and the static sensors determine their locations by receiving signals from the moving anchors.
3. Mobile anchors and mobile sensors: In this category, both the anchors and sensors are mobile. The mobile anchors and sensors work together to estimate their respective locations through interaction and signal measurements.

These different categories reflect the diverse scenarios and configurations encountered in mobile WSNs. Tables 4, 5 and 6 summarize the classification of localization based on mobility.

3.1 Mobile Sensors and Static Anchors

3.1.1 Received Information Based Localization Algorithms

These algorithms aim to estimate the coordinates of mobile sensor nodes by utilizing information gathered from anchor nodes. The subsequent sections provide a detailed description of typical algorithms in this context.

3.1.2   PTA (Power Tuning Anchors)

[23] proposed the PTA algorithm to address localization in mobile WSNs. In this algorithm, beacon nodes broadcast their information, including their maximum power level. A mobile node receives signals from the beacon nodes and identifies three adjacent beacons that form a triangular shape. The mobile node then sends a request to these three anchors, asking them to re-transmit with reduced power. Upon receiving acknowledgement from the mobile node, each of the three beacons decreases its power level by one and transmits the anchor signal again, this process continues until none of the selected beacons transmit any signal. The mobile node selects two beacons with power levels just above and below the received beacons. This algorithm improves the accuracy and success rate of localizing mobile nodes but increases the overall cost of the network.

3.1.3   Fingerprint and the RSSI Techniques

In [24], a proposed an event-triggered scheme that utilizes the IR fingerprint and RSSI techniques. In this scheme, when a beacon node receives a signal from adjacent beacons, it records the location of the anchors and the signal power. These records, including coordinates and RSSI values are stored in a fingerprint database. When a beacon node receives the record of its ith neighbor, it saves its own location and RSSI value. The beacon node then estimates the distance from its ith neighbor. Using the measured distance, the beacon node searches the fingerprint database for the best RSSI match. The scheme provides a low average localization error of mobile nodes that is moving at a low average speed in a network that has large number of beacon nodes. However the cost of communication and equipment will increase.

3.1.4   Self-adapting Localization for Mobile Nodes

In [25], a dynamic localization scheme called SALMN (Self-Adapting Localization for Mobile Nodes) to address the localization problem of mobile nodes is proposed. This approach allows a mobile sensor node to accurately determine its coordinates by generating a motion model. Specifically, when there are either two beacon nodes or exactly one beacon node within the communication field, the mobile sensor node can perform localization. I.e., at a given time t(i), the mobile sensor node's position is denoted as $(x\_t(i), y\_t(i))$. It moves with a speed $V\_t(i)$ and a direction angle $\theta\_t(i)$. The interval to the next localization execution is represented as $\triangle T\_t(i)$. The localization of the mobile sensor at the next time can be determined from a motion model [25]. SALMN offers improved accuracy in determining the locations of mobile nodes, resulting in a relatively high localization success rate. Additionally, this scheme contributes to extending the network's lifetime, thereby enhancing its overall efficiency and longevity.

Table 4. Comparison of Mobile sensors and static anchors Localization Methods

Method	PTA (Power Tuning Anchors)	Fingerprint and RSSI Techniques	SALMN (Self-Adapting Localization for Mobile Nodes)
Algorithm Description	Beacon nodes transmit signals at different power levels, and mobile nodes request beacon retransmissions with reduced power until no signals are received	Utilizes fingerprint database and RSSI values to estimate distances and select the best RSSI match	Mobile sensor node determines its coordinates based on a motion model, taking into account speed, direction angle, and time intervals.
Localization Accuracy	Improved accuracy and success rate	Low average localization error for slow-moving nodes in a large network	Better accuracy and high localization success rate.
Cost	Increases overall cost of the network	Increased cost of communication and equipment	No specific cost implications mentioned.
Advantages	Improved accuracy and success rate	Low average localization error for slow-moving nodes	Better accuracy, high localization success rate, and extended network lifetime

3.2   Mobile Anchors and Static Sensors

3.2.1   Measurement Confidence Based Localization Algorithms

The primary concept behind these algorithms is to assign confidence values to the measured distances. By prioritizing high-confidence distances, the localization algorithm can effectively and accurately determine the location of each sensor, thereby enhancing the overall accuracy of the localization process [26].

3.2.2   Virtual Ruler

The virtual ruler technique, proposed in [27] offers a solution for mobile sensor localization. This scheme involves a group of beacons that move around a group of static sensors, capturing multiple distance measurements from different perspectives. By assigning a confidence value C to the estimated distance, the technique mitigates statistically incorrect measurements. The confidence value is determined as $C = N + \lambda \times k\_max$, Where N is the total number of distance measurements to the same group of sensors, λ is the weighting coefficient, and k_{max} is the exact measured distance between two nodes. The proposed scheme offers the advantage of obtaining long-range distance measurements while staying within energy limitations. However, it needs additional equipment to estimate the moving direction of sensor nodes through radio signals (AoA) and it assumes a constant speed for anchor nodes, which may not always hold true in practical scenarios.

3.2.3   Geometric Localization Algorithms

The following algorithms estimate the sensor node location depending on the geometry properties between mobile and static nodes. In [28], GPS- and Compass-free Directed Localization (GCDL) algorithm is proposed to address the localization problem of mobile nodes. GCDL does not rely on a digital compass and incorporates directional localization after two iterations of movement.

The algorithm divides nodes into two groups, with one group moving in a step-wise manner while the other remains static, as depicted in Fig. 1-a. Through geometric approaches, adjacent nodes are located for each group after two movement iterations, as shown in Fig. 1-b. Once neighboring nodes are identified, the sensors align themselves along a common axis to move as a cohort. Messages are exchanged among the sensors, containing estimated positions of their one-hop neighbors.

Upon receiving the messages, each node compares the coordinates of its neighbors with its own position and measures the skew in the local coordinate systems, as illustrated in Fig. 1-d. The calculated skew is saved by each node for its adjacent neighbors, enabling local corrections whenever direction messages are received. To move in the calculated direction, each group executes a Zigzag movement, as shown in Fig. 1-c. This scheme provides better scalability and maintains better connectivity.

In [29], RSSI-based geometric localization in WSN approach is presented. In this approach, a hybrid localization method for WSNs that combines the range-free DV-hop algorithm with the more affordable range-based algorithm using RSSI measurements is introduced. The authors introduce a new RSSI-based localization algorithm called disk-based multilateration (DML) which extends the multilateration algorithm by associating each RSSI value with a distance interval represented by a disk. This disk models the imperfections of RSSI measurements based on the transmitter node's position. Additionally, the paper proposes two hybrid algorithms, DV + DML and DMLDV, which combine the DV-hop and DML algorithms to leverage the benefits of both localization methods.

In [30], the geometry optimization problem is formulated as a constrained optimization problem, where the objective function aims to maximize the deter-

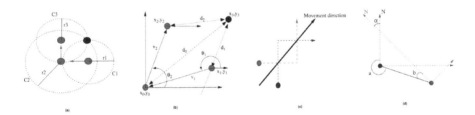

Fig. 1. Visual representations of the different steps involved in the GCDL algorithm [28].

Table 5. Comparison of Mobile Anchors and Static Sensors Localization Methods

Method	Properties
Measurement Confidence-Based Localization Algorithms	- Enhances overall accuracy of localization process - Prioritizes high-confidence distances - Improves localization with multiple beacons
Virtual Ruler	- Enables long-range distance measurements - Mitigates statistically incorrect measurements - Prioritizes distance values with higher confidence
GCDL (GPS- and Compass-free Directed Localization)	- Doesn't rely on a digital compass - Provides better scalability and connectivity
RSSI-based Geometric Localization in WSN	- Combines range-free and range-based algorithms - Considers imperfections of RSSI measurements - Leverages benefits of both localization methods
Geometry Optimization for Localization Systems	- Provides insights into optimal geometries for different configurations - Considers deployment constraints - Formulates optimization problem based on Fisher Information Matrix (FIM)
Geometrical Approach for Localizing Unknown Nodes	- Presents a novel geometrical approach - Provides mathematical formulation - Validated through simulations

minant of the Fisher Information Matrix (FIM). The constraints are defined by the irregular feasible deployment regions. To simplify the problem, maximum feasible angle and separation angle are introduced, allowing the transformation of the constrained optimization problem into an equivalent form. The optimal geometries are explored by examining the relationship between the minimum safety distance and the maximum feasible angle. The study initially focuses on optimal geometries for two and three sensors, and then extends the analysis to scenarios with arbitrary numbers of sensors and arbitrarily shaped feasible regions. This approach provides insights into achieving optimal geometries for localization systems with different configurations and deployment constraints.

The work in [31] introduces a novel geometrical approach for localizing unknown nodes. The mathematical formulation of this approach is presented in detail. The technique is validated through simulations of ten diverse scenarios, demonstrating the localization of three anchors and the unknown node.

3.3   Mobile Anchors and Mobile Sensors

In scenarios where both anchors and sensors are mobile, the localization procedure for algorithms becomes inherently complex. This complexity arises due to the unique challenges and considerations that need to be taken into account when dealing with mobile entities in the localization process. The proper handling of mobility in both anchors and sensors becomes of utmost significance to ensure accurate and reliable localization results in such dynamic environments.

3.3.1   Distributed Grid Based Localization

C. Sun et al. proposed an algorithm called DGL (Distributed Grid Based Localization) for localization, which relies on a power grid approach [32]. In this algorithm, when a sensor receives packets from anchor nodes, it establishes a coordinate system based on the position information provided by at least two anchors. The coordinate system is then divided into multiple square grids. Using the power level received from each anchor, the sensor adjusts its power level for communication within the predefined transmission radius range.

If the distance between the centroid of a grid and an anchor node falls within the transmission radius range, the sensor node contributes a vote to the power system and saves it. The sensor node calculates the centroid of all the grids with the highest votes, which is considered the estimated local position of the sensor node. However, there are limitations to the DGL algorithm. A sensor node cannot be localized if it receives less than two pieces of information from anchors or if the grid's votes are less than 50% of the anchor nodes' information received by the sensor node. The localization accuracy of the algorithm depends on the number of anchor nodes from which the sensor node receives information. If the number is too small, the localization error will be significant. Therefore, one of the main drawbacks of the DGL algorithm is its relatively long localization period, which affects its efficiency.

3.3.2   Timing Based Localization Algorithm

The key concept of the algorithms mentioned is that mobile sensor nodes esti-mate the propagation lag time of beacons, which are periodically transmitted by anchor nodes following a specific interval pattern. The estimated propagation lag time from the beacon anchors, along with the known dimensions of the anchors, is used to calculate the coordinates of unknown nodes. A detailed description of a specific algorithm can be found in the work of G. A. Shah et al. [33].

The proposed algorithm, known as TMSL (Timing-based Mobile Sensor Localization), is precise and efficient, relying on timing to calculate distances between nodes. The protocol divides localization into time periods, each consist-ing of four equal-sized slots for beacon transmission by four anchors. Anchors transmit beacons in specified orders within their slots.

When receiving packets from beacon anchors, the sensor establishes the Localization Base Time (LBT) for the current time period based on the ref-erence beacons received from the first two anchors at the beginning of the time phase. Once LBT is set, the sensor can determine the beacon's emission time by using information provided by the anchors, including the interval number and the elapsed lag since the beacon was scheduled for transmission. Using its local clock, the sensor node calculates the propagation time $t\_p1, t\_p2, ..., t\_pk$ for each beacon.

By calculating the average value of all the obtained propagation times $t\_\bar{p} = \frac{1}{k} \sum_{i=1}^{k} t_{pi}$ during the k time periods, the sensors estimate their distances to the anchors.

The TMSL algorithm offers several benefits in terms of localization accuracy and adaptability. One key advantage is that it effectively limits localization errors by considering the localization time, which is determined based on the expected velocity of nodes and the desired level of reliability. By appropriately setting the localization time, the algorithm can achieve reliable localization results while taking into account the movement speed of nodes and the required level of accuracy.

Simulation results have shown that the localization error remains consistent even when changing the density of nodes. This indicates that the algorithm is robust to changes in node density, and the localization accuracy is not signifi-cantly affected by variations in node density.

Although the localization error may increase with higher node speeds, it can be mitigated by increasing the desired level of reliability. This suggests that by prioritizing a higher level of reliability, the algorithm can compensate for the challenges posed by fast-moving nodes and maintain satisfactory localization accuracy.

Furthermore, the TMSL algorithm tackles the issue of beacon packet loss by increasing the beacon frequency, which is determined based on the expected speed of nodes and the desired level of reliability. Higher beacon frequency improves the localization precision of nodes, ensuring more accurate localization results. However, it is important to note that a higher beacon frequency comes at a cost in terms of bandwidth and energy consumption. The increased frequency of beacon transmissions requires more resources, leading to higher energy consumption and potentially affecting the overall network performance. Therefore, there is a trade-off between the localization precision achieved through higher beacon frequency and the associated costs in terms of bandwidth and energy consumption.

Table 6. Comparison of Mobile Anchors and Mobile Sensors Localization Methods

Method	Advantages	Disadvantages
Distributed Grid Based Localization (DGL)	- Relies on a power grid approach for localization - Establishes a coordinate system based on anchor nodes' position information - Considers power levels received from anchors for communication - Calculates centroid of grids with highest votes for estimated local position	- Sensor node cannot be localized with less than two pieces of anchor information - Localization accuracy depends on the number of anchor nodes' information received - Relatively long localization period affects efficiency
Timing-based Mobile Sensor Localization (TMSL)	- Precise and efficient algorithm based on timing - Calculates distances using propagation lag time of beacons - Considers localization time based on node velocity and desired reliability - Robust to changes in node density - Mitigates beacon packet loss through increased beacon frequency	- Higher beacon frequency leads to increased bandwidth and energy consumption

4   Conclusion and Open Challenges

Localization in wireless sensor networks is a dynamic research area that has seen numerous proposed schemes. This comprehensive review paper presents an overview of localization algorithms across different classifications. In this section, we summarize the challenges and perspectives that need to be addressed in localization, which can vary in different applications. These challenges include network scale, environmental changes, and the limitations of traditional localization strategies. Here, we highlight a few key insights that require further investigation:

Combining Different Non-radio Frequency Techniques: Incorporating non-radio technologies, such as visual sensors, can enhance the accuracy of existing localization algorithms. However, the additional equipment can be costly. Exploring cost-effective solutions for integrating these techniques is a promising future direction.

Integration of Various Solutions: Localization often involves the use of different types of wireless sensors, each with its own measurement characteristics. Integrating measurement strategies from various sensors can improve the overall positioning accuracy of the system .

Scalability: A scalable localization framework should perform effectively as the network expands. This includes geographical scaling, which increases the network coverage area, and sensor density scaling, which increases the number of sensors in a given area. Challenges such as signal collisions and the transition from 2D to 3D localization need to be addressed to ensure accurate and efficient scaling.

Computational complexity: Localization algorithms have hardware and software complexities that affect their efficiency. Achieving low computational complexity is crucial, especially for energy-constrained sensor nodes. Analyzing and representing the computational complexity of different localization algorithms is a challenging task that requires further research.

Accuracy vs. Cost Effectiveness: The accuracy of a localization system depends on the measurement methods used, and in range-free methods, the number of anchor nodes significantly impacts accuracy. Balancing accuracy and cost by achieving high accuracy with the fewest anchor nodes is an ongoing research problem.

4.1 Open Issues and Challenges

The discussed open problems and study issues in the context of localization in WSNs are as follows:

1. Variable Velocity of Sensor Node: Most mobility models used in research assume consistent velocity between two successive time intervals, which may not accurately represent real-life scenarios. Exploring the exchange of mobility information among nodes, where a sensor can send relative velocity information to neighboring sensors, could improve localization accuracy.
2. Mobile Nodes to Ensure Security: Leveraging mobility to enhance localization security is an interesting research concept. Incorporating mobile nodes as part of a secure localization scheme could help identify the presence of malicious nodes by localizing a mobile node positioned near them.
3. Anchor-Free Mobile Node Localization: While previous work has considered the mobility of both anchor nodes and sensor nodes, localizing a mobile node without anchors while ensuring high accuracy remains a challenging task.
4. Energy-Efficient Localization: Energy efficiency is a critical concern in wireless sensor networks. Few papers have addressed the transmission powers of anchor nodes, which play a crucial role in network localization. Further research is needed to understand the impact of anchor node power on localization performance, especially considering factors like mobile anchor nodes and the relative position of each anchor node.
5. Estimation of Unknown Parameters in Unknown Environments: There is a lack of literature discussing the derivation of road loss parameters in unknown environments. Existing work often relies on heavy mathematical assumptions, and additional research is required to address this problem in a lightweight manner.
6. Multiple Source Localization: Existing literature on multiple source localization lacks consideration of important factors. Synchronization between source and sensor nodes during localization is a significant challenge. Future exploration could focus on clock synchronization and developing schemes where a source can embed a signature in the signal it sends to sensor nodes.

7. Security and Privacy: With the numerous applications of sensor networks, security has become a major concern. Wireless sensor networks can be vulnerable to malicious attacks, compromising the trust and integrity of localization. Addressing security issues, such as protecting against tampering and false position estimation, is crucial in ensuring the overall integrity of sensor networks.

8. Mobility of Source and Sink Nodes: Most recent work on wireless sensor localization has primarily focused on either the source or sink nodes' mobility. Considering the mobility of both source and sink nodes is an area that requires further exploration in localization research.

By addressing these open problems and studying the associated issues, advancements can be made in the field of localization in wireless sensor networks, leading to more accurate, secure, and efficient localization techniques. Moreover, we can advance the field of localization in wireless sensor networks, enabling effective deployment in diverse applications and environments.

References

1. Khedr, A.M.: Effective data acquisition protocol for multi-hop heterogeneous wireless sensor networks using compressive sensing. Algorithms **8**(4), 910–928 (2015)
2. Osamy, W., El-Sawy, A.A., Khedr, A.M.: Effective TDMA scheduling for tree-based data collection using genetic algorithm in wireless sensor networks. Peer-to-Peer Netw. Appl. **13**(3), 796–815 (2020)
3. Khedr, A.M., Ramadan, H.: Effective sensor relocation technique in mobile sensor networks. Int. J. Comput. Netw. Commun. (IJCNC) **3**(1), 204–217 (2011)
4. Osamy, W., Salim, A., Khedr, A.M., El-Sawy, A.A.: IDCT: Intelligent data collection technique for IoT-enabled heterogeneous wireless sensor networks in smart environments. IEEE Sens. J. **21**(18), 21099–21112 (2021)
5. Osamy, W., Khedr, A.M., Salim, A., AlAli, A.I., El-Sawy, A.A.: Recent studies utilizing artificial intelligence techniques for solving data collection, aggregation and dissemination challenges in wireless sensor networks: a review, Electronics **11**(3), 313 (2022). MDPI
6. Aziz, A., Singh, K., Osamy, W., Khedr, A.M.: An efficient compressive sensing routing scheme for internet of things based wireless sensor networks. Wireless Pers. Commun. **114**, 1905–1925 (2020)
7. Osamy, W., Khedr, A.M., Salim, A., Ali, A.I.A., El-Sawy, A.A.: Coverage, deployment and localization challenges in wireless sensor networks based on artificial intelligence techniques: a review. IEEE Access **10**, 30232–30257 (2022). https://doi.org/10.1109/ACCESS.2022.3156729
8. Oliveira, L.L.D., Eisenkraemer, G.H., Carara, E.A., Martins, J.B., Monteiro, J.: Mobile localization techniques for wireless sensor networks: Survey and recommendations. ACM Trans. Sens. Netw. **19**(2), 1–39 (2023)
9. Lalama, Z., Boulfekhar, S., Semechedine, F.: Localization optimization in WSNs using meta-heuristics optimization algorithms: a survey. Wirel. Personal Commun. 1–24 (2022)
10. Pal, A.: Localization algorithms in wireless sensor networks: current approaches and future challenges. Netw. Protoc. Algorithms **2**(1), 45–73 (2010)

11. Nazir, U., et al.: Classification of localization algorithms for wireless sensor network: a survey. In: 2012 International Conference on Open Source Systems and Technologies (ICOSST). IEEE (2012)

12. Alfawaz, O., Osamy, W., Saad, M., et al.: Modified rat swarm optimization based localization algorithm for wireless sensor networks. Wirel. Pers. Commun. **130**, 1617–1637 (2023). https://doi.org/10.1007/s11277-023-10347-x

13. Priyantha, N.B., Balakrishnan, H., Demaine, E., Teller, S.: Anchor-free distributed localization in sensor networks. In: Proceedings of the 1st International Conference on Embedded Networked Sensor Systems, pp. 340–341 (2003)

14. Priyantha, N., Balakrishnan, H., Demaine, E., Teller, S.: Anchor-free distributed localization in sensor networks. In: 1st International Conference on Embedded Networked Sensor Systems, pp. 340–341 (2003)

15. Jing, N., Zhang, B., Wang, L.: A novel anchor-free localization method using cross-technology communication for wireless sensor network. Electronics **11**(23), 4025 (2022)

16. Aka, A.C., et al.: An efficient anchor-free localization algorithm for all cluster topologies in a wireless sensor network. Int. J. Comput. Commun. Control **18**(3), 4961 (2023)

17. Aka, A.C., et al.: Anchor-free localization algorithm using controllers in wireless sensors networks. In: International Conference on e-Infrastructure and e-Services for Developing Countries. Cham: Springer Nature Switzerland (2022)

18. Mesmoudi, A., Feham, M., Labraoui, N.: Wireless sensor networks localization algorithms: a comprehensive survey (2013). arXiv preprint arXiv:1312.4082

19. Mekelleche, F., Haffaf, H.: Classification and comparison of range-based localization techniques in wireless sensor networks. J. Commun. **12**(4), 221–227 (2017)

20. Singh, S.P., Sharma, S.C.: Range free localization techniques in wireless sensor networks: a review. Procedia Comput. Sci. **57**, 7–16 (2015)

21. Singh, S., Shakya, R., Singh, Y.: Localization techniques in wireless sensor network. Int. J. Comput. Sci. Inf. Technol. **6**(1), 844–850 (2015)

22. Jabbar, S., Aziz, M.Z., Minhas, A.A., Hussain, D.: A novel power tuning anchors localization algorithm for mobile wireless sensor nodes. In: Proceedings of the 10th IEEE International Conference on Computer and Information Technology, pp. 2441–6 (2014)

23. Singh, P., Saini, H.S.: Average localization accuracy in mobile wireless sensor networks. J. Mob. Syst. Appl. Serv. **1**(2), 77–81 (2015)

24. Wang, J., Han, T.: A self-adapting dynamic localization algorithm for mobile nodes in wireless sensor networks. Procedia Environ. Sci. **2011**(11), 270–4 (2014)

25. Gholami, M., Cai, N., Brennan, R.W.: An artificial neural network approach to the problem of wireless sensors network localization. Robot Comput. Integr. Manuf. **29**(1), 96–109 (2013)

26. Sabra, A., Fung, W.-K., Radhakrishna, P.: Confidence-based underwater localization scheme for large-scale mobile sensor networks. In: OCEANS 2018 MTS/IEEE Charleston, Charleston, SC, USA, pp. 1–6 (2018). https://doi.org/10.1109/OCEANS.2018.8604878

27. Ssu, K.F., Ou, C.H.: Localization with mobile anchor points in wireless sensor networks. IEEE Trans. Veh. Technol. **54**(3), 1187–97 (2005)

28. Akcan, H., Kriakov, V., Brönnimann, H., Delis, A.: Managing cohort movement of mobile sensors via GPS-free and compass-free node localization. J. Parallel Distrib. Comput. **70**(7), 743–757 (2010). ISSN 0743-7315

29. Achroufene, A.: RSSI-based geometric localization in wireless sensor networks. J. Supercomput. **79**(5), 5615–5642 (2023)

30. Fang, X., et al.: Improving localization accuracy under constrained regions in wireless sensor networks through geometry optimization. Entropy **25**(1), 32 (2022)
31. Zaidi, M., Bouazzi, I., Thafasal Ijyas, V.P.: Fast WSN localization method based on three anchors and simple geometric technique: mathematical modeling. In: 2022 IEEE 9th International Conference on Sciences of Electronics, Technologies of Information and Telecommunications (SETIT). IEEE (2022)
32. Shah, G.A., Akan, O.B.: Timing-based mobile sensor localization in wireless sensor and actor networks. Mob. Netw. Appl. **15**(5), 664–79 (2010)
33. Erol-Kantarci, M., Oktug, S., Vieira, L., Gerla, M.: Performance evaluation of distributed localization techniques for mobile underwater acoustic sensor networks. Ad-hoc Netw. **9**(1), 61–72 (2011)
34. Moore, D., Leonard, J., Rus, D., Teller, S.: Robust distributed network localization with noisy range measurements. In: 2nd ACM Conference on Embedded Networked Sensor Systems, pp. 50–61. Baltimore (2004)
35. Sottile, F., Spirito, M.: Enhanced quadrilateral-based localization for wireless Ad-hoc networks. In: Fifth Annual Mediterranean Ad Hoc Networking Workshop, Lipari (2006). Sensors, IEEE Wireless Communications and Networking Conference, pp. 3798–3803 (2007)
36. Mistry, H.P., Mistry, N.H.: RSSI based localization scheme in wireless sensor networks: a survey. In: 2015 Fifth International Conference on Advanced Computing & Communication Technologies (ACCT), pp. 647–652. IEEE (2015)
37. Sarigiannidis, G.: LOCALIZATION FOR AD HOC WIRELESS SENSOR NETWORKS. M.S. thesis TECHNICAL UNIVERSITY DELFT, THE NETHERLANDS, AUGUST (2006)
38. Fu, Y., et al.: The Localization of Wireless Sensor Network Nodes Based on DSSS. Electro/Infor. Tech., 2006 IEEE Int'l. Conf, pp. 465–69 (2006)
39. Niculescu, D., Nath, B.: Ad hoc positioning system (APS) using AOA. In: IEEE INFOCOM (2003)
40. Oguejiofor, O.S., Aniedu, A.N., Ejiofor, H.C., Okolibe, A.U.: Trilateration based localization algorithm for wireless sensor network. Int. J. Sci. Mod. Eng. **1**, 21–27 (2013)
41. Santos, F.: Localization in wireless sensor networks. ACM J. Name **5**, 1–19 (2008)
42. Simic, S., Sastry, S.: Distributed localization in wireless ad hoc networks. Technical Report UCB/ERL, vol. 2 (2002)
43. Savvides, A., Park, H., Srivastava, M.B.: The bits and flops of the N-hop multilateration primitive for node localization problems. In: Proceedings of 1st ACM International Workshop on Wireless Sensor Networks and Applications, pp. 112–121 (2002)
44. Saad, C., Benslimane, A., König, J.C.: AT-Family: Distributed methods for localization in sensor networks, pp. 1–32 (2007)
45. Capkun, S., Hamdi, M., Hubaux, J.P.: GPS-free positioning in mobile ad hoc networks. Clust. Comput. **5**(2), 157–167 (2002)
46. Widyawan, M., Pesch, D., et al.: Influence of predicted and measured fingerprint on the accuracy of RSSI-based indoor location systems. In: Proceedings of 4th Workshop on Positioning, Navigation and Communication, Hannover, Germany (2007)
47. Chen, S.-T., et al.: An indoor collaborative coefficient-triangle APIT localization algorithm. Algorithms **10**(4), 131 (2017)
48. Zhang, B., Jiao, Z., Li, C., Yao, Z.: Efficient location-based topology control algorithms for wireless ad hoc and sensor networks. View Issue TOC **16**(14), n/a–n/a (2016)

49. Ssu, K.-F., Ou, C.-H., Jiau Ou, H.C.: Localization with mobile anchor points in wireless sensor networks. IEEE Veh. Technol. **54**(3), 1187–1197 (2005)
50. Kamila, N.K.: Handbook of Research on Wireless Sensor Network Trends, Technologies, and Applications. Technology and Engineering, pp. 589 (2016)
51. Han, G., Xu, H., DuongJin, T.Q., Fang Jiang, T.: Localization algorithms of wireless sensor networks: a survey. **52**(4), 24192436 (2013)
52. Chelouah, L., Semchedine, F., Bouallouche-Medjkoune, L.: Localization protocols for mobile wireless sensor networks: a survey. Comput. Electr. Eng. **71**, 733–751 (2017)

The Relationship Between Digital Economy and International Regulatory Affairs: A Survey

Adham Khudaykulov[✉]

Tashkent State University of Economics, Toshkent, Uzbekistan
a.khudaykulov@tsue.uz

Abstract. International regulation is concerned with the instigation of rules and directives designed to govern and control at a global level in order to protect, preserve and maintain important issues which if not controlled, may be open to abuse, corruption and the endangerment of countries, economies and people. International directives are imposed on selected countries, although some may wish to opt-out. Economics is concerned with the balancing of a limited set of resources and the distribution of these resources. Regulation at any level may alter the nature of this distribution and as a result, may change the prosperity of economies, government and people and this ensures that regulation is imperative. Regulation at an international level may account for changes in national government as they may be required to alter their strategies, even at a cost which they may not be able to incur. This paper, presents a survey to five overview idea about the relationship between international regulatory affairs and the economics.

Keywords: digital economy · regulation

1 Introduction

The importance of international regulation cannot be understated [1]. The efficiency of the global markets for example cannot be compromised in the absence of such rules and markets rely on international policy makers to implement regulations to ensure the effective working of these global banking systems [2]. There are always externalities or missing markets in any economy and economic theory underpins this fact. Regulation is expected to revise these externalities and, in this manner, add to productivity and development. Practically speaking, governments additionally intercede and regulate in economies where market exchanges are seen to promote socially unacceptable levels of distortions in manner in which wealth is distributed, or there is an expectation desire that people in general ought to have admittance to specific merchandise and benefits (e.g. social insurance and education) regardless of their ability to pay (these are more commonly called merit goods) [3].

Economic theory does not give any credence or add value in the discussion on efficient markets in the light of regulation, nor does it add any value any discussion on missing markets, therefore, we must rely upon the research by academics (limited it may be) which has been proposed in this field. That's why in this paper, we are going

© The Author(s), under exclusive license to Springer Nature Switzerland AG 2024
Y. Koucheryavy and A. Aziz (Eds.): NEW2AN/ruSMART 2023, LNCS 14543, pp. 383–390, 2024.
https://doi.org/10.1007/978-3-031-60997-8_34

to discuss the assignment and the estimation of the relationship between international regulatory affairs and the economics.

2 Research Methodology

This paper investigates the influence of the international regulatory on the digital economy. Thus, this research is framed according to this aim and abiding by scientific guidelines [4].

Research methodology consists of several steps:

In the first step the papers were searched through the reliable databases, namely Web of Science and Scopus, and collected.

In the second step all the collected papers were sort out in accordance with relativeness to the topic.

In the third step selected papers were investigated and their contend was analysed.

In the final step all collected ideas and results from the studied papers were discussed and prospects of the international regulation in the digital economy contest were proposed.

3 Discussion

This section discusses research conducted in the sphere of the international regulation in the framework of the digital economy.

Majone (1994) has commented on the 'regulatory' state in his research. He states that there are naturally going to be distinct advantages arising from countries which are very well regulated and these advantages will lead to the prosperity of that country. These benefits are social as well as economic in their nature and in order for them to be considered as advantages, they must be greater than the costs of both implementing and running them [5].

For many, the results of international regulation misses the mark of the normal advantages of regulation intervention as far as the enhanced of economic performance is concerned. Regulation may be driven by particular vested parties campaigning for changes from government in order to reap advantages, Stigler [6]; Peltzman, [7]. Regulation is necessary to ensure that effective governance is possible but this is not always the case. There are instances where governance has not lead to economic prosperity and may have cited that this is due to bureaucracy or more specifically and commonly called 'red tape'. If red tape is eradicated, then citizen of countries will not seem to be at a disadvantage as firms will be able to perform to their maximum both globally and on the international markets. Thus, the eradication of this red tape is vital for economic success. The level and dynamics of corruption in selected countries can be seen in Table 1. The OECD and the World Bank have continued to be integral advocates of the drive to ensure the removal of red tape from industry, and they have been instrumental in raising awareness to countries so that they can understand that the issue of 'better regulation' is one that all countries should adhere to [8].

There exists an issue whereby the speed at which changes have been made and the level to which changes has had an effect. Generally, within the OECD nations, there have

Table 1. Dynamics of the estimated control of corruption in selected countries (2016–2021 years) [9]

Country Name	2016	2017	2018	2019	2020	2021
Albania	−0.44898	−0.45826	−0.52415	−0.54337	−0.55193	−0.55592
Armenia	−0.63775	−0.61445	−0.38573	−0.20382	0.020228	0.07215
Azerbaijan	−0.83187	−0.88563	−0.83199	−0.82996	−1.05708	−0.82758
Kyrgyz Republic	−1.07196	−1.04869	−0.93416	−0.93625	−1.09955	−1.12473
Tajikistan	−1.14809	−1.32874	−1.40997	−1.33004	−1.32786	−1.33822
Uzbekistan	−1.18131	−1.16738	−1.05924	−1.02622	−1.05037	−0.80808
Vietnam	−0.45735	−0.59939	−0.48885	−0.52432	−0.35173	−0.28578

been differences in the rate to which pace has changed and the way in which change has been implemented continues to be documented. The end result in implementation of regulation is that there must be a positive outcome in economic progress. What we need to know, however, is how the different international policy reforms work and how their implementation has exceeded the costs incurred. This is vital and proof is needed so that the policy makers are able to provide their own designs based on the proven effective policies which have been effective in augmenting change in economies. This proof needs to be open and countries may take advantage of policy regulations that work very well and these results should be used for transparency and accountability purposes. This is essential for effective regulation [10, 11].

As much as good international regulation can have a positive effect on economies, poor regulation, or hastily arranged regulation may have the converse effect. The consequences of poor regulation may give rise to an increase in welfare costs or more significant economic costs which dampen economic growth and reduce the capacity for firms to be competitive. Domestic or even foreign entrepreneurship with often difficult barriers to entry may be a consequence of poor regulation and this is a focal point to national enterprise and hence growth. New entrepreneurs should be encouraged to enter the market with few impediments and grow, thus contributing to the national economy. If regulation becomes difficult to comply with and administrative costs are unnecessarily high, then it is likely that the burden on these firms will be too great to overcome. The state thus has the duty to remove what is referred to in the literature as the 'regulatory burden' [12].

There is a form of measuring how international regulatory reforms impact the economy and this is known as the 'causal chain analysis'. Researchers use this to understand what they call the 'how' and 'why'. This form of analysis performed by researchers allows policy makers to understand the effects of their regulatory changes and the impact of these. Some have used 'Regulatory Independent Analysis' (RIA) in order to understand impacts, however, the main fact that is widely agreed upon is that whatever type of governance exists, this must lead to better economic performances following what they call 'better regulation'. The consequence of regulation must be that transparency and accountability must be better served and these must be essential traits which lead to higher GDP, more competitive markets and a better platform for orchestrating business [13].

Those involved in the 'better regulation' propositions are concerned with a variety of issues including how the policies changes are implemented and the outcome of these. They would like to ensure that the best practices are used to the assurance that they will lead to transparency and accountability amongst other measures. The issue also identifies that many interventions which serve to slow down regulation are kept to a minimum and that the relevant and right people are appointed in strategic places at the heart of central government. The important aspect of regulation is to ensure that all the separate parts of the regulatory framework are working effectively and that all the complex and diverse systems within the operations are pulled together and working effectively. One can certainly open up all the different parts of the different systems and identify a causal chain but that is too repetitive and the examination of all parts separately is pointless. The different components all serve to perform one function, and that is to contribute to the theory of what researchers describe as 'better regulation' [14]. In Fig. 1 the quality of administration in selected countries can be seen.

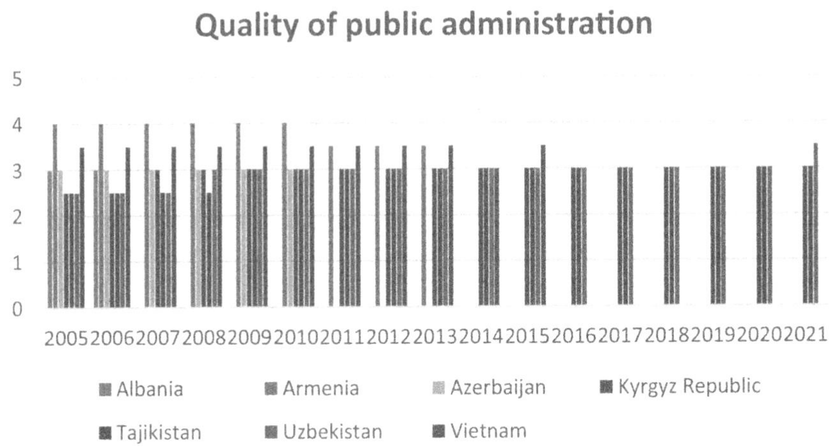

Fig. 1. Dynamics of the quality of public administration in selected countries (2005–2021 years) [9]

Economics is generally concerned with relationships and how different components of the ideas researchers are attempting to establish work with each other. This usually takes the form of measurement and the impact of regulation in economies is one such research debate. The causal chain analysis examines these relationships, as long as the important financial information is accessible. In a perfect world, the impacts and relationships will be measured using monetary values. Valuation of this nature permits the analysis of variation in relationships and testing to be contrasted and included with give a solitary measure of their interconnectedness and impact. However, practically speaking, the measurement of the economic impact might not always be measurable in terms of a monetary value and therefore a more qualitative assessment may be a more desirable measurement. By applying the appropriate analysis, one can observe relationships to particular regulatory relationships. Many empirical studies observe the policy intervention by forming an analysis of what the theory is expected to show with the actual results of the test – that is - in the absence of the intervention. The counterfactual is usually not known and hence may be estimated for example on trends in economic growth [15].

The following looks at a few of the results on international regulation and from this, it may be possible to draw on certain conclusions when attempting to establish a relationship between international regulation economics. In their use of OECD level data, [16] productivity was compromised when regulation in the production markets were administered and this was because of the fact that technology in an increasing globalised world was delayed. The same product market regulation was tested by Conway et al. [17] in order to show how productivity was affected and they found that the effect was negative. Feldman [18] in a more recent study to the previously mentioned researchers analysed seventy three countries between 2000 and 2003 and established that unemployment was a consequence of greater regulation in employment law. Jacobzone et al. [19], by examining the relationship between regulation and governance that there was a major positive impact on employment, GDP, and labour productivity after the implementation of international regulatory management systems.

Other major studies include Loayza et al. [20] who established a negative impact in the wake of international regulation. Their examination took the form of a cross-country regression technique to assess economic growth. Their methodology was unique in that they produced a range of indicators which included entry and exit parameters and international trade and measured regulation intensity for each index. They further established that where fiscal regulations had been implemented, there was no adverse effect on economic growth but neither was there a positive effect recorded. The relationship between regulation and productivity was found to be negative but to a much lesser extent. This led to the assumption that institutions which perform better tend to have the effect of reducing negative impact of how regulation affects economic performance.

A competent and popular database used by researchers is the 'World Bank's Doing Business' database which serves to ascertain the causal relationship between economic growth and regulation which are aimed at businesses. Djankov et al. [19] used this database in their examination of one 183 countries (a much larger sample than used by many researchers previously) and analysed the costs of business start ups. The study does not stipulate whether or not these are businesses which have been started from new or established businesses which are forming new subsidiaries. The factors examined in this study were for example, changes to employment laws, cross border trading, contract and legal aspects relating to business law, taxation, obtaining credit and more issues to name a few. Within this database was a ranking methodology which ranked all countries in terms of their cost of doing business in light of the changes in regulation [21, 22]. The samples were taken between 1993 and 2002 and the methodology used an index based on aggregation and panel data regression. The results in this test were that there exists a major relationship between the two variables – business regulation and economic growth in that any move from the worst to the best percentage quartile resulted in a 2.3% increase in economic growth [23].

The determination of a relationship between international regulation and economics is not straight forward. The relationships are context specific. However, badly designed regulation can be harmful to the government objectives. As with the EMU, policy makers should bear in mind that one-size-fits-all may not hold for all countries. It is also difficult to provide a firm quantitative assessment of the relationship between regulatory change and economics. Thus the importance of regulation policy and management in the form of improved regulation outcomes rather than measured evidence of the impact on economies. This provides a more robust relationship narrative for the researcher.

4 Conclusion

In general, governments additionally intercede and regulate in economies where market exchanges are seen to promote socially unacceptable levels of distortions in manner in which wealth is distributed, or there is an expectation desire that people in general have to admit specific merchandise and benefits (e.g. social insurance and education) regardless of their ability to pay (these are more commonly called merit goods). The OECD and the World Bank have continued to be integral advocates of the drive to ensure the removal of red tape from industry, and they have been instrumental in raising awareness to countries so that they can understand that the issue of 'better regulation' is one that all countries should adhere to. The efficiency of the global markets for example cannot be compromised in the absence of such rules and markets rely on international policy makers to implement regulations to ensure the effective working of these global banking systems. This is vital and proof is needed so that the policy makers are able to provide their own designs based on the proven effective policies which have been effective in augmenting change in economies. The results in this test were that there exists a major relationship between the two variables – business regulation and economic growth in that any move from the worst to the best percentage quartile resulted in a 2.3% increase in economic growth. Regulation at any level may alter the nature of this distribution and as a result, may change the prosperity of economies, government and people and this ensure s that regulation is imperative. This proof needs to be open and countries may take advantage of policy regulations that work very well and these results should be used for transparency and accountability purposes. If regulation becomes difficult to comply with and administrative costs are unnecessarily high, then it is likely that the burden on these firms will be too great to overcome. The factors examined in this study were for example, changes to employment laws, cross border trading, contract and legal aspects relating to business law, taxation, obtaining credit and more issues to name a few.

References

1. Khudaykulov, A.: The relationship between economics and international regulatory affairs in transition economies and neutrosophic sets: a Review. Int. J. Neutrosophic Sci. **21**(3), 64–74 (2023)
2. Usmanova, A.: The impact of economic growth and fiscal policy on poverty rate in Uzbekistan: application of neutrosophic theory and time series approaches. J. Int. J. Neutrosophic Sci. **21**(2), 107–117 (2023)
3. Ruiz, D.P., Silva, G.P., Ibrahim, M.: Single valued neutrosophic sets approach for assessment wind power plant. Int. J. Neutrosophic Sci. **23**(1), 205–215 (2024). https://doi.org/10.54216/IJNS.230118
4. Usmanova, A., et al.: Utilities of artificial intelligence in poverty prediction: a review. Sustainability **14**(21), 14238 (2022)
5. Majone, G.: The rise of the regulatory state in Europe, west European politics, Vol. 7. N o. **3**, 77–101 (1994)
6. Stigler, G.J.: The theory of economic regulation. The Bell J. Econ. Manage. Sci. **2**(1), 3 (1971). https://doi.org/10.2307/3003160
7. Peltzman, S.: Toward a more general theory of regulation. J. Law Econ. **19**(2), 211–240 (1976)
8. Salim, A., Osamy, W., Aziz, A., Khedr, A.M.: SEEDGT: Secure and energy efficient data gathering technique for IoT applications based WSNs. J. Netw. Comput. Appl. **202**, 103353 (2022). https://doi.org/10.1016/j.jnca.2022.103353
9. World Bank. World Development Indicators (2023). https://datacatalog.worldbank.org
10. Salim, A., Ismail, A., Osamy, W., Khedr, M.A.: Compressive sensing based secure data aggregation scheme for IoT based WSN applications. PLoS ONE **16**(12), e0260634 (2021)
11. Aziz, A., Singh, K., Osamy, W., Khedr, A.M.: Optimising compressive sensing matrix using chicken swarm optimisation algorithm. IET Wirel. Sens. Syst. **9**(5), 306–312 (2019)
12. Alisherovna, U.A.: Whether a higher e-government development index means a higher GDP growth rate? In: ACM International Conference Proceeding Series, pp. 467–472 (2021).https://doi.org/10.1145/3508072.3508168
13. Hampton, P.: Reducing Administrative Burdens: Effective Inspection and Enforcement. HM Treasury, London (2005)
14. Usmanova, A.: An Empirical Investigation of the Relationship Between E-government Development and Multidimensional Poverty. In: Koucheryavy, Y., Aziz, A. (eds.) Internet of Things, Smart Spaces, and Next Generation Networks and Systems: 22nd International Conference, NEW2AN 2022, Tashkent, Uzbekistan, December 15–16, 2022, Proceedings, pp. 471–480. Springer Nature Switzerland, Cham (2023). https://doi.org/10.1007/978-3-031-30258-9_42
15. Usmanova, A.: Impact of E-government on Poverty Rate: A Cross-Country Empirical Assessment. In: Koucheryavy, Y., Aziz, A. (eds.) Internet of Things, Smart Spaces, and Next Generation Networks and Systems: 22nd International Conference, NEW2AN 2022, Tashkent, Uzbekistan, December 15–16, 2022, Proceedings, pp. 462–470. Springer Nature Switzerland, Cham (2023). https://doi.org/10.1007/978-3-031-30258-9_41
16. Nicoletti, G., Scarpatta, S.: Regulation, Productivity, and Growth, OECD Evidence, Policy Research Working Paper 2944, World Bank, Washington D.C (2003)
17. Conway P., De Rosa, D., Nicoletti, G., Steiner, F.: Regulation, competition and productivity convergence, OECD Economics Department Working Paper No. 419, OECD, Paris (2006)
18. Feldmann, H.: The unemployment effects of labor regulation around the world. J. Comp. Econ. **37**(1), 76–90 (2009)
19. Djankov, S., McLiesh, C., Ramalho, R.M.: Regulation and growth. Econ. Lett. **92**, 395–401 (2006)

20. Jacobzone S., Steiner, F., Ponton, E.: Assessing the Impact of Regulatory Management Systems, OECD Working Papers on Public Governance No. 17, OECD Publishing Paris (2010)
21. Loayza, N.V., Oviedo, A.M., Serven, L.: Regulation and Macroeconomic Performance. The World Bank (2005)
22. Usmanova, A.: The impact of financial development and unemployment on poverty rate in the context of digital economy in Uzbekistan. In: ACM International Conference Proceeding Series, pp. 684–689 (2022).https://doi.org/10.1145/3584202.3584306
23. Aziz, A., Osamy, W., Khedr, A.M., Salim, A.: Chain-routing scheme with compressive sensing-based data acquisition for Internet of Things-based wireless sensor networks. IET Netw. **10**(2), 43–58 (2021)

Author Index

Printed in the United States
by Baker & Taylor Publisher Services